Barry Stimmel, MD

Alcoholism, Drug Addiction, and the Road to Recovery
Life on the Edge

More pre-publication
REVIEWS, COMMENTARIES, EVALUATIONS . . .

"Dr. Barry Stimmel's book represents a significant advance in the relatively short list of scholarly works on the science of addiction medicine written for the general public. What makes it most noteworthy is that it joins an even shorter list of books written with exhaustive and authoritative medical expertise which do not represent a view in favor of, or against, mood-altering drugs on a moral or dogmatic level.

Dr. Stimmel's book is a fair, balanced, and scientifically accurate work. It gives, in clear language without 'medicalese' or jargon, the information people need to have in order to make informed choices regarding the use of mood-altering chemicals by themselves, their families, and others in their community. In addition, it gives a frank critique of public policy in this area.

The book is written in a clear and concise style, is well referenced, and contains a very useful glossary of terms relating to alcohol and drug abuse. It covers not only recognition of addiction problems but approaches toward their treatment, both for the affected individual, and for their families and loved ones. This book belongs in the library of any individual interested in what is arguably the number one public health issue in the United States, as well as in the library of health professionals who wish to give their patients and clients a highly useful reference."

Alan A. Wartenberg, MD
Medical Director,
Addiction Recovery Program,
Faulkner Hospital,
Boston, MA

"Dr. Barry Stimmel has written a marvelously comprehensive book exploring the complex issues of drug use. He has done it clearly and without jargon, providing a useful overview of adverse effects, potential for dependency, and treatment options. This is a wise and passionate book filled with advice and opinions as well as scientific facts."

Robert L. DuPont, MD
President, Institute
for Behavior & Health, Inc.,
Rockville, MD

The Haworth Medical Press®
An Imprint of The Haworth Press, Inc.
New York • London • Oxford

Alcoholism, Drug Addiction, and the Road to Recovery
Life on the Edge

HAWORTH Therapy for the Addictive Disorders
Barry Stimmel, MD
Senior Editor

Alcoholism, Drug Addiction, and the Road to Recovery
Life on the Edge

Barry Stimmel, MD

The Haworth Medical Press®
An Imprint of The Haworth Press, Inc.
New York • London • Oxford

Published by

The Haworth Medical Press®, an imprint of The Haworth Press, Inc., 10 Alice Street, Binghamton, NY 13904-1580.

PUBLISHER'S NOTE
Medicine is an ever-changing science. As new research and clinical experience broaden our knowledge, changes in treatment and drug therapy are required. While many suggestions for drug usages are made herein, the book is intended for educational purposes only, and the author, editor, and publisher do not accept liability in the event of negative consequences incurred as a result of information presented in this book. We do not claim that this information is necessarily accurate by the rigid, scientific standard applied for medical proof, and therefore make no warranty, expressed or implied, with respect to the material herein contained. Therefore the patient is urged to check the product information sheet included in the package of each drug he or she plans to administer to be certain the protocol followed is not in conflict with the manufacturer's inserts. When a discrepancy arises between these inserts and information in this book, the physician is encouraged to use his or her best professional judgment.

Cover design by Jennifer Gaska.

Library of Congress Cataloging-in-Publication Data

Stimmel, Barry. 1939-
    Alcoholism, drug addiction, and the road to recovery : life on the edge / Barry Stimmel.
        p. cm.
    Includes bibliographical references and index.
    ISBN 0-7890-0552-2 (alk. paper)—ISBN 0-7890-0553-0 (alk. paper)
    1. Drug abuse. 2. Alcoholism. 3. Drug abuse—Treatment. 4. Alcoholism—Treatment. 5. Narcotic addicts—Rehabilitation. 6. Alcoholics—Rehabilitation. I. Title.

HV5801 .S78 2001
362.29'18—dc21
                                                                                    2001024339

To Matthew and Alexander

ABOUT THE AUTHOR

Barry Stimmel, MD, is currently Dean for Graduate Medical Education at the Mount Sinai School of Medicine at the City University of New York. He is the Katherine and Clifford Goldsmith Professor of Medicine (Cardiology) in the Department of Medicine and in the Department of Medical Education and has served as Dean of Academic Affairs, Admissions, and Student Affairs at the School of Medicine for over twenty years. A practicing internist and cardiologist, Dr. Stimmel is also Executive Director of the Narcotics Rehabilitation Center at the Mount Sinai Medical Center. He is the Editor of the *Journal of Addictive Diseases* and the author over 100 articles and several books dealing with drug abuse, the effects of mood-altering drugs on the heart, and pain control. In addition, Dr. Stimmel lectures extensively on issues concerning medical education, substance abuse, and pain management.

CONTENTS

Preface

The use of alcohol and other mood-altering drugs permeates all levels of our society, from the poor to those with the resources to disguise their problem or surreptitiously seek treatment. Whether it is alcohol, nicotine, prescription or over-the-counter medications, or illicit drugs, the effects of addiction on the individual are great, and the cumulative effects on society staggering. In terms of life and death, it has been estimated that almost half a million people in this country die each year from illness, injuries, or homicides related to tobacco, alcohol, or illicit drugs. Annual U.S. expenditures for treatment and prevention have been calculated at more than $2.9 billion. However, this is but a fraction of our costs. The annual cost for untreated alcohol and drug problems has been estimated at $166 billion. Smoking costs related to shortened lives and medical care are estimated at $130 billion annually, and costs due to excessive alcohol consumption are put at $100 billion a year. Considering all this, the total impact on the U.S. economy each year has been estimated to be $414 billion.

Public concern over the use of illicit substances has always been considerable, with 82 percent of Americans viewing illicit drug use as a major problem in 1996. In fact, between 1979 and 1996, illicit drug use ranked among the ten top problems facing our society. Concern over illicit drug use, however, is related not only to the financial costs to society or to the untoward effects on the user but also to the public's concern with crime. This fear is not unwarranted, as a 1998 Bureau of Justice report found that the proportion of state inmates using drugs in the months prior to their arrests rose from 50 percent in 1990 to 57 percent in 1997. More important, the proportion of inmates reporting being under the influence of alcohol or drugs when actually committing violent crimes was 42 percent for alcohol and 29 percent for drugs (as reported in *The New York Times,* January 6, 1999, p. A14). Unfortunately, although recognizing that a problem exists, people often ignore the involvement of thier own families or loved ones.

Although 82 percent of people consider illegal drug use a problem for society and 43 percent recognize it as a crisis nationwide, only 27 percent see it as a problem for their local community and merely 6 percent as a crisis among teenagers in their own schools. Yet, a 1996 Gallup Poll reported that 45 percent of Americans know someone with a drug problem. This blindness to the problem can also be demonstrated by a survey conducted by the *Washington Post,* which found that although nine out of ten parents reported having a serious talk with their teenagers about illegal drugs, only half of their teenagers said they had had such a conversation. This failure to identify the problem at hand, of course, does not apply to the inner cities, where illicit drug use in communities and schools is recognized as a major problem, and frustrations grow due to the inability to adequately address the issue.

Use of a licit mood-altering substance, especially with respect to tobacco, has only relatively recently become a major public and legislative concern. Yet, even so, as discussed in Chapter 15, the initiatives to curb such use always seem to falter. Eliminating use of all mood-altering drugs from our culture is impossible. It is not even desirable, because many are medically valuable. But there are considerable differences in the psychological and physical effects of various drugs as well as in the effects someone using a particular substance might have on other people.

Many books have been published over the past decades addressing the use of mood-altering substances. Some have been written for specialists in the field of addictive behaviors, others for health care professionals, and still others for the general public. Few, however, have attempted to explain why a person uses such substances, the effects of such use, the difficulties encountered in trying to remain drug free, and the differences among the multitude of current treatments that are available. Indeed, even today, despite the impressive advances in our knowledge of the brain and behavior, many still view excessive drug use as a moral issue, and those who engage in it as having "weak wills."

The pharmacological effects, medical complications, and behaviors resulting from the use of mood-altering drugs can be complex, but they can be understood, and everyone should know them. Knowledge of the adverse effects of such drugs, why they are used excessively and compulsively, how to identify persons at risk, available resources for users, and the problems encountered when one tries to remain drug free help us form an appropriate response to the "drug problem" on both individual and societal levels.

This book was conceived to accomplish these objectives by enabling persons with little or no background in science or health care to understand the often complex issues of drug use. The information is presented clearly, concisely, and without jargon. Considerable research and professional experience provide the underpinnings of the book, but no academic references are included in the text. Instead, a selected bibliography is given in a separate section at the end. Publications by individuals mentioned in the text are listed in this section. To allow a more comprehensive overview of the material, a few citations refer to secondary rather than primary sources. For those interested in a more thorough or technical view, several general works used in writing the book are also listed. Since the first edition, references have been updated to provide the reader with the most recent information and much new material has been added. Of particular value, especially to parents, may be the section on addressing drug use in your children and Appendix B, which provides a list of common street drug names. Although it is impossible to be totally comprehensive, as new names appear on the street daily, this list may help to quickly identify the type of drug used. Equally important, it can provide one with information to proceed to the appropriate chapter in the book to become better informed about the drug's adverse effects, potential for dependency, and treatment options.

This book attempts to present a nonjudgmental view of the effects of all licit and illicit mind-altering substances. This approach is sure to offend the "abolitionists," who believe all use of such substances is harmful, at best sinful, at worst criminal; as well as the "libertarians," who view benignly any drug use by informed adults. Lest there be a misunderstanding about my own personal views on the use of these substances, I believe that any substance taken primarily to produce a profound mood-altering effect—other than for defined medical reasons—is inappropriate or risky, but not criminal. Acts associated with or resulting from such use, however, may be criminal, and those who commit such acts should be held accountable. Some may disagree. But I hope that, chapter by chapter, the book will create a better understanding of the effects of mood-altering substances and the reasons many continue to use them despite the personal consequences. Unless we understand the nature of dependency and addiction and the forces (including poverty, homelessness, and feelings of isolation even among the affluent) that promote such behavior, we will never even approach a solution to one of our most persistent and pervasive problems.

Acknowledgments

This book could not have been written without the knowledge provided by many in the sciences, the health professions, and the media, as well as my own personal experiences with those who have inappropriately used mood-altering drugs. With the former groups I have liberally provided references to their work. With the latter, I feel privileged to have been of some assistance in helping them confront their problems. On a more concrete level, I am thankful to Patricia Bruno, who participated in the typing of the manuscript, and to Suzanne Crow and the reference staff of the Levy Library for the tedious and far from rewarding task of checking doubtful references. I am especially thankful to Karen Fisher of The Haworth Press for copyediting the entire manuscript, and to my assistant, Mary Kennedy, for incorporating the many, penultimate changes needed to make the book as up-to-date as possible. Finally, as always, I am greatly indebted to my wife, Barbara, for her numerous suggestions concerning the format of the text, the content concerning psychotherapy, and the final title.

PART I:
BASIC CONCEPTS

Chapter 1

Who Uses Drugs?

From the first beginning of our knowledge of man, we find him consuming substances of no nutritive value, but taken for the sole purpose
of producing for a certain time a feeling of contentment, ease, and
comfort: Such a power was found in alcoholic beverages and in some
vegetable substances, the same that are used for this purpose at the
present day.

Lewin, *Phantastica:
Narcotic and Stimulating Drugs*

One of the features that most distinguishes humans from other species is
our ability to adapt to and alter environments to promote our survival. But
we often fail to recognize that we have been altering our internal milieu
since prehistoric times—experimenting with a wide variety of plants and
substances to improve our psychological and physical well-being. At times,
the resulting experiences were so profound that the mood-altering substances became integrated into a culture's religious practices or way of life.

The history of the poppy, for example, begins in antiquity. Its seeds and
pods have been found in the area of the Stone Age Lake Dwellers. The
poppy was cultivated between 5000 and 3000 B.C. by the Sumerians in Mes-
opotamia (present-day Iraq) to provide opium, known as *gil,* meaning "happiness and joy." Similarly, *Cannabis sativa* (marijuana) has been known almost since the beginning of recorded history. Practically every human
malady has been treated with one form or another of this plant. Alcohol and
psychoactive substances found in plants also have been used since prehistoric times. Caffeine, cocaine, and nicotine have all been used for centuries,
sometimes playing integral roles in different cultures. More recently, advances in technology have been applied to synthesizing mood-altering substances. New and highly potent synthetic products are available, along with
those "primitive" substances that probably will be around forever.

Our concern over drugs often focuses on the mood-altering substances
outlawed by society. Yet to understand why millions of people choose to
break the law to consume these drugs, the use and effects of all mood-alter-

ing substances taken for nonmedical purposes must be considered. These include drugs obtained in supermarkets and liquor stores, those prescribed by physicians, and "street drugs."

We must also consider the accuracy of statistics about drug use. Determining legitimate medical use of mood-altering drugs is difficult because reporting may violate confidentiality between physician and patient. Illegal drug users are not apt to identify themselves; users of alcohol are not necessarily alcoholics. As a result, most data are gathered from a cross section of the population and applied to the general population. This is far from a precise technology. Some surveys review data from people entering treatment programs or from pharmaceutical databanks that keep track of prescribed medications. In addition, a considerable number of epidemiological surveys have been conducted by investigators interested in the use patterns of specific drugs or drug use among specific populations. But these surveys may vary greatly in their definitions of current use and lifetime use. Moreover, in any cross-sectional survey, groups at high risk for drug use (high school dropouts, the homeless, the unemployed) may not be included. Most of the data in the book are from relatively few sources (see Appendix A) and must be viewed as estimates rather than absolute figures. Each source is updated on a regular basis, with several being available on the Web site of the National Institute on Drug Abuse. Readers are encouraged to review the most recent reports to obtain more specific information.

DRUGS AND THE YOUNG

Fortunately, since 1979, which was the year of the greatest drug use among teenagers, in general, the incidence of illicit drug use has decreased. The Monitoring the Future Survey in 2000 revealed that the use of marijuana, amphetamines, tranquilizers, heroin, and alcohol has remained steady, while the use of Ecstasy and steroids has increased, and the use of inhalants, Rohypnol, crack, and crystal methamphetamines has decreased somewhat. These figures, however, do not give cause for optimism, as overall drug use is higher now than in 1992. At present, 6 to 10 percent of twelve- to seventeen-year-olds are felt to be current users of illicit drugs, excluding marijuana. The Monitoring the Future Survey in 2000 estimated that approximately 49 percent of twelfth-grade students had used marijuana in their lifetime, with 3 percent current users and 6 percent daily users.

Of equal importance is the perceived availability of these drugs to teenagers. The Monitoring the Future Survey in 1999 reported easy availability to teenagers of cocaine (59 percent), marijuana (90 percent), heroin (35 percent), amphetamines (59 percent), and Ecstasy (40 percent). Despite the War on Drugs, these figures were relatively unchanged from those seen ten years ago.

The use of illicit drugs, however, pales when compared to that of licit drugs. Approximately 25 percent of students are estimated to have smoked cigarettes before the age of thirteen, with 34 percent of twelfth graders and 18 percent of ninth graders being current smokers and an additional 8 percent and 5 percent, respectively, currently using smokeless tobacco. Almost one-third of the students surveyed purchased their cigarettes in a store or gas station without any difficulty. The use of alcohol is equally if not more impressive. Approximately 31 percent of students initiated drinking before age thirteen, with 5 percent of twelfth graders being current drinkers of alcohol and 33 percent having consumed five or more drinks at least once during the thirty days prior to the 1999 survey. The use of drugs by the young is of special importance, as surveys have noted that if a person does not use alcohol, tobacco, or marijuana by age twenty, there is little likelihood that such use will ever occur.

ADULTS AND DRUG USE

The National Household Survey on Drug Abuse (NHSDA) has shown a decrease in illicit drug use among all age groups, races, and both sexes from a high of 25 million in 1979 to approximately 14.8 million in 1999, with 35 percent of the population twelve years of age or older having used an illicit drug at least once in their lives. Although marijuana is the most popular illicit drug used by 75 percent of current illicit drug users, 6.4 million Americans are currently using other illicit drugs with or without marijuana.

Tobacco consumption remains alarmingly high. In the 1999 National Household Survey, 30.2 percent or 66.8 million persons were current users of a tobacco product. The lifetime prevalence of cigarette use did not change significantly between 1985 and 1998, although there was a significant decrease in lifetime use of "any illicit drugs." Similarly, while the past-month prevalence rates for any illicit drug decreased significantly between 1985 and 1998, the prevalence of cigarette use remained about the same.

Pinning down use of mood-altering substances in older adults is difficult. Some researchers estimate that the number of alcoholics age sixty and above is slowly rising. And health professionals are recognizing late-onset alcoholism more and more often, a problem that may grow as the number of older people increases.

Inappropriate (nonmedical) use of physician prescribed psychotherapeutic drugs is also of concern. The 1998 National Household Survey on Drug Abuse found 12 percent, or 23.5 million, of the U.S. population to have used these drugs nonmedically, with 3.4 million using them within the month before the survey. Adults between the ages of twenty-six and thirty-four had the highest lifetime prevalence rate, 22 percent.

ETHNICITY AND DRUG USE

A long-standing societal perception is that drug use has always been major among poor African Americans and Hispanics. Epidemics of heroin use in lower-income areas have been documented. So have high rates of poverty and broken homes, which unquestionably play substantial roles in promoting drug use.

More than likely, our perceptions about drug use are related more to socioeconomic levels and the conditions under which drugs are taken than to racial and ethnic differences. After all, individuals with similar drug dependencies—but with greater economic resources—can hide their drug use more effectively.

Contrary to popular perception, minorities in general do not have a significant higher use of licit and illicit drugs than the general population. But certain differences may exist with respect to specific drugs. Alcohol use, for example, is of great concern among the Native American population. Use of inhalants among Native Americans is also frequent, with up to 30 percent trying these substances, compared with less than 10 percent of the general population. Hispanic youths tend to have intermediate rates of use. African Americans, however, are at much greater risk in contracting AIDS with intravenous drug use. However, the absolute rates of drug use by ethnicity are not really as important as increasing the research effort to define differences in susceptibility to drug use, regardless of ethnic background. It is more than fair to say that neither race nor ethnicity protects someone from using mood-altering substances or condemns someone to use them.

DRUGS AND THE WORKPLACE

Approximately 65 percent of young adults entering the workforce have probably used illegal drugs, and 10 to 23 percent of all U.S. workers may continue to use dangerous drugs while working. In a 1989 nationwide survey of employers, 80 percent identified alcohol and other drugs as significant problems in their organizations. This is not surprising as a 2000 report by the Schneider Institute for Health Policy noted, that of full-time employees, over one-third are smokers, 20 percent reported binge-drinking within the past month, and 12 percent used illicit drugs within the past year. A separate study reported 8 percent to be current users of illicit drugs.

A survey by the National Institute on Drug Abuse found that 10 to 20 percent of all job seekers applying to private corporations were actively using drugs. Eight percent of the men admitted getting high on marijuana while working, and 2 percent did so on cocaine. In a survey of over 800,000 cocaine users, 68 percent were employed full time, with 14 percent holding part-time jobs. A 1996 NHSDA survey estimated 6.1 million users of illicit drugs were gainfully employed. Although it is generally recognized that alcoholism affects productivity in the work place, a study highlighted the adverse effects of even casual drinking. Sponsored by the National Institute for Alcoholism and Alcohol Abuse and the Robert Wood Johnson Foundation, this survey of 14,000 employees at seven major corporations showed that 59 percent of alcohol-related productivity problems were caused by casual drinkers. Further, managers were more likely to drink alcohol during the workday than hourly workers (25 percent versus 8 percent, respectively).

With the increased use of urine testing over the past several years, there has been a decrease in the percentage of the workforce using illicit drugs. In 1985, 17 percent of full-time and 15 percent of part-time employees reported current use of illicit drugs as compared to 28 percent of those unemployed. In 1993, these percentages had decreased to 7 percent, 10 percent, and 14 percent respectively. Although it is a stretch to consider a cause-effect relationship, it is of interest that the incidence of heavy alcohol use diminished much less, decreasing from 8 to 7 percent for full-time and 10 to 7 percent for part-time employees, while actually increasing from 8 percent to 14 percent for those unemployed. Those who use drugs are more likely to miss time from work, switch jobs more frequently, and are terminated more often. Alcoholism alone is thought to be responsible for 500 million lost work days each year.

Alcohol plays a well-documented and publicized role in accidents, homicides, and suicides. Almost 50 percent of all traffic fatalities are alcohol related. Intoxication is a factor in approximately one-third of homicides and deaths from boating and aviation accidents. Nearly half of those in prison were intoxicated when they committed their crimes. Becoming increasingly evident is the role of other substances, notably marijuana and cocaine, in plane crashes, train wrecks, and, of course, automobile accidents.

DRUG USE AMONG THE AFFLUENT

The relationship between drug use and socioeconomic status is elusive. Data on drug use are frequently gathered from large federally funded programs, and these programs typically serve people from the lower or middle economic groups. People with sufficient financial resources avoid entering such programs. Instead, they seek treatment from the psychiatric departments of voluntary hospitals or private treatment facilities, often located in secluded areas.

From available information, however, it's clear that the rich are as susceptible as the poor to the effects of drug dependency. Indeed, a number of studies have suggested that excessive drinking is more prevalent among the affluent. In a study of more than 630 members of Alcoholics Anonymous, 35 percent were in managerial and professional positions.

In one well-conducted 1984 study of New York State householders, consistently high usage rates of illicit substances turned up among those with annual incomes of $50,000 or more. The upper-income group tended to favor marijuana, sedatives, tranquilizers, and cocaine. In the six months prior to the survey, 25 percent of those surveyed used one of those substances, compared with 17 percent of the general population. The favorite combination of substances was marijuana and alcohol, used by 14 percent of the group as opposed to 10 percent of the general population.

Use of alcohol and mood-altering drugs by members of the health, legal, and education professions is not new but has recently become a genuine cause for concern. As noted by Blum and Associates, psychiatrists (along with other mental health professionals) and lawyers were among the first to use hallucinogens for nontherapeutic reasons. They were often introduced to these drugs—particularly LSD—by friends who were using them as part of legitimate research projects. These observations demonstrate that inappropriate use of mood-altering drugs can occur despite professional status or awareness of their adverse effects.

SUMMARY

The use of licit and illicit mood-altering substances is widespread and respects neither ethnic nor socioeconomic boundaries. Such use occurs at all ages and among all populations. Virtually all family constellations have been affected by a member who uses some mood-altering drug to excess. Due to the ubiquity of mood-altering substances and the pleasure derived from them, their use can never be eliminated. However, it is essential to continue to expand our knowledge of the effects of these drugs and the most effective ways to assist people using them excessively, and, most important, to develop much more effective means of preventing inappropriate use among adults and initiation of use among teenagers.

Chapter 2

Classifying Mood-Altering Drugs

Mood-altering drugs can be classified by their availability or perceived harm to the public, effects perceived by the user, action on the brain, actual mood-altering effects, and legitimate medical use.

TYPE OF CLASSIFICATION

Availability or Perceived Public Harm

This classification separates substances into three categories—those that can be bought in stores, those that require a physician's prescription, and those that are considered illicit. It is valuable in determining the risk that society assigns to particular drugs, but it really doesn't help in understanding their effects. Despite their assigned risk, some illicit substances have only relatively minor effects—unless they're consumed frequently, or in large quantities, or are contaminated with other substances.

The User's Perception

Drugs are often classified by users with street jargon such as uppers, downers, mind messer-uppers, and spacers. Such categories are also not an entirely clear means of classification. Some drugs fall into several categories, depending on the person describing their effects, and substances that produce markedly different physiological effects are sometimes grouped together. What's more, a drug's effects vary with the user, the setting in which it's used, frequency of use, quantity, and how it is administered.

Frequency of Use

Another classification separates drugs by frequency of use (Table 2.1). This classification is also less than optimal in explaining the mechanisms of drug action. In addition, it doesn't clarify the similarities between several of

TABLE 2.1. Classification of Mood-Altering Drugs by Frequency of Use

---

Caffeine
Alcohol
Nicotine
Depressants, Barbiturates, Benzodiazepines
Opioids
Stimulants
Hallucinogens
Inhalants

Source: "Dispelling the Myths About Addiction." Washington, DC: Institute of Medicine, National Academy of Science, 1997.

the separate groups, which often allow substitution of one drug for another without addressing dependency. A prime example of this is alcohol and the drugs in the depressant, barbiturate benzodiazepine group.

Primary Action on Brain Receptors or Neurotransmitters

The action of mood-altering drugs on the brain is the basis for an essential classification for physicians and researchers. But it is less helpful to the public than classification by the actual effects experienced when taking drugs. This is especially true as it has now been shown that many different drugs can have similar effects on neurotransmitters, although the manifestations of their mood-altering effects may differ considerably.

Primary Mood-Altering Effect

The actual mood-altering effect of a drug is the classification that health professionals generally accept. But controversy can arise over placement of a drug in a particular group because that can mask critical similarities among groups. For example, both narcotics (opioids) and drugs in the alcohol-barbiturate-sedative group are central nervous system (CNS) depressants. Although combining them can result in severe breathing problems or even death, the drugs in each group initially affect mood quite differently. Nevertheless, this classification is useful. All drugs in a group have similar psychotropic effects and can usually be interchanged easily using equivalent doses, except that such minor stimulants as nicotine and caffeine are not equivalent to the much more potent amphetamines and cocaine.

Legitimate Medical Use

The existence of appropriate medical indications for a drug's use is one of two criteria for classifying drugs under the federal Controlled Substances Act of 1970. The other is its potential for inappropriate use. This is perhaps the least useful classification in understanding a drug's effects. However, knowledge of a drug's legitimacy is of critical importance in avoiding legal penalties associated with its use.

DIFFERENCES AND SIMILARITIES AMONG DRUG GROUPS

The characteristics of each drug group (Table 2.2) are discussed in detail in subsequent chapters, but several points should be mentioned here.

Interchangeability Within a Group

Interchangeability is important when considering treatment. For example, any drug in the CNS depressant group mimics the effects of alcohol. So substituting a minor tranquilizer, say, diazepam (Valium) or chlordiazepoxide (Librium), allows an alcohol-dependent person to avoid withdrawal symptoms, hide the dependency by eliminating alcohol from his or her breath, and yet remain dependent as well as achieve a high essentially indistinguishable from that of alcohol. Since dependency on the tranquilizer continues in the same way as dependency on alcohol; little is gained by substitution alone. Yet gradually reducing the dosage of the tranquilizer or barbiturate can detoxify someone with alcohol dependency.

Opioids

Dependency on any drug in a group can then be maintained by any other drug in that group (Chapter 3). Depending on the potency of the specific drug, however, more or less of the second drug may be needed. A heroin-dependent person may be maintained on methadone, meperidine (Demerol), or proproxyphene (Darvon) without going into opioid withdrawal. But much higher doses of meperidine or proproxyphene are needed to obtain the same effect as methadone. Although all opioids are interchangeable and can be substituted for one other if the doses are equivalent, nevertheless, problems can arise. Some have both opioid (agonist) and antiopioid (antagonist) properties. When such a drug is given to someone dependent on a pure opioid agonist, immediate withdrawal is possible. Drugs with dual properties displace the pure narcotic from receptors in the brain, as do antagonist-

TABLE 2.2. Mood-Altering Drugs by Primary Effect

Group	Examples
Central nervous system depressants	Alcohol; chloral hydrate; barbiturates; benzodiazepines (Ativan, Dalmane, Valium, Librium, Xanax, Serax, Halcion, etc.) hypnotic sedatives (Parest, Quaalude, Doriden); and other tranquilizers (Equanil, Miltown, Noludar, Placidyl, Valmid)
Narcotics (opiates)	Opium, codeine, heroin, morphine, Demerol, pethidine, Dilaudid, methadone, Percocet, Percodan, Darvon, Tussionex, fentanyl, Lomotil, Numorphan, agonist-antagonists (Talwin, Stadol, Buprenex, Temgesic, Nubain)
Stimulants	Amphetamines, caffeine, cocaine, nicotine, Preludin, Ritalin, diet pills, khat
Hallucinogens (psychedelics)	Amphetamine variants (2,5 DMA, PMA, STP, MDA, DOM, MMDA, TMA, DOB); LSD, mescaline, peyote, phencyclidine and analogues, psilocybin, psilocyn, and miscellaneous compounds (DMT, DET)
Cannabinoids	Marijuana, hashish, THC
Inhalants and volatile solvents	Nitrous oxide, various paints and paint thinners, glues
Antidepressants	
Tricyclic antidepressants	Amitriptyline (Elavil, Endep, Amitril, Emitrip) and related drugs
Monoamine oxidase (MAO) inhibitors	Isocarboxazid (Marplan), phenelzine (Nardil), tranylcypromine (Parnate)
Tetracyclic antidepressants	Maprotiline (Ludiomil)
Miscellaneous antidepressants	Trazodone (Desyrel), fluoxetine (Prozac)

only drugs. Substituting pentazocine (Talwin) for pain relief in a person who has been on meperidine (Demerol) for several days causes withdrawal—nausea, vomiting, and extreme discomfort (Chapter 12). Detoxification from a drug can be accomplished with any drug in a similar group, but not with drugs from another group. Thus narcotic (opioid) withdrawal cannot be treated adequately by alcohol or another CNS depressant.

Hallucinogens

Drugs classified as hallucinogens always cause hallucinations, even when relatively small amounts are used. Pharmacologically, hallucinogens include some amphetamine derivatives capable of causing hallucinations at extremely low doses. A number of drugs not classed as hallucinogens can also cause hallucinations in excessive amounts. Toxic doses of stimulants, narcotic antagonists, and even drugs not usually used inappropriately—steroids and drugs used to treat ulcers, for example—can produce hallucinations.

Marijuana

Cannabis (marijuana) and its synthetic analogue, THC, are considered a separate group. Drugs from other groups do not really produce identical effects. Although image distortions and hallucinations can occur at high doses, they are rare with common usage. Hashish, although more potent, has similar effects.

Stimulants

The potency of stimulants varies greatly. Nicotine and caffeine are obviously much less stimulating than amphetamines or cocaine. Khat, derived from the leaves of *Catha edulis,* is pharmaceutically distinct from other stimulants, but its actions are similar to those of amphetamines and cocaine—two extremely potent stimulants whose toxic effects are often indistinguishable.

Antidepressants

A common misconception is that the use of antidepressants does not lead to dependency. Recent evidence suggests that inappropriate use of certain antidepressants with a predominantly sedative effect, say amitriptyline (Amitril, Elavil, Emitrip, Endep, Enovil), may be considerable in those with a history of inappropriate use of mood-altering drugs.

Potential for Dependency

It should be emphasized that any drug in any group can be used inappropriately, but use alone does not automatically imply dependency. Drugs within a group can vary greatly in ability to produce habituation, dependency, and addiction. Even those with the greatest dependency-producing potential can, in theory, be used intermittently for long periods without producing dependency (Chapter 3). However, even when these drugs are consumed intermittently, their pleasurable effects often encourage greater use (positive reinforcement), and that can lead to dependency. The process is most common with the more potent central nervous system depressants, narcotics, and stimulants.

Too often, people begin taking drugs thinking they can easily control their drug use. Yet animal testing shows that habitual self-administration of narcotics, barbiturates, alcohol, and stimulants can develop quickly (Chapter 3). With some drugs, such as narcotics, use occurs at a steady rate once dependency has been established, mainly to prevent unpleasant withdrawal. With others, notably cocaine and amphetamines, the reinforcing effects are particularly great. Sometimes laboratory animals press levers up to 4,000 times to self-administer a single injection of cocaine. When given free access, the animals increasingly choose the substance over food and water, if necessary, until they die. In short, mood-altering drugs are neither equal in their effects nor equal in their potential to produce dependency.

Controlled Substances Act

The Controlled Substances Act of 1970 created five schedules for drugs (Table 2.3). Periodically, drugs are reclassified based on reports of increased inappropriate use or decreased effectiveness. The Drug Enforcement Administration within the Department of Justice is responsible for assuring compliance.

Schedule I

Schedule I drugs have the highest potential for inappropriate use and have no commonly accepted medical use in the United States. These drugs cannot be prescribed and are available only for research after special application to federal agencies.

Schedule II

Schedule II drugs have a currently acceptable medical use, along with a high potential for inappropriate use and for causing heavy psychological and physiological dependency. To prescribe Schedule II drugs, physicians must be registered with the federal Drug Enforcement Administration (DEA) and must comply with certain requirements.

TABLE 2.3. Schedules for Federally Controlled Substances

Schedule	Common Examples
I	Heroin, marijuana, LSD, DMT, DET, peyote, psilocybin, mescaline, hashish, dihydromorphone, methaqualone, nicocodeine, PCP
II	*Narcotics:* opium (pantopon), morphine, codeine, hydromorphone (Dilaudid), methadone (Dolphine), meperidine (Demerol, pethadol), oxymorphone (Numorphan), oxycodone (Percocet), fentanyl (Sublimaze)
	Stimulants: cocaine, amphetamine group, phenmetrazine (Preludin), methylphenidate (Ritalin)
	Cannabinoids: dronabinol (Marinol), nabilone (Cesamet)
	Barbiturates: amobarbital, pentobarbital, Seconal, etorphine hydrochloride
III	Paregoric, glutethimide (Doriden), methyprylon (Noludar), nalorphine, various weight-reducing pills
IV	Pentazocine (Talwin), dextropropoxyphene (Darvon), phenobarbital, chloral hydrate, ethchlorvynol (Placidyl), meprobamate (Miltown, Neuramate, Equanil, Sedabamate), benzodiazepines (Valium, Librium, etc.)
V	Drugs containing moderate quantities of narcotics, usually in antidiarrheal agents and cough suppressants, includes diphenoxylate preparations (Lofene, Logen, Lomotil, Lo-trol, Normil, Lomanate)

Note: For selected substances—schedule of a particular drug may change with time.

Schedule III, IV, V

Schedule III, IV, and V drugs have currently acceptable medical uses; their potential for inappropriate use and dependency is lower in each succeeding schedule. Schedule V drugs may, under certain well-defined conditions, be dispensed without a prescription if that practice doesn't conflict with other federal, state, or local laws.

Overreliance on Schedules for Dependency Risk

Many Schedule I and II drugs can produce a high degree of physical dependency and considerable withdrawal symptoms. But as noted earlier, any drug with mood-altering properties can be used inappropriately and produce intense "highs," depending on how much and how often it's used. So someone who needs to get high when the preferred drug is unavailable will take any available drug—in large quantities, if necessary—to obtain the desired effect.

Perhaps the most striking example was an episode of paregoric use in Detroit in the early 1950s. At that time, paregoric, commonly used to treat diarrhea, was sold over the counter. Addicts unable to get heroin bought paregoric, boiled it with the antihistamine tripelennamine, and injected it intravenously. Users called it blue velvet; its high was almost identical to heroin's.

More than two decades later, a similar use was perpetrated with the narcotic agonist-antagonist pentazocine (Talwin). Another substitute, propoxyphene (Darvon), was initially promoted as a nonnarcotic painkiller. But it is a derivative of methadone, and when taken in large doses can produce narcotic dependency and withdrawal symptoms. Drug users quickly spotted Darvon's mood-altering effects, but the public became aware of its potential for inappropriate use only recently.

The Controlled Substances Act has been a mixed blessing. It has helped highlight drugs that create dependency and withdrawal symptoms, but ironically has lulled the public and the medical profession into incorrectly believing that Schedule III, IV, and V drugs can be used with little concern about dependency.

Drug scheduling fosters other ironies. Drugs that some professionals deem worthwhile are considered by others to have no medical value. Some examples are as follows:

- Heroin, a Schedule I drug, is available in England as a potent pain reliever. But most doctors in the United States oppose making it available for terminal patients in excruciating pain.
- Buprenorphine, a noncontrolled opioid agonist-antidepressant analgesic, can be prescribed freely for pain. Yet it is one of the leading drugs of abuse in Australia, New Zealand, and, most recently, South Asia and France. When injected intravenously, it provides a high equal to that of heroin.
- Marijuana, medically useful in well-defined situations, is listed in Schedule I, while its principle psychoactive component, dronabinol (Marinol), and its synthetic counterpart, nabilone (Cesamet), are available as Schedule II drugs to ease nausea and vomiting following chemotherapy and are promoted as appetite inducers. Yet marijuana is felt not to be helpful in any of these situations.
- Peyote, a Schedule I drug, is not available for medical purposes. But until recently it was "approved" for use by various Native American groups in religious ceremonies. This freedom was revoked by a U.S.

Supreme Court decision in 1990, allowing federal and state laws to exclude exemptions for use of illicit drugs for religious purposes.

As stated previously, any drug that alters moods can be used inappropriately. That's not to say these drugs should be prohibited when there are medical reasons for their use. Risk of disabling dependency is low when a drug is taken for medical reasons for a defined period. Someone incapacitated by pain can be greatly helped by of opioids. But using any substance for the primary purpose of getting high carries the potential for habituation and—depending on the drug—addiction.

DESIGNER DRUGS

In the 1980s, a new group of substances was synthesized. These new drugs have effects similar to those of existing drugs but differ slightly in chemical structure (see Table 2.4). They've been termed designer drugs because their chemical structure is developed specifically to avoid accusations of illegal manufacture. Many designer drugs can produce potent highs with such small quantities that they're virtually undetectable in blood or urine tests. And the change in chemical structure often results in unanticipated—sometimes fatal—toxic effects.

TABLE 2.4. Designer Drugs

Street Name	Clinical Name	Class
China White	Fentanyl derivatives	Narcotic
Ecstasy, XTC, Adam, MDM, MDMA	3-4 methylenedioxy-methamphetamine	Hallucinogen
Eve, Love Drug, MDMA	3-4 methylene disxyamphetamine	Hallucinogen
Ice	Methamphetamine derivatives produced in smokable form	Stimulants
MPPP	Meperidine derivative: N-methyl-4 phenyl-4 propionoxy piperidine	Narcotic
MPTP	Meperidine derivative: N-methyl-4 phenyl-1,2,3,6 tetrahydropyridine	Narcotic
Marijuana	Synhexyl	Marijuana
PMA	Paramethoxyamphetamine	Hallucinogen

The three major groups of designer drugs are fentanyl (Sublimaze) analogs, meperidine (Demerol) analogs, and amphetamine analogs. Drugs in the first two groups are used instead of heroin; those in the third group in place of hallucinogens. By the late 1980s, methamphetamine derivatives in smokable form began appearing with increasing frequency as a substitute for cocaine.

These drugs are extremely potent. One fentanyl analog, for example, is 3,000 times more potent than the same amount of morphine; a meperidine analog is 25 times more potent than meperidine itself. For producers and dealers, the advantages of designer drugs are great. Since routine toxicology can't detect and identify these substances, they enjoy licit status for a while until laws can be passed making their production, sale, or purchase illegal. They're also fairly easy to manufacture—and with legally obtained chemicals. (This eliminates the necessity of becoming involved with criminal organizations to buy opium or the morphine base, cocaine, or marijuana.) And designer drugs are easy to market because they produce highs that are often indistinguishable from those of naturally derived products. The biggest advantage, however is the enormous profit. By 1986, the annual market for these substances ran to an estimated $1 billion.

Designer drugs carry significant risks. Overdosing is common; users often do not realize that the new drug may be 1,000 times more potent than the drug they usually take. Side effects of a meperidine analog (MPPP) include drastic loss of muscle control (similar to symptoms of Parkinson's disease, which can lead to permanent neurological damage). Serious complications from the amphetamine analogs Eve and Ecstasy vary from extreme restlessness and agitation to convulsions.

The National Narcotics Act of 1984, part of the Comprehensive Crime Control Act, an early effort to put legal restraints on designer drugs, wasn't particularly effective. As a result, the more stringent Anti-Drug Abuse Act of 1986 contains the Controlled Substance Analogue Act, which requires that any analogue of a Schedule I substance be included as a controlled substance in Schedule I.

CLUB DRUGS

Most recently, the use of several types of drugs by young adults and teenagers has appeared on the "street scene," cutting across all socioeconomic levels. This category includes drugs such as LSD, Ecstasy, Rohypnol, methamphetamine, Ketamine, and GHB. Rohypnol and GHB are also called "date rape" drugs due to their ability to cause sleepiness and amnesia. The Monitoring the Future Survey in 2000 reported Ecstasy to be used by over

81 percent of 12th graders. These drugs will be discussed more fully in succeeding chapters.

PERFORMANCE-ENHANCING DRUGS

Athletes often use drugs to improve their performance. They take stimulants to give them more energy, narcotics to relieve pain, and anabolic steroids, cortisone, and growth hormone to increase muscular strength. Drugs
in the third category don't produce mood changes, but their excessive use
can affect behavior (Chapter 20).

SUMMARY

In the following chapters, the effects of specific drugs in the body are discussed in considerable detail, as are their potential for and treatment of dependence, regardless of specific classification. Ultimately this is the critical
knowledge needed when addressing inappropriate drug use.

Chapter 3

Habituation, Dependency, and Addiction

Although mood-altering substances have been used since antiquity, clear definitions and terminology for their effects weren't developed until the early 1980s. Some terms still have not been accepted fully by the drug-treatment community. One reason is the emotional response generated in various individuals by such terms as "dependency," "addiction," and "addict."

Recognizing the need for clear and uniform terminology, the American Medical Association established a special task force in 1983 to survey ninety-nine experts in various professions. That first attempt produced a common—though not perfect—vocabulary. The effort also provided a core of understanding for developing a consensus about patterns of use of mood-altering drugs. To help clarify the AMA's terminology, some additional definitions have been provided by the author.

DEFINING TERMS

Patterns of mood-altering drug use form a ten-stage continuum: nonuse or abstinence, appropriate use, misuse, experimental use, abuse, habituation, psychological and/or physical dependency, addiction, withdrawal, and finally, craving.

Nonuse or Abstinence

Nonuse denotes just that—not using a substance at all. Abstinence refers to nonuse of a mood-altering dependency-producing drug that had previously been used.

Appropriate Use

Appropriate use is using a substance for sound reasons in an accepted and approved manner. But "appropriate" is a relative term. These are recognized and approved uses for drugs sanctioned by the Food and Drug Administration and indications recognized by physicians that may not yet be formally approved by the FDA.

Minor tranquilizers are appropriate treatment for extreme anxiety that is otherwise uncontrollable. Medical consensus also holds that mood-altering drugs are appropriate in a variety of situations, such as stimulants for hyperactivity syndrome in children, opiate (narcotic) analgesics for unremitting pain unresponsive to nonnarcotic analgesics, cocaine as a topical anesthetic, major tranquilizers for severe anxiety, antidepressants for severe depression, and sleeping medications for incapacitating insomnia.

Other uses for mood-altering drugs are accepted—though not unanimously—by the medical community. They include stimulants to lessen the need for morphine in cases of acute postoperative pain, antidepressants for chronic pain, marijuana for controlling nausea following chemotherapy, antidepressants for cocaine users, and methadone for heroin users.

Misuse

Misuse is taking a drug for its prescribed purpose, but not in the way it is supposed to be taken. Two examples are taking sleeping medication more frequently than prescribed in order to sleep longer, and using more analgesics than indicated for headache in the hope of getting faster and better relief.

Experimental Use

Experimental use may be unintentional misuse or abuse. But more commonly it's a conscious effort to see what effect the drug will have. Experimental use implies trying a drug only once or twice. This type of use is quite common in adolescents.

Abuse

Abuse or inappropriate use is taking a drug for other than its intended purpose and/or in a way other than that prescribed. It's also use of any illicit drug that can result in physical, psychological, economic, legal, or social harm, either to oneself or to others. Abuse begins as experimental use, progresses to casual or intermittent use, and then moves along the continuum to more serious patterns of use. Drugs of abuse can be classified by their potential for dependency (Chapter 2). It should also be noted that abuse is perhaps an inappropriate term as one cannot literally abuse an inert substance. Nonetheless, it is commonly applied to inappropriate use of mood-altering drugs and is so used here.

Habituation

Habituation is the result of continued casual use and can be characterized as the need to take a drug at given times to avoid the anxiety associated with not taking it. At this stage, the intervals between uses are long enough to prevent dependency. Habituation doesn't usually progress to dependency or addiction but is frequently observed in weekend drinkers, in smokers who need a cigarette on awakening, and even in the many people who need a morning cup of coffee to "get started."

Dependency

Psychological and/or physical dependency usually follow habituation to a substance with high potential for dependency (see Table 3.1). Typically, dependency is characterized by three responses:

1. The need to take a drug to experience its pleasurable effects
2. The appearance of behavioral changes—psychological and/or physiological—when the drug is abruptly discontinued
3. The need continually to increase the dose and/or frequency of use to sustain its initial effects

TABLE 3.1. Dependency Potential of Commonly Used Drugs

Drug	Psychological	Physical	Withdrawal
Alcohol	4	4	4
Other CNS depressants	2-4	2-4	2-4
Narcotics	3-4	3-4	3-4
Stimulants			
Caffeine	1	0-1	0-1
Tobacco	3-4	3	0-2
Amphetamines	4	2	1-2
Cocaine	5	2	1-2
Marijuana	2-3	1	2
Hallucinogens	2	0	0
PCP	2	1	1
Inhalants and volatile solvents	2	0-1	0

Scale: 0-5, with 5 indicating most severe degree of dependency.

Psychological Dependency

Psychological dependency is an emotional state of craving a drug, either for its positive effects or to avoid the negative effects caused by its absence. All mood-altering drugs can create psychological dependency.

Psychological dependency often motivates drug-seeking behavior. A common misconception is that drugs with low degrees of physical dependency are less likely to be used inappropriately. Cocaine, for example, is thought to produce little physical dependency, but no drug is more psychologically reinforcing. Trying to differentiate the "addictive potential" of drugs by their degree of physical dependency is of little value.

Physical Dependency

Physical dependency is reached when the body has adapted to a drug and cannot function normally without it. Unpleasant symptoms—withdrawal—appear when drug use is suddenly discontinued. Physical dependency is associated with many medications and is usually—but not always—characterized by increasing tolerance to one or more effects of the drug. In fact, dependency is acceptable if the drug is for a specific medical condition and is necessary to maintain normal functioning. For example, individuals with epilepsy are dependent on barbiturates prescribed to prevent seizures. Discontinue the medication, and they suffer withdrawal. On barbiturates or similar drugs, however, they function without having their lives disrupted by seizures. Similarly, people with chronic or incapacitating cancer pain are able to resume normal, productive lives with the use of narcotic (opiate) analgesics. Their dependency on these drugs may be quite pronounced, and they may need increasingly high doses to function normally, but they rarely take the drugs for their euphoric effect. Problems begin when a person becomes dependent on the euphoria or high produced by the drug and takes it solely for that purpose.

It is ironic that dependency on non-mood-altering drugs is not only viewed as extremely beneficial by society but in fact is responsible for our leading longer and more productive lives. Just to cite a few examples: diabetics' dependency on insulin, asthmatics' dependency on bronchodilators, and the dependency of those with heart disease on multiple medications.

Tolerance

One definition of tolerance is physiological adaptation to the effects of a drug. In other words, the user needs larger and larger quantities to obtain the same effect and can consume those greater doses without untoward side effects. Tolerance to any drug in a particular class is usually accompanied by cross-tolerance—that is, tolerance to other drugs in that class. Tolerance to barbiturates, for example, would be accompanied by cross-tolerance to benzodiazepines or alcohol. Tolerance of the various effects of a specific drug may develop at different rates. A person may become tolerant to the sedative and euphoric effects of barbiturates relatively quickly, but tolerance to the lethal level rises much more slowly. The result can be an overdose when the person tries to get high with those drugs.

Different groups of drugs produce tolerance at different rates and intensities, depending on their potency, quantity taken, and the individual's sensitivities. For example, both narcotics (opiates) and CNS depressants—such as alcohol—can lead to a high degree of dependency and tolerance, and withdrawal follows if they are suddenly discontinued. But withdrawal from alcohol is much more severe than withdrawal from narcotics, and if untreated may cause death.

Cocaine generates very rapid psychological dependency. Its markedly positive (euphoric) and short-lived effect fosters development of dependency because the user immediately wants to repeat the experience. Dependency on alcohol develops over a much longer period, and with responsible use may never develop. Nevertheless, the degree of physical dependency on alcohol is much greater than on cocaine; so is the severity of withdrawal.

Addiction

Addiction, characterized by the compulsive use of a substance resulting in physical or psychological dependency, is usually but not always accompanied by increased tolerance. The person is unable to restrict drug use. As addiction develops, individuals lose control over intake and invest their energies in obtaining the drug. Today, the drug with the greatest addictive potential is cocaine or crack.

"Addiction," unlike "dependency," is always used in the negative sense. Within this powerful negative context, many people lose the ability to see the addict as a person, to understand the physiological changes occurring in the body as a result of continued drug use, to think clearly about appropriate approaches to addiction, or to recognize the effectiveness of many existing treatments. Putting addiction in perspective requires a look at two other features associated with dependency.

Craving

Craving is the need or compulsion to continue to take a dependency-producing drug even after abstinence has been achieved. Initially thought to be a purely psychological process, advances in neurobiological research, as described in the following, have isolated areas in the brain responsible for craving. Craving is now accepted as the most common reason for resuming drug use.

Withdrawal

Withdrawal is what happens after a drug-dependent person abruptly stops taking the drug. The resulting physiological changes vary according to the kind of drug it is or the degree of dependency on it. Withdrawal can always be suppressed by the drug that caused the dependency or by another drug in the same group when cross-tolerance exists.

EFFECTS OF DRUGS ON THE BRAIN

In general, most behavior is modified by chemical substances called neurotransmitters acting on the brain and other parts of the nervous system. Neurotransmitters, contained in nerve cells (neurons), may be released to transmit information to other cells. Although production and destruction of neurotransmitters may vary with the specific substance, simply put, neurotransmitters are usually synthesized in the neuron by a variety of enzymes acting on basic precursor substances. Once synthesized, neurotransmitters are stored in vesicles in a nerve ending and released after an electrical impulse passes through the nerve or by the action of a specific substance given to the body (Figure 3.1). Once released into the space between nerve cells (synapse), a neurotransmitter moves across the synapse and attaches itself to a receptor site located on a postsynaptic neuron. Specific receptors exist for each neurotransmitter, with the fit described as a "lock-key" interaction. This combination initiates a chain of biochemical events that ultimately results in either excitation or inhibition.

The neurotransmitter may then be (a) broken down by enzymes at the receptor site, (b) released into and metabolized at the area of the synapse, or (c) returned to the originating neuron to be broken down by enzymes located in the cell. Mood-altering drugs can therefore affect the neurotransmitter-receptor reaction in a variety of ways (Figure 3.2). They may interfere with the enzymes required to synthesize the drug in the neuron or, once the drug is synthesized, may prevent it from being stored in the vesicle, resulting in its being broken down in the nerve cell prior to being released into the synapse. Drugs may cause a release of neurotransmitters from the vesicles into the synaptic space or increase the number of receptors for certain neurotransmitters. A given drug may occupy the receptor site, preventing neurotransmitter-receptor binding and resulting in an increased concentration of the transmitter in the synaptic space. When this occurs, the drug may mimic the effect of the neurotransmitter or may be "neutral," that is, not

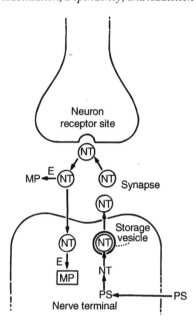

FIGURE 3.1. Functioning of neurotransmitter at receptor sites. PS = precursor substance; NT = neurotransmitter; E = enzyme; MP = metabolic product, the substance formed when NT is broken down.

cause any interaction. Uptake of the neurotransmitter may be inhibited or breakdown of the transmitter may be prevented through the drug's action in blocking the enzymes responsible for the degradation. Although receptor sites for specific mood-altering drugs such as opiates, benzodiazepines, and marijuana have been identified, almost all mood-altering drugs affect neurotransmitter-receptor interactions in a variety of ways. These are discussed more fully later.

Neurotransmitters related to mood-altering drug action include the endogenous endorphins and enkephalins (opiates), dopamine (nicotine, alcohol, cocaine, opiates, and other stimulants), gamma-aminobutyric acid (alcohol, benzodiazepines), norepinephrine (opiates, stimulants, LSD), epinephrine, and 5-hydroxytryptamine or serotonin (alcohol). Drugs that mimic or enhance the effect of the body's own neurotransmitters are termed agonists. Drugs that prevent the neurotransmitter or a like substance (drugs) from combining with a receptor are termed antagonists. Drugs may also act independently of receptor activity. Some may combine with smaller molecules in the cells. Others, such as those used in cancer chemotherapy, may be incorporated into the genetic material of cells.

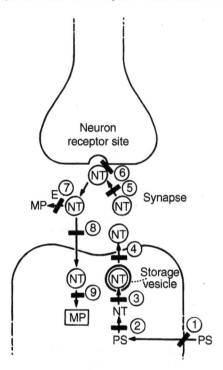

FIGURE 3.2. Sites of possible interference of mood-altering drugs with neurotransmitter-receptor interactions. PS = precursor substance; NT = neurotransmitter; E = enzyme; MP = metabolic product as breakdown of NT. (1) Inhibition of uptake precursor substance; (2) inhibition of synthesis of NT; (3) prevention of storage of NT in vesicle; (4) prevention of release of NT from vesicles in nerve terminal into synapse; (5) prevention of NT-receptor binding; (6) actual binding of drug with receptor; (7) prevention of breakdown of NT either in synapse or after return to cell (9); (8) prevention of uptake of NT at neuron.

Also located in the brain are anatomical areas called pleasure or reward centers. When subjected to stimulation of these centers during laboratory experiments, animals continue the pleasurable effects by pressing a lever to receive direct electrical stimulation or a mood-altering drug, say, cocaine. Although, as noted in Chapter 2, distinct differences exist between groups of mood-altering drugs, all have a commonality in enhancing neurobiological circuits, which includes an activation of the mesolimbic dopamine system in the part of the brain extending from the midbrain ventral tegmental area (VTA) to the nucleus accumbens (NA) and the medial frontal cortex (MFC) (Table 3.2) (Figure 3.3).

TABLE 3.2. Effects of Mood-Altering Drugs on Neurotransmitters

	Endor-phins	Dopa-mine	Serotonin	Acetyl-choline	GABA	Norepine-phrine
Alcohol	±	+	+			
Cocaine	1	+	+	+	+	+
Opioids	+	+	+			+

Although the opioid receptors are primarily responsible for the euphoria associated with heroin, the endorphins and enkephalins are also believed to be in some way associated with alcohol dependency and craving. Dopamine is felt to be the major neurotransmitter in the reward system of the brain acted on by nicotine, alcohol, opioids, and stimulants. Glutamate has been associated with drug-seeking behavior, often responsible for relapses after abstinence has been achieved. Serotonin has also been implicated in producing dependency as well as craving. Serotonin as well as corticotropin-releasing factor in the pituitary and hypothalamus have been associated with cocaine, opiate, and ethanol withdrawal. Physical signs of withdrawal seen after abruptly discontinuing alcohol or opioids, however, are mainly due to an outpouring of norepinephrine from cells located in the locus coeruleus of the brain. It should be emphasized that although it has now been demonstrated that drugs from different groups have common sites of action, it is their action on "nonshared" sites that explains the differences seen when they are taken for a mood-altering effect. All of these findings help explain the basis for dependency as well as why people continue to use drugs. They will be reviewed again in Chapter 4.

Development of Dependency: A Practical Explanation

A grasp of how dependency develops is the key to understanding why it's so hard to stop using a particular drug. The course of heroin use best illustrates the process (see Figure 3.4).

When someone injects heroin for the first time, the amount of the drug reaching the brain slowly rises. The rate of rise depends on the strength of heroin, speed and amount of its consumption, and the body's ability to metabolize it. Initial use may result in an uncomfortable feeling that reaches a peak and then slowly diminishes. But with subsequent use, the effect is pleasurable and promotes continued use.

Tolerance buildup is avoided if the user spaces the heroin injections so that the brain isn't consistently exposed to concentrations of the drug. The pleasurable effects are achieved, but the person won't become dependent.

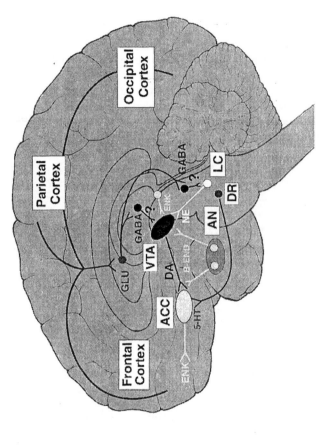

FIGURE 3.3. Mesolimbic system as it is involved in addiction to drugs. ACC, nucleus accumbens; VTA, ventral tegmental area; AN, arcuate nucleus; LC, locus coeruleus; DR, dorsal raphé; GLU, glutamate; GABA, gamma-aminobutyric acid; ENK, enkephalin; NE, norepinephrine; DA, dopamine; β-END, beta endorphin; 5-HT, 5-hydroxytryptamine (seratonin).

Source: Brick, J. and Erickson, C. (1998). *Drugs, the Brain, and Behavior: The Pharmacology of Abuse and Dependence,* p. 163. Reprinted by permission of The Haworth Press, Inc.

Users who take heroin that way are known as "chippers." They inject once or twice a week without becoming physically dependent. Similarly, using alcohol in that manner—a pattern termed "binge drinking"—does not lead to physical dependency (see Figure 3.4, graph A).

Trouble comes when the user takes more of the drug while levels of previous doses are still in the brain tissues stimulating the pleasure centers. That's when a tolerance threshold (TT) begins to develop. The user gets a high when the threshold is crossed (see Figure 3.4, graph B). Dropping the drug level below the threshold results in withdrawal symptoms.

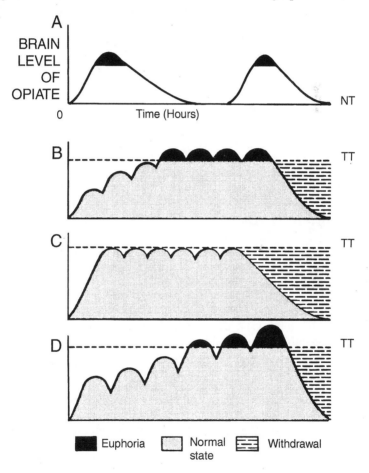

FIGURE 3.4. The development of dependence and withdrawal.
Note: NT = nontolerant; TT = tolerance threshold

Taking the drug at constant doses at regular intervals raises the threshold so that a high is no longer experienced (see Figure 3.4, graph C). Rather than stop the drug, lose the highs, and face withdrawal, the user injects more heroin and/or shortens the time interval between injections (see Figure 3.4, graph D). That pushes the drug level above the threshold and allows a high to be produced.

This simplified description points up some important facts about drug use:

- Tolerance to the high from most drugs continues to rise with constant administration, thus necessitating greater and greater intake to achieve a high.
- When the amount taken is much higher than the tolerance threshold, the result is overdose and possibly death.
- When the tolerance threshold is slowly increased, the user can be maintained on very high levels of the drug—levels that could kill a nontolerant person.
- Tolerance to specific effects of a drug may not occur at the same rate.
- When tolerance to the high is reached faster than tolerance to the lethal dose, escalating drug use may cause death.
- When the tolerance threshold is gradually lowered by giving smaller and smaller doses of the drug (detoxification), withdrawal will follow with relatively little discomfort.

Neurobiological Correlates

On a molecular level, dependency is produced by changes in the messenger system of the cellular network, the cyclic adenosine monophosphate system (cAMP). Chronic use of opiates and other mood-altering substances cause an upregulation of this system. When use is suddenly discontinued, the upregulated system continues to function, resulting in hyperactivity and withdrawal. This initiates drug-seeking behavior associated with an increase in dopamine release in the nucleus accumbens in part facilitated by the neurotransmitter glutamate. Opioids exert these effects by binding to the opioid receptors in the VTA, the NA, and the MFC; other mood-altering drugs do so by directly blocking neurotransmitter reuptake. Opioids and some other mood-altering drugs also inhibit a part of the brain called the locus coeruleus, whose cells secrete norepinephrine. Chronic use of these drugs results in an adaptation of those cells to the inhibition. As discussed previously, when those drugs are abruptly discontinued, there is excessive neuronal excitation with an outpouring of norepinephrine from the locus coeruleus, which is responsible for the signs and symptoms of withdrawal. Finally, it is important to remember that the degree of euphoria is facilitated by the rate of drug delivery to the brain. This is why heroin users usually progress from snorting to injecting and cocaine users move from snorting to freebasing (crack).

Chronic use of these drugs produces long-term changes in the brain that, depending on the actions of the specific drug, affect bodily functions responsible for physical dependency. Other changes with repeated use result in a tolerance to the effects of those drugs in the reward center of the brain, resulting in increasing amounts of the drug being needed to produce a similar high. Finally, conditioning effects occur in the memory circuits of the brain that produce a craving for the drug after abstinence is obtained or even withdrawal symptoms when a person is placed in an environment where withdrawal from the drug has occurred.

These concepts become quite important in understanding not only why people use mood-altering drugs but the rationale behind existing treatment modalities. In the ensuing chapters, these relationships are reviewed and clarified. It is ironic that while science continues to define with precision the receptors, biochemical changes, and neuronal circuits that are associated with dependence on virtually all mood-altering drugs, the public perception of drug addiction as a moral or predominantly social problem remains unchanged, as does the overall feeling of futility about successful treatment.

Chapter 4

Why People Use Drugs

The topic for a panel at a national meeting of experts on drug use was "Why do people take drugs?" The panelists—a psychologist, psychiatrist, general physician, sociologist, and a drug user—were allotted ten minutes each. All the professionals ran overtime, of course. Finally, the moderator asked the user to describe why he took drugs.

"They give me great pleasure" was all he said.

Despite the vast amounts of time, effort, and money spent trying to discover why people use drugs, no uniformly accepted theory can consistently predict drug dependency. The "feel-good" response is only a partial answer to a complex question; drug use often continues long after the pleasure has gone. In fact, studies have demonstrated that psychostimulant drugs may produce more euphoria in the nonaddicted than the addicted individual. But the pleasure provided by those substances must never be underestimated, and that answer must be taken seriously.

INITIATING DRUG USE

Data from the 1995 National Household Survey on Drug Abuse stated that over 70 million Americans have used some illicit drug during their lifetime. This does not include the additional millions who consume alcohol to excess or who smoke. Although once drug use is established the pathways described below come into play, our greatest success will be in preventing the initiating of such use. There have been many explanations of why one begins to use mood-altering drugs.

A 1997 survey by Louis Harris and Associates of why people feel one would use illicit drugs revealed only three factors given as major reasons by a majority of those surveyed. These were peer pressure, poor parenting, and drug dealers trying to expand their markets. Unfortunately, few of us actually have paid attention to what those who engage in this activity say. A survey of youths who had used illicit drugs gave five reasons for such use: (1) to feel grown up, (2) to fit in and belong, (3) to take risks and rebel, (4) to relax and feel good, and (5) to satisfy curiosity.

People start using drugs for a variety of reasons. Some are looking for a pleasurable experience. Others like the excitement associated with illicit drug use. And others just want to escape their reality. Many, or even most, will become neither addicted nor even frequent users. However, although initiation of drug use is volitional, continued use effects demonstrable changes in the brain that not only are long lasting but, when the drug is discontinued, can disturb an individual's homeostasis to the degree that a craving occurs and a return to drug use quickly follows. Dependency in the case of many mood-altering drugs is thus an actual medical illness and must be recognized as such to provide effective therapy. The reasons that drug use is continued are related to four basic factors (Table 4.1), whose biological determinants have been fairly well defined. Similarly, environmental and psychological forces that also play a role in continued use are increasingly being recognized. All these factors must be considered in addressing drug use. The challenge that remains, however, is clearly defining those features that separate the majority of persons who experiment with mood-altering drugs from those whose continued use leads to dependency and addictions.

BIOLOGICAL DETERMINANTS

Genetic Susceptibility

Scientists and clinicians have been searching for many years for a genetic disposition to chemical dependency. In animals, genetic susceptibility clearly can be shown to exist. Lewis-strain rats have been bred to readily self-inject drugs, whereas the Fisher 344 strain resists self-injecting behavior. When compared to "normal rats," the amount of dopamine released is

TABLE 4.1. Why People Use Mood-Altering Drugs

	Site	Clinical Manifestation
Pleasure (Euphoria)	Nucleus Accumbens (NA)	Inability to control use despite negative consequences
	Ventral Tegmental Area (VTA)	
Fear of Withdrawal	Locus Coeruleus	Continued drug use even in absence of euphoria
Drug Craving	Multiple Brain Sites	Abstinence often followed by relapse, especially under stress

markedly increased with the Lewis-strain rats, whereas the dopamine released by self-injection in the Fisher 344 rats is well below normal.

In humans, hereditary patterns have long been recognized in the development of alcoholism (see Chapter 7) but, until recently, not clearly demonstrated in relation to other drug dependencies. Studies of the familial patterns in both alcoholism and other forms of drug dependency have produced variable results; however, all have found a higher prevalence of both alcoholism and drug dependency among family members with those disorders than among the general population. Studies have revealed a 6.7-fold increase for substance abuse, a 3.5-fold increase for alcoholism, a 5.1-fold increase for unipolar depression, and a 7.6-fold increase for antisocial personality among first-degree relatives of patients dependent on opiates when compared to relatives of control patients. Similarly, twin studies have also found higher rates of alcoholism among twins than among siblings and higher rates among monozygotic than among dizygotic twins. It has also been suggested that a low level of response to consumption of alcohol may be familial and may predispose to alcoholism in later life.

Most recently, investigators have discovered two genes that have been implicated with the ability to prevent nicotine dependence from developing. Allele 9 of the dopamine transporter gene (SLC6A3) is believed to enable persons to discontinue smoking 1.5 times more frequently than those individuals lacking this gene. Alleles for gene CYP2A6, believed in active form to enhance the metabolism of nicotine, when present in an inactive form may diminish the chances of one becoming nicotine dependent by increasing the duration of unpleasant effects of nicotine.

The identification of receptors and neurotransmitters in the brain has led many researchers to propose that the use of mood-altering drugs is a response to a genetic defect causing an abnormal balance between the neurotransmitters and receptor sites. Taking a mood-altering substance might correct this imbalance but at the same time compel the individual to continue to take the drug in order to feel well. However, to date, the number of studies addressing these issues is small and more are needed to demonstrate a direct genetic heritability utilizing specific action of individual drugs on gene function.

Neuronal Circuits and Neurotransmitters

One of the first hypotheses on the biochemical basis of addiction to drugs other than alcohol dealt with heroin dependency. The idea of giving methadone to heroin users was developed by Drs. Vincent Dole and Marie Nyswander, who believed that once heroin use was regularized, certain biochemical changes occurred in the body, resulting in a need or craving to take heroin or opiates in order to function normally. But whereas heroin is a short-acting drug producing "highs" because of rapidly changing levels in the brain, methadone, being a long-acting opiate, could satisfy this craving and allow a return to normal homeostasis.

The identification of opiate receptors in the brain and the presence of endorphins and enkephalins soon led to the hypothesis that those deficient in neurotransmitters or opiate receptors would be predisposed to anxiety and anger. To curb these feelings, opioids or other mood-altering substances would be taken. The feeling of well-being produced by the drug would then reinforce its continued use. There has been no convincing evidence, however, that heroin addicts have deficiencies in either endorphins or opiate receptors. However, over the ensuing years, the neuronal circuits, neurotransmitters, and receptors through which all mood-altering drugs exert their effects on the brain have been clearly defined and the commonality shared by different groups of drugs recognized (Chapter 3). Further, the major reasons why people take mood-altering drugs and are often unable to abstain from their use once drug free (Table 4.1) have been linked with these biological determinants. These observations have in turn stimulated new forms of therapy. However, an overreliance on biological determinants will distract attention from the coexisting factors accompanying continued drug use, which must be addressed in order for treatment to become successful.

PSYCHOLOGICAL FACTORS

Psychological explanations for drug dependency range from classic analytic theory to more superficial explanations of personality. But an "addictive" personality has never been clearly defined. Characteristics commonly seen in the drug-dependent are seen just as frequently in those without signs of alcohol or drug problems. However, some experiences can increase (or decrease) the likelihood that someone may use or become dependent on drugs. Indeed, if one can diminish the chances of experimenting with mood-altering substances, one can make the greatest impact in decreasing addiction.

Parent-Child Interactions

Deficient parent-child interactions such as lack of intimacy, failure to praise a child's achievements, criticism, inability to set clear limits on behavior, lack of closeness between parents, and lack of communication are all associated with drug use. A positive family relationship usually deters the initiation of drug use, or at least minimizes chances that drug experimentation will progress to inappropriate drug use.

Contradictory and sometimes hypocritical attitudes often exist about licit and illicit drug use. Many parents are quite aware of the dangers of illicit drug use and aren't reluctant to advise against it. But they may have a benign attitude toward alcohol or nicotine. They may be heavy drinkers themselves and even provide alcohol for their children's parties. The message that "drinking as I do is all right" is one reason excessive alcohol use by parents is often associated with problem drinking among adolescents.

It's a small step from excessive alcohol use to illicit drugs such as marijuana or other substances. But that progression isn't automatic. Although most people who use heroin or cocaine have tried marijuana first, the overwhelming majority of marijuana users don't progress to heroin or cocaine. If one believes in the gateway concept of addiction, it is alcohol and nicotine that are the true gateway drugs.

The importance of developing a strong family bond cannot be overemphasized. This relationship is increasingly difficult to achieve, especially when both parents work or in single-parent families. Lack of appropriate role models in the family leads to increased reliance on peers and other adults.

Peer Relationships

Drug-related behavior in the absence of a secure family bond is strongly associated with drug experimentation among friends. Peer influence is especially strong during early adolescence, when the sense of appropriate and inappropriate behavior is established. And peer influence is particularly powerful when it comes to marijuana and cigarette smoking. Conversely, inability to form adequate peer relationships—alienation from others and such antisocial behavior as chronic anger or fighting—also places a child at risk for illicit drug use.

Adults As Role Models

The impact of adult role models other than family members seems to be strong, particularly in the absence of good parent-child relationships. In general, children tend to make role models of people they view as successful, usually in terms of financial success or physical prowess. When athletes endorse beer and smokeless tobacco, for example, they promote approval of the product, encourage its use, and even associate the product with success. Surveys of teenagers have revealed that a majority believe that our culture glamorizes smoking and drinking, with over 40 percent feeling that illicit drug use is also glamorized. In fact, those who deal drugs may appear glamorous and daring. Dealers have large sums of ready money, and the excitement of "making it" on the street is a strong incentive for youths who have little else to occupy their time.

ENVIRONMENT AND CONDITIONING

Environmental stimuli can promote continued drug use through its association between drug taking and the actual effects of the drug on the brain. Anticipating a high when injecting heroin often results in a high even when the substance injected contains only contaminants. In settings associated with drinking, study subjects tend to get high consuming drinks not containing any alcohol. Associating pleasurable situations with prior drug use can also create a craving. Ex-smokers, for example, will often experience the greatest desire for a cigarette when having morning coffee or when having an alcoholic drink in the late afternoon or evening. All those occasions were moments of pleasure associated with cigarettes. Even withdrawal can be conditioned. Former heroin addicts returning to neighborhoods where they had previously "shot up" begin to experience drug craving, even if they have been abstinent for prolonged periods. In an experimental setting, merely showing videotapes of someone undergoing withdrawal to former heroin users often makes them uncomfortable. Craving promotes recidivism and must also be addressed.

Stress and increasing anxiety are known to not only increase drug-taking behavior but to lead to relapse in both animal models and humans. An atypical responsiveness to stress has been documented in both former heroin- and cocaine-dependent persons. Stress, when combined with environmental drug-associated stimuli and the biological determinants of craving, can easily facilitate relapse.

CONCLUSION

Psychological and environmental factors play a considerable role in both developing and maintaining an addiction. At times, the actual pharmacological addiction to a drug is not the most relevant or important problem. These features must be acknowledged and effectively addressed if one is to be successful in both prevention and treatment. Unfortunately, all too often in an attempt to provide a quick, inexpensive solution to the immediate problem, only one of these determinants is addressed. The expected failure makes us feel that treatment for drug dependency is futile. In fact, as demonstrated in Chapter 6, appropriate treatment for drug addiction is no less successful than our treatments for other chronic disorders.

Our failure to recognize this is most apparent in our government's response to addressing illicit drug use. Although the funds allocated to this effort increase annually, enforcement still rules the day. Approximately 66 percent of all federal funding is devoted to enforcement, with prevention, treatment, and research accounting for 12 percent, 18 percent, and 4 percent respectively. Yet, our efforts to limit the supply of drugs reaching this country appear to be unrelated to either their availability on the street or the numbers of drug users. Recognizing that addiction is a chronic, often relapsing disorder and targeting prevention, treatment, and research for the majority of government support would be the first step in the right direction to effectively addressing illicit drug use.

Chapter 5

Identifying Inappropriate Drug Use and Drug Dependency

Differentiating between acceptable drug use—smoking, social drinking, or even occasional marijuana use—and problem use of drugs is far from easy. Most of those who become habituated to and dependent on drugs follow a fairly standard progression: cigarettes and/or alcohol to marijuana, then on to other mood-altering substances with greater dependency potential. Yet the majority of those who smoke or drink don't follow that path. Understanding why some people progress from socially acceptable behavior to illicit drug use is extremely important. Unfortunately, a behavior pattern that consistently leads to drug use is yet to be determined.

SIGNS AND SYMPTOMS OF DRUG USE

Early signs of drug use tend to be similar, regardless of the drug. Behavior at school or work often changes; the person has trouble paying attention; levels of efficiency fall dramatically; work or study habits change; and there is a lack of concern about physical appearance or dress. At home, the person may appear distracted, often expresses anger, and loses interest in his or her usual pursuits. Someone injecting usually wears long sleeves to hide needle marks. Unexplained absences sometimes occur, leading to defensiveness and anger when questioned. The need for money begins to surface; the person often tries to borrow from friends, relatives, co-workers, and employers. Most important: the circle of friends may change with the new group often including one or more people known to use drugs.

Identifying a user of mood-altering drugs is essential if help is to be offered before patterns of drug-taking behavior become established. Although a variety of questionnaires are used by health professionals to identify persons at risk or impaired by alcohol and drug use, a very simple test that can be self-administered is an adaption of the CAGE questionnaire (Table 5.1). CAGE is a mnemonic representing the four questions asked, "cut down," "annoyed," "guilty," and "eye opener." The test takes less than thirty sec-

TABLE 5.1. Adaptation of the CAGE Questionnaire to Identify Inappropriate Alcohol or Drug Use

---

1. Have you ever felt you should cut down on your drinking or drug use?
2. Have people annoyed you by criticizing your drinking or drug use?
3. Have you ever felt bad or guilty about your drinking or drug use?
4. Have you ever had a drink or used drugs first thing in the morning to steady your nerves or to get rid of a hangover or feeling of fatigue (eye opener)?

---

onds, and if one positive answer is given a person can be considered at risk for developing an alcohol or drug problem. Two or more positive answers indicate a problem exists.

In addition to the general signs and symptoms of use of mood-altering drugs, specific signs may be seen, depending on the type of substance consumed.

Alcohol and Other Central Nervous System Depressants

There are a number of signs of excessive use of alcohol:

- Obvious impairment in individual relationships and social functioning, plus need for "social drinking" early in the day
- Decreased productivity in school or at work
- Increasing absenteeism
- Loss of control over amount consumed
- Possible binge drinking sprees

Symptoms of the physiological effects of alcohol may include increasing anxiety and tension, inability to sleep, chronic heartburn, and rapid heart rate.

Other central nervous system depressants such as the benzodiazepines (Valium, Librium), glutethimide (Doriden), and methaqualone (Quaalude) produce the following symptoms: occasional drowsiness, slurred speech, inability to concentrate, and altered perceptions. When the drug is not readily available, those symptoms may alternate with periods of increased anxiety, sweating, and agitation. Judgment is often impaired, as are motor skills. The symptoms are quite similar to those of alcohol intoxication.

Stimulants

Stimulant dependency is most often associated with weight loss (despite a voracious appetite at times), difficulty sleeping and concentrating, hyperactivity, and impulsivity. Stimulant-dependent people have difficulty maintaining a conversation. Pupils may be dilated, and vision may be blurred. When use stops abruptly, extreme fatigue may set in with long periods of sleep. With extreme use, paranoia and even hallucinations can occur.

Those who snort cocaine also have nasal irritations, alternately manifested by a running nose and nasal stuffiness. Weight loss may be pronounced at times, associated with loss of interest in food. The pupils are often dilated; coughs and colds may be present. Crack, when used in high doses, frequently intensifies all those signs and symptoms, sometimes leading to sudden death.

Narcotics (Opioids)

Narcotic use is readily identifiable when the individual is high, or immediately after an injection when he or she is sleepy or drowsy. But once the high has subsided, it's very hard to tell if someone is using narcotics. The user may establish behavior patterns that indicate a frequent need to take drugs and become anxious and irritable anticipating the next dose. The user's eyes are watery, and the pupils are often constricted, even between injections. Signs of injections—track marks or drug paraphernalia—are obvious clues, but they are often hidden. Detection is difficult when narcotics are taken orally. Associated signs include chronic physical problems, including hepatitis or being HIV positive, and recurrent skin infections. In the absence of the drug, withdrawal signs can be seen, such as increasing anxiety, tearing of the eyes, running nose, nausea, and, at times, vomiting.

Marijuana

Intermittent or sporadic use of cannabis is far from unusual but is also hard to detect. Frequent use produces a dreamy state with no desire for productive activity, the antimotivational syndrome. The smoker may have a distorted sense of time and distance and feel considerable anxiety. Appetite is often increased. Physical signs include red eyes, dry mouth, rapid heartbeat, and facial pallor.

Hallucinogens

Hallucinogen use is relatively easy to identify when the user is observed soon after the drug is taken. A hallucinogen high may produce euphoria, anxiety, panic, and odd behavior. Even hours later, the user may experience visual hallucinations and lose the sense of self. Persons on a hallucinogen may have trouble expressing thoughts or describing events. Phencyclidine (PCP) can cause extreme hyperactivity, mood disturbance, and sometimes impulsive or violent behavior and "pressured" speech. Such behavior may last for hours.

Inhalants

Breathing volatile substances is most likely to be done by children and adolescents, and by adults who have specific access to such substances in the workplace. Signs of inhalant use can include sneezing, coughing, nosebleeds, and difficulty concentrating.

ADDRESSING DRUG ABUSE IN YOUR CHILDREN

One of the most frequent fears expressed by parents is the concern over their children using mood-altering drugs. This fear is understandable as virtually every child, during high school and even earlier, is exposed to nicotine, alcohol, marijuana, stimulants, and hallucinogens. Studies have consistently documented the use of these drugs by children even prior to entry into high school. Adolescence, the age of rebellion par excellence, is a time when your child is especially susceptible to the influence of peers. Unfortunately, drugs are readily available in and around most school yards, city and suburbs alike. How does a parent then approach this problem in an attempt to protect a child from reckless experimentation with drugs and how does a parent satisfactorily address the issue when drug use becomes a regular part of a child's daily activities?

As a start, it is essential that at all times an open line of communication be kept with one's child. With respect to the use of mood-altering drugs, discussions concerning the problems associated with their use can and probably should begin long before a child will be exposed to these temptations. Such discussions are most effective when a parent is nonjudgmental and truthful. It is important to emphasize that by the time they reach junior high school, most children will actually know more about drugs than their parents, having been exposed to this information in health education courses. It is important, therefore, that parents be informed not only of the dangers of such drug use but also of the relatively few side effects that some mood-altering drugs may produce so as not to overdramatize the consequences of such use, which can, in the end, result in a child disregarding the parent's opinion. It is also important to remember that children are quickly able to detect the hypocrisy in a parent's words when they differ from parental action. It is very difficult for children to believe adverse effects of marijuana when lectured by parents who smoke or drink to excess. The hazards of such "drug-taking" behavior are well known. The physical effects of marijuana appear to pale in comparison. Setting an example is essential.

On the other hand, it is important to remember that adolescence is a time of experimentation. The fact that a child uses a drug once does not mean that such use will continue if a good relationship exists between parent and child that recognizes exploration into the effects of such use in an open and nonconfronting manner. Attempts to deny the pleasurable experience of taking some drugs create barriers in communication that ultimately prove a deterrent to calmly discussing the reasons why such use is dangerous even while pleasurable.

Often parents are unaware of their child's drug use until it has become established and has started to interfere with function. This is most often due not to disinterest or uninvolvement on the part of the parents but rather to an unconscious denial that their child could be using drugs. Even when drug use is identified, help is often not sought because of continuing denial on the part of the parents. Many parents have a tremendously difficult time accepting the need for professional help in the face of drug use. It is easier to blame the child's attitude and cling to the hope that if he or she would just "shape up," things would be fine. Unfortunately, this is rarely the outcome.

Drug use among children occurs under a variety of circumstances, usually starting with their peer group. Friends may change, with new and possibly older acquaintances appearing on the scene. Disinterest in formerly appropriate and pleasurable activities may occur. These telltale signs should lead to worry. Changes in a child's behavior including a lackadaisical attitude toward school, frequent distractions, returning home at night and going immediately to his or her bedroom so as not to be seen all raise concern. The presence of associated physical signs such as dilated pupils, confused thinking, or the smell of cigarettes, marijuana, or fumes (when inhalants are involved) are frequent indications of use. Finally, the actual documentation of drug use, such as calls from school or finding drugs or drug paraphernalia in the child's room, leaves no room for mistake.

The parental approach should be direct and reasoned rather than angry and confrontational. Even if a child admits to such use, this confession is most often accompanied by a denial of its frequency or its importance. It is worse when an angry denial of drug use is followed by a refusal to discuss the issue further. In these situations, the temptation often exists for the parent to immediately document drug use either by requiring the child to provide a urine specimen or by clipping off hair for analysis, which can in fact indicate recent or past use. This course of action, however, will almost certainly prevent the parent from establishing a relationship that allows for assistance. It is much more effective to engage the child in a discussion concerning reasons for using the drug and the effects of such use with respect to functioning rather than overemphasizing the dangers of becoming an addict with an accompanying list of the destructive effects the drugs will have on the child's body.

On discovering a child's drug use, parents often vacillate between the temptation to minimize the problem and a draconian approach to eliminating their use. Neither approach is productive and both are dangerous. It is important that the frequency and intensity of drug use be assessed and limits be set. If the use is merely experimental, then hopefully discussion with a parent or even a family friend whom the child respects should be quite helpful. If frequent use exists and function has already been impaired, it is essential that professional help be obtained. Information concerning referrals can usually be obtained from the school's guidance counselor, a family physician, or friends who have had similar problems. In fact, discussing the issue with a close friend can be quite helpful, as not infrequently they too have encountered this problem and may have helpful advice. It is essential not to let feelings of shame, guilt, denial, or the need to blame others for this problem interfere with obtaining effective and prompt assistance.

LABORATORY AIDS TO IDENTIFY
ALCOHOL AND DRUG USE

There are a variety of laboratory tests to identify the use of alcohol and other mood-altering drugs (Table 5.2). Some of these tests provide indirect evidence of such use where as others identify the specific drug as well as the level of use. In general these tests are used to (a) confirm recent use, (b) validate suspicions about such use, (c) provide information about the cause of associated medical conditions and, more recently, (d) eliminate individuals who are felt to be using illicit substances from the workforce.

Abnormal Liver Chemistries

Since excessive alcohol use can seriously damage the liver, a suggestive sign of excessive alcohol consumption is elevation of the enzyme gamma-glutamyltransferase (GGTP) and, less commonly, carbohydrate-deficient transferrin (CDT) and aspartate amino transferase (AST). However, a variety of conditions unrelated to alcohol and other drug use can cause eleva-

TABLE 5.2. Laboratory Tests to Detect Alcohol and Drug Use

Abnormal liver chemistries
Breathalyzer test for alcohol
Concentrations of alcohol and other drugs in blood
Hair analysis
Saliva analysis
Urine testing

tions of the GGTP including hepatitis, diabetes mellitus, gall bladder disease, and pancreatic cancer, making this test less useful as a marker for alcoholism. At times it may be helpful if elevated in the known presence of alcoholism as an indicator of increasing consumption.

Breathalyzer Test for Alcohol

The breathalyzer test, which documents recent drinking, is quite effective, being used mainly by law enforcement in cases of vehicular accidents or preventive road checks and less frequently, in some emergency rooms.

Detection of Drugs in Body Fluids and Hair

Modern analytic techniques allow the detection of drug use in blood, sweat, saliva, hair, and urine. Since drug elimination from these fluids and from hair occurs at different rates depending on the fluid used and even in the absence of current use, past use can be detected. Although most drugs are cleared from the bloodstream relatively rapidly, drugs can be detected in the urine for two to four days, in saliva for twelve to twenty-four hours, in sweat for one to four weeks, and in hair for months.

Blood Concentrations of Alcohol and Other Drugs

Analyzing the presence as well as the level of alcohol and other drugs in the blood provides definitive evidence of drug use. The blood alcohol concentration is used in all states to define impairment while driving and is discussed more fully in Chapter 7.

Analysis of Hair and Saliva

Analysis of saliva for detecting drug use is not commonly used. However, analysis of hair is becoming more attractive to detect past drug use, as drugs can be detected in hair for up to several weeks or months following their use. This is due to the low metabolic rate of the hair shaft as well as the stabilizing components of the hair shaft. Although not widely used, analysis of hair may be of value in determining the accuracy of self-reports of abstention.

Urine Testing

Historical Background

Urine tests to detect drug use have been available since the late 1970s. The issue of widespread testing did not become a major public concern until

1986, when President Ronald Reagan issued an executive order requiring all federal agencies to achieve a "drug-free workplace." Congress subsequently required implementation of that order to include testing all job applicants, plus employees suspected of drug use. The mandatory requirements specify testing for marijuana, cocaine, opiates, amphetamines, and phencyclidine.

The Department of Transportation also requires the testing of private employees involved with mass transit. This group comprises employees of businesses that do work for the Federal Aviation Administration, Federal Highway Administration, Federal Railroad Administration, U.S. Coast Guard, Urban Mass Transit Administration, and the Special Research and Special Program Administration (including workers operating pipelines and those who produce and store liquid natural gas). All told, more than 4 million employees are affected.

In a decision that accelerated the move toward mandatory testing of new employees outside of federal agencies and the military, the U.S. Supreme Court in March 1989 upheld the constitutionality of drug testing over challenges by employees of the U.S. Customs Service and the Federal Railroad Administration. However, as far as local municipalities are concerned, in June 1990 a federal judge declared the mandatory urine testing of all New York City Transit employees unconstitutional, deciding that mandatory testing was appropriate only for "safety sensitive positions." In November 1990, the U.S. Court of Appeals in the District of Columbia struck down regulations allowing the Department of Agriculture to test employees suspected of off-duty drug use if such use did not impair performance.

According to a 1984 survey by the Employees Management Association, only 3 percent of the surveyed companies conducted urine tests of job applicants or new employees. By 1988, the numbers had risen to 30 percent, with 21 percent also testing current employees. Moreover, half of the larger Fortune 500 companies engaged in urine testing in 1988, compared with only 18 percent in 1985. Fueled in no small way by the Office of Management and Budget's 1989 directive to firms with federal contracts to screen all employees, many smaller companies began testing programs. In 1989, the Bureau of Labor Statistics estimated that 20 percent of Americans work in businesses with drug-testing policies. At present, urine testing for drugs in new hires has become the rule rather than the exception in most large corporations.

Common Urine Testing Techniques

It is important to emphasize that, with the exception of marijuana, a person's urine will be positive for drugs only if the drug has been used within the previous seventy-two hours. The test therefore does not identify dependency or inappropriate drug use, providing that the user can remain abstinent for several days. Urine testing on a scheduled basis is more helpful in sending a message that drug use will not be tolerated rather than identifying a frequent drug user. Random testing, however, often identifies such use. Marijuana, unlike other drugs of abuse, is fat soluble and can remain in the body longer than other drugs. Its metabolites can be detected for up to two weeks or longer depending on the frequency of use.

Most urine toxicology tests routinely identify the presence of sedatives-hypnotics, cocaine, marijuana, and opiates. Although other drugs such as alcohol, phencyclidine, and hallucinogens can also be easily identified, they are not part of routine screening as it is not felt that the prevalence of use of these drugs justifies the cost. Since social drinking is acceptable, the presence of alcohol could not provide useful information.

The most common techniques are thin-layer chromatography (TLC), enzyme immunoassay (EIA), and radioimmunoassay (RIA) for initial screening, and gas-liquid chromatography with mass spectrometry (GC-MS) for confirmation.

Thin-Layer Chromatography. In TLC, drugs or drug products (metabolites) in the urine are treated with solvents and then allowed to move by capillary action over a coated glass plate or plastic film. The coating contains mixtures of known drug compounds, each drug represented as a separate spot and serving as a standard. As the solvent-treated urine specimen moves across the plate, the substances separate and are identified by a spray that produces color reactions in the substances in the specimen and in the standard.

TLC can provide relatively rapid, simultaneous detection of a number of mood-altering drugs or their metabolites (Table 5.3) at relatively low cost. But the test is not extraordinarily sensitive, and its accuracy may depend on the skill of the technician in distinguishing the patterns and colors of the drugs being tested from other substances in the urine.

TABLE 5.3. Detection of Drugs by Thin-Layer Chromatography

Drugs Not Readily Detectable	Drugs Detectable After Use	
	After 3 to 12 Hours	After 24 or More Hours
Cannabinoids (marijuana)	Cocaine	Amphetamines
Phencyclidine (PCP)	Opiates	Benzodiazepines (Librium, Valium, Dalmane, etc.)
Hallucinogens	Pentazocine (Talwin)	Propoxyphene (Darvon)
		Nicotine
		Tricyclic antidepressants

Immunoassays. In immunoassay, a laboratory animal is injected with the drug to be tested so that its immune system develops an antibody to that drug. Serum containing the antibody (capable of binding to the drug) is drawn from the animal and placed in a test tube with a quantity of the drug— "labeled" with an enzyme or radioactive isotope. The urine specimen is added and the mixture incubated. During this time, the labeled and unlabeled drug compete for sites on the antibody, and a precipitate consisting of the antibody-drug combination is formed.

The amount of the unattached labeled drug remaining, or the amount of labeled drug attached to the precipitate, indicates the extent of drug use. Depending on the test used, the result is measured as the amount of enzyme activity remaining (EIA) or as remaining radioactivity (RIA). The fluorescence polarization immunoassay (FIA), another technique, involves the use of polarized light.

These tests are sensitive; they detect a number of substances (Tables 5.4 and 5.5) for which there are defined minimal threshold levels. Probably the most popular test in the United States is the EIA technique called the Enzyme Multiplier Immunoassay Test (EMIT). It provides an easily measured, fairly rapid analysis of drug use. Most recently, on-site kits have been developed that can provide a determination of commonly misused substances within three to eight minutes.

Confirmation Tests. Both laboratory errors and substances similar in structure to drugs being tested for can produce false positive results, so all positive results should be confirmed through more sensitive tests. Confirming tests using gas chromatography with mass spectrometry are exceptionally accurate, but expensive and complex. Used properly and consistently with every positive specimen, they virtually eliminate the possibility of false positive reactions.

Effectiveness of Urine Testing

A number of factors must be considered in evaluating the concept of widespread urine testing of those not known to be at high risk for drug abuse:

- Accuracy of the testing technique
- Meaning of false positive and false negative reactions
- Limits of detection
- Value of detection when employee is unimpaired at work
- Value of screening to help the substance abuser
- Risks to confidentiality when detected drugs were prescribed by physicians for specific medical conditions

TABLE 5.4. Drugs Detectable by Enzyme Immunoassay

Alcohol	Cannabinoids (marijuana)
Amphetamines	Cocaine and metabolites
Barbiturates	Methadone
Benzodiazepines	Methaqualone (Quaalude)
(Valium, Librium, etc.)	Opiates (by class)
	Phencyclidine (PCP)
	Propoxyphene (Darvon)

TABLE 5.5. Timetable for Detection of Drugs in the Urine by Immunoassay

Drug	Days*
Amphetamines	1 to 4
Barbiturates	3 to 4 (short acting)
	up to 30 (long acting)
Benzodiazepines	up to 30 days§
Cocaine (including metabolites)	2 to 3
Codeine (as morphine)	2 to 4
Heroin (as morphine)	2 to 4
Marijuana	
sporadic use	1 to 10
daily use	up to 30
Methamphetamine	2 to 4
Phencyclidine (PCP)	2 to 7

*Variation depends on whether use is acute or chronic.
§Depends on length of action of benzodiazepine.

Test Accuracy. Despite increasing use of urine screening, the accuracy of the tests leaves something to be desired. In 1985, the Centers for Disease Control (CDC), in conjunction with the National Institute on Drug Abuse, evaluated thirteen laboratories serving 262 methadone maintenance treatment programs. Error rates (false positives) on urines containing known drugs ran 11 to 94 percent for barbiturate, 19 to 100 percent for amphetamines, 0 to 33 percent for methadone, 0 to 100 percent for both cocaine and codeine, and 5 to 100 percent for morphine. In a subsequent study on 500 prospective hospital employees, 33 had initial positive results, but only 13 could be confirmed.

To rectify this high-error situation, the federal government initiated a certification program to identify laboratories believed capable of providing accurate test results in the high volume necessary. The hope is that enough laboratories with standard quality-assurance procedures can be certified to drastically cut testing errors.

Test accuracy depends on the sensitivity of the specific technique as well as on the laboratory-determined cutoff point for considering tests positive or negative. Sensitivity is the point at which a particular drug can't be detected, no matter how recently it was taken.

Because test reliability diminishes as the drug concentration in the urine decreases to the sensitivity threshold, a cutoff point is used in most laboratories (Table 5.6). Concentration of a drug below that point is read as negative, even if the substance is detected. In practice, to diminish the likelihood of false positives, the cutoff point is usually set above the sensitivity of a specific test. If an initial test is positive, a confirmation test should be run on the sample immediately. Certain over-the-counter preparations and other commonly used products have been known to produce false positive readings (Table 5.7).

False negative responses are equally important. Most false negative urine tests are the result of mechanical and logistical problems. Switching of specimens—intentionally or accidentally—obviously prevents a true read-

TABLE 5.6. Cutoff Levels for Drugs in Urine Immunoassay

Drug	Cutoff Level* Initial	Cutoff Level Confirmatory
Amphetamines	1,000	500
Barbiturates	200	200
Benzodiazepines	200	200
Cocaine (including metabolites)	300	150
Codeine	300	300
Heroin	300	300
Marijuana (cannabinoids)	100	15
Methadone	300	300
Opioids	300	300
Methamphetamine	1,000	500
Phencyclidine (PCP)	25	25

*Levels measured in nanograms (billionths of a gram) per milliliter (ng/ml), may vary in some laboratories.

TABLE 5.7. Substances Capable of Producing False Positive Results in Urine Immunoassay

Drug Tested For	Substance Causing False Positive Result
Amphetamines	Contac, Sudafed, diet pills, decongestants, antiasthma medications containing phenylpropanolamine and ephedrine
Opiates	Dextromethorphan cough syrups, poppy seeds*
Marijuana	Ibuprofen preparations (Advil, Haltran, Nuprin, Pamprin, Medipren, Trendar)§
Cocaine	Herbal teas, and substances listed for amphetamines
Methadone	Benadryl

*Three poppy seed bagels have produced morphine levels above 2,500 ng/ml and codeine levels above 200 ng/ml.
§These substances were initially identified only with EMIT, a technique since modified to eliminate such false positives.

ing. The newest automated analyzers can turn out 18,000 results per hour, so a mechanical switch is certainly conceivable.

Other ways of producing false negatives include diluting the urine to lower the concentration of a drug; using diuretics, a method well known to drug users and athletes; and changing urine acidity/alkalinity (pH). Acidifying urine can increase PCP excretion fivefold. Adding large quantities of salt to urine can also interfere with detection.

Limits of Detection. Other critical factors that determine test accuracy include the amount of drug taken, frequency of use, and elapsed time between use and submission of the specimen. The role of each factor varies from drug to drug.

A positive result indicates only that the identified substance was taken sometime before the test. It doesn't indicate either past or present impairment. For example, a single marijuana cigarette can yield a positive urine test for up to three days; a chronic user may test positive for up to a month after stopping. Cocaine is rapidly eliminated from the body, but its metabolites are detectable up to three days after a single dose. A single dose of amphetamine results in positive urine for one day; in a chronic user for three days.

Urine will be positive for morphine for several days after a heroin injection. But morphine is found in poppy seeds and a wide variety of drugs, so a single positive urine doesn't necessarily mean drug use.

Central nervous system depressants vary in how long they show up in urine tests. Intermediate-acting barbiturates can be detected for up to three days and some benzodiazepines for up to a month following chronic use.

Phencyclidine or its metabolites can be detected for up to a week with sporadic use and for several weeks in chronic users.

Home Testing Kits

Not infrequently, family members who suspect someone of drug use wish to learn the truth without subjecting the person to a laboratory visit or even without letting the person know testing is occurring. Most often this involves a parent confirming a child's use of a mood-altering drug. Several kits are available for urine testing, ranging in price from $35 to $45. At-home hair-analysis kits are available as well. Depending on the kit, results can be made available immediately, or the specimen can be mailed to an outside laboratory. These tests are subject to all of the same problems as the standard tests and in addition are never preferable to establishing an open dialogue in which the use of drugs can be freely discussed.

Risks to Confidentiality

Perhaps the greatest ethical dilemma arises when a positive urine test results from a physician's prescription for a medical condition. A former heroin addict, functioning extremely well on methadone maintenance therapy, risks being dismissed following a positive urine test, even though it is legal for methadone to be prescribed and used. Detection of marijuana (THC) prescribed for nausea caused by chemotherapy violates a person's right to be treated for a serious disease without his or her employer's knowledge. Use of amphetamines for refractory depression falls within this realm as well. Under such circumstances, if performance isn't impaired, there's no justification for violating privacy.

Similar—though less important—situations arise with prescriptions for amphetamine-like drugs for weight loss or narcolepsy, cough suppressants or opiate analgesics for pain syndromes, use of cocaine as an anesthetic in dental or throat surgery, and, most common of all, use of central nervous system depressants for treatment of anxiety.

To ensure confidentiality, the results of all positive tests should be reviewed by a knowledgeable physician. Corporations employing urine testing have access to such physicians, who are called medical review officers (MROs). The MRO reviews positive tests to make certain that (a) the chain of custody has been followed, (b) the confirmation test was done appropriately, (c) the test is not likely to be a false positive, and (d) there is no medical or other legitimate reason for a positive result. If drug abuse is present, the MRO can make appropriate referrals for further treatment.

Perhaps the most important statement on urine screening was issued by the American Society of Clinical Pharmacology and Therapeutics (ASCPT) in 1988. This group of experts in testing agreed that a positive test provides only limited information on the drug dose or on whether its use was recent or chronic. Further, the pharmacological effect of the drug in the user—either at time of sampling, in the past, or in the future—cannot be determined. Concern was expressed that not all laboratories are following defined, high-quality testing standards.

The conclusion was that testing should be based on scientific or clinical evidence of behavioral changes that lead to impairment in the workplace. But the 1989 U.S. Supreme Court decision made clear that where public safety is concerned, testing even without suspicion of use is allowed. The ruling also applies to those indirectly involved with public safety—federal employees who intercept drugs, carry firearms, or have classified material authorization.

THE VALUE OF IDENTIFYING DRUG USERS

Use of illegal substances by people in sensitive positions, or in jobs critical to the safety of others, cannot be condoned. In fact, these people should not use any mood-altering drug, including alcohol, which is probably responsible for most of the breaches of security and accidents at work. The existence of a drug-testing program states clearly that such use will not be condoned and may serve as a deterrent to some employees. But when a person tests positive for, say, alcohol, but there's no evidence of impaired job performance, is further action warranted?

That's not an academic question. Some years ago, several transit system employees in a large city were summarily dismissed when methadone was found in their urine. Their dismissal was upheld by the U.S. Supreme Court, based on the ability of the transit system authority to hire and fire whomever it pleases.

Former President Reagan's executive order makes it clear that illegal drug use by itself is incompatible with federal employment. But again, if use is sporadic, recreational, and not accompanied by impairment, should a person be at risk of losing his or her job? The order establishes employee assistance programs (EAPs) and states that no employee can be discharged or disciplined if he or she voluntarily seeks counseling or treatment. Thus, identification may facilitate treatment. But it is unclear whether counseling is needed or effective for sporadic use of such drugs as alcohol or marijuana if such substances are not used on the job or when the person must report to work.

Chapter 6

Treating Drug Dependency

It is ironic that, although the neurobiology of drug dependency has become well defined, as have the reasons why people take drugs and why they often fail to remain abstinent when drug free, the public's general attitude toward treatment is one of extreme pessimism. As a result, despite the wide array of treatment modalities, the Substance Abuse and Mental Health Services Administration estimates that only 3 million of the approximately 16 million persons in need of alcohol or drug abuse treatment are receiving it.

In a National Household Survey on Drug Abuse, the percentage of people receiving treatment varied greatly with the type of drug used. Only 6 percent of marijuana users received treatment as compared to 14 percent of cocaine, inhalant, hallucinogen, and psychotherapeutic drug users and 40 percent of heroin users. Encouragingly, however, within each group heavy users were two to three times more likely to have received treatment than infrequent users. Contrary to what one might think, treatment cuts across all socioeconomic levels, with individual savings reported as a primary source of payment for 23 percent, private health insurance 30 percent, and Medicare or Medicaid 16 percent, with 28 percent of persons in treatment reporting the treatment to be free of charge.

AVAILABLE TREATMENT MODALITIES

As of 1997, over 14,500 facilities were providing treatment services for substance abuse. Of these, 60 percent were private nonprofit, 23 percent private for profit, 13 percent state or locally run, 3 percent federally operated, and 1 percent tribal operated. Of these facilities, slightly more than half were devoted solely to substance abuse treatment (54 percent), with the rest being part of mental health clinics (24 percent), community settings, or the criminal justice system. The variety of treatment available is considerable and often presents a confusing picture to someone in need of assistance. In general, these varieties can be arbitrarily grouped as (a) brief interventions, (b) pharmacological models, (c) psychological models, (d) sociocultural models, and (e) other forms of treatment, including acupuncture. Some approaches, although not considered treatment modalities, do indirectly benefit the drug user and can be effective in diminishing drug use. These include harm reduction, civil commitment, and drug courts. Each technique has specific advantages or drawbacks, depending on the drug used and an individual's needs. Many, although not all, treatment modalities have been adequately evaluated to allow an assessment of their effectiveness.

The treatment setting is also an important variable and can encompass several types of treatment modalities. Programs may be freestanding, part of mental health facilities, or attached to acute care hospitals. Inpatient or short-term residential programs, at times in acute care hospitals result in a twenty-eight-day stay. Long-term residential programs allow a person to remain for six months to a year, and therapeutic communities exist where an individual may live for several years. Outpatient treatment is the most commonly available treatment setting, responsible for almost 87 percent of persons in treatment. The treatment may vary in intensity from day care centers to weekly visits. In the sections that follow, a brief description is given of the more commonly available modalities. More detailed discussions will be provided, as appropriate, in the chapters dealing with specific drugs of abuse.

Brief Interventions

Brief intervention is probably the most cost-effective and certainly the easiest technique to use to assist a person at risk or who is actually using mood-altering substances. It involves having a physician or other health care provider assess and advise of the existence of a problem during a routine contact as well as suggesting what can be done immediately, if social dysfunction due to dependency does not already exist (Table 6.1). It has been estimated that such an approach can help 15 to 20 million heavy drinkers in this country. Brief interventions have been shown to decrease alcohol consumption by 20 to 50 percent. If considerable dependency exists, however, a much more intense intervention is needed.

TABLE 6.1. Components of Brief Intervention

Provide feedback on screening results, impairment and risks of continuing
    drug-using behavior
Inform as to safe consumption limits for alcohol
Assess readiness to change
Offer goals and strategies to effect change
Arrange for follow-up treatment if needed

Pharmacological Therapies

Pharmacotherapies to treat drug dependency are used (a) for detoxification to prevent withdrawal, (b) for maintenance, (c) to block the effects of specific mood-altering drugs, (d) to prevent drug craving, and finally (e) to treat coexisting psychiatric conditions (Table 6.2). Although many medications have been utilized to treat dependence on stimulants, hallucinogens, and inhalants, these drugs have not consistently been proven to be of value. However, effective drugs do exist for treatment of alcohol, opioid, and nicotine use.

Detoxification

In some instances, when actual physical dependence is not present, drugs can be withdrawn without any withdrawal symptoms. With other drugs, such as cocaine, methamphetamine, and marijuana, even in the presence of heavy and frequent use, specific withdrawal symptoms are rarely present. Agitation and anxiety, if severe, are usually managed with one of the benzodiazepines.

When physical dependence is present, detoxification is necessary. It should be emphasized, however, that detoxification is only the first step in starting therapy. It is not rehabilitation. An individual will usually request only detoxification for a number of reasons (Table 6.3). In addition to immediately benefiting the drug user, detoxification also provides a public good, as it diminishes the need for the user to engage in antisocial behavior in order to obtain money for drugs. Although detoxification is most often accomplished on an outpatient basis, for persons with complex medical problems, coexisting serious psychiatric difficulties, or without sufficient resources to participate in the detoxification process, inpatient hospitalization is required. Often, this results in a twenty-eight-day stay, during which time a therapeutic plan is developed and rehabilitation initiated.

Detoxification from alcohol in the presence of physical dependence is exceptionally important, as the alcohol withdrawal syndrome (delirium tremens) can often be fatal. Although a variety of drugs can be used in alcohol withdrawal (Chapter 7), the most common is the benzodiazepine chlordiazepoxide (Librium). Opioid dependence can be treated by detoxification with the long-acting opioid methadone. If a more rapid detoxification from opiates is desired, clonidine or lofexidine can be added to suppress the adrenergic overactivity responsible for withdrawal symptoms (see Chapter 12). Detoxification from nicotine dependence can be accomplished by use of the nicotine patch, gum, inhaler, or nasal spray. Detoxification from central nervous system depressants, such as benzodiazepines, barbiturates, carbonates, and chloral hydrate, can be accomplished by the use of a variety of drugs, including chlordiazepoxide and phenobarbital.

TABLE 6.2. Pharmacological Agents Used to Treat Drug Dependency

	Alcohol	Cocaine	Nicotine	Opiates
Detoxification	Benzodiazepines* Carbamazepine‡ (Tegretol) Valproate (Depakote, Depakene) Pheno-barbital Bromocriptine§ delta-Hydroxybutyric acid§		Nicotine patch, gum, or nasal spray	Clonidine Lofexidine Methadone Tetrodin‡
Maintenance		Coca leaves, Coca tea§	Nicotine/ Mecamylamine‡ Gumsmoke™	Buprenorphine Levo-alphamethadol (LAAM)* Methadone* Dextromethorphan‡
Blocking or Aversive Agents	Disulfiram* Calcium carbimide†			Naltrexone
Reduce Craving	Naltrexone Nalmefene‡ Acamprostate Tiapride	Amantadine§ Bromocriptine§ Cyclazocine‡ Disulfiram‡ Endabuse (ibogaine) Mazindol§ Methylphenidate§ Pergolide§ Selianine (Eldepryl)‡	Bupropion Gamma vinyl-GABA† Lazabemide‡ Lobeline‡ Selegine‡ Methoxalen‡	
Coexisting Psychiatric States	Antidepressants Anxiolytics (Buspirone)			Anxiolytics Antidepressants
Vaccines		Cocaine conju-gates§		Morphine 6 hemisuccinate BSA‡

*Drugs of choice
§Unproven
†In animal experimentation—not yet shown to be effective in humans
‡In various stages of clinical trials

TABLE 6.3. Benefits of Detoxification

Protects from the hazards of seeking illicit drugs
Encourages user to consider a larger and more productive therapeutic relationship
Allows existing medical problems to be readily identified and addressed
Permits the user to get his or her life in order once the cycle of drug use has been broken

---

Maintenance

Maintenance therapy, used for opiate (heroin) dependence, is based on the theory that maintaining one on a long-acting, pharmacologically pure drug does not alter cognition or motor activity and allows the body's disturbed physiology resulting from repeated frequent injections of heroin to recover, while enabling the individual to focus on the reasons for becoming dependent. Those drugs currently approved for maintenance therapy are the agonist drugs methadone, levo-alpha acetyl methadol (LAAM), and the agonist/antagonist buprenorphine. The use of these drugs is discussed more fully in Chapter 12.

Although nicotine products are currently available for use only in detoxification, it is conceivable that these products, devoid of the risks of smoking, may ultimately be promoted as maintenance therapy. Indeed, the tobacco industry is currently developing devices that heat rather than burn tobacco derivatives. These products, while delivering a comparable dose of nicotine, markedly diminish the amounts of carcinogens consumed by smoking. The utility or desirability of such agents, of course, remains to be seen.

Antagonists and Aversive Agents

Drugs that block the action of mood-altering agents are termed antagonists, whereas those drugs that prevent their use by producing undesirable effects when the mood-altering drug is taken are called aversive agents. Disulfiram (Antabuse) prevents use of alcohol by interfering with its metabolism, causing the substance acetylaldehyde to accumulate in the blood. Acetylaldehyde causes flushing and headache within fifteen minutes and nausea within thirty minutes of drinking (Chapter 7). Naltrexone is a pure opioid antagonist that blocks the effects of heroin injection without causing euphoria (Chapter 12). When taken daily it can effectively prevent heroin injection. However, with both naltrexone and disulfiram, effectiveness is directly dependent on a person agreeing to take the drug on a daily basis.

Prevention of Craving

Many of the drugs that reduce craving have only recently been developed, although they are being used with increasing frequency. Methadone, by maintaining a steady level of opioid in the system as well as a high tolerance threshold, eliminates the craving for heroin. Bupropion, an effective antidepressant, has been approved by the Food and Drug Administration to eliminate craving in nicotine dependency and may well reduce the likelihood of a return to smoking after abstinence has been achieved. Experimentally, in the animal model, Vigabatrin, a drug used for the treatment of epilepsy, has been shown to block drug-seeking behavior for alcohol, morphine, amphetamines, and nicotine in animals through its ability to increase the concentration of aminobutyric acid. Naltrexone, nalmefene, and acamprosate have been shown to reduce the craving for alcohol. Since acamprosate, unlike naltrexone and nalmefene, does not act on the opioid receptors, if further trials prove it effective, it may be possible to combine it with these drugs (Chapter 7). Although in animal experiments a variety of drugs have been shown to be effective in diminishing cocaine craving through actions on the dopamine (D_1) receptors and by blocking the dopamine transport system, nonetheless, to date in clinical trials these drugs have not been consistently proven to be helpful. An exception may be the use of disulfiram (Antabuse) which has been shown to decrease cocaine craving. It has been suggested that the pills made from coca leaves may be helpful in reducing cocaine craving; however, this hypothesis remains to be demonstrated satisfactorily.

Peripheral Blockers

Most recently, research has been underway to develop means of preventing mood-altering drugs from reaching the brain, thereby eliminating their effects. Development of antibodies to cocaine through a vaccine and synthesizing or enhancing enzymes in the body that increase metabolism or breakdown of mood-altering drugs are currently underway to reduce the effects of illicit drugs or to treat drug overdose.

Nonpharmacological Therapies

While therapy with a specific drug is usually targeted toward abuse of a single mood-altering agent, nonpharmacological approaches cut across groups of drugs, with several techniques being available for use in one individual in either the inpatient or ambulatory setting (Table 6.4). They can also be used with pharmacotherapy to allow the person to (a) address the issues that led to drug use, (b) enhance compliance with a particular regimen,

(c) better understand the factors leading to relapse, and (d) develop necessary skills to improve interpersonal functioning. A variety of such techniques exists, unfortunately, some often in conflict with one another.

Acupuncture

Acupuncture has been used for several years—primarily for narcotic addiction (Chapter 12) but for other addictions as well. This is not surprising, as it has been documented that acupuncture releases endorphins as well as other neurotransmitters. Proponents claim good success rates in decreasing withdrawal symptoms, promoting general relaxation, and enhancing the ability to remain drug free. But those claims have not often been evaluated objectively. The National Acupuncture Detoxification Association was formed in 1985 to evaluate and support acupuncture in treating drug dependency. As of this writing, only a few well-designed studies have been conducted. A recent National Institute of Health Consensus Panel reviewed all published data pertaining to acupuncture in the treatment of various disorders. The panel concluded that although acupuncture has not been demonstrated to be effective in smoking cessation, it may be useful as adjunct or alternative therapy in the treatment of opiate addiction.

TABLE 6.4. Nonpharmacological Approaches to Drug Use

Acupuncture
Brief Interventions
Psychological
  Behavioral Interventions
    Aversive Conditioning
    Cognitive Therapy
    Contingency Management
    Coping Skills
    Relaxation Techniques
    Relapse Prevention
    Voucher Therapies
  Comprehensive Outpatient Treatment
  Counseling and Employee Assistance Programs
  Family Therapy
  Group Therapy
  Marital Therapy
  Psychodynamic Approaches
Sociocultural
  Residence Houses
  Self-Help Groups
  Spirituality

Psychological Models

Behavioral Therapies. Behavioral therapies are based on the belief that dependence on mood-altering drugs is a learned behavior, maintained and reinforced by conditioning caused by the drugs independent of other psychosocial conditions. It teaches the user to understand the relationship between the thought process that initiates the intent to use and the actual use. Therapy is directed toward developing behaviors that are incompatible with drug use and avoiding situations associated with a high risk of recidivism. Behavioral therapies range from cognitive therapy to contingency contracting (an agreement between patient and therapist that results in rewards and/or punishment) to aversive conditioning to extinguishing conditioned behavior.

Cognitive therapy focuses on the processes that lead to and sustain drug use, subsequently assisting in development of skills needed to prevent such use. Contingency contracting allows an agreement to be reached between patient and therapist permitting rewards and/or punishment based on the patient's behavior. This technique has been used successfully in assisting (a) patients on methadone maintenance to comply with program rules, (b) those dependent on alcohol to continue to take Antabuse, and (c) those with cocaine dependence to remain abstinent. In general, the programs that are the most successful utilize positive rather than negative reinforcement.

Conditioning techniques attempt to diminish drug use either by providing a way to relax and resist the drug craving or by associating the use of the drug with discomfort. Aversive conditioning diminishes use or the desire to use drugs through the administration of unpleasant stimuli such as electroshock or use of a pharmacological agent as discussed previously. Relaxation techniques, biofeedback, and desensitization procedures are other forms of conditioning that are also employed. Unlike the classic psychotherapeutic approach, conditioning is usually a time-limited process.

Coping skills or relapse prevention therapy teaches a person how to recognize situations that place one at high risk for drug use. These techniques have been incorporated into most successful treatment programs. Studies have demonstrated the effectiveness of relapse prevention therapy when combined with other techniques.

Voucher therapy provides persons who consistently produce urine free of illicit drugs with a voucher each time such a specimen is submitted. The vouchers can be exchanged for food or retail goods and increase in value the longer urine remains drug free.

Comprehensive Outpatient Treatment. Outpatient programs offer a variety of services, from drop-in centers to free clinics and formal counseling. They provide educational, medical, psychological, and rehabilitative services related to substance use, and may meet other medical needs of the community. Such programs account for half of the people in treatment, and they allow easy access for those unwilling or unable to make a greater time commitment. In that respect, they can serve as the second step after detoxification.

Counseling and Employee Assistance Programs. Counseling is conducted by trained counselors, social workers, and psychologists, as well as by those without formal degrees whose experience and training have equipped them for the job. In itself, counseling is the most basic form of therapy. It deals with the practical problems of both client and family members, providing support and appropriate referrals.

In the workplace, counseling is offered through employee assistance programs, which serve as resources for those identified as having an alcohol or a drug problem. A good EAP provides education to employees and their families about alcohol and drug use, and develops among management a better general knowledge of drug dependency and how to spot it before it becomes a major problem. Unfortunately, even though there are an estimated 10,000 EAPs across the United States, and despite evidence that they are effective for both employer and employee, only 30 percent of the workforce has access to these programs.

Group, Family, and Marital Therapies. These therapies involve patients and significant others and allow participants to openly express feelings and share painful experiences. When combined with the guidance of an experienced group leader, additional support can be provided to the drug user as well as those not using drugs to gain a better understanding of dependency of craving and abstinence. Involvement of family members has been shown to have a positive effect on compliance and retention as well as maintaining abstinence.

Psychodynamic Approaches. In the past, the use of intensive psychotherapy as the sole method of addressing use of alcohol and other drugs of abuse had not been adequately evaluated and, on an anecdotal basis, was found to be less than effective. However, this was perhaps due to the inability to identify those persons most likely to be helped by these techniques. At present, psychotherapy provided by psychologists, social workers, rehabilitation counselors, and/or psychiatrists may be part of a comprehensive outpatient program or just a one-to-one relationship with a therapist. It can vary in intensity, depending on the client's needs and the particular training and belief of the therapist. By allowing the client to understand his or her behavior, a rationale for change is developed. Initially thought to be ineffective because of the severe personality disturbances accompanying addiction, psychotherapy, alone or in combination with other modalities, is now known to be helpful especially in those with moderate levels of psychopathology.

Sociocultural Approaches

Residential Therapeutic Communities. Changing the personal character-istics that led the drug user to take drugs is the target of residential therapeu-tic communities (Chapter 12). Since the first such program, Synanon, was founded in the 1950s, a large number of programs have been developed. As described by George De Leon, therapeutic communities can be distin-guished from other forms of treatment in two main ways:

1. Almost all their primary therapists and staff have themselves com-pleted a recovery process. As successful role models, they offer con-tinuous support as they instill appropriate behavior backed by their own rehabilitation experience.
2. Addiction or drug use is viewed more as a symptom than as a problem. Detoxification, therefore, becomes a preliminary step toward entering the therapeutic process, rather than the goal. The ultimate objective is being able to cope with stress without needing any pharmacological support.

As a result of that philosophy, many therapeutic communities—unlike other treatment facilities—are amenable to admitting people with multiple drug problems, including alcohol. The therapeutic experience may require liv-ing in the community for up to two years and passing through successive stages of increasing responsibility, ending in the reentry phase: maintaining contact with the community while living outside it and being engaged in productive activity. Commitment to the process must be total, so there is a high dropout rate.

Self-Help Groups. Alcoholics Anonymous, formed in 1935, is perhaps the oldest of the self-help groups. At present, a number of such groups exists not only for drug users but for family and friends as well. They are usually available in major cities and even smaller communities and are open to all. The only qualification for admission is the self-recognition of a dependency and the desire to be helped. The process is often coupled with a religious or spiritual approach toward achieving a drug-free state. Due to the commit-ment of their successful members who are always available to supply addi-tional support, many treatment programs utilize these groups for additional support. Unfortunately, attempted evaluations of the effectiveness of this approach as a therapeutic modality have only occasionally supported this use. This is in large part due to the voluntary nature of these groups and the anonymity of participants, which result in an inability to obtain membership lists. Nonetheless, the popularity of these groups is considerable and for cer-tain persons they may be lifesaving.

Spirituality. Spirituality, while far from being a recognized treatment modality, may be a major force in recovery and rehabilitation. It is important to emphasize that spirituality does not require belief in a particular religion but rather the acceptance of the existence of a higher being or a universal force. To some extent, some self-help groups consider a lack of spirituality as a precursor of addiction, with a refocusing on spirituality as a primary means of recovery. Spirituality, however, may take many forms, which makes an evaluation of its effectiveness quite difficult (Table 6.5).

A recent conference on spirituality held by the National Institute of Health Care Research reviewed all of the available evidence in the literature concerning spirituality and classified claims as: strongly supported by evidence, reasonable, less well confirmed, or not accompanied by any evidence. On the basis of this review, the panel addressing addiction felt it was reasonable to conclude:

- Involvement with religion or spirituality is predictive of lesser problems with alcohol or other drugs of abuse.
- Involvement with Alcoholics Anonymous is associated with better outcomes.
- Denominations that take a strong stand against alcohol use are less likely to have problem drinkers, even among those who drink.
- Meditation-based interventions were associated with a lesser incidence of alcohol or drug problems.

The panel, however, was unable to conclude that:

- Members of AA consistently attributed their recovery to spiritual factors.
- Interceding with prayer improves outcome.
- Individuals in treatment for alcoholism or drug abuse had a lowered sense of meaning of life.
- Religious involvement was minimal in persons with substance abuse problems.
- Spirituality was associated with an increased success in stopping smoking.

What one can conclude from these findings is that for some people spirituality may be quite helpful in assisting in the transition to abstinence. Thus, it should be encouraged when a person expresses an interest or feels it is of value. Like other modalities, spirituality does not have to stand alone but can be part of a comprehensive, individualized approach to rehabilitation.

TABLE 6.5. Spirituality Techniques

Clarifying values
Cognitive approaches to spirituality issues
Communal worship
Dance therapy
Meditation
Quest experience
Spiritual directions
Repetitive prayer
Twelve-step fellowships
Self-help groups

EVALUATION OF TREATMENT

Despite the wide array of treatment modalities, until recently, evaluation of their effectiveness has not been satisfactory. Published studies were often subject to serious criticism. This is not surprising, as it is often difficult to find treatment and nontreatment groups adequately matched for age, sex, socioeconomic levels, and reasons for seeking treatment. The incentive to enter treatment is often related to the need for keeping a job, staying out of jail, or maintaining a family. Underlying associated psychopathology, differing methodology, and varying lengths of follow-up can all distort outcome results.

As managed care continues to make inroads into the mental health field, including substance abuse, evaluation through outcome monitoring will become increasingly important. The most confusing aspect of evaluating treatment effectiveness, however, has not been a lack of interest but rather a lack of clarity in defining the parameters to use in evaluation. The effectiveness of treatment can be defined by a variety of factors, which basically can be grouped as: (a) individual parameters of success, (b) societal benefits, and (c) effectiveness as compared with treatment for other forms of chronic disease (Table 6.6). When all of these parameters are taken into account, the conclusion is that regardless of type of treatment employed, regardless of drug of abuse, or regardless of length of time in treatment, treatment is more effective than nontreatment, with successful efforts increasing proportionately to the time in treatment. Some examples of several more recent studies follow.

The Drug Abuse Treatment Outcome study (DATO) followed 10,010 drug abusers in 100 programs consisting of outpatient clinics, methadone maintenance programs, long-term residential programs, outpatient drug-free programs, and short-term inpatient programs. In all these modalities, drug use significantly decreased by at least 50 percent from twelve months before treatment began to twelve months after treatment despite the steady decline in retention support services that occurred due to decreased funding

TABLE 6.6. Parameters to Be Used in Evaluating Treatment Effectiveness

---

Individual Parameters
  Successful completion of program
  Significantly decreasing drug use as compared to untreated
  Ability to remain abstinent
  Improved social functioning
  Improved employment

Societal Parameters
  Reduction in crime
  Diminished expenditures for health care and law enforcement

Comparative success with other chronic disorders

---

over the study period. Differences in retention did exist among programs, with those programs having the more severely disturbed clients and the poorest prognosis, and those clients in programs receiving additional support services having the greatest chance of remaining abstinent. A similar study sponsored by the Substance Abuse and Mental Health Service Administration of 4,411 underserved hard-to-reach groups found that treatment also decreased illegal drug use by 50 percent.

These findings are of particular interest, as it has been commonly held that matching a treatment modality with an individual's characteristics would optimize the chances of success. However, another study by the National Institute of Alcohol Abuse and Alcoholism (Project MATCH), which randomly assigned 1,726 patients with alcohol or other drug dependencies to twelve-step facilitation therapy, cognitive-behavior therapy, or motivational enhancement therapy, found little benefit was obtained by matching patient characteristics and outcome, with more than 90 percent of patients in all programs completing all sessions. Regardless of type of therapy, all clients substantially diminished their drinking, with these differences maintained for up to three years posttherapy.

A larger study by the Department of Veterans Affairs involving alcoholism reported similar findings. Regardless of type of treatment, participation is associated with increased rates of abstinence, decreases in alcohol and drug use, and improvement in psychological functioning. Those involved in more professional counseling sessions after inpatient treatment had, not surprisingly, better outcomes. On the other hand, psychosocial outcomes were poorer for those with psychotic or anxiety depressive disorders.

On a statewide level, similar results have been reported. As one example, in California an evaluation of treatment programs from 1992 to 1994 found alcohol and illicit drug use to diminish by 40 percent with treatment, accompanied by a one-third decrease in hospitalizations. Most impressive is a study from the Women and Children's Branch of the Center for Substance Abuse, which found that of women in treatment for substance abuse, 95 percent had uncomplicated drug-free births, with 75 percent of women who successfully completed treatment remaining permanently drug-free, and 46 percent obtaining employment. The children also showed beneficial effects from their mothers' treatment, with 65 percent being returned from foster care and 84 percent who participated in the treatment with their mothers having improved performance in school.

Since the effectiveness of matching patients to specific programs had been questioned, a study by McLellan and colleagues attempted to evaluate outcome by matching patients' problems with specific targeted therapeutic services. These investigators found that when this was done, the matched patients were more likely to complete treatment and have better six-month outcomes than those patients receiving standard care treated in the same programs.

Societal Benefits of Treatment

It is not often realized that the total annual cost of untreated drug dependency exceeds $400 billion due to lost productivity, health care, welfare, and law enforcement costs.

Contrary to common belief, treatment for drug dependency is exceedingly cost effective when compared not only to the treatment of other chronic diseases but also to the alternative to treatment: incarceration. As documented by the Physicians Leadership on National Drug Policy, annual treatment costs can range from $1,800 for outpatient care to $6,800 for residential long-term treatment centers. This compares quite favorably with an annual cost of $25,900 for incarceration (Table 6.7). Yet, despite the rela-

TABLE 6.7. Costs of Treatment versus Prison

	Annual Cost per Person
Regular Outpatient	$1,800
Intensive Outpatient	$2,500
Methadone Maintenance	$3,900
Short-Term Residential	$4,400
Long-Term Residential	$6,800
Incarceration	$25,900

Source: Data obtained from Physician Leadership on Drug Policy, *Journal of the American Medical Association* 279 (1998): 1149.

tively low costs of treatment, spending on substance abuse treatment is minimal compared to the total expenditures on personal health care. In 1996, substance abuse treatment represented only 1.3 percent of spending on personal health care and 16 percent of the portion spent on behavioral health care.

Treatment is also accompanied by a considerable reduction of criminal activity as well as hospitalizations for illness. Data on criminal activities from the National Treatment Improvement Evaluation Study revealed arrests due to selling drugs to have decreased from 64 to 14 percent, muggings from 49 to 11 percent, and overall arrests from 48 to 17 percent with treatment. In New York City's Drug Alternative to Prison Programs, there was an 8 percent recidivism rate six months after the program completion, compared to 40 percent recidivism for those who were incarcerated. In California, for every dollar spent on drug treatment programs, seven dollars were believed to have been saved, for a total of $1.4 billion in savings, mostly due to reduction in crime, although medical costs were also impressively diminished. Costs decreased by 58 percent for drug overdose, by 44 percent for mental health problems, and by 25 percent for total days hospitalized. A study of treatment effectiveness in prisoners revealed that subsequent arrests after discharge decreased by 50 to 60 percent, and later drug use was decreased by 50 to 70 percent.*

Comparison with Effectiveness of Treatment and Other Chronic Disorders

It should be clear from the data just discussed that virtually all studies show that not only is treatment more cost effective than nontreatment, but in addition, on an individual basis, significant improvements occur in abstaining from drug use and enhancing social functioning. Yet, in any study, certain percentages of persons continue to use drugs or cannot complete the treatment process. This observation has led to a general pessimism on the part of the public with respect to treatment effectiveness, and, correspondingly, often an unwillingness to adequately support new programs with appropriate ancillary services. In fact, despite the data demonstrating treatment effectiveness, appropriate support services for federally funded programs are diminishing, and insurance companies and managed care groups are whittling away at covered benefits for drug users.

Treatment for substance abuse is no less effective than that of other chronic diseases. If one looks at three common disorders, asthma, adult-onset diabetes, and hypertension, less than 30 percent of patients with these conditions comply with advice concerning dietary or behavioral change,

---

*National Institute on Drug Abuse <www.nidh.hih.gov> February 16, 2001.

with those from the lowest socioeconomic groups and those with associated psychiatric problems having the poorest records. Even with respect to medication regimens, less than 50 percent of insulin-dependent adult diabetics and approximately only 30 percent of hypertensive and asthmatic persons take their medicines appropriately. Recurrence of symptoms occurs each year in these groups and is quite high, ranging from 30 to 80 percent. Associated complications due to poor medical control are well known and have serious consequences, not only to the individual but to society as well, as they are quite costly. Yet despite comparable data concerning compliance, we do not consider treatment of these disorders as questionable and, in fact, billion of dollars are gladly spent each year, not only for treatment, but for basic and clinical research. It is our failure to recognize that drug dependency is a similar chronic relapsing disorder that prevents us from recognizing the value of treatment and the need to provide even greater support.

AFTER TREATMENT

The depression that can follow completion of treatment for drug dependency has been described by Dr. Forest Tennant as the post drug-impairment syndrome (PDIS). On returning to the community at large, the individual feels fragile in the face of the everyday stresses of life and has difficulty relating to friends and concentrating on ordinary problems. Craving, the urge to resume drug use, begins to surface. The intensity of the syndrome varies and doesn't always cause problems. But certain steps can help minimize its effects and thus maximize chances for successful abstinence. Counseling during the last phases of treatment, and afterward, is of prime importance. So is community involvement and job placement. A job provides a purpose in life and lessens the amount of aimless free time that breeds a craving for drugs. A strong social environment, especially a stable family unit, is also essential. The lack of such an environment is particularly significant for the homeless. Many are amenable to entering treatment facilities, but they quickly go back to drug use when they're released.

THE LAW AND DRUG TREATMENT

It may seem oxymoronic to associate law enforcement with the treatment of drug use. Indeed, in the past laws have been used mainly as deterrents to illicit drug use and as punishment for those convicted of possession and sales. The cost of these efforts is considerable, as exemplified by the $30 billion crime bill that became law in September 1994, which allowed for hiring 100,000 new police officers and spending $8.7 billion in building new prisons. Much of this was directed toward the drug user and seller. In 1993, over 25 percent of inmates in state and federal prisons were incarcerated for drug offenses, with 60 percent of federal prisoners serving drug sentences. This has occurred despite the observations that adding treatment is four times more effective than adding law enforcement, eight times more effective in reducing cocaine use than increasing sentences for such use, and fifteen times more effective in reducing the social costs associated with cocaine use than law enforcement efforts.

Perhaps as a result of these observations, over the past several years there has been considerable interest on the part of many, including law enforcement officers and judges, to use the law not as punishment but as a means of making persons dependent upon drugs more amenable to treatment through increasing society's tolerance of the use of illicit drugs without encouraging or promoting such use. In fact, it now appears that entering treatment under legal auspices is associated with outcomes as favorable as seen when treatment is initiated voluntarily. Current use of the legal system has included:

1. Pretrial services programs
2. Civil commitment
3. Increased use of drug courts
4. Intensive supervised probation
5. Decriminalization for simple possession
6. Limitation or authorization of a regulated drug market
7. Harm reduction

Pretrial Services Programs

Pretrial services provide to judges a complete profile of the arrestee to allow the judge to determine whether the person stands a good change of being rearrested or of causing harm to the community if he or she is released. Release is based on the agreement to enter and remain in a drug treatment program for at least six months. If the program is successfully completed, the charges are dropped.

Civil Commitment

Coercing a person into treatment and abstinence with "or-else" threats of jail or job loss is effective only to the extent that the person has something to lose by not complying. Civil commitment entails forcing drug users into therapy regardless of their desire for help in lieu of prison sentences. It is not a new idea. By 1938, facilities to treat and rehabilitate narcotic offenders had been established at Lexington, Kentucky, and Fort Worth, Texas. Ostensibly under the auspices of the U.S. Public Health Service, the facilities were in fact supervised by the Federal Bureau of Narcotics and the Justice Department. The result was closer to a prison than a rehabilitation center. In 1944, the Public Health Service Act led to a program for management of narcotic dependency at these centers. Since then, thousands of persons entered the hospitals at Lexington and Fort Worth. But while these facilities produced a great deal of clinical research on the complications and effects of narcotics, their effect on rehabilitation has been minimal, with relapse rates as high as 90 percent.

A number of states have experimented with varying forms of civil commitment. Under California's 1962 Metcalf Voker Law, arrested narcotics addicts could request civil commitment in lieu of prosecution. Charges would be dropped if they successfully completed this program and then practiced abstinence and good behavior over the next three years. The California civil commitment program established comparable guidelines, allowing a person to request commitment in a state rehabilitation center from several months to years. In 1966, the Narcotic Addict Rehabilitation Act (NARA) empowered the federal government, rather than states, to commit narcotic users not previously charged with any criminal offense. But those committed under this act had a high recidivism rate, with up to 45 percent using an opiate almost as soon as they left the program. To date, the general experience with civil commitment has been unsatisfactory.

Advocates of civil commitment programs say they can be successful only when rehabilitation facilities are available and effective and when those who leave treatment prematurely are forced to return to the legal system for sentencing. As concern over escalating drug use has risen, so has consideration of civil commitment. A number of states currently have civil commitment laws varying from those that let parents commit children suspected of drug use to those that commit individuals convicted of violating state drug laws. New York State, for example, has developed large drug treatment compounds, or "campuses," on federal lands for rehabilitating addicts after civil commitment, as well as for those seeking voluntary treatment. A variety of treatment strategies may be implemented on these campuses along with stringent sanctions against those who have been committed but leave before completing therapy.

Drug Courts

Evolving from civil commitment, in the late 1980s and early 1990s, a number of states started experimenting with drug courts, which arrange specific treatment plans for nonviolent offenders arrested for drug use or possession. These courts remove low-level offenders from the usual criminal justice system and establish a nonadversarial process focused on treatment and rehabilitation. Free from incarceration, participants are required to attend treatment sessions, have their urine checked frequently for drugs, and participate in rehabilitation and clinical vocation training. Most programs involve thirty to sixty days of intensive treatment followed by one year or more of supervision. As of 1997, thirty-eight states have initiated such programs, which have processed over 45,000 people.

Although failure to participate results in sanctions and ultimate incarceration, in fact, evaluations of these programs by the Office of Justice have been quite favorable. Recidivism for the 70 percent of persons who complete the treatment process is less than 4 percent, compared to a 45 percent arrest rate within two to three years for those arrested for possession and traditionally processed. Costs, compared to bringing persons to trial and incarceration, are much lower, and the lightening of the load on the criminal justice system is considerable. The effectiveness of this program is best demonstrated by the support given to it by police chiefs as well as judges.

Intensive Supervised Probation

Programs of supervised probation provide intensive surveillance through electronic monitoring devices or curfews. Often they may be instituted following an early or conditional discharge when a person has agreed to complete a formal rehabilitative program. The costs of this program are less than incarceration but obviously greater than those of traditional parole. However, the rate at which new crimes are committed is also less than that seen with traditional paroles—but higher than that for traditional probation. Most instructive is the recent experience in Arizona, the first state to direct all those arrested for drug use into treatment programs. Of the first 2,622 persons diverted into treatment through probation, 77.5 percent subsequently were drug free on urine testing. Although this is a preliminary finding, it documents the effectiveness of treatment over incarceration and is quite cost effective, with a $2.5 million saving realized in its first year of operation.

Decriminalize Simple Possession of Illicit Substances

Although we have done little to stem the flow of illicit drugs into our country, we have become too efficient in arresting those who use these substances. Of the one million drug arrests each year, 250,000 (25 percent) are for simple possession of marijuana, which, incredibly, is the fourth leading cause of arrest. Drug arrests have risen considerably out of proportion to arrests for other types of crimes by a factor of three or four.

Seventeen percent of persons in federal prisons are first-time offenders arrested for possessing small amounts of drugs. Incarceration for simple possession is not only remarkably expensive, clogging our criminal justice system, and overcrowding our prisons, but in addition is completely ineffective as a deterrent. Indeed, most knowledgeable persons involved with law enforcement have conceded that mandatory prison sentences and incarceration for simple possession or minor drug sales serves neither the individual nor our society.

Simply by decriminalizing simple possession and having those convicted of "real" crimes actually serve out their sentences, the crime rate would decrease. Furthermore, by establishing rehabilitation programs rather than prisons for minor offenders, a further decongestion of our prisons would occur. In fact, due to mandatory minimum sentencing laws, many are spending far more time in prison for simple possession than they would have if sentenced for violent crime. Simple possession of a teaspoon of crack (cocaine) carries with it a mandatory minimum federal court sentence of five years without parole. Unlike serious drug offenders, these individuals are far less likely to commit new crimes when released. In addition, in order to accommodate those serving mandatory sentences, at times, far more violent offenders are released. An agreement to serve time in rehabilitation, with an automatic prison sentence for those who do not fulfill this commitment, would also decongest the judicial system. It is realized that the effectiveness of "rehabilitation camps" as compared to prisons has not yet been evaluated, and preliminary data have not shown great differences.

Although not generally realized, we have already had considerable experience with the effects of decriminalization. In the 1970s, ten states decriminalized simple possession of marijuana. Not only did those states considerably reduce their law enforcement costs, but in addition, the number of persons using marijuana did not increase. Neither was there any evidence of a detrimental effect on the community at large.

Decriminalization versus Legalization

It should be emphasized that decriminalization is quite different from legalization, which, if implemented, would permit the sale of all formerly illicit substances. Without entering into the myriad arguments both for and against legalization (Table 6.8), two observations are important. First, the general premise advanced by advocates of legalization is that it would reduce crime without increasing use of formerly illicit substances. Whereas one might argue the effects of legalization on crime, it is counterintuitive to consider that increased availability will not lead to increased use. Whether one cares if more people use these drugs is a different issue, but history has repeatedly demonstrated that considerable increases in use will occur.

Second, despite our failure to restrict the availability of illicit drugs, all evidence suggests that, in fact, illicit drug use by our nation's youth has

TABLE 6.8. Arguments For and Against Legalization of Illicit Drugs

Advocates	Opponents
People have and will continue to use illicit drugs.	Continued illicit drug use does not justify legalizing a harmful activity.
People have the right to pursue behavior that may harm them as long as it does not affect others.	Use of illicit drugs does affect others in a multitude of ways unrelated to their legal status, including child neglect and antisocial behavior. The majority has the right to create laws reflecting values. Most of society will regard legalization as morally wrong.
Funds currently used for enhancement could be better used in prevention, education, and treatment.	There is no reason to believe any financial savings would go where they are needed.
Current enforcement has little impact on criminal activities and slight deterrent effect.	Enforcement has not been effective due to the manner in which it has been pursued.
The failure of Prohibition should serve as a lesson, with legalization of illicit drugs carrying the same benefits and risks.	Prohibition reduced many complications related to alcohol. Many illicit drugs have far greater potential for antisocial behavior than alcohol as well as a much smaller likelihood of their consumption being controlled.
Crime would decrease as the cost of drugs would plummet.	If drugs were more readily available, use would increase, productivity would decrease, and crime might well increase to provide users with money for other needs. At present, more than 50 percent or violent crime is committed under the influence of drugs.
Workable models of legalization exist in other countries.	Cultural differences prevent these models from being pursued here. Those countries with the most lenient laws are rethinking their approach to drug use.
Legalization would not be accompanied by an inordinate increase in drug use.	There are currently 50 million smokers and 18 million alcoholics, yet only 2 million cocaine users. The potential for increase in use is enormous.
Legalization still would not permit access to drugs by children.	At present, children's access to alcohol and tobacco is rampant. Access to other drugs would be similarly difficult to control. Low cost would facilitate purchases.
Education would prevent individuals from unknowingly using substances with adverse effects.	The mere act of legalization implies a certain approval by society. Similar to children's perceptions concerning alcohol, the complications associated with use of these drugs would be trivialized.

Source: Stimmel, B. *Drug Abuse and Social Policy in America: The War That Must Be Won.* New York: The Haworth Press, Inc., 1997, pp.140-141.

considerably declined. The driving force behind this decline appears to be student realization of the harm caused by these drugs. Even with respect to marijuana, the drug consistently having the most advocates for legalization, the majority of students feel that this drug should not be legalized. Students have increasingly viewed the use of illicit substances as dangerous, in no small part due to their illicit status. This feeling can be contrasted with students' use of licit substances, such as alcohol and tobacco, which are currently responsible for more adverse effects than all of the illicit drugs combined and whose use has remained stable or even slightly increased. In fact, despite the widespread publication of the adverse effects of tobacco, a 2000 Monitoring the Future Survey found only 60 percent of eighth graders felt that risk existed with smoking a pack of cigarettes a day. Since the time of greatest risk for using mood-altering drugs is during adolescence, legalizing illicit substances would provide exactly the wrong message at a time when demand continues to decrease.

Decriminalization for use or simple possession, however, would have the effect of recognizing the user as one in need of assistance, not punishment. In addition to being more socially productive, decriminalization is also exceptionally cost effective and would allow impressive savings that could be better applied to prevention and rehabilitation. This would also have the effect of clarifying the issue when one is arrested for a crime and is obviously under the influence of a mood-altering substance. The actual offense can be appropriately addressed without focusing on whether the drug use should be a mitigating factor.

Although many benefits are associated with decriminalization, the distinction between possession for personal use or for use by others is often less than easy to define. In addition, it might well send a mixed message concerning the appropriateness of refraining from use of these substances. At the least, such a policy directed at simple possession would decongest our courts and overcrowded prison system and result in considerable savings that could be well directed toward prevention and treatment. Decriminalization need not eliminate sanctions or supervision, but rather confinement.

Limitation: Authorizing a Regulated Drug Market

Limitation would make certain drugs available, but only under certain circumstances and to certain people. Further, those who would be permitted to distribute those substances would be clearly defined, with the options being a medical or a nonmedical model. Limitation under the medical model has existed for many years in England, specifically restricting prescription of drugs to physicians who may provide them to persons felt to be physically dependent.

Authorization of a regulated drug market would give a specific drug the status of alcohol or tobacco, but this, in reality, is limited legislation. Proponents of this approach argue that use of the drug would not substantially increase, crime would diminish as would drug dealing, and due to the low costs involved, the profit margin would be greatly decreased; however, there is no good evidence that this would occur. In fact, it is difficult to believe that use would not increase, especially among the young, despite their purchases of these drugs remaining against the law. In this regard, it is of interest that in Switzerland, which has among the most liberal policies on drug use of any country, when a referendum was held to legalize all drugs in 1998 it was defeated by almost three-quarters of those voting.

Although decriminalization remains controversial, and legalization, even when restricted to marijuana, is not considered a possibility by the majority, the other alternatives to traditional imprisonment for simple possession or street sales offer real possibilities for decongesting our prisons and encouraging minor offenders to enter treatment. They also place a greater burden on the individual for determining his or her future and as such should be seriously considered.

Harm Reduction

While drug courts and civil commitment have had increasing public approval and are considered quite useful ways of encouraging drug users to enter treatment, harm reduction as an initial step to rehabilitation remains quite controversial. The concept of harm reduction in and of itself is quite benign. Harm reduction involves instructing the drug user in ways to diminish the risks associated with drug use while providing information concerning treatment and rehabilitation. Indeed, some harm reduction techniques, such as providing information concerning the effects of drinking and driving, the number of drinks that cause impairment, and the use of condoms to prevent transmission of sexual diseases, are taught in most schools. Other harm reduction techniques, such as information concerning ways to disinfect needles, the risks of needle sharing, ways to reduce high-risk behavior, and recognizing the presence of symptoms indicating more serious diseases, are also met with general public acceptance. It is the harm reduction technique utilizing needle exchange to decrease the risk of transmission of the HIV virus that has aroused public controversy and concern.

The concern of our government in endorsing harm reduction as a formal strategy is considerable. As described by Nadelman, in December 1994, the U.S. delegation refused to sign any statement by the U.N. Drug Control Program that contained the term harm reduction. In 1995, our State Department successfully pressured the World Health Organization not to release a report showing that traditional use of coca leaf in Peru was relatively harmless. Although needle exchange programs are well recognized internationally and, in fact, exist throughout the United States, in this country they are still small in number and underfunded, as the federal administration maintains a ban on the use of funds for such programs. Although the concept of needle exchange is discussed more fully in Chapter 12, suffice it to observe that despite the conclusions of the Centers for Disease Control and Prevention, the National Academy of Sciences, and an independent committee established by Congress in 1997 that there is no doubt that needle exchange programs are effective, (along with a report by the President's Advisory Council on HIV and AIDS urging the president to immediately end the ban on federal funding for these efforts), as of the current writing, the administration still withholds funds for these programs.

Harm reduction techniques, in fact, are important treatment modalities. In addition to providing information concerning the use of the drug and the ways that one may decrease risks with such use, they are often the first meaningful interpersonal contact with the drug user that does not require a commitment to discontinue drug use. This often establishes a bond with another person that can be a vital link to entering treatment. The intensity of this interaction can best be demonstrated by quoting one person for whom harm reduction was the only way to become healthy:

> In my desperation, I tried drug treatment programs, but they made me feel like I was a junkie. Worse than that, I was a woman junkie and they treated me like I was a bad mother, a bad woman. Drug treatment wasn't for me. Oh, no! I started hanging out at the lower east side harm reduction center needle exchange program and this is where it all started happening. This was a big change in my life. I found myself getting involved and learning about myself and about my drug use. I started going to support groups and volunteering my time in helping others and learning about substance abuse and HIV/AIDS. At the same time, I learned how to manage my drug use while dealing with life itself. This is the first place that I was accepted for who I was and not looked down upon for my drug use. (Milau, E. "It's About Respect." *Harm Reduction Communication,* Spring 1998 (6): 5.)

PART II:
MOOD-ALTERING DRUGS

Chapter 7

Alcohol

If, when you say whisky, you mean the devil's brew, the poison scourge, the bloody monster that defiles innocence, yea, literally takes the bread from the mouths of little children; if you mean the evil drink that topples the Christian man and woman from the pinnacles of righteous, gracious living into the bottomless pit of degradation and despair, shame and helplessness and hopelessness, then certainly I am against it with all of my power.

But, if when you say whisky, you mean the oil of conversation, the philosophic wine, the stuff that is consumed when good fellows get together, that puts a song in their hearts and laughter on their lips and the warm glow of contentment in their eyes; if you mean Christmas cheer; if you mean the stimulating drink that puts the spring in the old gentleman's step on a frosty morning; if you mean the drink that enables a man to magnify his joy and his happiness, and to forget, if only for a little while, life's great tragedies and heartbreaks and sorrows; if you mean that drink, the sale of which pours into our treasuries untold millions of dollars, which are used to provide tender care for our little crippled children, our blind, our deaf, our dumb, our pitiful aged and infirm, to build highways, hospitals and schools, then certainly I am in favor of it.

state senator addressing Mississippi legislature, 1958
(From Goodwin, *Alcoholism: The Facts*)

Alcohol remains the one mood-altering substance viewed with considerable ambivalence by the American public. It's been around since the founding of the country, when its use was widespread and considered almost a necessity at every social gathering. The erratic or rowdy behavior associated with excessive drinking during the eighteenth century was blamed more on a person's companions than on the drinking itself. Average Americans then consumed greater quantities of alcohol than they do today.

Concern over the adverse effects of alcohol developed during the nineteenth century and grew into the temperance and prohibitionist movement, culminating in 1919 with ratification of the Eighteenth Amendment (prohibiting the production, sale, and transportation of alcohol for use in beverages) and passage of the Volstead Act to enforce it. Prohibition lasted until 1933, when the Twenty-First Amendment repealed the Eighteenth.

Since then, drinking has become an accepted part of our way of life. But there is still controversy. Advocates claim that moderate social drinking facilitates communication, allows a person to relax after a hard day, assists those unable to sleep, and diminishes chances of heart attack. Critics say that drinking increases antisocial behavior that puts the user and public at risk, causes severe illness and death, places unborn children at risk, and facilitates the use of illicit drugs. Although mild to moderate drinking has not been shown to be harmful, without question, excessive consumption of and dependency on alcohol is associated with a wide array of adverse psychological, physical, and societal effects.

PATTERNS OF USE

In 1987, the average per capita consumption of pure alcohol (in all beverages) by Americans was 2.54 gallons. Take the one out of three nondrinkers out of the calculation, and per capita consumption jumps to almost 4 gallons. That's equivalent to 56 gallons of beer, 20 gallons of wine, or 6 gallons of distilled spirits. Not to be overlooked is that almost half the alcohol was consumed by only 10 percent of the population. These figures are lower than those reported in the previous three decades. Nonetheless, that year over 1.4 million people in this country were treated for excessive alcohol consumption or dependency. More recently, as documented in the 1999 National Household Survey on Drug Abuse, approximately 105 million of the 47.3 percent, U.S. household population age twelve and over had consumed alcohol, and 20 percent of persons had engaged in binge drinking at least once within the month preceding the survey.

It is estimated at present that 44 percent of U.S. adults are drinkers, 22 percent former drinkers, and 34 percent abstainers. Approximately 13 percent of the population are either excessive drinkers or physically dependent on alcohol. Alcohol use among the young remains high, with 35 percent of twelfth graders reporting drinking five or more drinks in a row on at least one occasion in the two weeks prior to the 2000 Monitoring the Future Survey. Availability of alcohol is high, with over 90 percent of seniors in high school reporting easy availability of purchase. This is despite the observation that thirty-one of the fifty states have laws prohibiting the consumption of alcohol beverages by individuals under the age of twenty-one. Binge drinking on college campuses has long been recognized as a major problem. It is estimated that as many as 23 million people engage in binge drinking, with 11 million drinking five or more drinks in a row on five or more days a month, with the lifetime prevalence of alcoholism ranging from 14 to 23 percent. Even among the elderly, alcohol consumption is prevalent, being seen in 14 percent of elderly persons admitted to emergency rooms, with problem drinking reported as high as 49 percent in nursing homes. Rates of alcohol-related admissions to acute care hospitals match rates of admission for heart attacks.

COSTS OF DRINKING

As discussed below, excessive alcohol use is responsible for a multitude of medical problems—up to 40 percent of general medical hospital admissions—and taking perhaps 20 percent of the nation's total expenditure for medical care, depending on the specific survey. Estimates of alcohol-related deaths range from 50,000 to 200,000 per year. Many of these deaths are unrelated to the chronic medical complications of alcohol and include accidents, homicides, and suicides—where alcohol is implicated in about half the cases. One study demonstrated a significant relationship between number of drinks per occasion and incidence of fatal injury: those who had five or more drinks were more than twice as likely to die from injuries as those who drank less. Alcoholism also places one at risk for using other drugs by a factor of seven. Mental disorders are also associated with excessive alcohol consumption, with 37 percent of those who abuse alcohol having a coexisting mental disorder.

Excessive drinking doesn't affect only the drinker. Approximately 40,000 newborns each year are at risk of fetal alcohol syndrome (Chapter 19), one of the three leading causes of birth defects. Up to 15 million school-age children live with at least one alcoholic parent. Altogether, about 28 million (one out of every eight) Americans are children of alcoholics. Many experience a wide variety of emotional problems that often last well into adulthood.

Excessive alcohol use also puts children, in general, at risk. A survey by the National Council on Alcoholism indicated that almost 30 percent of fourth graders were encouraged by peers to try alcoholic beverages. One-fourth of all motor vehicle deaths between 1995 and 1996 among children under fifteen years of age involved alcohol, and almost two-thirds of passenger deaths involve an illegally drunk driver having a child in the driver's car.

Although violent behavior is related to alcohol abuse, with both parties frequently being intoxicated, this is not always the case. One survey found that nondrinkers living with alcoholics had almost a twofold risk of being the victim of homicide. Half of those arrested on criminal charges are believed to have been drinking while committing the crime.

Traffic accidents are the leading cause of death in young adults. Of the 41,967 traffic fatalities in 1997, alcohol was implicated in approximately 39 percent, with 50 percent of driving fatalities related to alcohol used by drivers ages twenty-one to thirty-four. Roughly half the daytime fatalities on weekends involve drunk driving. The numbers climb to about 60 percent on weekend nights. Alcohol and other drugs are believed responsible for more than a half million nonfatal injuries per year; two out of five Americans will be involved in an alcohol-related accident in their lifetimes, and nearly half of all fatally injured drivers will have significant levels of alcohol in their blood. Total cost to society for these accidents is approximately $74 billion a year.

Alcohol has been associated with a variety of other disorders, ranging from multiple drug dependency to gambling to food addictions to depression. Although sexual dysfunction is common in alcoholics, the consumption of alcohol, especially by the young, has been associated with participation in high-risk sexual activity and, correspondingly, sexually transmitted diseases.

COMMON ALCOHOLIC BEVERAGES

The three basic types of alcoholic beverages are wines, beer, and distilled spirits. Fermented fruit juices and their distillation produce brandies; addition of sugar or other flavorings produces liqueurs or cordials. Wines, dessert wines, wine coolers, and sherry or port can be produced by varying the quantity of alcohol or sugar. This results in a total of seven groups of beverages (Table 7.1): beers and ales, distilled spirits, liqueurs (brandies, cordials, port, sherry), table wines, dessert wines, wine coolers, and hard cider. The volume of alcohol in those beverages varies, so consumption must be compared in terms of absolute alcohol. For example, one ounce of absolute alcohol is considered equal to two cans of beer, or two glasses of wine, or two 1.5-ounce drinks of distilled spirits. The term "proof," used to describe potency, refers to twice the alcohol content by volume. Thus a drink that is 80 proof is 40 percent alcohol.

However, the definition of a "standard drink" can vary greatly by country, from 8 grams of ethanol in England to 19.75 grams in Japan. In the United States a standard serving is considered to contain 14 grams of ethanol and is found in 12 ounces of beer, 5 ounces of wine, or 1.5 ounces of spirits. The concept of equivalency is important because of the common misconception that a glass of wine or beer has less alcohol than a mixed drink or a "shot." In fact, all have roughly the same quantity of alcohol. A person who drinks two double shots a day is consuming a considerable

TABLE 7.1. Alcohol in Common Beverages

Beverage	Percent By		Amount per Serving	
	Volume	*Proof*	*Ounces*	*Grams*
Beers and ales	3-6	6-12	0.36-0.72	10-20
Distilled spirits	25-50	50-100	0.52-0.75	7-21
Hard ciders	8-15	16-30	0.32-0.60	9-17
Liqueurs	20-55	40-110	0.30-0.90	6-15
Wines				
Dessert wines	15-20	30-40	0.45-0.6	14-17
Table wines	8-14	16-28	0.32-0.56	9-17
Wine coolers	1.5-3	3-6	0.12-0.24	3-7

Note: Based on serving sizes of 12 ounces for beer, 5.4 ounces for table wine and hard cider, 3 ounces for dessert wine, 8 ounces of a wine cooler, and 1.5 ounces for liqueurs and distilled spirits.

quantity of alcohol, but no more than someone drinking four beers or four glasses of wine.

Popularity of particular alcoholic beverages changes. In 1988, beer accounted for 51 percent of the alcohol consumed, wine 14 percent, and distilled spirits 35 percent. Wine coolers, the newest type of beverage, were increasingly consumed through most of the 1980s until their popularity began to lessen. It is important to realize that even some "nonalcoholic" drinks may not be completely alcohol free but contain less than 0.5 percent alcohol. Those sensitive to alcohol should make certain the beverage is labeled alcohol free rather than nonalcoholic.

Over-the-Counter Medications

A large number of over-the-counter (OTC) medications—antihistamines, cough syrups, mouthwash, asthma medications, and other drugs—contain alcohol in varying amounts, up to 60 percent in some. The alcohol content of these drugs is usually of little concern because they're taken in relatively small quantities. But not always. Someone with asthma or chronic bronchitis who takes 3 tablespoons of a theophylline elixir four to five times a day is consuming up to 1.5 ounces of pure alcohol. That's roughly equivalent to 10 ounces of table wine, 2.4 ounces of distilled spirits, or 30 ounces of beer. In such instances, especially in the presence of other underlying medical problems, the alcohol could produce adverse effects.

HOW ALCOHOL IS HANDLED BY THE BODY

Alcohol's effects on the brain depend on quantity consumed, rate of absorption and distribution, which in turn are affected by body weight, metabolism, elimination, and the sensitivity of particular tissues to alcohol or its metabolites.

Absorption of Alcohol

Alcohol is readily absorbed into the bloodstream from the stomach and intestinal tract (about 25 percent of alcohol from the stomach; the rest from the small intestine). The rate of absorption, however, varies greatly among people, as well as in the same person, depending on a number of factors. They include the pattern of drinking, rate of consumption, tolerance to alcohol (based on previous exposure), presence of food in the stomach, and type of beverage as well as genetic differences. Food in the stomach can decrease the blood alcohol level by about 30 percent whereas an empty stomach results in a markedly increased absorption.

Distribution of Alcohol

Once absorbed, alcohol is quickly distributed throughout the body, with the concentration in the brain about the same as in the bloodstream. However, for a given quantity of alcohol, blood alcohol concentrations are less in a heavier person than in a thin one.

Metabolism of Alcohol

Almost all alcohol is metabolized completely (broken down) in the liver. New research, however, has demonstrated that alcohol begins to be metabolized first in the stomach, not in the liver as previously believed. This first breakdown results from the action of the enzyme alcohol dehydrogenase. When the enzyme's action is diminished—as happens when drinking on an empty stomach and in chronic alcoholics—the body's tissues receive greater amounts of alcohol, and its mood-altering effects are felt earlier and more intensely.

It has been demonstrated that women tend to have less alcohol dehydrogenase in their stomach linings and therefore absorb more alcohol than men. Thus women tend to become more intoxicated than men and are more vulnerable to the damaging effects of alcohol on the liver. If a woman is pregnant, there can be potentially detrimental effects on the fetus with even small quantities of alcohol consumed. Of equal or greater importance is that women who drink more than two drinks a day have a higher relative risk for death (RR = 1.3) than men, whose risk of death was not greater than non-drinkers until their consumption exceeded four drinks per day. The increased risk in women was related to alcohol-related liver disease.

Alcohol is mainly oxidized by enzymes in the liver, forming acetaldehyde. Two enzyme systems are involved in the metabolism of alcohol to acetaldehyde: the microsomal enzyme oxidizing system (MEOS) and alcohol dehydrogenase. Alcohol dehydrogenase accounts for most of the metabolic process at low blood alcohol levels. As the levels increase, the MEOS becomes more active, an important phenomenon because of the effect that the system has on metabolism of other drugs. The MEOS also breaks down several other drugs, and the effect of alcohol on this system can result in alcohol-drug interactions that either increase or diminish the effects of the other drugs. When isoniazid (INH), a drug used to treat tuberculosis, is metabolized by the MEOS, a metabolite toxic to the liver is produced. For that reason, adverse effects of INH are common in alcoholics. The commonly used painkiller acetaminophen is acted upon in a similar manner. Since Tylenol and other similar drugs are taken in large doses by alcoholics to relieve headaches, the potential for liver damage exists. It is important to note that once activated, the MEOS may remain active for some time, even in the absence of alcohol. So toxic effects can result when acetaminophen is taken for withdrawal symptoms.

Although long-term administration of alcohol activates the MEOS, acute drinking of a large quantity of alcohol has the opposite effect. Thus the metabolism of other drugs usually deactivated by the MEOS is inhibited. That affects tranquilizers, barbiturates, and methadone, the blood and brain levels of which are enhanced with consumption of large amounts of alcohol. So when someone who has been drinking large quantities of alcohol takes one of those drugs to get to sleep, the potential for overdose is real. Acetaldehyde is an intermediate substance produced when alcohol is metabolized. Acetaldehyde is extremely toxic. When it accumulates in the bloodstream, it can cause flushing, headaches, and rapid heartbeat. This reaction is the basis of the disulfiram (Antabuse) reaction and the reason why Antabuse is used to prevent drinking.

A diet consisting mainly of alcohol lacks vitamins and minerals. Relying on alcohol as the main source of calories (even when caloric intake is adequate) leads to deficiencies and breakdown of the body's protein stores, resulting in a number of medical complications. Even when a healthy diet is eaten, chronic alcohol use can prevent the body from effectively using the nutrients, impairing absorption as well as metabolism of vitamins, proteins, carbohydrates, and minerals.

Approximately 2 percent of alcohol is excreted unchanged through the kidneys and the lungs. Excretion through the breath reflects the alcohol concentration in the blood, the basis of the Breathalyzer test for intoxication.

Normal or Low-Risk Drinking

The widespread "social" consumption of alcohol associated with its proven beneficial effects in reducing anxiety and stress, as well as the recognized ability of moderate drinking to decrease risk of coronary artery disease, peripheral vascular disease, and "all cause" mortality, when compared to nondrinkers raises the question as to how many drinks are good for you.

This is an extremely important question and not easy to answer. The 2000 guidelines promoted by the Department of Health and Human Services and the National Institute on Alcohol Abuse and Alcoholism both state that weekly limits of alcohol consumption should be no more than two drinks daily for men and one drink daily for nonpregnant women.

A standard drink, as noted earlier, would consist of 14 grams of alcohol which can be found in 12 ounces of beer, 5 ounces of wine, or 1½ ounces of 80 proof spirits. It was further recommended that those weekly limits not exceed 4 drinks for men or 3 drinks for nonpregnant women on any one day. Individuals in poor health, the elderly, and those on medications that might interact with alcohol should adjust these limits downward.

Intoxication

Alcohol is popularly perceived as a stimulant. It isn't. It's a depressant. As consumption progresses, the areas in the brain that normally inhibit behavior are depressed, leaving unopposed those brain centers that facilitate behavior. Virtually everyone has witnessed the strong antisocial behavior that sometimes results with large quantities of alcohol. But as the amount consumed increases, general central nervous system depression sets in. So at low doses alcohol appears to be a stimulant, until its actual depressant effects become visible as the dose increases.

How fast an individual becomes intoxicated depends on many factors— body weight, food in the stomach, alcohol metabolism rate in both stomach and liver, tolerance to specific alcohol, beverage strength, other mood-altering drugs in the system, and even the environment.

Blood Alcohol Levels

The most common way to correlate impairment with alcohol consumption is through alcohol content in the body. Alcohol is easily measured in the breath, blood, and urine, but blood alcohol level is the standard measurement for impairment and intoxication. Breathalyzer tests are frequently administered by police and are both quick and fairly accurate in pinpointing blood alcohol concentrations. Blood alcohol levels (BAL) are expressed as milligrams per deciliter (mg/dL), grams per deciliter (g/dL), or more commonly as percent by volume. In most states, intoxication is defined as a blood alcohol concentration of 100 mg/dL (0.10 g/dL), or 0.10 percent. Performance can be affected at much lower levels. In various studies, 14 to 68 percent of tested subjects were diagnosed as intoxicated with blood levels of 0.05 to 0.10 percent. On an individual basis, impairment may be detected at levels as low as 0.02 percent, with euphoria seen at 0.03 percent in nontolerant persons (Table 7.2, 7.3). Clearly, using a 0.10 percent BAL to define the threshold for driving while intoxicated is not very helpful.

The blood alcohol level can be affected by a number of factors. As body weight increases, more drinks can be consumed prior to reaching a given BAL. Women, as noted above, have higher BALs than men. Consuming the same number of drinks over a period of time will result in a diminished BAL. Food in the stomach also greatly affects BAL. A BAL of 0.10 percent can be reached quickly after two glasses of wine (or equivalent) on an empty stomach; after three glasses if drunk an hour or two after a meal. Four ounces of whiskey on an empty stomach result in a BAL of 0.67 to 0.92 percent; the same amount after a meal would result in a BAL of about 0.3 to 0.5 percent.

TABLE 7.2. Approximate Blood Alcohol Percentage in Men by Weight and Number of Drinks

Drinks	Body Weight in Pounds								
	100	120	140	160	180	200	220	240	
0	.00	.00	.00	.00	.00	.00	.00	.00	Only Safe Driving Limit
1	.04	.03	.03	.02	.02	.02	.02	.02	Impairment Begins
2	.08	.06	.05	.05	.04	.04	.03	.03	Driving Skills
3	.11	.09	.08	.07	.06	.06	.05	.05	Significantly Affected
4	.15	.12	.11	.09	.08	.08	.07	.06	
5	.19	.16	.13	.12	.11	.09	.09	.08	Possible Criminal Penalties
6	.23	.19	.16	.14	.13	.11	.10	.09	
7	.26	.22	.19	.16	.15	.13	.12	.11	Legally Intoxicated
8	.30	.25	.21	.19	.17	.15	.14	.13	
9	.34	.28	.24	.21	.19	.17	.15	.14	Criminal Penalties
10	.38	.31	.27	.23	.21	.19	.17	.16	

Source: National Clearinghouse for Alcohol and Drug Information, Rockville, MD.
Note: Subtract .01 percent for each 40 minutes of drinking.
One drink is 1.25 oz. of 80 proof liquor, 12 oz. of beer, or 5 oz. of table wine.

TABLE 7.3. Approximate Blood Alcohol Percentage in Women by Weight and Number of Drinks

Drinks	Body Weight in Pounds									
	90	100	120	140	160	180	200	220	240	
0	.00	.00	.00	.00	.00	.00	.00	.00	.00	Only Safe Driving Limit
1	.05	.05	.04	.03	.03	.03	.02	.02	.02	Impairment Begins
2	.10	.09	.08	.07	.06	.05	.05	.04	.04	Driving Skills Significantly Affected
3	.15	.14	.11	.10	.09	.08	.07	.06	.06	
4	.20	.18	.15	.13	.11	.10	.09	.08	.08	Possible Criminal Penalties
5	.25	.23	.19	.16	.14	.13	.11	.10	.09	
6	.30	.27	.23	.19	.17	.15	.14	.12	.11	
7	.35	.32	.27	.23	.20	.18	.16	.14	.13	Legally Intoxicated
8	.40	.36	.30	.26	.23	.20	.18	.17	.15	
9	.45	.41	.34	.29	.26	.23	.20	.19	.17	Criminal Penalties
10	.51	.45	.38	.32	.28	.25	.23	.21	.19	

Source: National Clearinghouse for Alcohol and Drug Information, Rockville, MD. Data supplied by the Pennsylvania Liquor Control Board.
Note: Subtract .01 percent for each 40 minutes of drinking.
One drink is 1.25 oz. of 80 proof liquor, 12 oz. of beer, or 5 oz. of table wine.

The Morning After: The Hangover

The most common occurrence experienced by those who drink excessively, or at times even by those who drink sporadically and only moderately, is the morning-after "hangover." Although the symptoms of a hangover have been suggested to be signs of a mild, early alcohol withdrawal process, in fact this does not appear to be the case.

Hangover symptoms, well known to many, include headache, fatigue, loss of appetite, varying degrees of gastrointestinal upset including nausea and diarrhea, dry mouth, and tremulousness. The exact causes of the hangover have been debated, but significant factors include the production of increased acetaldehyde, a metabolic breakdown product of alcohol, and the various congeners seen in many alcoholic beverages, such as whiskey, wines, and liqueurs.

Physiologically, the hangover is associated with increased secretions of a variety of hormones, including the antidiuretic hormone aldosterone, renin, and cortisol. Its effect on the antidiuretic hormone which is responsible for urine secretion and fluid balance, is directly opposite to that of alcohol, which, in fact, stimulates urine production disproportionately to the volume of fluids taken in. As a result, dehydration is a common accompaniment of the hangover and is responsible for the dryness of the mouth. Although not often realized, the cognitive and motor deficits during a hangover can be considerable and may affect performance during the day. Symptoms are increased in severity in the presence of coexisting chronic medical conditions, especially cardiovascular disorders, fatigue, hunger, or dehydration.

The amount of alcohol consumed within a specific time that results in a hangover is five to six drinks for a man or three to five drinks for a woman, which, within a relatively short time and on an empty stomach, will consistently produce a hangover. The hangover intensity may also be related to the type of alcohol consumed. It is felt that the cognitive deficits often seen are related to the congener content. "Clear" liquors, such as vodka or gin, are associated with less frequent hangovers than mixed drinks and liqueurs.

A number of treatments have been suggested for "curing" a hangover. The most common, and perhaps most pleasing to those who drink excessively, is the use of an "eye opener" or the "hair of the dog," namely, consumption of alcoholic beverages. Other more appropriate supportive measures include a mild analgesic for headache and increased fluid ingestion to combat the dehydration. There have been attempts to study the effects of drugs used concurrently with alcohol ingestion to diminish the chances of a hangover. Of the substances studied, Vitamin B6 has been the only one to date that has been shown to somewhat reduce hangover symptoms when taken concurrently with alcohol ingestion.

Since there is no effective treatment for the rapid relief of hangover symptoms, the best way to prevent a hangover from occurring is to carefully moderate one's drinking patterns to prevent excessive alcohol from being consumed and to make certain that drinking does not occur in the presence of dehydration or a lack of food.

EFFECTS OF ENVIRONMENT

What an individual expects from a drink and the setting in which it's consumed are also important determinants of intoxication. People who don't know they're drinking alcohol become intoxicated at a slow rate. People who think they're drinking beverages containing alcohol (but which don't) show remarkable mood changes. A person can become high drinking in a social setting more quickly than when drinking alone. Compared with people who don't anticipate positive mood changes from alcohol, those who expect pleasurable effects tend to be more likely to become heavy drinkers, to drink when confronted with stress, and to be less able to handle stress when they're abstinent.

Alcohol is metabolized in an adult at a rate of approximately one-fourth to one-third of an ounce (7 to 10 grams) per hour—about equal to two-thirds to one ounce of distilled spirits, or 8 to 12 ounces of beer. Limiting consumption to the rate of metabolism can keep a person's BAL under 0.10 percent. Genetic variations cause some people to metabolize alcohol much more slowly than others. These people rarely get drunk because even one glass of wine can produce headache, flushing, or dizziness.

As tolerance develops, larger quantities of alcohol must be consumed to produce intoxication. Tolerance results from either a more rapid metabolism rate or a function of alcohol on the central nervous system. With tolerance, some people can appear to perform at acceptable levels with a BAL higher than 0.20 percent. But tolerance doesn't always rise to lethal levels of blood alcohol, so respiratory depression and death can follow soon after rapidly drinking large quantities of alcohol. Drinking large amounts in a relatively short time can also cause an alcoholic blackout, an acute loss of memory surrounding the immediate drinking episode without impairment of long-term memory.

INTERACTION WITH OTHER DRUGS

As a central nervous system depressant, alcohol exhibits cross-tolerance and cross-dependence with all other CNS depressant drugs. As discussed earlier, chronic drinking increases activity of the MEOS in the liver that breaks down CNS depressants, making higher dosages necessary to provide the same effect. But when alcohol is taken acutely, or the BAL rises swiftly, the MEOS is inhibited, and the person is then susceptible to the combined depressant effects of alcohol and the other CNS depressant. Overdose is a frequent complication, so taking sleeping pills after a night of heavy drinking can be hazardous.

Alcohol can also interact with other drugs, including oral anticoagulants, anticonvulsants, antidepressants, and painkillers. When interacting with drugs for diabetes, a marked lowering of blood sugar (hypoglycemia) can result. The same effect is likely with insulin, because alcohol can decrease the rate at which insulin is broken down in the body.

The use of aspirin and alcohol may increase the chances of gastrointestinal bleeding, especially in persons with a history of peptic ulcers. Medications taken by people with peptic ulcers or hyperacidity, called histamine H^2 receptor blockers (Tagamet, Ranitidine), may also affect alcohol metabolism by decreasing the activity of the enzyme alcohol dehydrogenase in the stomach. As discussed in the section on Antabuse, a drug used to prevent drinking, a number of drugs have Antabuse-like activity and, in susceptible individuals, can cause adverse reactions when a person taking these medicines drinks. The Food and Drug Administration now requires that alcohol warnings appear on all over-the-counter drugs containing analgesic or antipyretic ingredients, advising those who consume three or more alcoholic beverages a day to consult a physician concerning the safety of taking these products.

DEPENDENCY AND WITHDRAWAL

Alcohol consumption on a chronic basis affects a variety of neurotransmitters, including increasing dopamine release, inhibiting effects of glutamate on N-methyl-D aspartate (NMDA) receptors, potentiating effects of gamma-aminobutyric acid (GABA) receptors, and influencing noradrenergic receptors. Abstinence results in removal of the inhibitory action of alcohol on these receptors, with an increased level of neurotransmitters, resulting in the signs and symptoms of withdrawal. Chronic and excessive alcohol consumption leads to dependency and then leads to severe withdrawal symptoms when drinking stops. The lifetime risk of withdrawal in problem drinkers has been estimated at 14 percent; however, up to half of problem drinkers may experience various symptoms of withdrawal.

Untreated, the withdrawal reaction progresses through four stages, based on severity of symptoms. Withdrawal can be prevented by treatment with appropriate medications—or even with alcohol. Indeed, detoxification from alcohol should never allow symptoms to progress further than the stage at which medical help is first sought (Table 7.4).

TABLE 7.4. Alcohol Withdrawal Signs and Symptoms

Stage 1	Stage 2	Stage 3	Stage 4
Agitation and anxiety	Fever	Persistent hallucinations	Hallucinations: severe
Tremors	Chest pain	Excitability	Hyperthermia
Sweating	Nausea and vomiting	Minor seizure activity	Delirium
Tachycardia	Disorientation		Seizures
Insomnia	Intermittent hallucinations		Death
Mild elevated blood pressure	Hypertension		

Stage One usually sets in from six to twelve hours after the last drink and is due to hyperactivity of the autonomic nervous system. Anxiety, restlessness, increased heart rate, sweating, difficulty sleeping, and increased blood pressure are common. At this point, if dependency is not extreme, the discomforts may be minor and treatable without medication, but with reassurance.

Stage Two begins after twelve hours, often peaking at twenty-four to thirty-six hours. It combines Stage One symptoms with visual and auditory hallucinations, notable because of relatively clear intervals. When not hallucinating, the person is well oriented and aware of having hallucinated. Medical treatment should always be given.

Stage Three begins from twelve to forty-eight hours after the last drink. Seizures may occur. In susceptible individuals, these may come as early as seven hours after the last drink.

Stage Four begins up to seventy-two to ninety-six hours after consumption. However, seizures may be seen in up to six days. This is when delirium and tremors (delirium tremens, or DTs) appear, characterized by increasing confusion, disorientation, agitation, and paranoid hallucinations. Without treatment, the DTs can persist for several days and result in death up to 50 percent of the time, especially when there is an underlying medical problem. Recovery usually takes five to seven days. However, long-term effects, such as depression, anxiety, fatigue, and disturbances of sleep, may last much longer, for up to a year, and may be responsible for the relapse to alcohol often seen after abstinence has been achieved.

DTs should never be allowed to develop because withdrawal symptoms can be treated so effectively in their earliest stages. The rare cases that occur today are the result of not recognizing during the early stages of withdrawal that the person is dependent on alcohol. A person may begin to experience withdrawal but deny an alcohol-dependent problem, try to hide it from family and friends, feel capable of "going it alone," or may just be too embarrassed to seek medical help.

That is why family and friends of a chronic drinker should be alert to withdrawal symptoms. When that person stops drinking and starts to develop a rapid heart rate, shortness of breath, chills, low-grade fever, or nausea with recurrent vomiting and/or abdominal pain, immediate medical attention is necessary. The treatment of withdrawal from alcohol is discussed below.

ADVERSE EFFECTS

When used excessively, alcohol is a toxic drug responsible for both acute and chronic complications (Table 7.5). Such problems involve a variety of systems and organs in the body.

TABLE 7.5. Complications of Heavy Alcohol Use

Acute Use	Chronic Use
Gastrointestinal tract and liver Gastritis and peptic ulcer,* dilated and bleeding esophageal veins, pancreatic inflammation (pancreatitis), liver failure	Gastrointestinal tract and liver Gastritis, dilated esophageal veins (portal hypertension), peptic ulcer, malabsorption, diminished esophageal motility, fatty liver, cirrhosis with liver failure, pancreatic cysts and inflammation (pancreatitis)
Heart Irregularities of rhythm, elevated blood pressure, cardiomyopathy	Heart Enlargement (cardiomyopathy), high blood pressure, stroke
Metabolic abnormalities	Nutritional General malnutrition, anemia
Decreased temperature	Infections Lungs and urinary tract
Allergic reactions Flushing, urticaria, headache	Cancer Mouth, larynx, esophagus, pancreas, liver, stomach, colon, breast
Neurological effects Intoxication, blackouts, withdrawal	Neuropsychiatric effects Wernicke's encephalopathy, Korsakoff's psychosis, cerebellar degeneration, polyneuropathy, optic neuropathy, myopathy, dementia, central pontine degeneration, Marchiafava-Bignami disease

*Usually when taken with a gastric irritant such as aspirin.

Gastrointestinal Tract and Liver

Even mild social drinking can cause impairment of motor function and gastrointestinal upset, felt as heartburn. Increased short-term use, even a single episode, can cause inflammation of the stomach (gastritis) with abdominal pain and bleeding, peptic ulcers, and inflammation of the pancreas. When an episode of heavy drinking is superimposed on chronic complications, such as enlarged esophageal veins (portal hypertension) and liver disease, severe bleeding and liver failure can occur. It is estimated that 10 to 35 percent of heavy drinkers develop alcoholic hepatitis and 10 to 20 percent cirrhosis.

Not uncommon are such accompanying problems as decreased absorption of nutrients, diminished intestinal activity, fatty liver, cirrhosis with liver failure, and pancreatic cysts and inflammation (pancreatitis). Most of those complications are seen in people who have been drinking large amounts of alcohol for long periods, but recent evidence suggests that such damage can show up in susceptible people after much less drinking. Chronic liver disease and cirrhosis is a frequent cause of death in alcoholics.

Cardiovascular System

Chronic alcohol consumption can lead to enlargement of the heart (cardiomyopathy). Although this condition is seen only in 1 to 2 percent of excessive drinkers, it can cause heart failure and death. Even nonchronic alcohol use has been associated with rises in blood pressure, and an increased incidence of stroke shows up among those who drink more than 300 grams (about 10.5 ounces) a week. It is estimated that 5 to 24 percent of hypertensive patients may have elevated blood pressure because of alcohol consumption—in this instance, three drinks per day.

A number of studies, however, have demonstrated that minimal to moderate drinking can have a protective effect against coronary artery disease, as opposed to no such effect from either abstinence or heavy drinking. One reason may be that alcohol increases the blood levels of one type of high-density lipoprotein (HDL). HDLs are believed to be a protective factor in preventing heart attacks. But some say that the type of HDL that is increased by alcohol has no connection with the protective factor and that any significant decreases in heart attacks occur only among those who already have heart disease. However, the reduced risk of heart attack among light or moderate drinkers remains a consistent finding. A reduced risk of severe narrowing (stenosis) or obstruction of the coronary arteries with moderate alcohol consumption has also been noted. Studies have also shown that after heart attacks, persons consuming small to moderate amounts of alcohol have lower mortality rates than nondrinkers. Similarly, it is believed that mild or moderate alcohol consumption is associated with a diminished risk of ischemic stroke and peripheral vascular disease. However, the association of heavy drinking with increased death rates from coronary heart disease, stroke, and other causes has been noted in all studies.

Even in healthy people, acute consumption of alcohol causes an increased heart rate, with irregular heart rhythms also reported, particularly in regular drinkers. This phenomenon is known as the "holiday heart syndrome" because it was first described following drinking during the Christmas-New Year holiday season.

Neuropsychiatric Effects

A wide variety of neuropsychiatric complications have also been noted with excessive alcohol intake, ultimately leading to dementia and inability to function. Researchers have demonstrated that even two drinks can temporarily alter brain function and affect memory. Chronic neurological effects of excessive alcoholism are well known (Table 7.5). Wernicke's encephalopathy, primarily due to thiamine deficiency, consists of disordered cerebral function, including memory impairment, confabulation, organic psychosis, paralysis of eye muscles, and difficulty walking. Treatment with thiamine can reverse many of those symptoms, but residual effects may remain, including Korsakoff's psychosis, a memory disorder associated with apathy.

A more severe and much less common syndrome, Marchiafava-Bignami disease, is characterized by inability to walk, dementia, and muscle spasticity. Difficulty walking and speech disturbances associated with long-term drinking are because of degeneration of the cerebellum. Destruction of another part of the brain, the pons, leads to paraplegia and inability to speak or swallow (central pontine myelinolysis).

Cognitive deficits can be demonstrated in chronic alcoholics following detoxification. Approximately 50 to 70 percent of people with long-term alcohol dependency show impairment in cognitive function, including problem solving, memory, and perception. Although this may be related to the presence of coexisting disease, notably cirrhosis with low levels of encephalopathy, such findings have been observed in individuals without any evidence of severe liver disease. In such cases, CAT scans of the brain have revealed structural abnormalities. Some of these deficits have diminished when the person stopped drinking. Extensive studies on this aspect of alcoholism have recently begun, and in the future it will be the subject of much research.

Alcohol and Sleep

It is commonly believed that a drink before retiring will not only have a calming effect but will facilitate sleep. While on an individual basis this may be correct, in fact, alcohol can disturb normal sleep patterns. After an initial stimulant effect when drinking, drowsiness may occur and the time required to fall asleep may well decrease. However, the usual sleep pattern is disturbed, and not infrequently awakening will occur, with difficulty returning to sleep. Consuming alcohol in the afternoon can also have a similar effect, resulting in increased loss of sleep at night. The elderly have a natural decrease in restful sleep as part of the aging process, with awakenings being quite frequent. Consumption of alcohol to facilitate sleep may have a paradoxical effect, with increased wakenings and morning fatigue.

If excessive alcohol is consumed, sleep disturbances are quite frequent, consisting of difficulty falling asleep, frequent awakenings, and a decrease in quality of sleep. In persons with obstructive sleep apnea (OSA), excessive alcohol consumption can result in an increased frequency of the apnea and a greater degree of obstruction. Persons with OSA who consume more than two drinks per day are at a fivefold risk for fatigue-related traffic crashes as compared to those with OSA who do not drink. Disturbed sleep patterns in alcoholics during withdrawal are also quite common. However, even after abstinence has been achieved, sleep may not return to normal for some time.

Other Effects on the Body

Almost every system can be affected by long-term excessive drinking. Next to nicotine, excessive alcohol consumption is associated with the most serious and widespread complications of any mood-altering drug. In combination with smoking, alcohol has been associated with increased risk of cancer of the head and neck, esophagus, pancreas, stomach, colon, rectum, liver, and even the breast.

Endocrinological effects of alcohol have been described for almost every hormonal system in animal studies. The relevance of some of these observations to humans remains to be determined. But it has been frequently observed that chronic alcohol intake can alter hormonal function relating to human sexuality. Men can show decreased levels of testosterone, a female pattern of hair distribution, and breast enlargement. Impotence isn't uncommon. As Shakespeare put it, "It [drink] provokes the desire, but it takes away the performance."

In women, menstrual abnormalities and infertility are the most common effects. Alcohol causes fetal alcohol syndrome, a condition seen in 0.1 to 0.3 percent of live births, with the most serious effects resulting from the daily consumption of four or more glasses of an alcoholic beverage during pregnancy. But much smaller amounts also can have deleterious effects (see Chapter 19).

The nutritional disturbances that go with heavy drinking include less attention to a balanced diet, substitution of alcohol calories for those usually obtained from carbohydrates, protein, and fat in other foods, diminished absorption of other nutrients, loss of appetite, vomiting, and deficiencies of fiber, protein, calcium, iron, folate, zinc, and vitamins A, B1 (thiamine), B6 (pyridoxine), and C.

Disorders of peripheral nerves (peripheral neuropathy) and muscles (myopathy) are fairly common. Symptoms and signs include numbness, tingling or burning in the extremities, and muscle cramps, tenderness, and weakness. Chronic alcoholism affects the immune system, predisposing the drinker to common and uncommon infections.

DIAGNOSIS

Inordinate drinking is bad for your health; occasional or responsible drinking has minimal, if any, proven adverse effects. But the dividing lines between responsible use, excessive use, and alcoholism are often fuzzy, even to experts in the field.

Some believe heavy drinking means having more than one ounce of pure alcohol (two drinks) a day. Others focus on the amount consumed per occasion (five drinks or more) and frequency of consumption, with heavy drinkers defined as those who take five or more drinks at one time more than once a week. As noted earlier, the National Institute on Alcohol Abuse and Alcoholism has defined moderate drinking as two or fewer drinks a day for men, one drink per day for women and one drink per day for those over sixty-five, with at-risk drinking defined as consuming over fourteen drinks per week or four drinks on any occasion for men and over seven drinks per week or more than three drinks per occasion for women.

The National Council on Alcoholism has developed a list of signs and symptoms for diagnosing alcoholism, divided into definitive and probable groups (Table 7.6). Both the American Psychiatric Association (APA) and the World Health Organization (WHO) have established a more quantitative definition of inappropriate use of alcohol, separate from alcohol dependency. The new WHO guidelines and the APA guidelines have moved closer

TABLE 7.6. Signs and Symptoms of Alcoholism

Definite	Probable
Physical dependency on alcohol, with tremors, hallucinations, seizures on abstinence	No control of consumption
	Surreptitious and/or morning drinking
Mental changes directly related to alcohol	Repeated, conscious attempts at abstinence
Major effects on brain	Medical excuses from work for a variety of reasons
Alcohol-associated complications	Shifting from one type of alcoholic beverage to another
Drinking despite strong medical or social contraindication	Loss of interest in activities not associated with drinking
Blatant, indiscriminate use of alcohol	
Consuming one-fifth gallon of whiskey or alcohol equivalent in beer or wine daily for more than one day	Rages and suicidal thoughts with drinking
Alcoholic blackouts	Drinking to relieve insomnia, anger, fatigue, depression
BAL over 0.15 percent without gross evidence of intoxication, or 0.30 percent at any time	

Source: Modified from National Council on Alcoholism guidelines.

together to allow for unified diagnostic criteria. A consensus of these guidelines now defines inappropriate use of alcohol as a harmful, maladaptive state characterized by at least one of the following:

- Continued use despite knowledge of alcohol causing actual psychological or physical harm to the user
- Recurrent use in situations in which alcohol is physically hazardous

According to the guidelines, a pattern of inappropriate use must exist for at least one month or recur repeatedly over a longer period for a diagnosis to be confirmed. By comparison, the guidelines consider alcohol dependency to exist in the presence of at least three or more of the following for at least one month or frequently over a year:

- Compulsion to drink
- Loss of control in managing alcohol use
- Alcohol taken to relieve or avoid withdrawal symptoms
- Presence of a physiological alcohol withdrawal state
- Evidence of tolerance, with markedly increased amounts of alcohol needed to achieve intoxication or the desired effect
- Progressive neglect of social, occupational, or recreational activities
- Continued use despite knowledge of adverse consequences
- Frequent intoxication or withdrawal when expected to fulfill major social obligations or when alcohol use is known to be hazardous
- Prolonged periods spent drinking or recovering from the effect of drinking

A number of questionnaires that can even be self-administered have been developed to identify problem drinkers early (Table 7.7). These tests are quite simple to administer and, in the medical setting, can be quite helpful in identifying a problem or a potential problem. This is not unimportant, as surveys have shown that up to 50 percent of patients with alcohol problems may not be detected by their general physicians. Laboratory tests that identify liver dysfunction secondary to alcohol consumption may also be helpful, but are far from specific as the liver can be abnormal in a variety of disease states.

Most important, however, is early recognition of inappropriate alcohol use by family, friends, teachers, or employees. Some of the early signs of alcoholism, however, are not difficult to spot (Table 7.8). They include periods of depression alleviated by taking a drink, needing several quick drinks in order to relax (accompanied by increased anxiety if alcohol isn't available), marked increase over previous drinking, drinking at inappropriate times, and undue denial or anger when questioned about drinking behavior.

TABLE 7.7. Questionnaires That Identify Alcohol Abuse

Test	Positive Score	Sensitivity (Percent)	Specificity (Percent)
CAGE	2	61-100	77-96
TWEAK	2	79	83
B MAST	6	30-78	80-99
AUDIT	8	38-94	66-90

AUDIT = Alcohol Use Disorder Identification Test
B MAST = Modified Michigan Alcohol Screening Test

TABLE 7.8. Early Signs of Drinking Problems

Anxiety relieved by drinking
Frequent job and/or residence changes
Gulping drinks
Choosing jobs that facilitate drinking
Frequent traffic violations and/or accidents
Social disorganization in family
Complaints by spouse about drinking
Denial
Depression alleviated by drinking

Frequent changes of job, absences for nonspecific medical reasons, accidents at work or when driving, or coming to work with alcohol on one's breath should all serve as warning signs.

REASONS FOR EXCESSIVE DRINKING

The greatest controversy in trying to determine the reasons for alcoholism centers on the roles of nature and nurture, or genetics versus environment. Many studies have shown that alcoholism is three to five times more common among children whose parents were alcoholic, regardless of whether they were reared with biological or adoptive parents. Other studies have shown a predominance of alcoholism among adopted children whose biological parents were alcoholics. One of the largest studies included 862 men and 913 women adopted between 1930 and 1949. The incidence of alcohol dependency among the adoptive parents showed no association with increased risk of alcohol dependency among the children. Excessive alcohol consumption among the biological parents, however, was linked to an increased risk for alcoholism among the children.

Twin and half sibling studies have also suggested a genetic component to alcoholism. Studies of the drinking habits of twins would appear to be a good way to build a case for genetic determinants of alcoholism. But one must be aware of confounding variables such as social interaction between twins, even when living with separate adoptive parents, as well as the environment in which twins may live when reaching adulthood, especially the stability of their own family unit. Investigators who have reviewed these factors have found that identical twins tended to have more social contact with each other during adulthood than fraternal twins. This frequent social contact seemed to affect their drinking patterns. However, it did not fully explain the strongly similar drinking habits; there must still be a significant genetic contribution. This finding existed only for men, not women. With respect to women twins, marital status appears to play a role, with genetic factors accounting for 60 to 75 percent of the variance in drinking habits in twins who are not married, but only for 31 to 59 percent of the variance in those who are married.

In reviewing twin studies, two distinctive patterns or types have been observed (Table 7.9). Type I appeared when at least one biological parent consumed large quantities of alcohol and the situation in the adoptive home was similar. Both men and women were three times more likely to develop alcoholism than those in a control group. This high-risk group is termed "milieu-limited," meaning that a drinking-conducive environment had to have existed. Excessive drinking in this group usually developed after age twenty-five, with the person experiencing frequent guilt over his or her drinking. These people can seldom abstain from drinking, but they are less likely to be antisocial when they drink.

Type II (male-limited) were men whose biological fathers abused alcohol. Their risk of alcoholism existed regardless of environment—from 17 to

TABLE 7.9. Genetic Patterns of Alcoholism

Characteristics	Milieu-Limited (Type I)	Male-Limited (Type II)
Age of onset	After 25	Before 25
Ability to abstain	Infrequent	Frequent
Aggressive behavior and arrests when drinking	Infrequent	Frequent
Loss of control	Frequent	Infrequent
Guilt over drinking	Frequent	Infrequent

18 percent had problems later on in life, compared with fewer than 2 percent of those who didn't fit that pattern. Women who matched that pattern appeared to develop increased anxiety in later life, but not actual alcoholism. The men began drinking before age twenty-five and were frequently able to abstain for periods of time. But they consistently engaged in aggressive behavior, were often arrested while drinking, and rarely experienced guilt over their drinking episodes.

However, more recent studies have been unable to confirm the existence of a Type II pattern of primary alcoholism. It is now believed by many in the alcohol field that those thought to have Type II alcoholism have a primary personality disorder with a secondary drinking problem. This inability to validate what had been previously considered a characteristic of primary alcoholism illustrates the difficulties inherent in separating genetic from environmental influences.

Ability to Metabolize Alcohol

Support for the genetic theory has been found in the observation that different ethnic groups metabolize alcohol at different rates—because of variations in enzyme activity. Asians and Native Americans metabolize alcohol at a much slower rate than other groups. That leads to an increased concentration of acetaldehyde in the body, resulting in a strong adverse reaction to only small amounts of alcohol. It could be assumed, therefore, that such cultures would have a lower incidence of alcohol use. But this is not so.

The adverse biochemical reaction is unarguable, but improper use of alcohol among Native Americans is high; indeed, it is one of their leading causes of death. And while excessive drinking is relatively rare among Asians, the 1980s saw an increase in drinking, especially in those cultures that are developing highly competitive industrial societies. Even though the rate at which alcohol is metabolized may be genetically determined, it appears there is still insufficient evidence that this metabolism is related to excessive drinking.

Other Genetic Factors

Other genetic factors have been identified in laboratory studies. But their relationship to an inevitable genetic predisposition to alcoholism remains to be determined. Recently, a gene thought to be responsible for placing one at risk for alcoholism was identified in the brain of deceased alcoholics. The dopamine D2 receptor gene (DRD2) was identified in 77 percent of the brains of dead alcoholics as compared with 28 percent of nonalcoholics. However, a more recent study was unable to confirm a linkage between the DRD2 gene that encodes the D2 receptor and alcohol dependence. Gene loci on the 5HT and GABA genes have also been reported, with a threefold and fivefold greater risk of developing alcoholism. All of these studies, however, are preliminary, and confirmation is needed.

Neurophysiology

Studies have also found differences between children of alcoholics and other children in tests of general intelligence, memory, attention, and organizational abilities. These studies involved relatively small samples, so it's hard to ascertain whether genetic influences or environment played a role in the findings.

Environmental Effects

The evidence is convincing that a genetic risk for excessive drinking exists in some people. Yet it's clear that such patterns do not follow a simple Mendelian distribution, which would make alcoholism in a parent the basis for predicting with certainty the proportion of children who will become alcoholic. In a study of genetic and social determinants in adolescent alcohol use, family influence was found to be quite important, accounting for 40 to 50 percent of the variance in men and 58 percent in women. More than 80 percent of children in the male-limited susceptibility group do not go on to abuse alcohol. Nor do the majority of alcoholics fit either pattern. Fewer than half of children of alcoholics develop drinking problems, and an even smaller proportion become dependent on alcohol.

So environment is important in fostering improper use of alcohol. This includes the family, peers, role models, and society's view of alcohol consumption—favorable if consumed in reasonable amounts in social settings.

ALCOHOLISM: A DISEASE
OR A PSYCHOLOGICAL DISORDER?

Almost everyone involved in treating alcoholism now considers it a disease. This includes groups such as the American Medical Association, the American Psychological Association, the American Psychiatric Association, the American Society of Addiction Medicine, and the World Health Organization. But when does inappropriate use of alcohol in increasing quantities become a disease rather than a social or psychological disorder?

In the strictest sense, excessive alcohol consumption fits the commonly acknowledged definition of "disease": a change of normal body function as demonstrated by specific signs and symptoms whose causes are known or unknown. Excessive alcohol use, of course, is recognized as causing a host of changes in the body. But there's no question that alcoholism also fits the definition of "disorder": a derangement or abnormality of function caused by a specific agent.

Why the disagreement? Is it just over semantics? Opponents of the alcoholism-is-a-disease school say that the term "disease" tells alcoholics they're victims, helpless to control their drinking, and doomed to continuing alcoholism if they should take even one drink. That relieves the alcoholic of personal responsibility to control his or her behavior. Critics of the disease model say that because alcoholics can control their drinking for varying periods, because most people with genetic predisposition to alcoholism don't become alcoholics, and because large numbers of alcoholics may not even have a predisposition, clearly alcoholism is not a disease. These observations, however, are really independent of the disease model.

Proponents of the disease model correctly observe that alcoholism, similar to other forms of drug dependence, is a chronic medical condition that conforms to the characteristics of other chronic diseases even with respect to outcome following appropriate treatment. Recognition by the alcoholic of the medical model should no more relieve him or her of personal responsibility than knowledge of having diabetes relieves the diabetic of the responsibility to control his or her carbohydrate intake.

As for mandatory insurance coverage for treatment, it should hardly matter whether alcoholism is a disease or a disorder because impaired function, whether the result of a character disorder, generalized anxiety, or alcohol, should be covered in the same way as organ system damage because of high cholesterol (coronary artery disease), nicotine consumption (lung cancer), or liver disease (alcohol). Unfortunately this is not the case. Insurance coverage for alcoholism or other drug dependencies is inadequate. Recognition of alcoholism as a disease by the insurance companies would add support to providing appropriate coverage as exists for other diseases.

Recognizing that excessive drinking can cause a definable syndrome, then, neither negates the disease concept nor relieves an individual of responsibility for his or her behavior. Simply acknowledging the existence of the medical model would allow more energies to flow into prevention programs and assessment of treatment alternatives with appropriate coverage by third-party payers for effective treatment.

Prevention

Many prevention efforts can help to diminish excessive drinking behavior. They include general education campaigns for those most likely to identify potential problems, particularly teachers, health care professionals, and employers, and intervention techniques aimed at such high-risk groups as children of alcoholic parents.

Raising the economic and social costs of drinking can also be effective. Such efforts include increasing the cost of alcoholic beverages, raising the legal drinking age, establishing severe penalties for driving while intoxicated, and establishing shared liability between drinker and server when an accident occurs.

Although several studies of advertising alcoholic beverages have documented their positive effect in increasing alcohol consumption, others revealed no consistent relationship. However, advertising, especially on television, may be more pernicious in encouraging children and adolescents to drink. Although alcohol accounts for only 6 percent of total beverage use in the United States, it is the third most common drug used on television and the most frequently depicted beverage. Those portrayed drinking in print and on television are often role models for children as well as adults.

Treatment

Each of the many approaches for treatment of alcoholism has its advocates and detractors. Unfortunately, until recently few have been objectively evaluated. On an anecdotal basis, however, compelling evidence of effectiveness has been offered by advocates of various treatments. The authors of an extensive review of treatment-outcome studies concluded that the approaches that appeared to be most effective had one common characteristic: they were rarely used consistently in all treatment programs!

Competition among treatment facilities for funding and for patients has often prevented rational dialogues among professionals who advocate different approaches and has also stymied attempts at objective studies to document effectiveness. The best solution would be to have a comprehensive array of services from which anyone needing therapy could select the most appropriate. Available therapeutic options used alone or in combination include:

1. Brief intervention
2. Inpatient detoxification and subsequent rehabilitation
3. Outpatient detoxification and rehabilitation
4. Such self-help groups as Alcoholics Anonymous and Al-Anon
5. A variety of drug therapies
6. Short-term and long-term behavioral therapy
7. Controlled drinking

Brief Intervention

The use of brief intervention techniques by physicians and other health providers to identify potential or actual problems with excessive alcohol consumption, is discussed in Chapter 6.

Detoxification and Short-Term Rehabilitation

An inpatient setting for detoxification isn't always necessary, but it becomes so when a person simply cannot stop drinking or has a severe underlying medical problem such as heart disease or uncontrolled high blood pressure that can make ambulatory detoxification risky. In addition, detoxification may be more effective an inpatient setting if the person does not have an adequate support system.

A complete medical assessment and relevant laboratory tests are performed before inpatient detoxification. Diet is adjusted, including vitamin supplements when appropriate, and a suitable therapy to follow withdrawal is chosen. Detoxification by itself rarely eliminates the drinking problem; it must be considered just a first step in the entire rehabilitative process.

Detoxification is usually accomplished with a drug in the benzodiazepine group (Librium, Valium, Serax, or Ativan), Librium being most frequently used due to its better ability to reduce seizure activity. Doses are high enough to keep the person comfortable during the first few days, then decreased about 25 percent a day, subject to considerable variation. When dependency is low and withdrawal symptoms minimal, medication is often not needed. That's preferable because developing dependency on other depressants is always a concern in those who are alcohol dependent.

Drugs called beta-blockers (Inderal, Tenormin) have been assessed for control of withdrawal symptoms, as early withdrawal from alcohol and several other mood-altering drugs is associated with increased activity of the sympathetic (adrenergic) nervous system; and the beta-blockers prevent this activity. In outpatient use, for example, the beta-blocker atenolol (Tenormin) has lowered the intensity and shortened the duration of withdrawal symptoms, and lessened the craving for alcohol. However, the use of beta-blockers has also been associated with a slightly increased incidence of delirium.

Clonidine, which has been used to treat hypertension and also to prevent symptoms of heroin withdrawal, has also been shown to be helpful in alcohol withdrawal when used with a benzodiazepine. Carbamazepine and valproic acid are anticonvulsants commonly used in Europe for withdrawal symptoms. They are effective in mild to moderate withdrawal but no more effective than the benzodiazepines, which have few side effects. Side effects of the anticonvulsants include nausea, gait disturbances, and possible liver damage.

The major tranquilizers, phenothiazines and haloperidol, have also been used to treat withdrawal but are not routinely effective and, in fact, have been shown to be associated with an increased risk of seizure activity. Gamma hydroxybutyric acid (GHB) has been shown to be effective in suppressing the signs of the alcohol withdrawal syndrome as well as reducing alcohol craving and maintaining abstinence, being able to suppress anxiety more rapidly than the benzodiazepines. However, GHB has also been shown to have a high potential for abuse with adverse effects, including seizures. It is frequently used to promote euphoria or build muscle. Its use cannot be recommended until more clinical trials are undertaken, demonstrating its effectiveness and relative safety.

Other agents used during detoxification include magnesium, thiamine, and multivitamin preparations. Although magnesium levels are diminished during withdrawal, studies comparing the use of magnesium and benzodiazepines with the use of only benzodiazepines have not revealed any different outcome between the two groups. Thiamine deficiency is quite common in alcoholism and since thiamine deficiency can contribute to Wernicke's encephalopathy and Wernicke-Korsakoff syndrome, supplementation with thiamine is always indicated.

As noted previously, withdrawal symptoms may persist for a number of weeks after detoxification has been accomplished. This protracted withdrawal most often manifests as anxiety, insomnia, and, at times, a craving for alcohol. During this time support is essential. It should also be noted that subsequent withdrawal episodes may often be associated with more severe symptoms. This is termed the "kindling effect." It therefore becomes quite important to treat withdrawal as early as possible to prevent symptoms from developing and progressing.

Inpatient versus Outpatient Treatment After Detoxification

Whether to treat alcoholics as inpatients or outpatients is a long-standing controversy among health professionals. Sometimes, the patient makes an independent decision. But that decision is usually based on how the options were presented or the presence of adequate medical insurance to cover an inpatient stay

Inpatient treatment, with detoxification plus four to eight weeks on a rehabilitation unit, is the established method of dealing with alcoholics. But as far back as 1965, both the American Psychiatric Association and the National Association of Mental Health recognized the value of outpatient treatment, stating that outpatient clinics should be the backbone of services. By no means does this constitute a call to eliminate all inpatient treatment, which is clearly necessary for some. Rather, it reflects evidence that for the majority of alcoholics, who do not develop severe withdrawal symptoms, well-run outpatient programs have the same success rates at one-eighth to one-tenth the cost of inpatient programs, which nevertheless continue to dominate initial treatment of alcoholics.

Pharmacological Approaches

Disulfiram Therapy. Disulfiram (Antabuse) has been used since the 1940s. Antabuse inhibits the breakdown of alcohol in the body, which results in high levels of acetaldehyde. Elevated blood levels of acetaldehyde cause nausea, vomiting, sweating, restlessness, flushing, chest pain, headaches, increased heart rate, palpitations, generalized weakness, and changes in blood pressure, which if severe can cause loss of consciousness or seizures. However, when used appropriately, the untoward effects produced when alcohol is consumed are of sufficient intensity to deter drinking but not result in serious adverse effects.

Disulfiram becomes partially effective within an hour of administration, and its effect lasts four to seven days. Even small amounts of alcohol will produce a bad reaction in five to fifteen minutes, which can last from thirty minutes to several hours. Just the fear of a disulfiram reaction is enough to motivate most people to refrain from alcohol. The dose used in many disulfiram programs is actually too low to cause a severe reaction. Many people on disulfiram, when told what they can expect if they use alcohol, have never challenged its effect.

Side effects of disulfiram include allergic skin reactions, drowsiness, fatigue, occasional impotence, and a metallic aftertaste. More severe, but unusual, side effects are loss of coordination, behavioral disturbances, seizures, bleeding into the brain, liver dysfunction, and damage to the optic nerve. Disulfiram can also intensify the effects of other medications (Table 7.10). Many of these drugs are widely prescribed, so a careful medical history should be taken before starting disulfiram therapy. Some drugs act similarly to disulfiram and produce a mild disulfiram-alcohol type reac-

TABLE 7.10. Drugs That Interact with Disulfiram

Generic Name	Brand Name
Barbiturates	Amobarbital, phenobarbital, Seconal
Benzodiazepines	Ativan, Librium, Serax, Xanax
Caffeine	Coffee, tea
Metronidazole	Flagyl
Phenytoin	Dilantin
Rifampin	Rifadin, Rimactane
Theophylline	Bronkosol, Elixophyllin
Tricyclic antidepressants	Elavil, Tofranil
Warfarin	Coumadin

tion when alcohol is consumed (Table 7.11). A disulfiram reaction can occur when any beverage containing alcohol is consumed, including those not usually thought of as containing alcohol, such as cough medications.

Disulfiram must not be given in the presence of an acute infectious disease, asthma, respiratory insufficiency, cardiac disease, epilepsy, psychosis, liver or renal disease, or pregnancy. A history of prior adverse reactions to disulfiram itself, or an allergy to rubber, are also absolute contraindications.

To be most effective, disulfiram must be taken daily (usually a 250 to 500 milligram dose), thus requiring motivation for continued use. Disulfiram capsules have been developed to be implanted in the body, but this form of treatment is still not widely used. At times, the drive to drink can be so great that some may continue to drink even while on the drug.

New studies have generated less enthusiasm for disulfiram as the sole, long-term therapy for alcoholism. Little or no evidence exists to indicate that disulfiram—unaccompanied by another therapy—has any marked beneficial effect in helping to sustain abstinence. It's now considered most effective for short-term use to prevent drinking while the individual starts outpatient therapy.

TABLE 7.11. Drugs That Cause Antabuse-Alcohol Reactions

Generic or Group Names	Brand Names
Amitriptyline	Elavil and others
Calcium carbimide	Temposil
Cephalosporins	Cefaclor, Keflex, Duricef
Chloramphenicol	Diabinese
Griseofulvin	Grisactin, Grifulvin, Gris-PEG, Fulvicin
Metronidazole	Flagyl, Protostat
MAO inhibitors	Pargyline, Nardil, Parnate
Nitrofurantoin	Furadantin, Nitrofan, Macrodantin
Phenylbutazone	Azolid, Butazolidin
Procarbazine	Matulane
Quinacrine	Atabrine
Sulfonylureas	Orinase, Dymelor, Apo-Tolbutamide, tolazamide, Ronase, Tolinase, Apo-Chlorpropamide, Diabinese, Glucotrol, DiaBeta, Micronase

Note: Reaction varies depending on dose, individual sensitivity, and quantity of alcohol consumed.

Lithium Carbonate. Lithium, a drug used for manic depression, has been under evaluation as a treatment for alcoholism, typically in conjunction with other therapies. But its effectiveness still remains to be proven. Those studies that were well controlled were unable to demonstrate effectiveness in either depressed or nondepressed alcoholics.

Naltrexone (Revia)/Nalmefene. Naltrexone is a pure opioid antagonist that has been shown to reduce alcohol craving as well as decrease the alcohol high. Several studies have demonstrated the effectiveness of naltrexone and, when combined with counseling, naltrexone is associated with a higher rate of abstinence. Naltrexone, however, may be associated with a variety of side effects including nausea, headache, dizziness and, when given to an individual who has an unknown dependence on opioids, may precipitate opiate withdrawal. It also has the capacity to cause liver damage when given in excessive doses, and its use is therefore contraindicated in persons with active liver disease. Despite the potential side effects of naltrexone, its use has been found to be quite helpful. Even in a primary care setting, as compared to a specialist alcohol treatment center, it has been found to be effective in maintaining abstinence and helping clients complete a treatment program.

Nalmefene is also a pure opioid antagonist that, in a single study, has been found to be effective in diminishing relapse to alcohol.

Acamprosate. Acamprosate has been used in the treatment of alcohol dependence in Europe and is felt to enhance one's ability to remain abstinent. Studies have consistently demonstrated its ability to reduce frequency of drinking as well as to enhance abstinence. To date, there has been little experience with it in the United States.

Drugs That Affect Neurotransmitter Activity. The discovery of the role that neurotransmitters and receptors may have in promoting drug use, including alcohol (Chapter 4), has led to the development of drugs that may affect those receptors and neurotransmitters particularly sensitive to alcohol. Much of this work still remains experimental; however, some of the findings may well prove to have future application. Bromocriptine, a dopamine agonist, has been suggested to reduce both alcohol craving and consumption. Drugs reducing uptake of serotonin by nerve cells also diminish alcohol consumption. These drugs include fluvoxamine, fluoxetine, citalopram, and the nonbenzodiazepine antianxiety drug buspirone. As discussed previously, GHB has also been suggested as an aid in maintaining abstinence. Odansetron (Zolfran), when combined with psychotherapy, has been found effective in decreasing alcohol consumption and increasing days of abstinence in alcoholics who began drinking excessively before the age of twenty-five. Studies utilizing these agents, however, have yielded mixed results as to their effectiveness.

SUMMARY

Although a number of pharmacological agents are currently being promoted to assist in both achieving and maintaining abstinence, randomized, controlled studies demonstrating their effectiveness are few (Table 7.12). In general, disulfiram appears to be helpful but less effective than previously thought. Naltrexone and acamprosate have increasingly shown to be helpful. With respect to the other agents, much more evidence is needed.

TABLE 7.12. Evaluation of Controlled Studies of Efficacy of Pharmacological Agents Used in Treatment of Alcoholism

Agent	Mechanism of Action	Evaluation*
Acamprosate§	Interacts with glutamate receptors and calcium channels	A
Calcium carbimide§	Aversive agent	C
Disulfiram	Inhibits alcohol dehydrogenase	B
delta-hydroxybutyric acid§	Sedative	I
Lithium	Affects phosphoinositide signaling Enhances serotonin activity in the brain	C
Naltrexone	Opioid antagonist	A
Nalmefene	Opioid antagonist	I
Tiapride§	Dopamine D_2 antagonist	I
Serotonergic Agents Citalopram, fluoxetine, fluvoxamine	Selective serotonin uptake inhibitor	I
Buspirone	Serotonin agonist	I
Ondansetron, ritanserin	Serotonin antagonist	I

Source: Adapted from Garbutt, J.C., West, S.L., Carey, T.S., Lohr, K.N., and Crews, F.T. Pharmacologic treatment of alcohol dependence. A review of the literature. Journal of the American Medical Association 281(1999): 1318-1325; Swift, R.M. Drug therapy for alcohol dependence. New England Journal of Medicine 340(1999): 1482-1490.
*A = Good evidence of effectiveness; B = Fair evidence—data sufficient but insufficiencies between drug and placebo, making evaluation difficult; C = Poor evidence that drug no more effective than placebo; I = insufficient or inadequate data.
§Not available at present in United States.

Nonpharmacological Therapies

Alcoholics Anonymous and Al-Anon

Alcoholics Anonymous (AA), founded in 1935 by two former alcoholics, remains a self-supporting, nonprofessional, nondenominational, multiracial self-help organization with over 73,000 groups worldwide. Its only requirement is for a participant to want to stop drinking. AA's Al-Anon, a separate but parallel program, is for family or friends whose primary concerns are to keep AA members sober and help others achieve sobriety.

AA has no affiliation with any organization or institution, takes no political stand on any issue, and does not allow members to identify themselves for any political purpose. The basic premise of participation is acceptance of an alternate way of life without drinking and acknowledgment that alcoholism is an incurable, progressive disease that can be managed only through abstinence. The nondenominational, yet religious, nature of this group is apparent in its twelve-step program. The first step is an admission of being powerless over alcohol. Full participation requires considerable soul-searching and total commitment—not easy tasks.

AA was initially thought best able to help healthy, stable, middle-class, severe alcoholics. But its current membership probably mirrors the general population of drinkers, and its presence is ubiquitous, sponsoring over 36,000 groups in the United States. Directories are available from any local AA chapter. Anonymity is the basic requirement for participation. AA structure contains three major components: (a) *meetings* that occur several times a week, which participants are expected, but not required to attend; (b) *sponsorship* by a member who has maintained sobriety to assist new members in refraining from drinking; and (c) *fellowship,* which provides the environment for participants to share their experiences and expectation. Some people can be helped through periods of acute stress by attending only a few meetings; others can't adjust to the process and find it of little value. But the many who continue to participate are intensely committed to the program and profoundly believe in its effectiveness.

AA's abstinence approach leaves many chapters with an unkindly view of dependency on other mood-altering drugs, even when prescribed by a physician. Thus, former heroin users with alcohol problems who are on methadone maintenance may have trouble joining AA or may be pressured to detoxify from methadone. Also, since many alcoholics may have underlying psychological disorders that require psychotropic medication, discouraging the use of such drugs can prevent an individual from staying abstinent.

Evaluations of AA's effectiveness have produced varying results. Among the reasons for this is the voluntary, informal nature of the organization and the difficulties in obtaining membership lists due to its commitment to anonymity. Its success is connected to the long-standing commitment of members, who serve as sponsors of new members. The cost of treatment compares quite favorably with other forms of therapy. Yet the dropout rate can be high. In one study of people who attended an AA meeting one month after being discharged from a detoxification unit, only 11 percent were still participating a year later. In other studies, 68 percent dropped out before the tenth meeting. But of those who attended regularly, an estimated 26 to 50 percent remain abstinent after one year.

This success rate matches those of other treatments. AA is most effective in conjunction with other therapies, such as individual or group therapy, or Antabuse. Such a combination may well increase the possibility of success.

Counseling and Psychotherapy

Counseling, family therapy, marital or couples therapy, and forms of recognized individual psychotherapy have been used for a long time, alone or in combination with other therapies. Psychotherapy may be exceptionally helpful for those drinkers with underlying psychological disturbances. Family therapy, to identify the settings that promote drinking and help family members relate appropriately to the problem, is also valuable.

Motivational Enhancement Therapy (MET)

This therapy is based on the belief that the capacity for change lies within the client and can be expressed through individualized feedback provided by the therapist. It is felt by some to be among the most cost-effective treatment modalities.

Employee Assistance Programs

Recognition of the effects of excessive drinking in terms of days lost, inadequate job performance, and high health care costs has led to development of programs in the workplace that help identify and refer employees with drinking problems. Most large companies have such programs, staffed by trained personnel. When an employee voluntarily seeks help from an EAP and follows EAP staff recommendations, the situation is kept confidential from the employer. But if the employee is referred by a supervisor and doesn't follow the recommendations, a "pink slip" may result. Evidence to date suggests that EAPs provide valuable resources for early identification of problem drinkers and subsequent referral to long-term therapy.

Behavioral Therapy

Studies of short-term therapy based on negative conditioning (aversive therapy) designed to control drinking behaviors have produced mixed results. Aversion therapy, based on producing physical or emotional discomfort when in a setting that promotes drinking, remains controversial. But several studies have supported the effectiveness of some of these approaches.

Controlled Drinking

Probably no treatment has aroused more controversy than training the alcoholic to control his or her drinking. Proponents of the abstinence approach believe that the term "controlled drinking" is itself a fallacy because it's impossible to moderate an alcoholic's drinking patterns. "One drink, one drunk" and "One drink is too much, and two are not enough" embody the prevailing philosophy of the alcohol-treatment community in the United States.

The fear that de-emphasizing recovering alcoholics' ability to abstain might cause them to revert to alcoholism may be warranted. But several studies suggest that some alcoholics can moderate their drinking behaviors, either as part of a controlled-drinking program or by returning to drink at greatly reduced levels. Formal programs of controlled drinking exist in other countries but not in the United States, where approaches other than abstinence have not met with either public or professional acceptance.

In many instances, chronic drinkers have been able, over time, to moderate their drinking. But in equal—if not greater—numbers of instances, drinkers have lapsed into excessive alcohol consumption, believing they have failed. As treatment methods and evaluation techniques become more refined, well-designed, objective studies of controlled drinking may be undertaken.

Chapter 8

Central Nervous System Depressants and Antianxiety Agents

The central nervous system depressants comprise a variety of chemically unrelated compounds, all capable of altering mood. Their effects are generally similar to those of alcohol, and withdrawal symptoms are often indistinguishable from those of chronic alcoholism.

The first drug in this group to be synthesized was chloral hydrate, in 1832. Several years later, barbituric acid, parent drug of the barbiturates, was developed. The first drug, barbital (Veronal), was introduced into clinical practice in 1903, with phenobarbital following close behind. The ability of these drugs to produce sedation, relieve insomnia, and decrease seizure activity resulted in their ready acceptance by the medical profession.

Their adverse effects weren't widely recognized until the late 1940s, when health professionals realized that such drugs could cause highs and dependency. Yet their popularity continued. More than 2,500 barbiturates were synthesized; fifty were available for medical use. In 1976 an estimated 18 million prescriptions were written for barbiturates, enough to allow each adult in the United States twenty-four doses of 100 milligram pills. Barbiturate usage has since declined considerably with development of newer agents. In 1950, meprobamate (Equanil, Miltown) came on the market as an effective tranquilizer. It was promoted as having lower potential for dependency and fewer prominent side effects than the barbiturates. But it quickly became apparent that chronic use could induce meprobamate dependency.

Chlordiazepoxide (Librium), first of the benzodiazepines, appeared in 1961. Since then, more than 3,000 benzodiazepines have been synthesized, with more than twenty-five in clinical use. The ability of benzodiazepines to relieve anxiety, relax muscles, prevent seizure activity, and treat sleep disturbances resulted in remarkable acceptance by both the medical profession and the public.

In 1967, prescriptions for psychotropic drugs added up to 17 percent (170 million) of the 1 billion written, with Librium and Valium accounting for one-third (or 56 million) of that number. More than 70 million prescriptions were written in 1972 for those two drugs combined, and an estimated 7 percent of all adults between the ages of eighteen and twenty-five were taking some kind of tranquilizing drugs.

Concern over inappropriate prescriptions for these drugs led the FDA in 1975 to classify diazepam as a Schedule IV drug, permitting no more than five refills within a six-month period, and recommending reevaluation of need after four months of continuous use. But that measure did little to stop use. Four years later, the percentage of eighteen- to twenty-five-year-olds who had ever used tranquilizers had risen to 15 percent.

Flurazepam (Dalmane), introduced in 1970 for treatment of sleep disorders, was responsible for 7 million prescriptions by 1976. In 1978, more than 68 million prescriptions were written for the benzodiazepines (half for Valium) despite increasing concern over adverse effects reported even with "appropriate" use. That statistic was accompanied by another: diazepam ranked second only to alcohol in combination with other drugs in drug dependency-related episodes treated in emergency rooms nationwide. In 1985, prescriptions for benzodiazepines reached 61 million, with more than 8 million written in New York State alone. Over the years, these drugs have remained an important part of the physician's pharmacological armamentarium.

Nonmedical use of these drugs appears to be on the decline. However, the 2000 Monitoring the Future Survey reported that barbiturates had been used by 6 percent of twelfth graders within the past year with a similar percentage reporting non-medically prescribed tranquilizer use. The 1999 National Household Survey on Drug Abuse found over 4 million persons aged 12 and older (1.8 percent of the population) to be current nonmedical users of psychotherapeutics. These drugs included tranquilizers and sedatives (1.3 million users), pain relievers (2.6 million users), and stimulants (0.9 million users). All CNS depressants have similar side effects, but they vary considerably in potential for overdose and intensity of the withdrawal syndrome.

PATTERNS OF USE

Depressant drugs are prescribed for a number of reasons. Perhaps the most common reason for appropriate use is their ability to relieve stress and facilitate sleep. Until recently, the ease of getting a prescription introduced many people to their beneficial effects. The positive mood-altering effects of the depressants often led to continued use, first for anxiety, then to feel comfortable, and ultimately in a few individuals to get high.

A paradoxical stimulant effect is seen as tolerance develops in people taking depressants on a regular basis. A heightened high can be reached when additional doses are taken irregularly, thereby reinforcing continued use. At times a depressant is taken to counteract the actions of other drugs that are being simultaneously used, such as cocaine or amphetamines.

Use of one CNS depressant to intensify a high from another can also occur. Excessive drinkers, fearful of having alcohol on their breath during working hours, may switch to a depressant drug to avoid detection. It offers a high and affects behavior in almost the same way as alcohol. Drinking a great deal of alcohol sometimes results in increased awareness several hours later, along with difficulty sleeping. This often leads to taking a depressant to facilitate sleep. When alcohol is unavailable, those who use illicit narcotics and those on methadone maintenance programs may also take depressants to enhance or produce a mood-altering effect.

Combining CNS depressants and alcohol or narcotics accentuates the respiratory depressant effects of these drugs. That's why depressants are frequently identified in overdose cases. Diazepam (Valium) is perhaps the most commonly improperly used prescription drug seen in emergency room admissions and is the legal drug most commonly found in deaths resulting from unnatural causes, such as multiple drug overdose and accidents. Although the benzodiazepines have a relatively low overdose potential when taken alone, the consequences can be deadly when they're taken in combination with alcohol or other CNS depressants.

These drugs can best be described by dividing them into four groups: barbiturates; nonbarbiturate hypnotics and sedatives; miscellaneous central nervous system depressants; and benzodiazepines, the group most often prescribed and most frequently used inappropriately.

BARBITURATES

The barbiturates can be classified by duration of their action: ultrashort, short, intermediate, and long acting (Table 8.1). Those with an ultrashort duration of action include hexobarbital (Evipal), methohexital (Brevital), thiamylal (Surital), and thiopental (Pentothal), and are administered by injection to produce rapid anesthesia. They are rarely used inappropriately. But short- and intermediate-acting barbiturates are frequently used to get high.

Absorption from the gastrointestinal tract varies when barbiturates are taken orally. Ultimately, they're widely distributed in the body and metabolized in the liver. They produce a generalized depression, with mood-altering effects ranging from mild sedation and euphoria to coma. The latter is caused by marked depression of the brain's respiratory center as a result of overdose.

The effects of barbiturates and related hypnotics and sedatives on the heart and blood vessels are relatively minor. So are their actions on other organ systems, except for the liver. As is the case with alcohol, they can interfere with other drugs metabolized in the liver and increase or decrease the effects of the other drugs.

TABLE 8.1. Common Nonmedically Used Barbiturates

Brand Name	Generic Name	Street Name
Long Acting		
Luminal, Phenobarbital, Barbita, Solfoton	Phenobarbital	Barbs, Beans, Biscuits, Blockbusters, Bullets, Downers, Downs, Dolls, Fool Pills, Goofballs, Green Dragons, Greenies, Mexican Reds, Pajao, Pink Ladies, Purple Hearts, Rojo, Sleeping Pills, Stumblers
Gemonil	Metharbital	
Mebaral	Mephobarbital	
Intermediate Acting		
Amytal	Amobarbital	Bluebirds, Blue Devils, Blue Heaven, Blues
Alurate	Aprobarbital	
Butisol	Butabarbital	
Lotusate	Talbutal	
Short Acting		
Nembutal	Pentobarbital	Nebbies, Minbies, Yellow Jackets, Yellows
Seconal	Secobarbital	Red Birds, Red Devils, Reds, Seccies
Ultra Short Acting		
Brevitol	Methohexital	
Evipal	Hexobarbital	
Surital	Thiamylal	
Combinations		
Tuinal	Amobarbital, Secobarbital	Christmas Trees, Rainbows, Tooies, Tuiys
Tri-barbs, SBP	Phenobarbital, Butabarbital, Secobarbital	

Tolerance, Dependency, and Withdrawal

Tolerance for barbiturates develops easily, as they have a relatively narrow tolerance-toxicity ratio. That is, someone tolerant to a given dose of barbiturates may show little mood-altering effect, but even a slight increase above the tolerance threshold can result in intoxication and overdose. Considerable cross-tolerance exists among all hypnotic and nonbarbiturate sedatives and alcohol. Withdrawal from any of these drugs can be relieved immediately by administering any other drug in the group.

Abruptly stopping high doses of barbiturates and related drugs leads to the characteristic severe withdrawal syndrome indistinguishable from that seen with alcohol. Depending on the barbiturate or hypnotic, symptoms appear within ten to twenty-four hours with the short-acting drugs, or within two to three days with longer-acting drugs. Restlessness and anxiety appear first, accompanied by cramps, nausea, and vomiting. Next come tremors of the hands and feet, followed by seizures and ultimately hallucinations, delirium, disorientation, increases in blood pressure, and—if untreated—collapse of the respiratory and cardiovascular systems. Hallucinations can reappear for several months after withdrawal has been completed.

NONBARBITURATE HYPNOTICS AND SEDATIVES

A number of nonbarbiturate hypnotic and sedative drugs with potential for excessive use are listed in Table 8.2. Several of the more common ones are discussed below.

Glutethimide (Doriden)

Doriden was promoted as a nonaddictive alternative to barbiturates when it was introduced in 1954. But its potential for inappropriate use was quickly recognized. Although its CNS depressant effect is similar to that of the barbiturates, it is particularly long-lasting, with a half-life (the time it takes to eliminate half of a substance in the blood) of up to 100 hours. Severe withdrawal symptoms and prolonged aftereffects can show up in people who are dependent on even moderate doses. One of the combination of drugs appearing on the street, "hits" (500 milligrams of glutethimide and 60 milligrams of codeine), is particularly dangerous as both drugs can depress the central nervous system's respiratory center.

Chloral Hydrate

This medication was one of the earliest hypnotic-sedative drugs used to treat alcohol withdrawal, anxiety, and insomnia. With the alternative of available benzodiazepines today, chloral hydrate is rarely prescribed. Historically, it was used as a knockout potion (a Mickey Finn). Taking alcohol and chloral hydrate results in decreased breakdown of the alcohol (by the chloral hydrate) and enhancement of chloral hydrate activity (by the alcohol).

TABLE 8.2. Nonbarbiturate Hypnotics and Sedative Drugs

Brand Name	Group*	Generic Name	Street Name
Ambien	NBH	Zolpidem	
Doriden	NBH	Glutethimide	Hits†
Equanil, Meprospan, Miltown, Neuramate	C	Meprobamate	
Noctec§ Aquachloral	CH	Chloral Hydrate	Green Frogs, Knockout Drops, Peter
Noludar§	NBH	Methyprylon	
Optimil§	NBH	Methaqualone	
Paxarel	NBH	Acetylcarbromal	
Parest§	NBH	Methaqualone	
Paraldehyde, Paral	O	Paraldehyde	
Placidyl	NBH	Ethchlorvynol	Plastivil
Quaalude§	NBH	Methaqualone	Ludes, Mean Greens, Quads, Quas
Sopor§, Somnafac§	NBH	Methaqualone	Soapers, Soaps
Valmid	C	Ethinamate	

*C = Carbamate; CH = Chloral hydrate; NBH = Nonbarbiturate hypnotic; O = Other
§No longer legally manufactured
†Combined with codeine

Methaqualone

Formerly manufactured under the brand names Quaalude, Sopor, Parest, Optimil, and Somnafac, this drug was withdrawn from legal use in the United States and classified as a Schedule I drug in 1973. Nevertheless, methaqualone continued to be sold illegally. Its use continued to grow, and not even the diversion of some legal supplies to the street was enough to meet the demand. In 1979 approximately 100 tons of methaqualone were smuggled into the United States from Colombia. By 1981, methaqualone was considered the most common street drug after marijuana. Use was often associated with automobile accidents because it causes drowsiness and lack of judgment. Like other nonbarbiturate hypnotic and sedative drugs, methaqualone was at first considered nonaddictive. But it was quickly discovered to produce heightened feelings of pleasure and became known as the "love drug"—a term now reserved for Ecstasy (Chapter 9).

Meprobamate

Meprobamate is a carbamate derivative that acts selectively at multiple sites in the central nervous system. It is commonly used as a tranquilizer, an anticonvulsant or a muscle relaxant. Its effectiveness and long-term use is similar to other antianxiety agents. Its potential for both physical and psychological dependence is known. Withdrawal symptoms occur within twelve to forty-eight hours after discontinuing the drug, and last for another two days, with seizures occurring in cases of severe dependency. Similar to other antianxiety agents, the mood-altering effects of the drug can be potentiated by alcohol and by concurrent use of other central nervous system depressing agents.

Carisoprodol

Recently, a muscle relaxant, carisoprodol (Soma), has been brought to the attention of the Drug Abuse Advisory Committee because one of its metabolites is meprobamate. Whether the amount of meprobamate produced is sufficient to cause Soma to be placed in a controlled drug schedule is as of yet unclear. However, the Drug Enforcement Administration reported over 200 instances of seizure or illegal purchase of Soma over the last several years in twenty-seven states. As of this writing, the potential for abuse of Soma is being evaluated.

OTHER CENTRAL NERVOUS SYSTEM DEPRESSANTS

Gamma Hydroxybutyrate

Gamma hydroxybutyrate (GHB) is a central nervous system depressant used as an anesthetic in several countries. In the United States, it is considered to be an "orphan" drug without any proved indication for its use. Proposed uses include treatment for narcolepsy and cataplexy as well as treatment of hallucinations. On the street, it has been used by bodybuilders and as a psychoactive agents in night clubs and rave parties.

Initially GHB was believed to have steroid-enhancing effects through its stimulation of growth hormone. However, although this action has never been confirmed, it is still used by some weight lifters. It is also used by alcoholics to decrease craving for alcohol. When L-tryptophan was taken off the market in 1990 due to its adverse effects, its replacement was GHB, which was marketed as a sedative due to its anesthetic qualities. At that time, sales were accompanied by a warning that combining its use with alcohol as well as taking more than the recommended dose was quite dangerous.

GHB acts by increasing the levels of dopamine at nerve terminals in the brain as well as by affecting the opioid receptor system. It is a relatively short-acting drug, with excretion being almost complete within the first hour of ingestion. Toxic effects may be severe and range from vomiting to respiratory depression, seizures, and coma. All of these effects can be enhanced by use of alcohol which, unfortunately, is frequently present in places where GHB is taken. It has been estimated that only one to six teaspoons of GHB, when taken with alcohol, can produce pronounced coma and respiratory depression within fifteen to thirty minutes in susceptible individuals. The respiratory depression may be short lived, lasting no longer than one to two hours. Recovery, if artificial respiration is quickly applied, is usually spontaneous, with amnesia of the entire event. Treatment of GHB overdose, therefore, is mainly supportive with ventilatory assistance essential for survival in severe cases. Withdrawal symptoms consisting of tremors, insomnia, and anxiety in persons using large amounts of GHB for prolonged periods have also been reported.

In the United States, GHB is produced in clandestine laboratories and sold on the street in liquid or powder form under a variety of names, including grievous bodily harm, Georgia home boy, GIB, liquid Ecstasy, liquid X, easy lay, salty water, cherry menth, organic Quaalude, Somatomax, GHB, and GBH. Its anesthetic properties resulting in amnesia have allowed it to be slipped into drinks and consumed unknowingly, thereby giving it an additional name of "date rape." By 1997, reports of GHB use had appeared in twenty-seven states, with California, Florida, Georgia, and Texas being most prominent.

Although the use of GHB has been prohibited, related drugs, gamma butyrolactone (GBL) and 1,4 butanediol, which are industrial and household solvents, have been marketed in health food stores as effective in inducing sleep, relieving depression, increasing athletic and sexual performance, and releasing growth hormones. Once ingested, both solvents are converted into GHB and may even be more toxic than GHB due to a better bioavailability, resulting in better absorption from the gastrointestinal tract. Cases of GBL toxicity and 1,4 butanediol have been reported, resulting in the Food and Drug Administration asking all manufacturers to withdraw products containing GBL in 1999.

BENZODIAZEPINES

For the most part, benzodiazepines have replaced barbiturates and other nonbarbiturate hypnotics and sedatives in medical practice. A variety of benzodiazepines are available (Table 8.3). It's hard to consistently find differences among them, except with those used for sleep disturbances, which

TABLE 8.3. Benzodiazepines

Brand Name	Onset Time*	Duration§	Generic Name
Ativan	I	IA	Lorazepam
Centrax	S	LA	Prazepam
Clonopin	I	LA	Clonazepam
Dalmane†	I-R	LA	Flurazepam
Doral†	I	LA	Quazepam
Halcion†	I-R	SA	Triazolam
Librium, Mitran, Reposans 10, Libritabs	I	IA	Chlordiazepoxide
Paxipam	S	IA	Halazepam
ProSom	I	I	Estazolam
Restoril†	I	IA	Temazepam
Rohypnol			Flunitrazepam
Serax	S	IA	Oxazepam
Tranxene, Gen-Xene	R	LA	Clorazepate
Valium, Dizac, Zetran	R	LA	Diazepam
Valrelease	S	LA	Diazepam
Versed	I	SA	Midazolam
Verstran	S	LA	Prazepam
Xanax	I-R	IA	Alprazolam

*R = Rapid; I = Intermediate; S = Slow
§LA = Long acting; IA = Intermediate acting; SA = Short acting
†Sleep medications

are relatively short acting. This causes considerable confusion for both physicians and patients in choosing the best drug with the least potential for dependency.

The benzodiazepines are thought to affect a particular neurotransmitter, gamma aminobutyrate (GABA), in the limbic, mesencephalic, and neocortical reticular systems. Benzodiazepine receptors have also been identified in the brain. Benzodiazepines are absorbed at varying rates, with onset of action ranging from fifteen to thirty minutes, depending on the drug. Levels of benzodiazepines accumulate quickly in the brain and blood, then decrease as the drug is distributed to other organs and metabolized until a steady state is reached. That's the point at which the amount taken is equal to the amount that's been broken down and eliminated.

Considerable mood-altering effects can be experienced during the initial period of changing brain levels. Early side effects include drowsiness, impaired thinking, diminished memory, reduced motor coordination, and slurred speech (Table 8.4). The effects differ depending on individual susceptibility, but they tend to subside after several days of consistent use. Unlike the barbiturates and other nonbarbiturate hypnotics and sedatives (such as Doriden), benzodiazepines alone rarely produce fatal overdose. But when benzodiazepines are taken with other CNS depressants, including alcohol, fatal overdose is a real possibility.

Tolerance, Dependency, and Withdrawal

Even under medical supervision, persistent use of benzodiazepines can result in dependency and withdrawal. The incidence of withdrawal has been difficult to document because the withdrawal symptoms are similar to the indications for which these drugs are prescribed (Table 8.5). They include nausea, loss of appetite, anxiety with associated depression, depersonalization, and abnormal perception or sensation. Seizures or psychotic behavior rarely may occur with barbiturate withdrawal.

The severity of withdrawal can be linked to dosage, duration of treatment, and to the particular benzodiazepine. Ativan and Halcion have shorter half-lives and their metabolites have no activity, so they produce earlier

TABLE 8.4. Side Effects of Benzodiazepines

Drowsiness
Reduced level of consciousness
Impaired intellectual function
Impaired memory
Reduced motor coordination
Slurred speech

TABLE 8.5. Benzodiazepine Withdrawal Symptoms

Anxiety*	Muscle aches*	Nausea
Dizziness*	Tremor*	Loss of appetite
Irritability	Sweating*	Depression
Insomnia*	Difficulty in concentration*	Depersonalization
Fatigue*	Increased sensory perception	Abnormal perception or sensation of movement
Headache*	Seizures§	Psychotic behavior§

*Common in anxiety states for which benzodiazepines are prescribed
§Rare

withdrawal symptoms that can be harder to treat. Taking short-acting benzodiazepines regularly to get to sleep may, paradoxically, result in early-morning awakening. Those symptoms may be mild signs of withdrawal.

One extensive review of benzodiazepine withdrawal cases reported that withdrawal occurred 40 to 50 percent of the time with short-term use and 40 to 100 percent of the time with use longer than one year. But when the symptoms for which these drugs were prescribed were considered, withdrawal after short-term use occurred no more than 5 percent of the time, and after long-term use no more than 50 percent of the time. Eliminating such symptoms as anxiety, irritability, insomnia, muscle aches, and tremors can be misleading because they're typically seen in withdrawal from most CNS depressant drugs, including alcohol. In fact, these withdrawal symptoms have been reported to appear in patients who used medically indicated daily doses of benzodiazepines for as few as six weeks. The Food and Drug Administration has emphasized that studies of the effectiveness of benzodiazepines in treating anxiety for more than four months have not been performed.

Potential for Inappropriate Use

Without question, benzodiazepines are extremely valuable psychotherapeutic agents. They've been used successfully to treat a variety of disorders, including generalized and specific anxiety, panic attacks, sleep disorders, muscular and seizure disorders, and withdrawal symptoms from alcohol and other CNS depressants. They're also used to relax patients before they receive general anesthesia. However, these drugs may not always be the best course of action, even when legally prescribed. A study of 119 patients on prescribed benzodiazepines found that one-third suffered from major depression and should have been taking antidepressants instead. Another 25 percent had panic disorders that were not relieved by the drug. A subsequent study by the Food and Drug Administration revealed that some patients had been taking the drugs for years without medical supervision, despite their increased vulnerability to severe dependency and withdrawal after the first six months of use.

It is important to emphasize that the elderly may be at particular risk for reaction to benzodiazepines even when legally prescribed. The elderly, in fact, are major users of these drugs, with 35 percent of all prescriptions for benzodiazepines being written for persons over sixty years of age. Hemmelgarn and colleagues, in a study of motor vehicle crashes associated with benzodiazepine risk, found that one out of every five older drivers was taking benzodiazepine, with the risk of a crash increasing by 28 percent with long-term use and by 50 percent within the first seven days of therapy. This increased risk at the beginning of treatment was present only in users of long-acting benzodiazepines and was not associated with the use of short-acting drugs.

Some benzodiazepines—diazepam, for example—are believed effective in treating certain muscular disorders, but their frequent use for lower back pain syndrome is controversial: the benefits may be attributable to decreased anxiety over the pain, rather than to actual relief of the muscle spasm. Their use in panic attacks, while effective for associated anxiety, does nothing for the underlying condition; antidepressants and other psychotropic drugs are probably a better choice as they are associated with a much better outcome in treating mixed anxiety-depressive syndromes. As awareness of their potential for inappropriate use expands (Table 8.6), prescriptions for benzodiazepines continue to decrease.

TABLE 8.6. Concerns Over Regular Use of Benzodiazepines

Produces dependency and withdrawal
Easily used inappropriately
- Among most common drugs identified in emergency room admissions
- Commonly used in suicide attempts
- Most commonly found legal drug in deaths due to unnatural causes
- At least 25 percent of patients exceed prescribed dose, use it for other than prescribed reasons, or get it from nonmedical sources
- Impairs motor skills, especially when driving
Exposes certain populations to increased risk
- Withdrawal in newborns whose mothers had therapeutic levels in third trimester
- Greater susceptibility to adverse reactions in the elderly, including hip fractures due to falls
- Use with other CNS depressants increases depressant effects

---

MISCELLANEOUS ANTIANXIETY AGENTS

Buspirone (BuSpar)

Buspirone is an antianxiety agent unrelated pharmacologically to the barbiturates, benzodiazepines, or other central nervous system sedatives. Used for the short-term treatment of anxiety, to date it has shown no potential for abuse or diversion. It appears not to increase alcohol-related impairment of motor or mental functions. However, its relatively recent appearance on the market suggests caution in its prescription for individuals with known drug dependency problems.

Rohypnol

Rohypnol (flunitrazepam) is a potent benzodiazepine used for treating severe sleep disorders and extreme agitation. Although rarely prescribed in this country, street use of the drug, under the name of rophies, R2s, Mexican Valium, rib, roach or rope, or the fort me pill, first appeared in 1993 in South Florida, with reports of persistent use now appearing in other states as well. Associated with amnesia, the original drug product, similar to GHB, when diluted was colorless and odorless and therefore able to be easily slipped into an unsuspecting person's drink. As a result, initial reports of complications associated with its use were also frequently accompanied by charges of date rape.

In an attempt to prevent its unknowing consumption, the manufacturer of Rohypnol has agreed to a reformulation that will make it more difficult to dissolve and when dissolved, to release a blue color, allowing it to be recognized. However, if the drug is added to a dark mixed drink or a dark beer, this probably would be less than helpful. Knowing ingestion of Rohypnol occurs quite frequently, as it can potentiate the effects of alcohol as well as diminish inhibitions. It can also be used on the street to diminish withdrawal symptoms from alcohol or other benzodiazepines.

After ingesting Rohypnol, sedation can occur within twenty to thirty minutes, with a peak effect in one to two hours. Although the sedative effect lasts up to eight hours, psychomotor disturbances can exist for up to twelve hours after ingestion. Side effects are similar to those seen with consumption of other benzodiazepines, including psychological and physical dependence.

Chapter 9

Powerful Hallucinogens, Phencyclidine, and Ecstasy

Because plants containing hallucinogenic substances can be grown in almost any climate, hallucinogens have been used throughout the world from the earliest of times. In North and South America, they have been used predominantly by Native Americans as part of religious observances. Peyote (mescaline), for example, continues to be used in that role today, and until recently its legal status has been upheld. The Native American Church of North America has been instrumental in repealing individual state laws prohibiting its use in peyote ceremonies. One researcher extensively reviewed peyote use by the Navajo as part of their religious practice and found no adverse reactions associated with it.

Development of lysergic acid diethylamide (LSD) by Albert Hoffman at Sandoz Laboratories in Switzerland in 1943 marked the beginning of serious interest in synthetic hallucinogenic drugs. Dr. Hoffman accidentally ingested LSD twice during its production. He found those first two experiences distinctly unpleasant, but they clearly demonstrated LSD's potent psychedelic properties. Since then, LSD and its related compounds have been widely studied by basic researchers and psychiatrists. Enthusiasm for the beneficial effects of LSD was so great at first that some researchers encouraged friends and associates to take it for recreational purposes. Suggestions for its approved use began to flourish. They ranged from military applications (to incapacitate an enemy) to use as a palliative in cases of terminal cancer (Table 9.1). Some faculty members at many universities promoted LSD, leading to widespread use on college campuses during the 1960s. By the 1970s, an estimated 1 to 2 million Americans had taken LSD, and it ranked sixth in substance-involved crises at drug treatment centers. The response of society to use of LSD and related drugs, however, was far from enthusiastic and permissive. Concern focused on the immediate side effects and the adverse emotional reactions that occurred long after the drug had been taken. The prevailing campus theme, "Turn on, tune in, and drop out," contributed to public disapproval. LSD was classified as a Schedule I drug in the 1970s.

TABLE 9.1. Early Proposed Uses for LSD

Military application; brainwashing and/or disabling enemy forces
Aid in psychotherapy
Treatment of alcoholism
Treatment of opiate dependency
Palliation of cancer
Recreational use

LSD and related compounds are relatively easy to synthesize. As a result, illicit production and distribution, which began in the mid-1960s, reached such a peak that the United States had an oversupply. LSD became the only drug illicitly synthesized in the United States and exported to Canada and Europe. As a result of its classification as a Schedule I drug and the adverse publicity surrounding its use, recreational use began to decline by the end of the 1970s, but by 1982 approximately 21 percent of young people between the ages of eighteen and twenty-five reported having tried it at some time in their lives. Estimates of use by high school students have remained low nonetheless. The 2000 Monitoring the Future Survey reported 8 percent of twelfth graders to have used a hallucinogen within the past year, and 2.6 percent within the thirty days preceding the survey. The 1999 National Household Survey on Drug Abuse reported an estimated 1.2 million new users of hallucinogenic drugs, with the rate of initiation among users aged 12 to 17 almost doubling between 1991 and 1996 (14.5 to 25.9 per 1,000 potential new users).

CLASSIFICATION

Classifying a substance as a hallucinogen is not as simple as it seems. At first, the term "psychedelic" was used to describe all agents that produce visual hallucinations, usually accompanied by intensified perception or insight, and sometimes the kind of bizarre behavior and loss of contact with reality seen in psychoses. Thus hallucinations can be caused by a variety of drugs, many of which share few, if any, pharmacological characteristics. Several mood-altering drugs are not primarily hallucinogens but produce hallucinations when taken in increased amounts. Still others have that effect when taken by susceptible people in small doses or in combination with other mood-altering drugs. The hallucinogen classification in this section includes substances taken primarily to produce visual hallucinations and/or intensified perceptions. Although the effects of these substances themselves may differ in intensity, the psychological effects are fairly uniform: feelings of tranquillity, developing new meanings to life or watching one's life go by, harmony with humankind and the environment—in short, mind-expanding sensations. That can be contrasted with the effects of heroin: introversion, an inward focus, and a "return-to-the-womb" environment.

Pharmacologically, it's best to classify hallucinogens according to their action on a specific neurotransmitter site (Chapter 4). But for practical purposes, classification by the subjective experiences they produce can be more helpful (Table 9.2). Thus hallucinogenic drugs can be classified as those that produce:

- Effects almost identical to those of LSD
- Effects similar but not identical to those of LSD
- Experiences in addition to those with LSD
- Completely different effects from LSD (such as phencyclidine, Ecstasy)

Herbal Preparations

Many herbal preparations commonly used as teas contain mood-altering substances (Table 9.3). They have low potential for inappropriate use and are consumed infrequently, but purchasers may be unaware that they contain hallucinogens. Depending on the tea and quantity drunk, the effects may vary from mild dysphoria (feeling somewhat under the weather) to actual hallucinations.

Ephedra

Recently, a Chinese herb containing ephedra (ma huang), which was originally promoted as a dietary supplement to control weight and increase energy, has been offered as a drug that can be used recreationally. The feelings obtained when taking this drug have been described as quite similar to those of MDMA (Ecstasy). Hence, the street name, the original herbal ex, cloud nine, and liquid ecstasy. Although the sales of this substance cannot be adequately tracked, since its initial labeling as a dietary supplement freed it from FDA regulation, in 1996 one company reported selling over 15 million units. Initially, advertising promoted it as an extremely safe agent providing a natural herbal high. Similar to other drugs containing ephedrine, ephedra can cause irregular heartbeats, hypertension, and adverse psychological reactions. In fact, many toxic reactions have been reported from its excessive use. Since many taking this substance are unaware of the psychoactive effects, these symptoms may be quite disturbing and frightening. For those who are taking the drug specifically to get high, inappropriate use of excessive doses can result in severe reactions. As a result of intervention by the Federal Trade Commission, sales of the drug are now accompanied by a warning concerning the adverse effects of ephedrine.

TABLE 9.2. Hallucinogens by Similarity to LSD Effects

Effect	Duration (Hours)	Group	NS*	Street Name
LSD-like				
LSD	12	Indolealkylamines	S	Acid, Barrels, Blotter, Blue Cap, Blue Cheer, Blue Dots, California Sunshine, Cherry Top, Camel, Candles, Cube-D, Dragon, King Tut, Man, Microdot, Mr. Natural, Orange Sunshine, Owsleys, Pape Acid, Purple Haze, 25, Wedges, White Lightning, Window Panes, Zigzag
Mescaline (peyote)	4	Phenylethylamines	A	Big Chief, Buttons, Cactus, Mesc, Mescal
Psilocybin	6	Indolealkylamines	S	Magic Mushroom, Shroom, Silly Putty
Morning glory seeds	—	Indolealkylamines	S	Glory, Mexicana
Similar to LSD				
DOM	Days	Phenylethylamines	A	Peace, Serenity, STP, Tranquility
DMT	1-2	Indolealkylamines	S	Businessman's Special
LSD-like plus other properties				
MDA§	Varies up to days	Phenylethylamines	A	Love Pill
MDMA§		Phenylethylamines	A	Ecstasy
MDEA§		Phenylethylamines	A	Eve
Different from LSD Effect				
Atropine, Scopolamine		Cholinergic	C	
Muscarine		Cholinergic	C	
Physostigmine		Cholinergic	C	

Effect	Duration (Hours)	Group	NS*	Street Name
Phencyclidine	Varies up to days	Arylcyclohexylamines		Angel Dust, Crystal, Cyclone, DOA, Dust, Elephant, Goon, Itog, Killer Weed, Krystal, Loveboat, Mint, Monkey Dust, Peace Pill, PCP, Peace Scuffle, Sherman, Supergrass, Superkool, Superpot, Surfer, T, Tac, Tran Q, Weed

Source: W. R. Martin and J. W. Sloan, "Pharmacology and Classification of LSD Hallucinogens," *Drug Addiction II: Amphetamine, Psychotogen and Marihuana Dependence,* ed. W. R. Martin. Berlin: Springer-Verlag, 1977, pp. 305-308. Permission granted by Springer-Verlag Gmbh & Co. KG.
*(NS) = Neurotransmitter receptor sites: A = Adrenergic, C = cholinergic, S = serotonergic
§Designer drug (see Chapter 2)

Ayahuasca

Ayahuasca is a brown-reddish liquid extracted from a mixture of leaves from plants growing in the Amazon. These plants contain several alkaloids, the active one being dimethyltryptamine, which is responsible for its hallucinogenic effect. Although infrequently seen in this country, it has been reported to be used in Europe for its hallucinogenic effects.

LSD-like Drugs

Hallucinogens are believed to exert their behavioral impact by modifying effects of the neurotransmitters, or messengers of the brain (Chapter 4). Depending on the drug, action on a particular neurotransmitter may be more or less pronounced.

The physiological effects of hallucinogens on the heart and blood vessels can appear within a few minutes as increased blood pressure and heart rate (sometimes accompanied by tremors), dilated pupils, elevated temperature, hyperactive reflexes, and sweating. Those signs may be accelerated when the substance is in the amphetamine (phenylisopropylamine) group (Table 9.2).

Visual hallucinations and perceptual changes appear in one to two hours. The user becomes either hypervigilant or withdrawn, perhaps changing from one condition to the other. There may be a fear of personality fragmentation, prolonged afterimages, and greatly altered time perception (feeling that the hours-long "trip" has lasted only minutes). Mood changes can range from excitability (especially with amphetamines) to tranquillity. A calming

TABLE 9.3. Hallucinogenic Plants in Herbal Teas

Plant		
Popular Name	*Scientific Name*	*Hallucinogenic Effect*
Catnip	*Nepeta cataria*	Mild
Ephedra		Mild-Moderate
Juniper	*Juniper macropoda*	Strong
Kavakava	*Piper methysticum*	Mild
Mandrake	*Mandragora officinarum*	Moderate
Nutmeg	*Myristica fragrans*	Moderate
Periwinkle	*Cathacanthus rosens*	Moderate
Thorn Apple	*Datura stramonium*	Strong
Yohimbe	*Corynanthe yohimbe*	Mild

Source: R. K. Siegel, "Herbal Intoxication: Psychoactive Effects from Herbal Cigarettes, Teas and Capsules," *Journal of the American Medical Association* 236 (1976): 473-476. Copyrighted 1976, American Medical Association.

effect may appear after several hours, together with detachment and control. A clearing of mood sets in after twelve hours.

Different hallucinogens vary in duration of their effects. DMT, which has relatively short duration, is called the businessman's special. Drugs in the amphetamine group can produce effects lasting anywhere from three hours to two days. Differences in potency also exist. LSD is more than 100 times more potent than psilocybin, and 1,000 times more potent than mescaline.

ADVERSE EFFECTS OF HALLUCINOGENS

Use of hallucinogens doesn't result in physical dependency, but there is a high degree of tolerance to the behavioral effects after several doses. Cross-tolerance exists among LSD-like drugs, but not with other hallucinogens. For that reason, a person tolerant to LSD who takes a higher dose of an unrelated hallucinogen may suffer severe toxic effects. Fatal reactions are rare and probably attributable to contaminants in the drug. Street purchases may contain strychnine, amphetamines, or PCP, among other adulterants.

Adverse psychological reactions, however, are common. They include panic reaction, suicide, post-LSD depression, flashback, and psychotic behavior. Panic reaction—what is called a "bad trip"—is the most frequent adverse effect. Why some people almost never have a bad trip while others have one every time they take the drug is unclear. The individual's expectations undoubtedly influence the experience. So does the environment in which the drug is taken, as well as prior personality disorders. Taking a hallucinogen in too great a dose or with other mood-altering drugs can also cause a bad trip.

Suicide is a possibility during an extreme panic reaction, particularly when LSD is mixed with amphetamines. Panic reaction can be treated by placing the person in a quiet environment and providing reassurance that recovery will occur. Tranquilizers can be used but are rarely needed.

Physicians who are unfamiliar with the panic reaction caused by hallucinogens sometimes treat the condition with phenothiazines (Thorazine, Stelazine, etc.). Not only is this unnecessary, but when the panic reaction is caused by hallucinogens in the amphetamine group, it sometimes leads to intensified excitability and a drop in blood pressure. Treatment with phenothiazine is also associated with increased flashbacks.

Flashback is the phenomenon of a currently drug-free user suddenly returning to the mood-altering state of a prior trip. It's called a "free trip" and happens to 10 to 15 percent of users. Flashbacks are more frequent among those who have combined hallucinogens with other drugs, or who are under extreme stress or anxiety. The precise cause of flashbacks is not clear. They can occur several times for up to a year following the last LSD use.

Post-LSD depression can last for months. Whether a cause-and-effect relationship exists is uncertain. Hallucinogens have also precipitated psychotic behavior; again, whether that behavior might have surfaced without use of these drugs is not known.

ECSTASY

When MDMA (3,4-methylenedioxymethamphetamine) was patented in Germany in 1914, its synthesis was part of a process to identify compounds with potential therapeutic efficacy. However, as described by Cohen in his excellent and comprehensive review, this substance "lay fallow" until tested by the U.S. Army in 1950 during a series of animal experiments. It is of interest that at this time, another drug, MDA (3,4-methylenedioxyamphetamine), later to appear on the streets as Eve, was also tested but was found to be too toxic to nerve terminals to be of value.

MDMA is a less toxic derivative of MDA. Although classified as a hallucinogenic amphetamine, it usually does not cause either visual or auditory hallucinations unless taken with other mood-altering substances. Its action, similar to other psychoactive agents, is primarily on the neurotransmitters, mainly serotonin, but it may effect dopamine and norepinephrine as well.

The use of MDMA on the street, under the name of Ecstasy, began in the late 1960s, but did not reach the notice of the government until 1986, when it was placed in Schedule I. Since that time, its use has continued to increase, and it is currently one of the more popular illicit drugs, seen on college campuses, in bars, and in other social settings. The 2000 Monitoring the Future Survey reported the annual use of Ecstasy to have increased among 12th graders from 5 percent in 1996 to 8 percent in 2000, with 50 percent reporting easy availability. The usual dose is one to two tablets. It is used most frequently during raves, all-night affairs of drinking, singing, and dancing. As its use has increased, clandestine laboratories have developed to meet the demand, and at present the drug is sold on the street under various names, including E, XTC, Adam, doctor, rhapsody, raven, and biscuit (see Appendix B). The increasing use of this drug can best be illustrated by the number of tablets seized, increasing by 700 percent in three years, from 381,000 in 1997 to over three million in 1999, with a $40 million shipment of 2.1 million tablets seized in July of 2000. The profit margin for this drug is extremely high. Ecstasy costs only a few cents to make but can sell for up to $25 to $50 retail.

Users of Ecstasy report it allows them to be more open-minded, close to others, blissful, able to love, and able to "break down barriers." These feelings can occur within twenty to forty minutes after taking Ecstasy and can be heightened by music, with the high lasting between three and eight hours. Similar to other psychoactive agents, the setting can often determine the quality of the experience, ranging from exceptionally energizing to blissful.

Adverse Reactions

Unfortunately, as described by Cohen, the use of Ecstasy can also be accompanied by a variety of adverse reactions, some quite severe. The onset of its psychoactive effects is accompanied by the effects seen when any stimulant is ingested. There is a rapid heart rate, pupillary dilatation, and mild headache often followed by more disturbing symptoms, such as muscle tension, low back pain, involuntary clenching of the teeth, vomiting, blurred vision, and sudden elevation of blood pressure. Far from achieving a blissful high, users of Ecstasy can develop depression, panic attacks, paranoia, psychoses, mood swings, depersonalization reactions, memory losses, catatonic states, and, similar to LSD, flashbacks weeks after taking the drug. Treatment of the psychological disturbances is usually supportive. However, in extreme cases serotonin uptake inhibitors, such as fluoxetine, may be used beneficially.

Severe medical complications, such as strokes, convulsions, hyperthermia, degeneration of muscle cells (rhabdomyolysis), bleeding liver failure, kidney failure, and death, have all been recorded. These adverse effects are more likely to appear in settings such as raves, where people are agitated, hot, drinking alcohol or using other drugs, and dehydrated. However, even when adequate fluids are consumed, it has recently been shown that Ecstasy stimulates secretion of a hormone (arginine vasopressin) that retains water. This can lead to a marked lowering of salt content in the blood (hyponatremia), with serious adverse effects. Chronic use has been demonstrated to lead to damage to the neurons in the brain that produce serotonin (5-HT), with resultant memory loss. Most recently, in England use of Ecstasy during pregnancy has been associated with a significantly increased risk of congenital defects, consisting mainly of cardiovascular and musculoskeletal abnormalities. Even in situations that are less hectic, individuals with medical conditions, such as high blood pressure, heart disease, diabetes, asthma, seizure disorders, or underlying psychological disturbances, will be at particular risk. Adding to the risk is a finding that these pills may not contain Ecstasy or may have other substances added to them. An analysis by Baggott and Sferios of 107 pills from across the United States found only 63 percent to contain MDMA or a related substance. Dextromethorphan (DXM), a synthetic opioid used to suppress coughing, was seen in 21 percent at considerably higher doses than used therapeutically. It is entirely possible that some of the serious adverse effects reported in Ecstasy users may be related to a DXM overdose. Clearly, the agony that accompanies the Ecstasy suggests this is a drug that should be taken with extreme caution, if at all.

PHENCYCLIDINE

Phencyclidine (PCP) was first used by veterinarians in the 1950s as an anesthetic. Because it provided relief from pain (and some loss of memory) without significantly depressing the respiratory or cardiovascular systems, it was also used as an anesthetic for humans. But reports of disorientation, excitability, delirium, and even hallucinations upon awakening from anesthesia began to appear. By 1965, the adverse effects were well documented, and PCP was discontinued for human use. For a time it remained available for animal use under the brand names Sernyl, Synalar, and Sernylan, but it is no longer available.

Mechanism of Action

Among the effects of PCP and related drugs are stimulation, depression, analgesia, and hallucinations. The reinforcing properties are probably the result of a combination of these effects, but none seems to dominate. Laboratory animals won't self-administer LSD or similar compounds, but they'll readily self-administer PCP, become tolerant, and undergo withdrawal when chronic use is stopped. Almost all neurotransmitters are affected by PCP, and PCP is believed to bind with the sigma receptor, a type of opiate receptor. Independent PCP receptors probably exist as well.

Patterns of Use

PCP wasn't popular when it first appeared on the street around 1965. It was usually taken when dealers successfully passed it off as one of the more sought-after hallucinogens or put it in marijuana. PCP use increased from 1973 to 1979, tapered off until 1981, then rose again. Seven million people had used PCP by 1979; approximately 8.3 million by 1982. This was most apparent in metropolitan areas. In 1989, PCP was the second most frequently used drug in Washington, DC. Although its use has diminished over the ensuing years, nonetheless, in the 1998 Monitoring the Future Survey, approximately 4 percent of twelfth graders reported ever using PCP, with 2 percent reporting its use in the thirty days prior to the survey.

PCP and its analogs are easily manufactured, making it difficult to identify and eliminate illicit laboratories. In liquid form, PCP can be mixed with a beverage, but it is most commonly sprayed over other mood-altering substances. As a liquid, it may contain volatile solvents that can contribute to acute reactions. PCP may be sold as cigarettes with thick brown wrappers that absorb the drug, or in small aluminum packages, from which it can be hand-rolled into cigarettes or placed in pipes.

Drugs sold as PCP are often mixed with stimulants, narcotics, or—most often—small amounts of marijuana. Of the PCP street samples that have been analyzed, up to half were contaminated with other drugs. When intentionally mixed with cocaine (ghostbusters), it can produce marked antisocial behavior. When sold as powder (angel dust or flakes), it's typically 50 to 100 percent pure. When it goes by other names, such as rock crystals, it is only 10 to 30 percent pure. The average dose in a PCP cigarette is about 2 milligrams. In one survey, up to 36 percent of first-time users didn't know they had taken PCP.

Effects of PCP can be felt within five minutes; intoxication follows within fifteen to thirty minutes and lasts four to six hours. Craving after discontinuing the drug, as well as withdrawal, is possible.

Adverse Effects

As with other hallucinogens, the initial effects of PCP come from its stimulant properties (Table 9.4). These include increased blood pressure, rapid heart rate, and rapid breathing. Its other effects in the nervous system can produce flushing, wheezing, sweating, drooling, rapid eye movements,

TABLE 9.4. Immediate PCP Effects

Psychological

Combativeness
Visual hallucinations
Toxic psychosis
Disorientation

Autonomic

Rapid heart rate
Elevated blood pressure
Increased salivation
Respiratory depression

Neurological

Coma
Convulsions

Renal

Kidney failure

and constriction of the pupils. Users may appear clear-headed and oriented or may have slurred speech and exhibit bizarre behavior. This can happen even with small doses. Larger doses may result in extreme mood alterations. Doses higher than 20 milligrams can cause extreme rises in body temperature, convulsions, breathing problems, coma, and cardiac rhythm disturbances—any of which may be fatal. PCP cigarettes can cause seizures, coma, and respiratory failure within one hour.

The effects of PCP have been classified into major and minor complications. The major patterns (Table 9.5) are sometimes fatal. They include coma, catatonia (total unresponsiveness), and acute brain syndrome, manifested by delirium and memory loss. Minor complications are disturbing, but usually not dangerous: lethargy, bizarre behavior, agitation, violence, and a dreamy high.

An acute toxic reaction is directly related to the PCP level in the blood, but a psychosis marked by impaired judgment may not be. Those with prior personality disturbances seem to be particularly susceptible to this complication.

Psychotic episodes similar to schizophrenia may continue to appear after the acute reaction and can last from four weeks to several months. This can be followed by depression, again lasting four weeks to several months, which may lead to suicide or a return to PCP use.

TABLE 9.5. Major PCP Complications

Coma
Less than two hours to weeks
Extremely high temperatures and blood pressures

Catatonic syndrome
Mute and staring
Muscle rigidity
Seizures, delusions, hallucinations

Toxic psychosis
Hallucinations, paranoid behavior, delusions, agitation

Acute brain syndrome
Disorientation, lack of judgment, memory loss
without findings noted above

Chronic use of PCP has been associated with memory loss, bouts of depression, recurrent psychotic episodes, and a chronic brain syndrome called, in its most severe form, the "Alzheimer's disease of adolescence." This rare syndrome shows up as an inability to function and periods of forgetfulness.

Treatment

Treatment of PCP reactions depends on the symptoms. In many cases of mild intoxication, no treatment other than reassurance is needed. For seizures, diazepam (Valium) or a similar drug can be given. Psychotic behavior is treated with such antipsychotic medications as haloperidol (Haldol). Large doses of PCP can be washed out of the stomach through a nasogastric (nose-to-stomach) tube. A slurry of activated charcoal can also be given. Vitamin C (ascorbic acid) increases elimination of PCP in the urine.

Depending on the severity of the effects and the patterns of use, treatment for chronic PCP use can be short-term inpatient psychiatric hospitalization or outpatient substance-abuse programs.

KETAMINE

Ketamine, a veterinary anesthetic, is used on the streets as a liquid or a white powder (Special K) often mixed with tobacco. In large doses, it can cause effects similar to PCP. Toxic effects include delirium, severe hallucinations, hypertension, impaired motor function, and respiratory depression. Chronic use can result in impaired attention span and memory loss.

Chapter 10

Marijuana

Cultivation of *Cannabis sativa,* the marijuana plant, in both tropical and temperate climates can be traced back thousands of years. Its ability to alter mood and the use of its fiber in making linen, canvas, and rope have made it a desirable crop. Mood-altering effects are obtained through eating, smoking, chewing, or drinking. In the Americas it appeared as early as 1545, grown in Virginia around 1607 by the Jamestown settlers, and introduced into England about a decade later.

Throughout history, cannabis has been used to treat a variety of human complaints and disorders. In the United States, it was considered particularly effective for headaches, toothaches, and menstrual cramps. In fact, it was listed in the *United States Pharmacopoeia* until 1941, when its use was made illegal. From 1913 to 1938, the Eli Lilly and Parke-Davis pharmaceutical companies maintained a farm where a highly potent strain, *Cannabis americana,* was produced. Today, there are still some proposed medical uses for marijuana (Table 10.1), but, until recently, the only use that has been generally accepted is to prevent nausea and vomiting following chemotherapy for cancer. Both dronabinol (Marinol), the principal psychoactive substance in marijuana, and nabilone (Cesamet), a synthetic cannabinoid, have been approved for that purpose.

TABLE 10.1. Proposed Medical Uses of Marijuana

Analgesic
Anticonvulsant
Antianxiety agent
Antidepressant
Antiemetic
Appetite enhancer
Bronchodilator
Muscle relaxant
Preanesthetic agent
Sedative-hypnotic
To reduce intraocular pressure in glaucoma
To treat alcohol and drug dependency

REEFER MADNESS

The psychoactive effects of the plant were well known in the eighteenth and nineteenth centuries, but its use as a psychotropic agent was fairly limited in the United States until the 1920s, when the Eighteenth Amendment put an end to legal drinking. Interest in marijuana as a mood-altering substance suddenly grew. By the time Prohibition was repealed in 1933 and liquor once again became readily available, it was too late to stop the spread of the drug. In 1936 a film, *Reefer Madness,* made the public aware and concerned over its purported devastating effects. Public reaction led to efforts to restrict its accessibility. By 1937, marijuana had become illegal in forty-six states. Penalties for its use were similar to those for morphine, heroin, and cocaine. The attitude toward marijuana was so negative that it was erroneously classified as a narcotic. When it was realized this was not so, marijuana became labeled as a "stepping stone" to heroin use. Therefore, preventing its use was of such importance as to warrant severe penalties. It was designated a Schedule I drug along with heroin and LSD, being considered to have a high abuse potential and unsafe for use, even under medical supervision. Much of the public's thinking changed, however, as marijuana began to be perceived—especially by the young—as a relatively harmless substance whose adverse effects had been vastly exaggerated.

Spurred on by the increasing use of this drug, in 1970 Congress authorized funding for the National Commission on Marijuana and Drug Abuse. This commission ultimately found no serious adverse effects associated with marijuana use and, although it recommended retaining sanctions against its cultivation and sale, suggested elimination of criminal penalties at both federal and state levels for simple possession and use. This recommendation was endorsed by a variety of professional organizations, including the American Bar Association, the American Medical Association, the National Council of Churches, and the American Public Health Association. Commissions that were subsequently established in other countries also recommended the elimination of criminal sanctions for simple possession and use of marijuana. Over the next decade, physicians and other concerned individuals attempted to find a place for marijuana in the medical armamentarium and promoted transferring it from Schedule I to Schedule II to allow appropriate prescription by physicians. In 1988, after several years of hearings, the Drug Enforcement Administration's administrative law judge recommended that marijuana be reclassified as a Schedule II drug. In 1992, the DEA made a final ruling, rejecting this recommendation. The relative safety of marijuana, however, continues to be confirmed.

In the past on a state level, marijuana for medical use was approved by several states without much fanfare or public outcry. As an example, in 1980, the New York State Legislature passed and the governor signed a medical marijuana law that as never put into practical action. However, this complacency changed in 1996 when California approved the Compassionate Use Act (Proposition 215), allowing residents of the state to possess and cultivate marijuana for medicinal purposes when recommended by a physician for treatment of "cancer, anorexia, AIDS, chronic pain, glaucoma, arthritis, migraine, or any other illness for which marijuana provides relief." Arizona also approved a similar but even more comprehensive initiative regarding the use of any drug in Schedule I. However, this was quickly amended by the Arizona State Legislature to apply only to drugs approved by the Food and Drug Administration, thereby voiding the statute.

All of this thinking never permeated law enforcement agencies, which continued to consider marijuana as dangerous as other illicit substances. As reported by Zimmer and Morgan, since the National Marijuana Commission's report, over 10 million people have been arrested for marijuana offenses. In 1995, over 500,000 people were arrested for such offenses, with 86 percent of arrests being for possession. Minorities bear a disproportionate burden of these penalties. Although representing only approximately 20 percent of marijuana users, African Americans and Hispanics make up 58 percent of those sentenced under federal law. In 1996, nationwide arrests for marijuana doubled from 1992, reaching 642,000. In New York City, due to a mayoral initiative in 1998, the number of marijuana arrests rose from 27,264 in 1997 to close to 40,000, of which 80 percent were for possession rather than selling.

Disapprobation, however, is focused not only on those who use the drug. In response to the California initiative, which was strongly opposed by the Clinton Administration, the attorney general stated that the U.S. Attorney's Office in California would "continue to review cases for prosecution and drug DEA officials will review cases as they have to, to determine whether to revoke the registration of any physician who recommends or prescribes so-called Schedule I controlled substances." Federal legislation was introduced (Helms, Faircloth, SB 40), although fortunately not passed, proposing a minimum eight-year sentence in a federal penitentiary for any physician who would recommend medical marijuana to any patient under twenty-one years of age. The final act, however, was played out by the U.S. Supreme Court, which on May 14, 2001, unanimously found the manufacture and distribution of marijuana to be illegal under any circumstances. Clearly, it appears that reefer madness still exists.

PATTERNS OF USE

Despite the vigorous attack on marijuana, its use has increased consistently over the past decades, and it still remains the most commonly used illicit drug in this country. It is estimated that over 65 million Americans or approximately one-third of the population over twelve years of age have used this drug at least once, with 20 million smoking it within the past year, and 12 million within the past month. In 1998, 2.3 million persons were estimated to have used marijuana for the first time. It is estimated that approximately 10 percent of those who ever use marijuana become daily users, with another 20 to 30 percent using the drug weekly, with smoking ceasing by the mid- or late twenties. Although in 1990 the daily use of marijuana by high school students had diminished markedly since the previous decade, nonetheless the American Council on Education survey reported 26 percent of students had used marijuana one to five times. A 1997 survey of 17,592 students at 140 American colleges reported that 25 percent had used marijuana in the past year, with rates of use varying greatly among institutions, from 0 to 54 percent. Although marijuana use among high school students is on the decline, the 2000 Monitoring the Future Survey reports that 16 percent of all eighth graders and 37 percent of all twelfth graders have tried marijuana within the last year. Marijuana appears to be still very much with us and shows no evidence of disappearing from public view, despite its illegality and its association with potential incarceration. The following sections review what we know about the drug, as well as provide recommendations concerning both its use and misuse.

Marijuana Preparations

The strength of cannabis plants is determined by the concentration of delta-9-tetrahydrocannabinol (delta-9-THC), their major psychoactive substance. The delta-9-THC content ranges from 1.4 to 5 percent.

Four major mood-altering products are obtained from the plant (Table 10.2). Ganga comes from the dry leaves and flowering shoots. Hashish is a potent resin extracted from the top of the flowering plant; it contains 3 to 8 percent delta-9-THC. Repeated purification of hashish yields extremely potent hashish oil, containing up to 20 percent delta-9-THC.

Marijuana is obtained from both the flowering tops and cut and dried leaves and stems. Potency varies greatly, depending on the plant (Table 10.3). A 500-milligram, U.S.-produced marijuana cigarette may contain from 0.5 to 1 percent delta-9-THC. With marijuana imported from the West Indies, however, those numbers rise to 7 to 11 percent. In the late 1980s, law enforcement efforts lowered the amount of marijuana entering the United States. But that success was accompanied by a more than twofold increase in domestic production, which constitutes 25 percent of the marijuana available on the street. More significant, almost half the marijuana being harvested domestically is sinsemilla (from the unpollinated female plant), with a THC content of up to 14 percent. However, there is not a one-to-one rela-

TABLE 10.2. Marijuana and Related Substances

Product	Origin	Street Name
Ganga	Leaf preparations	Bhang, Charas, Dugga, Goma de Mota, Kif, Machohina
Hashish	Resin from top of flowering plant	Hash, Rope, Soles, Sweet Lucy
Marijuana	Usually flowering tops, but also dried leaves and stems	Acapulco Gold, Berkley, Boo, Brick, Grass, Hawaiian, Hay, Hemp, Herb, J, Jamaican, Jive, Joint, Key, Lid, Locoweed, Mary Jane, MJ, Mota, Mutah, Muggles, Pot, Reefer, Roach, Rope, Sativa, Sinsemilla, Skunk, Stick, Tea, Tocas Tea, Weed, Yerba
THC	Tetrahydrocannabinol	THC

TABLE 10.3. Delta-9-THC Content of Street Drugs

Substance	Percent by Weight
Hashish	3-10
Hashish oil	10-30
Marijuana cigarettes Jamaican	0.5-4
U.S.-produced	Under 1
Sinsemilla (U.S.)	7-15

tionship between increase in potency and increase in psychoactive effect, and with persistent use tolerance does develop. Phencyclidine, cocaine, hashish, or opium are sometimes mixed with, and sold as, straight marijuana. Of greater concern is the 1989 report by the Community Epidemiology Work Group of marijuana being laced with insecticides. Identified in Phoenix and called Wac, this preparation has been associated with unusual psychiatric symptoms.

Synthetic delta-9-THC, approved by the Food and Drug Administration to combat nausea and vomiting caused by cancer chemotherapy, is occasionally diverted to the street or produced in clandestine laboratories. A potent synthetic designer drug, Synhexyl, was available through the mid-1970s and prompted considerable research.

Smoking Pot

Marijuana can be smoked straight, mixed with tobacco, or eaten. Contrary to popular belief, marijuana smoke is carcinogenic, containing twice the amount of tar in tobacco. When smoked, the amount of delta-9-THC that is absorbed by the lungs depends on how much is lost through burning (perhaps up to 60 percent) or through exhaled air, and how much is retained when the breath is held. It is believed that the bioavailability of THC ranges from 5 to 24 percent, with as little as 2 to 3 mg reaching the bloodstream able to produce a high. From 50 to 60 percent of the THC may be delivered to the bloodstream. It's rapidly absorbed; a subjective effect is felt within minutes and continues for two to three hours.

When marijuana preparations are eaten and absorbed from the intestinal tract, first effects take thirty minutes to two hours to appear, with peak levels appearing in one to six hours. The amount of THC absorbed varies and is much less than with smoking because much is destroyed in the gastrointestinal tract and by early metabolism in the liver. However, oral ingestion produces an increased concentration of the THC metabolite 11-hydroxy-THC, which can cause a strong psychoactive effect. This is the reason why those who have tried Marinol for chemotherapy-related nausea frequently find the drug unsatisfactory, claiming it gets them stoned while they still remain nauseated.

Marijuana is fat soluble and enters many tissues, including the brain, heart, and liver. It's metabolized in the liver and excreted in the urine. Half of a single dose is eliminated in one day. In an infrequent user, marijuana can be detected in the blood for up to three days. In a frequent or heavy user, arbitrarily defined as smoking several joints a day, residual levels remain in the tissues and can be detected in urine for up to one month after the last use. Urine testing for marijuana will therefore detect the drug after its use has been discontinued.

TOLERANCE, DEPENDENCY, AND WITHDRAWAL

Tolerance to the mood-altering effects of marijuana is typical; chronic users can consume, and often need, increased quantities to obtain the same feelings. Acute intoxication from marijuana is rare but has become more common with the widespread availability of the more potent varieties. It can show up as impaired learning, diminished performance, acute panic reactions, and symptoms of acute toxic psychosis. Such symptoms can include visual hallucinations, delirium, and paranoia. However, it is important to remember that marijuana is frequently used in combination with other drugs, such as alcohol, tranquilizers, heroin, cocaine, and amphetamines. All of these drugs have profound mood-altering effects, with those in the alcohol-tranquilizer and opioid group being associated with physical dependency and withdrawal.

The dependency potential of marijuana is quite low. Infrequent use of low doses seldom leads to withdrawal. But after discontinuing frequent high-dose use, anxiety, irritability, tremulousness, loss of appetite, and sleeping difficulties—all compatible with mild withdrawal—may follow.

ADVERSE EFFECTS

Adverse effects of marijuana were first described in the 1894 Indian Hemp Drug Commission Report, still considered one of the best systematic studies of the subject. In the twentieth century, a number of commission reports and books attempted to define the effects of this drug. Some have been confirmed; others have not. However, virtually all natural and scientific commissions both in this country and abroad have concluded that the medical effects of moderate use are mild and the antisocial effects nonexistent.

Effects on the Central Nervous System

Marijuana's effects on the central nervous system vary greatly, depending on dose and the setting it's taken in. When smoked in a quiet environment, the most common positive feelings are euphoria and relaxation, accompanied by mild sedation. In a social setting, however, stimulation and increased activity are common. In such circumstances, users report keener visual and hearing abilities, and sometimes increased sexual arousal.

Taking marijuana when anxious can produce the opposite effect—an uncomfortable experience. Unlike alcohol, the high associated with a low dose of marijuana can be controlled; the person seems perfectly normal to an observer. Short-term memory can be impaired, however, and the transfer of information from intermediate to long-term memory can be slowed. Mental tasks involving complex thinking may be performed poorly.

Performance Requiring Coordination

Simple motor tasks may be accomplished, but complex ones, such as driving, are more difficult, with the degree of impairment directly related to the complexity of the task. A study of teenagers who smoked marijuana at least six times a month found them more than twice as likely to be involved in traffic accidents as nonsmokers. In California, one study reported detectable levels of delta-9-THC in 11 to 20 percent of drivers involved in fatal accidents. The levels were very low in most of the drivers, but alcohol was detected in 81 to 87 percent. Of those, 60 to 68 percent had levels high enough to cause intoxication. Those findings suggest that the combined effects of the two drugs might have precipitated the accidents. It has been suggested that although alcohol tends to make an individual engage in risky driving practices, marijuana tends to make one more cautious. Be that as it may, it is fairly safe to conclude that any drug that impairs short-term memory, even briefly, should never be used in association with operating a vehicle.

A study of airline pilot reactions under simulated flying conditions found that ten of nineteen had substandard performances after smoking one marijuana cigarette. Impairment continued for up to twenty-four hours, but when tested after twenty-four hours, the pilots believed they were not affected by the marijuana.

Memory Loss

Short-term memory loss is a consistent finding with acute marijuana use. Although this usually lasts only for the duration of intoxication, changes persisting for at least six weeks after discontinuing marijuana use have been noted by several investigators. Their studies related the memory loss to dose and frequency of smoking. Marijuana smokers with learning disabilities or other cerebral dysfunctions might be at particular risk.

The Antimotivational Syndrome

The ability of marijuana to produce the "antimotivational syndrome" (Table 10.4) has been widely discussed. Chronic intense use is unquestionably linked to impaired function, slowed thought, and loss of coordination. But whether intermittent use in low doses results in an irreversible step toward the antimotivational syndrome is not certain.

The effects of long-term or high-dose use of marijuana on the human brain remain to be clearly defined. In laboratory studies with monkeys, it has been reported that six months of administration of marijuana smoke resulted in damage to the portion of the brain related to intellectual function.

TABLE 10.4. Antimotivational Syndrome

Loss of interest, apathy, passivity
Loss of productivity and desire to work consistently
Fatigue
Low frustration threshold
Impairment in concentration
Lack of concern with appearance
Consistent marijuana use

However, a subsequent study was unable to confirm these findings. In humans, evidence of chronic brain damage with sporadic use of marijuana remains to be documented. Heavy use, however, has been associated with impairment of memory and of integration of complex information.

Of recent and great interest is the finding that the brain actually produces marijuanalike chemicals (endogenous cannabinoids) that may play an important role in the memory process.

Effects on the Lungs

Marijuana smoke, similar to tobacco smoke, is toxic to the lungs. Lethal pulmonary disease develops in laboratory animals tested with high-dose marijuana. In humans, asthma, bronchitis, and emphysema can follow hashish use or heavy use of marijuana. Studies demonstrate decreased pulmonary function in healthy volunteers after several weeks of heavy marijuana smoking. Burning and stinging of the mouth and throat, accompanied by a heavy cough, can occur even with infrequent use. Changes in the lung tissues with combined marijuana and cigarette smoking as a prelude to lung cancer have also been reported.

Effects on the Cardiovascular System

Effects of marijuana on the heart are mild, usually related to an increase in heart rate by 20 to 50 percent for up to three hours. Blood pressure rises slightly when lying down. However, pressure decreases if a person quickly stands and smokes. At such times, dizziness and loss of consciousness may occur. Recently, preliminary observations have suggested that these changes may increase the risk of having a heart attack by almost twofold within four hours after smoking marijuana. These observations, however, remain to be confirmed by other investigators.

Effects on the Eye

Marijuana's effects on the visual system usually consist of redness of the conjunctiva and a decrease in intraocular pressure (the pressure behind the eyes). This effect has led some to suggest that marijuana could be used to treat glaucoma, a condition in which the increased pressure can cause blindness.

Other Effects

Miscellaneous effects relating to marijuana use include a hangover, experienced the morning after smoking, a dry throat, and an increased appetite. In various experiments, marijuana has been shown to impair immune function, cause infertility in laboratory animals, and decrease sperm counts and blood testosterone levels in men. Disrupted menstrual cycles and complications with labor and delivery have been reported in women. Maternal exposure to marijuana has also been associated with one of several factors associated with cancer in childhood. These studies have all been faulted because they were done in laboratory settings using much higher doses of marijuana than usual, or with people prone to using other mood-altering drugs. So the practical value of the findings is unconfirmed. It is important to emphasize, however, that pregnancy should be a time when a woman abstains from all mood-altering drugs including marijuana.

Toxicity related to an overdose of marijuana is quite unlikely. As noted during the DEA administrative hearings, the medium lethal dose has been found to be 1:200,000 to 1:400,000, requiring a smoker to consume 20,000 to 40,000 times as much marijuana as is found in one cigarette. Administering marijuana by intravenous injection is rare, but the practice has been reported. It produces a severe toxic-allergic reaction, which can include nausea, vomiting, and diarrhea. These symptoms are frequently accompanied by shock, kidney failure, and alterations in the blood-clotting mechanism. Almost all such effects can be traced to the numerous unsterile substances found in the marijuana.

MOVING TO STRONGER DRUGS

Researchers studying marijuana use in adolescents say that experimentation with the drug sometimes leads from occasional social use to continued regular use, and finally on to cocaine, heroin, or hallucinogens. Almost every such study, however, has shown that alcohol and nicotine consistently preceded that kind of progression as well. So it's curious that many who are quick to claim marijuana as a cause of subsequent illicit drug use are reluctant to see a causal link with alcohol and tobacco. Since marijuana remains the most frequently used illicit drug, it is not surprising that those who use other illicit agents have also used marijuana. Inappropriate and frequent use of marijuana is neither benign nor harmless, but applying the same severe sanctions against its use as those against cocaine and heroin is unwarranted.

MEDICAL USES OF MARIJUANA

Those who argue for legalization of marijuana say that, at the very least, it should be available by prescription for disorders that can't be treated effectively with existing medications. Delta-9-THC has been proposed for a number of medical conditions (Table 10.1). Its adverse effects when smoked, however, make it preferable to use a pure form of THC, or one of the several synthetic cannabinoids now being studied. The latter would provide the desired outcome without the side effects that even pure THC can produce.

The most promising benefits appear to be marijuana's ability to alleviate nausea and pain and to stimulate appetite. These effects, combined with the drug's mood-altering action, make it particularly valuable for cancer patients and those with other wasting syndromes such as AIDS. As noted earlier, although synthetic THC in the form of dronabinol (Marinol) is commercially available, it is far less effective and less well tolerated. Recently, extremely potent antinausea medications, such as Zofran, also become available. However, the cost of taking these agents, for even a short time, is so high as to preclude their use by the majority of those in need of an effective antinausea medication.

Due to increasing public pressure to allow the use of marijuana to relieve the nausea associated with cancer chemotherapy, to improve appetite, and to diminish the pain associated with the AIDS muscle-wasting syndrome, the Institute of Medicine undertook an independent evaluation to determine if marijuana is effective in these settings. Their report concluded that, although marijuana smoke was indeed toxic, on an individual basis under close supervision, marijuana can be useful in alleviating the weight loss, pain, and nausea associated with AIDS. The recommendation was advanced that a safe inhalation device be developed for those in need of this drug. The panel also confirmed what many have previously observed—that no evidence exists implicating marijuana as a "gateway" to harder drug use. Perhaps in response to these findings, the Clinton administration, in May 1999, announced that the previous restriction on marijuana research (it could be funded only by grant funds obtained from the National Institutes of Health), would be lifted. This would allow the sale of government-grown marijuana to researchers regardless of their source of funding. Public initiatives to allow physicians to provide the best care for seriously ill patients also persist, despite the recent U.S. Supreme Court ruling prohibiting its use.

CONCLUSION

Based on all of the available evidence, occasional use of marijuana must be considered to be benign, with minimal addictive potential. Surveys reveal that most marijuana users begin to taper use of this drug in their late twenties, with only 2.5 percent even using it on an average of once a week or more. The penalties associated with its use appear out of proportion to its psychological, social, or medical effects. Although one cannot condone or promote its use by children, the same argument can be made of nicotine and alcohol, two clearly proven licit gateway drugs with far more toxic effects on the body and with a much greater potential for addiction.

Although the majority of the public is against the legalization of marijuana, the same cannot be said for its decriminalization or for its compassionate use, and most would agree that research into its effectiveness in alleviating pain and discomfort in people with chronic or terminal disease is long overdue. The need for supporting research can be perhaps best exemplified by a 1998 editorial in the prestigious British medical journal the *Lancet,* which concluded: "on the medical evidence available, moderate indulgence in cannabis has little ill effect on health, and that decisions to ban or legalize cannabis should be based on other decisions" ("Dangerous Habits," p. 1565). It is time to put the reefer madness of the late 1930s aside and to fairly evaluate the drug as well as to enable physicians to use their judgment with respect to its compassionate use.

Chapter 11

Opiates and Opioids

Cultivation of the poppy plant dates back to 5000-4500 B.C. when the Sumerians, living in what is now Iraq, cultivated the plant to extract its opium. Derived from the Greek work for onion, opium was the name subsequently given to the juice of the poppy. The first recorded reference to poppy juice was by the Greek philosopher Theophrastus in the third century B.C., but the medicinal value of opium was first described by Hippocrates, who praised it as a cathartic, styptic, and narcotic. By the seventeenth century, opium was being used throughout Europe; by the eighteenth century, it was being traded on a large scale. Increasing quantities were exported to the Far East, bringing prosperity to the many European countries that actively traded with China.

Profits from opium were so huge that the Opium Wars erupted in 1839 when China tried to stop importation of the drug. The Treaty of Nanking in 1842 legalized the Chinese opium trade. United States ships played a major role in transporting opium, but U.S. involvement with the drug wasn't limited to passive conveyance. During the nineteenth century, opiates were available in American grocery stores and pharmacies. They were dispensed freely by physicians and were consumed in numerous patent medicines. Invention of the hypodermic in the 1850s added injection as another way of taking opium, but smoking remained the prevalent method.

A German chemist isolated morphine from the alkaline base of opium in 1805, and several years later codeine was isolated in France. As concern about opium smoking escalated in the late 1800s, injectable morphine was touted as a cure for opium dependency. This "solution" had just the opposite effect: the number of people dependent on morphine increased dramatically, and the term "soldiers' disease" was coined during the American Civil War. Opium smoking began to decrease in the United States early in the twentieth century—about the time heroin was synthesized in England.

Early in this century, an estimated 400,000 Americans were dependent on opiates—roughly the same estimate as today. The Harrison Act in 1914 put an end to the most common method of treating opiate dependency—physician prescription of narcotics. This practice was replaced by the opening of community-based morphine clinics, which in turn were closed when the American Medical Association formally stated that prescription of opiates to maintain a dependency was not consistent with acceptable medical practice. Despite many local, state, and federal efforts to restrict importation and use of opium and heroin, consumption did not slack off until America's entry into World War II, when international drug traffic was severely limited. Toward the end of the war, fewer than 20,000 Americans were heroin dependent. When international shipping routes opened again at the war's end, heroin traffic flourished and in the 1960s reached epidemic proportions in many cities (Chapter 12).

OPIUM PREPARATIONS

Opium is derived by cutting the pod of the poppy plant to obtain a milky fluid. When air-dried, the fluid forms a thick brown mass that eventually becomes opium powder. The powder contains several alkaloids, including morphine and codeine. Legal opium preparations are still available today (Table 11.1). Morphine is approximately 10 percent and codeine 0.5 percent of dry opium, by weight. Originally, these naturally occurring substances and their derivatives were called opiates. Substances made through synthetic processes were termed opioids. But currently, owing to common usage, "opiate" and "opioid" are interchangeable and are also used to refer to receptors in the brain specific for these drugs as well as to those drugs that mimic as well as oppose their actions.

The natural opiates, the semisynthetic derivatives, and the synthetic opioids are all considered narcotics, defined as a drug that in moderate doses dulls the senses, relieves pain and induces profound sleep, but in excessive doses causes stupor, coma, or convulsions. Today "opioid" is the preferred term for these drugs. In a broader sense, however, "narcotic" refers to any drug that produces dependency; consequently, it has been used to describe cocaine, marijuana, alcohol, and amphetamines, depending on the locale.

TABLE 11.1. Licit Opium Preparations

Name	Contents
Brown's mixture	12 percent paregoric, alcohol, antimony, potassium tartrate, glycyrrhiza extract
Pantopan	Opium alkaloids; slightly less potent than morphine
Paregoric*	Camphorated tincture of opium, 45 percent alcohol
Tincture of opium	10 percent opium, 19 percent alcohol

*Used by mixing with an antihistamine and injecting (street name blue velvet).

It's misleading to use "narcotic" to encompass all dependency-producing drugs. In this chapter, the word refers only to the opioids or their antagonists, with only the licit opioids being reviewed. Heroin, the major illicit opioid, is discussed in detail in the following chapter.

ACTION OF OPIOIDS ON THE BRAIN

Among the narcotic drugs, morphine, the original derivative of opium, is considered the standard or prototype when discussing dependency, tolerance, and withdrawal. Its actions are relatively consistent and have been studied extensively. But all narcotics in equivalent doses can have similar effects, varying only in intensity and duration of action.

Common effects on the central nervous system include pain relief without loss of consciousness (analgesia), mood changes, drowsiness, nausea, and vomiting. Constriction of the pupils and respiratory depression can occur, depending on dose. With chronic or high-dosage use, hormones secreted from the pituitary gland may be affected.

Opiate Receptors

In 1973, scientists in three different laboratories identified certain nervous system receptors believed to be sites for opioid binding. Those findings have helped us better understand how opioids act on the brain and why people persist in taking them even in the absence of a pleasurable effect (Chapters 3 and 4). Eight receptors have already been identified, but many more are known to exist. The four considered most closely associated with opioid activity are the mu, kappa, delta, and sigma receptors.

The mu receptors are considered primarily responsible for the classic opioid effect of pain relief but also modulate euphoria, respiratory depression, sedation, and physical dependence. Kappa receptors are felt to play a role in opioid withdrawal, as well as having the ability to produce dysphoria, and also may moderate the sedative effects of the opioids. Several opioid agonist-antagonists are believed to preferably bind to the kappa receptors. Delta receptors are probably involved with the pleasurable or unpleasurable reactions associated with opioid use and to some extent analgesia. Sigma receptors are thought to relieve depression and may be the sites for such mood-altering drugs as PCP.

Opioid-like substances in the brain, pituitary gland, and other parts of the body were isolated several years after discovery of the opioid receptors. These substances, called endogenous peptides, are classified in three major groups: enkephalins, endorphins, and dynorphins. Although their exact roles have yet to be determined, they're being closely examined in connection with an individual's predilection for pain, and their effect in producing dependency and even in maintaining emotional well-being.

Agonists and Antagonists

Three major groups of drugs have been identified on the basis of opiate action on the receptors: (a) those that primarily alter mood and relieve pain (agonists), (b) those that displace or block opiates from receptors and have no mood-altering effects (antagonists), and (c) those that have both agonist and antagonist actions.

If agonist effects in the third group predominate, the drugs can alter mood and are susceptible to nonmedical use. That is important because, as discussed below, a number of agonist-antagonist painkillers are on the market. They've been touted as being able to provide effective pain relief with little or no risk of dependency. That is not the case.

EFFECTS OF OPIOIDS ON THE BODY

Except for its depressant effect on the brain and potential for overdose, the physical effects of morphine and other opiates are mild—probably less harmful physically than other drugs. Common effects of opiates will vary depending on the specific drug and individual susceptibility but include:

- Decreased secretion of stomach acid
- Decreased activity in the large and small intestines, resulting in constipation—one of the reasons opium and morphine are used to treat diarrhea
- Probable constriction of the gallbladder ducts
- Somewhat decreased urine flow as a result of action on muscles of the urethra and bladder
- Slowed labor and depressed fetal respiration when given to control predelivery pain

The liver metabolizes morphine but is minimally affected by it. In the presence of liver disease, however, increased levels of morphine may exist in the blood and brain—posing a risk for respiratory depression and an overdose reaction.

TOLERANCE, DEPENDENCY, AND WITHDRAWAL

Tolerance

Morphine tolerance develops at different rates, depending on the receptor involved. Tolerance to the analgesic or euphoric effects develops quickly, but tolerance to respiratory depression may remain unchanged. That makes opiate-dependent people more susceptible to respiratory depression when they take increasing quantities to get high.

Subtle physiological changes produced by opiates persist long after use is discontinued. Laboratory animals can have altered responses to pain up to twelve months after morphine withdrawal. Morphine-induced changes in the respiratory center can also persist in humans for prolonged periods. These changes can be measured in a laboratory setting but are not chemically important.

Dependency

Morphine and its related compounds can cause high degrees of dependency, tolerance, and withdrawal (Chapters 3, 4). When used inappropriately, addiction can develop quickly in both laboratory animals and humans. In humans, withdrawal can be brought on by a narcotic antagonist after taking only four to six pain-relieving doses of morphine or comparable drug per day for as few as three days. But when such drugs are used to control acute pain, the level of dependency is not great enough to outweigh the primary objective—relief of pain.

The reinforcing effects of morphine are not necessarily related to physical dependency. Rats that become dependent by drinking bitter-tasting morphine solutions will consume greater quantities of quinine solutions (also bitter) than other rats. By the same token, people who inject heroin cut with quinine often experience a high from quinine alone if they think the substance contains heroin. As with other mood-altering substances, expectations and the environment in which heroin is taken often greatly influence the pleasurable effects (Chapter 4).

Withdrawal

Physical signs of opioid withdrawal consist of early and late phases, with the time of appearance of each phase depending on the duration of action of the specific opiate. The user who realizes that another dose is unobtainable can develop anxiety considerably earlier than actual physiological symptoms. The resulting behavior is called "purposive," focused on obtaining the drug. Symptoms that can be objectively evaluated, independent of environment or other people, are "nonpurposive" (see Chapter 12).

OPIOIDS SUSCEPTIBLE TO NONMEDICAL USE

Almost all medically prescribed opiates can be used inappropriately, either to get high or to substitute for heroin or other opiates (Table 11.2). This is important to remember as opioids, when used as indicated by a physician, can significantly enhance the quality of life of someone in chronic pain. However, inappropriate use of any of these drugs can produce euphoria and markedly interfere with function, with the shorter-acting agents much more easily misused than the longer-acting opioids. Many medically prescribed opiates may be combined with other analgesics such as aspirin or acetaminophen in order to enhance pain relief. One solution used for many years, Brompton's Cocktail, contained cocaine in addition to heroin (or morphine), alcohol, and syrup. Originally used quite successfully for persons with severe pain due to cancer treatment, it has undergone numerous recipe changes over the years and has now finally given way to newer drug combinations.

Opium

Opium is commercially available in a variety of medications. Some years ago, paregoric, a camphorated tincture of opium commonly used for diarrhea, before the development of the synthetic drugs diphenoxylate (Lomotil) and Imodium, was a popular street drug. When paregoric was sold as an over-the-counter medication in the 1960s, heroin addicts regularly boiled it with the antihistamine tripelennamine. The mixture, sold on the street as "blue velvet," was injected. It was first believed that addition of the antihistamine reduced allergic reactions and gave the substance its distinctive smooth consistency. The understanding now is that the antihistamine probably allows greater uptake of opium in the brain. The mixture was so thick that peripheral veins quickly became clotted, and the larger veins in the neck were used. Scarring of the skin over the jugular veins became a sign of blue velvet use.

Morphine and Related Opioids

Codeine

A naturally occurring alkaloid of opium, codeine is found in raw opium in concentrations of 0.7 to 2.5 percent. It is a mild analgesic widely available in combination with acetaminophen (Tylenol), aspirin, and many commercial cough medicines. Codeine used appropriately is an extremely effective analgesic.

TABLE 11.2. Commonly Used Licit Narcotics (Opioids)

Common or Brand Name	Generic Name	Street Name	Potency*
Morphine and related opioids			
Duramorph PF, MSIR, RMS Roxanol, Uniserts, MS cotin	Morphine	Big M, Micro Dots, Miss Emma	1
Codeine			(0.3)
Dilaudid	Hydromorphone	First Line, Fours	6
Hycodan	Hydrocodone		No data
Synalgos-DC DHC plus	Dihydrocodeine	DHC	(0.5)
Levo-Dromoran	Levorphanol		5
Percocet§, Tylox§, Roxiprin§ OxyContin	Oxycodone	Morph, Percolators	2
Codoxy§, Percodan, Roxicet§, Roxicodone		Morphine	2
Numorphan	Oxymorphone	Goma	1
Demerol and related drugs			
Demerol	Meperidine	Cube	0.13
Lomotil	Diphenoxylate, atropine sulfate		
Nisentel	Alphaprodine		0.2
Fentanyl, Sublimaze	Fentanyl	China White	80-100
Methadone and related drugs			
Dolophine	Methadone	Disks, Dollies, Wafers	1
Darvon, Darvon-N, Darvocet§, Doxaphene§, Genagesic§, Profene 65, Propacet§, Wygesic§, E-Lor§	Propoxyphene	Pinks and Grays	0.5

*Compared with 10 mg morphine (injected), except for Percocet, Tylox, Percodan, Codoxy, and Doxaphene, which are taken orally
§Contains acetaminophen or aspirin

Dextromethorphan

Dextromethorphan is a disomer of the codeine analog levorphanol. Although when used as prescribed it lacks analgesic and addictive properties and is quite effective in suppressing cough through central action on the cough center in the brain, when taken in excess, dextromethorphan, or DXM as it is called on the street, can cause euphoria as well as hallucinations. The availability of this drug for such use has blossomed due to Internet sales, with poison control centers around the country recently reporting a marked increase of dextromethorphan overdoses. Its use is felt to be quite prevalent among teenagers due to its ready availability and the public conception of its benign nature. Toxicity is manifested by dysphoria, slurred speech, vomiting, respiratory depression, and convulsions.

Hydromorphone (Dilaudid)

Dilaudid is a semisynthetic derivative of morphine, approximately six to eight times more potent. It's an effective analgesic and can produce a high with a dependency similar to that of morphine when taken either orally or by injection.

Oxycodone and Its Combinations

Percodan, Percocet, Roxicet, Roxiprin, Tylox, and Codoxy are oral analgesics that contain oxycodone plus homatropine, aspirin, or acetaminophen (Tylenol). These commonly prescribed semisynthetic opiates produce a dependency similar to that of morphine when used continuously. Dependency occurs by rapidly escalating the oral dose or by dissolving the tablet in water and injecting the solution. A large amount of oxycodone and aspirin taken orally can cause gastric upset and bleeding, primarily a side effect of the aspirin, while large amounts of oxycodone and acetaminophen, especially in combination with alcohol, can cause liver damage.

OxyContin

OxyContin, a long-lasting form of oxycodone, was introduced in 1996 to better manage chronic pain. Although an effective analgesic, OxyContin is also an extremely potent one, with some preparations containing up to 160 mg of oxycodone as compared to 5 mg doses in the shorter-acting oxycodone preparations. Due in part to the lack of awareness of some physicians prescribing OxyContin, combined with the awareness of its potency and potential for abuse by many on the "street," diversion and abuse of OxyContin started to become a major problem over the past several years.

OxyContin can be chewed, crushed, snorted, or injected to produce a rapid high and an equally rapid dependency. The street market for Oxy-Contin rapidly expanded, with the 40 mg tablets retailing for approximately $300 in pharmacies, selling for $2,400 on the street. Because of this diversion, similar to that seen with inappropriate use of other "pure opioids," overdose deaths, often in combination with alcohol and other mood-altering drugs, are being reported. Treatment for OxyContin dependency is the same as that for dependency on other opioids (Chapter 12). As always, education and prevention are the optimal ways to address this issue. Such efforts must involve not only the public but physicians and other health care providers as well.

Demerol and Related Drugs

Meperidine (Demerol)

Demerol is one of the prototype synthetic opioids called phenylpiperidines. As an analgesic it is only one-quarter as effective as morphine and has a much shorter duration of action. Unlike morphine, Demerol in large doses may result in central nervous system toxicity, ranging from tremors to seizures. These toxic effects are primarily due to the accumulation of normeperidine, a toxic metabolite. Normeperidine is further metabolized in the liver and excreted in the urine by the kidneys, so individuals with liver or kidney disease may be particularly susceptible to its toxicity. The general belief that Demerol is a "mild" narcotic has made it one of the most widely prescribed analgesics. It can be taken orally or by injection. Chronic use several times a day can result in considerable dependency and tolerance.

Diphenoxylate (Lomotil)

Frequently used to treat diarrhea, Lomotil is a derivative of the group of drugs that contain meperidine (Demerol). It also contains atropine sulfate. Its potential to produce dependency is far less than morphine's, and it was once mistakenly thought not to be a narcotic. In that guise, Lomotil was briefly used as a maintenance agent to treat heroin dependency (Chapter 12).

Fentanyl

Fentanyl, another synthetic opiate in the phenylpiperidine group, is approximately 80 times more potent as a pain reliever than morphine. The drug initially was used mainly during anesthesia and in the immediate postoperative period. It is also now marketed in a patch form for use in chronic pain syndrome. In the early 1980s, a fentanyl analog, China white, was being sold on the street, primarily in Southern California. It was 50 to 2,000 times more potent than street heroin. Extremely small amounts provide a high. Compared with heroin, fentanyl provides, according to users, a subtler initial "rush," a longer period of sleepiness following injection, and a more gradual "comedown" (Chapter 12). However, it is far more deadly because of the possibility of overdosing.

Methadone and Derivatives

Methadone

Methadone, one of the phenylheptylamine group of synthetic opiates, was originally synthesized in Germany at the end of World War II when morphine supplies were not readily available. Through the next several decades it received considerable attention in the United States and became the drug of choice for treating chronic, unremitting pain. It was taken off the market soon after first being used as maintenance therapy for heroin addiction (Chapter 12) but became available again for pain relief in 1975.

Methadone is about equal to morphine in actions and potency, but much more effective when taken orally and slightly more potent when injected. Unlike morphine, methadone provides consistent analgesia without the need to rapidly increase the dose because it is widely distributed to body tissues and then slowly released into the bloodstream. These properties are most beneficial to patients in need of continuing pain relief—or maintenance therapy for heroin addiction (Chapter 12). Methadone also allows detoxification from opioids to proceed smoothly. Methadone is rarely used inappropriately when prescribed for pain relief. Its use in maintenance therapy, however, has created a street market, where it is sold to those who (a) do not want to enter heroin treatment programs, (b) want to "boost" their highs, or (c) want to slowly detoxify themselves from heroin without actually entering a treatment program.

Levo-Alpha Acetyl Methadol (LAAM)

LAAM is a long-acting methadone preparation developed specifically for use in maintenance therapy. It suppresses withdrawal symptoms for up to ninety-six hours on a single dose. LAAM is now available for use as a maintenance agent in the treatment of heroin dependency (Chapter 12).

Propoxyphene (Darvon)

Propoxyphene is a derivative of methadone but a less selective mu agonist than methadone or morphine. The drug, which like other opiates produces analgesia, is manufactured in various forms by many companies.

Shortly after propoxyphene was introduced, more than 31 million prescriptions were written, making it the third most commonly prescribed drug. Alone, or in combination with aspirin, phenacetin, or caffeine, in 1987, it ranked approximately fifteenth among the most commonly prescribed drugs in the United States. The analgesic effect is similar to codeine's but its potency is not as great. Propoxyphene is available as both a short-acting and long-acting agent; Darvon-N is the brand name for the latter.

Most physicians consider propoxyphene a relatively safe, nondependency-producing analgesic. But it is an opioid and can lead to dependency, tolerance, and withdrawal when taken in large doses. In addition, one of its metabolites, norpropoxyphene, may contribute to its toxicity, which includes, in addition to respiratory depression, delusions, hallucinations, and adverse cardiac effects. Dependency on the drug became well recognized, and in 1979 the Food and Drug Administration required that a warning of risks be placed on the labels of all products containing propoxyphene, and that printed information be made available to patients. Both toxic reactions and treatment of overdose reactions are similar to those seen with other opioids. Respiratory depressant effects of propoxyphene are also enhanced by alcohol or any other CNS depressant.

OPIATE AGONISTS-ANTAGONISTS

Opiate antagonists with no agonist properties rapidly displace opioids from the receptors in the brain. That action is extremely helpful in treating a pharmacological overdose and can be useful in diagnosing subtle opioid dependency by producing withdrawal symptoms. Efforts to develop an opioid analgesic that produced pain relief without dependency resulted in a new series of drugs with both agonist and antagonist properties (Table 11.3). Although these drugs can displace pure opiate agonists from receptor sites and produce withdrawal, they also have dependency-producing potential.

TABLE 11.3. Opiate Agonists-Antagonists

Brand Name	Generic Name	Potency*
Nubain	Nalbuphine	1
Stadol	Butorphanol	5
Dalgan	Dezocine	1
Talwin, Talwin NX	Pentazocine	0.3
Buprenex	Buprenorphine	25-30

*Compared with 10 mg morphine (injected)

Pentazocine (Talwin)

Talwin was initially promoted as a nonnarcotic analgesic with low risk of dependency. For a time, it was one of the most frequently prescribed analgesics. But its dependency-producing power was amply demonstrated in laboratories in clinical studies and among people for whom it was prescribed, and in some physicians and other professionals who had access to it. The drug quickly became available on the street, being either injected as a mixture with the antihistamine tripelennamine (street name Ts and blues) or injected alone as a heroin substitute. Typical illicit use involves crushing one or two 50 milligram tablets with a tripelennamine tablet, dissolving the powder in water, straining it through cotton, and injecting it intravenously.

The rush from injecting pentazocine is indistinguishable from that of heroin. But it is followed by dysphoria, or a low, and a repeat injection is needed to experience a high. Several injections may be needed. Frequent use can lead to withdrawal similar to that seen with pure opiates. Frequent injections have also caused seizures, apparently the result of tripelennamine's stimulation of the central nervous system.

Talwin is now a Schedule IV drug, which limits prescriptions to six months and requires accurate record keeping. In attempt to prevent inappropriate use, Talwin NX was developed, which contains pentazocine and the pure narcotic antagonist naloxone. When Talwin NX is taken orally, the poor absorption of naloxone in the gastrointestinal tract prevents naloxone from interfering with the analgesic effects of pentazocine. However, if injected intravenously, the naloxone will prevent the high obtained from pentazocine.

Newer Agonists-Antagonists

Some of these drugs have potencies five to forty times greater than that of morphine. They are promoted as having low levels of dependency and therefore can be prescribed without any of the restrictions usually applied to dependency-producing drugs. But since all these drugs have a mood-altering effect, dependency and subsequent addiction can follow. In fact, heroin addicts report that buprenorphine (Buprenex) has essentially the same mood-altering effects as heroin. Inappropriate use of this drug has already been reported. Another brand of the same agent, Stadol, has been diverted from pharmacies in the United States as well. Buprenorphine has been used as maintenance therapy in place of methadone to treat heroin dependency (Chapter 12). Although its effectiveness as a maintenance agent has been demonstrated, its potential for abuse warrants appropriate monitoring if its use becomes a recognized treatment modality.

PARTIAL OPIOID RECEPTOR AGONISTS

In an attempt to develop analgesic agents whose use would not be accompanied by dependency or addiction, scientists began to synthesize a variety of compounds that would have additional effects other than on the opioid receptors or perhaps would affect kappa and delta receptors rather than the mu receptor, which is felt to be responsible not only for the analgesic but also the dependency-producing effects of opioids. These efforts have led to development of several drugs, only one of which is available at the present time.

Tramadol (Ultram)

Ultram is an analgesic agent that acts through binding to mu opioid receptors, as well as preventing the reuptake of norepinephrine and serotonin at the nerve terminals. Tramadol has been shown to be an effective analgesic for moderate pain, although a potential for dependency and/or actual addiction also exists. Since its introduction, addiction has been reported and the manufacturer has now included in the drug information insert a warning against the development of drug dependency and addiction. However, unlike other analgesics released on the market, since Ultram was marketed as a nonscheduled drug, the manufacturer agreed to have an independent steering committee conduct prospective surveillance to detect abuse. Between 1995 and 1998, approximately 900,000 patients a month received this drug. The rates of abuse reported were extremely low, at 0.5 to 1 case per 100,000 patients, with 97 percent of cases of abuse occurring in persons with a past history of drug abuse or dependence.

Experimental Drugs

DPDPE is a substance produced by modifying an endogenous opioid that selectively stimulates the delta receptor and in animal experiments has been able to reduce pain, with a lesser potential for dependency than opioids. Biphalin, a drug believed to be more than 250 times potent than morphine in reducing pain in laboratory models, provides analgesia without significant physical dependence. It is felt that Biphalin acts by simultaneously stimulating both the mu and delta receptors. This is associated with analgesia but not with the side effects seen with only mu receptor stimulation. Both of these substances, however, have difficulty in crossing the blood-brain barrier, which would make them less than optimal analgesics. SNC 80, a delta receptor agonist, has been synthesized to produce analgesia even when given orally. Yet another substance, DOIPP, has been synthesized, which produces analgesia without the development of tolerance or dependency. This substance has been found to be 50 percent more potent than morphine when administered to the brain.

Although much additional work is needed before these compounds become available clinically, it still is important to emphasize that their ability to produce dependency and therefore the potential for misuse in humans, remains unknown and should be carefully evaluated prior to their acceptance as effective analgesics with a low potential for addiction.

Chapter 12

Heroin Addiction

Heroin (diacetylmorphine) is a morphine derivative with three to five times the potency of morphine. It is ironic that heroin, when first synthesized, was originally promoted as a safe drug to be used in the treatment of morphine dependence. This is not surprising, as the pharmacological effects of heroin and morphine are almost identical, with heroin being transformed into morphine within five minutes of injection. In fact, after forty minutes, concentrations of morphine in the blood may exceed those of heroin. The one major difference between injecting pure heroin and pure morphine is the greater speed at which heroin enters the brain (within fifteen to twenty seconds), perhaps precipitating an overdose, as 68 percent of an intravenous injection of heroin is absorbed into the brain compared with 5 percent of an intravenous morphine dose. Heroin is legally available by prescription in England and several other countries but classified as a Schedule I drug in the United States. As an illegal drug, it is supplied only by the street trade.

HEROIN FROM OPIUM: THE STREET TRADE

Preparing heroin from opium is a relatively simple process requiring little sophistication. Raw opium is dissolved in water and "purified" by adding lime salts, ammonium chloride, alcohol, and ether. The mixture is filtered to extract organic wastes, leaving "pure" morphine. This solution is combined with hydrochloric and sulfuric acids, charcoal dust, and water. It's filtered, heated, filtered again, then mixed with ammonia to facilitate separation of morphine. The process yields a brown morphine base, reduced about one-tenth in volume, ready for conversion to heroin.

Producing the morphine base requires only minimal laboratory equipment. Synthesis of heroin is more complicated, taking up to twenty-four hours to pass the base through cycles of mixing with acetic acid anhydride and chloroform to remove impurities. The resulting brown heroin is sold as is, or bleached and treated with hydrochloric acid. Baked and sifted, it becomes a white powder up to 90 percent pure.

Heroin may be sold at any point in the process (Table 12.1). Heroin number 1 is the crude morphine base used in producing more refined products. Heroin number 2 is used for smoking and injection, number 3 mainly for smoking. Many variations exist, and the composition of a specific heroin preparation may change with locality. Once the dealer gets the heroin, all pretense of quality control ceases. The drug passes through several more levels of distribution, and quality consistently decreases as it's cut with a variety of adulterants (Table 12.2), many of them poisonous. The most com-

TABLE 12.1. Types of Heroin

Street Name	Composition and/or Color	Method of Administration
Heroin preparations		
Number 1	Crude morphine base; tan/brown	Smoking
Number 2	White/gray	Injection and smoking
Number 3 White	May contain caffeine (30-50 percent) or small dose of strychnine (rarely); tan/gray	Smoking
Number 4	White to yellow	Injection
Black Tar	Higher-quality heroin	Injection
Iranian Heroin (Dava, Rufus, Persian Brown)	Heroin with adulterants, becoming dark, reddish brown powder	Injection
Red Chicken	Heroin and red dye, fentanyl	Smoking, injection
Heroin combinations		
Mexican Brown	Heroin and coffee	Injection
Bombitas	Heroin and amphetamines	Injection
Speedball	Heroin and cocaine	Injection
Designer heroin		
China White	Fentanyl analogues	Injection
Tango and Cash	Fentanyl analogues	Injection
MPPP, MPTP	Meperidine analogues	Injection
*Other illicit opiate preparations**		
Blue Velvet, Ts and Blues	Pentazocine, tripelennamine	Injection
Loads (Setups)	Codeine, glutethimide (Doriden)	Injection

*Used when heroin is unavailable

TABLE 12.2. Contaminants and Adulterants in Heroin

Amphetamine	Cotton fibers	Nicotine
Baking soda	Fuel oils	Parathion
Barbiturates	Gum resin	Procaine
Battery acid	Lactose	Quinine
Caffeine	Mannite (Mannitol)	Starch
Cocaine	Methapyriline	Strychnine

mon are sugar (lactose) and quinine. Lactose gives the heroin mixture a white color to suggest greater purity. Quinine's bitter taste is similar to heroin's and can confuse the buyer about the mixture's quality and actual heroin content. Dealers may also add coloring to identify their own particular brand or may mix in other mood-altering drugs, such as amphetamines (bombitas) and cocaine (speedballs). Adding such stimulants provides an immediate rush and may also decrease the period of sleepiness that immediately follows a heroin injection.

The concentration or purity of street heroin is unpredictable. Consequently, the user always risks a pharmacological overdose. However, there is no question that over the years the purity of street heroin has considerably increased. In 1984, envelope purity was less than 5 percent as compared to 59 percent purity of small heroin purchased in 1995. Many street names are given to heroin and its combinations (Tables 12.1, 12.3). Some are simply slang; others may refer to a particular type of heroin produced in a particular place. Names are changed regularly to promote sales. A form of heroin, black tar, originated in Mexico and contained much higher proportions of heroin (40 to 80 percent) than the usual samples of street heroin (2 to 6 percent). Black tar is difficult to dilute because of its gummy consistency, giving it a greater potential for overdose. It also attracts moisture from the air to form acetic acid, which can cause severe scarring when injected. Most recently, P-dope, a heroin of high purity cut with lidocaine or procaine, has appeared on the streets.

Some substances sold as heroin may really be designer drugs made by modifying a synthetic narcotic. Derivatives of fentanyl (China white, Tango and Cash) are 3,000 times more potent than morphine and produce a high indistinguishable from that of heroin. Analogues of meperidine (MPPP and MPTP) are also sold on the street as synthetic heroin. They may cause a syndrome resembling Parkinson's disease, which destroys neurons in the brain.

Patterns of Use

Heroin can be taken several ways: smoking, snorting or sniffing, injecting under the skin (skin popping), and injecting intravenously (mainlin-

TABLE 12.3. Street Names for Heroin

Bing	Dynamite	Mud
Boy Jive	Estuffan	Scat
Brown	Foolish Pleasure	Shit
Caballo	Funk	Skag
Chivo	H	Smack
Crap	Hombre	Sugar
Dead on Arrival	Horse	Sweet Jesus
Dope	Jive	Tango and Cash
Doo Doo	Junk	
Duke	La Bamba	

ing)—the most common method. Heroin levels peak in the serum within one minute after intravenous use, three to five minutes after intramuscular or intranasal use, and within five to ten minutes after subcutaneous injection. Frequent use of any of these techniques can result in dependency. Many heroin addicts began by sniffing the drug when they were teenagers. The recent increase in potency of street heroin and concern about HIV and AIDS with injection has not only resulted in an increased number of people snorting heroin but also in a more rapid progression from snorting heroin to injecting as well as a more rapid progression to dependency and addiction.

Mainlining causes the greatest degree of dependency and addiction. The heroin is usually dissolved in water, boiled and then filtered through cotton in a futile effort to remove impurities, and then injected. Shooting up is often a group activity, where a set of works (needles) may be used by dozens of people in one day without being cleaned between uses. This, of course, exposes the user to a wide variety of communicable diseases, including hepatitis and the human immunodeficiency virus (HIV), the cause of AIDS (Chapter 18).

GETTING HIGH AND COMING DOWN

Several seconds after injection of heroin, a flush and warmth are felt throughout the body as heroin enters the brain, followed by drowsiness. The user appears to be asleep at that point but can be aroused and will respond to questions. Next comes a high that can last for several hours, followed by a feeling of relaxation. At this time the user may function normally and except for constriction of the pupils, it is not always apparent that heroin use is present.

Since heroin is a short-acting drug, frequent injections are necessary in order to achieve euphoria. Each time heroin is injected, it rapidly occupies the opioid receptors. Although tolerance will develop with repeated injections, since the objective of the heroin user is to get high, repeated injections with larger quantities of heroin will occur and, as a result, the heroin user rarely is functioning appropriately. The time it takes for dependency to develop depends on several factors, including frequency, quantity of heroin injected, and even the user's expectations. Dependency can appear after several days of frequent injections, with early signs of withdrawal being due more to anxiety over obtaining another dose of heroin (purposive behavior) than to the actual signs and symptoms due to the physiological changes that occur after heroin use has stopped (nonpurposive behavior). Even after withdrawal has been completed, drug craving due to the heroin-induced disturbances in the neuronal systems may occur, making it quite difficult to remain abstinent.

Purposive behavior includes extreme nervousness or anxiety, demands for money and/or drugs, and an increased level of activity. This type of behavior peaks within twenty-four hours and can be modified greatly by a sympathetic observer and a calm environment.

Nonpurposive symptoms range from mild to severe (Table 12.4) and generally appear eight to twelve hours after the last injection. Untreated, the symptoms become intense within thirty-six to forty-eight hours, then gradually subside over the next week. Acute withdrawal symptoms can be eliminated at any time by administering an opiate. Late signs and symptoms of withdrawal, however, have been observed for up to two years following heroin use and consist of loss of energy, insomnia, and craving for opiates.

PREVALENCE

In the 1970s, it was estimated that approximately 400,000 people used heroin, with this number remaining fairly stable over the next ten years.

TABLE 12.4. Heroin Withdrawal Signs and Symptoms

Mild	Moderate	Marked	Severe
Yawning	Loss of appetite	Deep breathing	Vomiting
Tearing of eyes	Dilated pupils	Fever	Abdominal cramps
Nausea	Tremors	Restlessness	Diarrhea
Running nose	Gooseflesh*	Agitation	Muscle spasms§
Sneezing		Elevated blood	
Sweating		pressure	

*Termed "cold turkey"
§Termed "kicking the habit"

However, as the purity of heroin on the streets increased and concerns developed over the transmission of HIV through shared needles, heroin use by sniffing or snorting started to increase, and the age at which this use began decreased. Data from the 2000 Monitoring the Future Survey recorded a rise in lifetime prevalence of heroin use among twelfth graders from 0.9 percent in 1991 to 2.4 percent in 2000 with snorting being the predominant form of use. Data from the National Household Survey on Drug Abuse estimated that approximately 2.4 million persons used heroin at least once in their lifetime and approximately 455,000 used heroin at least in the past year, with 149,000 new users in 1998. Of the new heroin users, a large proportion were young (25 percent under eighteen) and were sniffing or snorting heroin rather than injecting it. Most recent estimates (1997) place the number of opioid-dependent persons in the United States as high as 600,000. It was estimated that among lifetime heroin users, the proportion of those who smoked, sniffed, or snorted heroin increased from 55 percent in 1994 to 82 percent in 1996, suggesting again that sniffing or snorting has become considerably more common. This was confirmed by data concerning persons using heroin admitted to emergency departments between twelve and seventeen years of age. Total emergency room admissions due to heroin use among persons ages twelve to seventeen increased by 277 percent between 1990 and 1994. In this cohort, the percentage sniffing, inhaling, or smoking heroin rose from 15 percent in 1991 to 41 percent in 1995, while the percentage associated with injecting decreased from 30 to 22 percent during this time.

Heroin addiction, of course, is not confined to the United States. It can be found in virtually all countries, with an estimated 8 million people using this drug each year. In those countries without a heroin problem, not infrequently there is a segment of the population who are dependent on opium.

ADVERSE EFFECTS

Many severe and often life-threatening complications result from heroin use (Table 12.5). The types of complication vary with patterns of use. Thus, while injection either by mainlining or skin popping (subcutaneous use) can be accompanied by virtually any complication, sniffing is associated with a lesser risk of overdose and infectious diseases. Virtually all are related entirely to impurities or contaminants in the drug, unsterile injection, and injection of an unknown strength of heroin.

Acute Fatal Reaction

At one time, the acute fatal reaction accounted for 80 percent of heroin addict deaths in New York City. Although death may strike so fast that the

TABLE 12.5. Complications of Heroin Use

Acute fatal reaction

Allergic and febrile reactions

Cardiovascular system
Rhythm disturbances, infarction of heart valves (endocarditis), inflammation of small arteries (vasculitis), inflammation and clotting of veins (thrombophlebitis)

Dermatological problems
Abscesses, ulcers, hyperpigmented areas, track marks, scarring, swelling

Endocrine system
Low blood sugar, sexual dysfunction

Gastrointestinal tract
Decreased stomach emptying, bile secretion, and intestinal activity; constipation

Hematological and immunological abnormalities

Liver
Hepatitis B, C, chronic liver disease

Immunological abnormalities including HIV infection and AIDS

Infections in multiple organ systems including tetanus and botulism

Respiratory system
Increased susceptibility to pulmonary infections; increased pressure in pulmonary vessels

---

user is often found with the needle still stuck in a vein and a hand on the syringe, this is felt to occur rarely. Most often death occurs one to three hours following an injection and is therefore preventable if medical assistance is promptly obtained. Unfortunately, this often does not happen despite the fact that most of these reactions occur in the presence of other people. Indeed, surveys have shown that 33 percent of heroin users had experienced an overdose in the past year, and 86 percent had been in the presence of someone with an overdose. Yet, an ambulance was called in less than half the cases. The failure to obtain help rapidly has been attributed to trust in house remedies and fear of police involvement.

For many years, such deaths were believed to result from a true pharmacological overdose, an understandable conclusion since a bag of heroin might contain from 0 to 10 milligrams of the pure drug. Accumulation of evidence, however, failed to support pharmacological overdose as the major cause of death. For one thing, postmortem toxicology reports were positive for morphine or heroin in only half the cases. When those drugs were detected, their levels were quite low, with other drugs also identified. The Medical Examiner's Office in New York City has found that half of those who die from an acute fatal reaction have detectable levels of blood alcohol, which in 25 percent of the cases exceeds 0.1 percent. Between 5 and 12 percent also had significant levels of benzodiazepines.

Second, when a group of people have shared heroin, only one might experience an overdose. The inferior quality of the heroin on the street or in the bags surrounding the deceased also make it unlikely that pharmacological overdose would occur in someone with high tolerance. Many factors unrelated to actual heroin concentrations may contribute to a death (Table 12.6). One of the most common is use of multiple drugs, including alcohol and other CNS depressants. Several postmortem studies of heroin addicts have shown alcoholic cirrhosis to be the most common form of liver disease, a finding that also implicates excess alcohol use in overdose reactions.

When the death is sudden, it is often associated with marked fluid accumulation in the lungs and brain, similar to severe allergic reactions to such drugs as penicillin. Considering the various adulterants and contaminants in heroin, allergic reactions might be expected. Another cause may be suppression of the gag reflex and aspiration of stomach contents into the lungs. This can happen when heroin is injected after a full meal and the user becomes sleepy. Suffocation and death follow. In some cases, contaminants (Table 12.2), notably quinine, can affect cardiac rhythm. When combined with heroin's depressant effect on the central nervous system and a drop in oxygen level, abnormal heart rhythms may be fatal. Of course, a true pharmacological overdose may sometimes be the cause of death. It may become more prevalent as more potent forms of heroin, including designer drugs, appear on the street.

Treating the Acute Fatal Reaction

Someone who is undergoing an acute reaction to heroin must be taken to a medical facility as quickly as possible. An open airway must be maintained, artificial respiration applied, and oxygen given, if needed. At the medical facility, the opiate antagonist naloxone should be administered im-

TABLE 12.6. Causes of Acute Fatal Reaction

Alcohol and multiple drug use
Allergic reaction
Aspiration of stomach contents
Changes in cardiac rhythms
Pharmacological overdose

---

mediately. If the problem is overdose, the drug will reverse the action of the heroin. Since the action of naloxone does not last longer than twenty to forty minutes, the person should be observed for several hours to make certain that signs of heroin toxicity do not recur. If, indeed, the reaction is secondary to an allergic phenomenon, multiple drug toxicities, or cardiovascular toxicity, then admission and careful monitoring are warranted. Admission with monitoring is also necessary if a long-acting opioid, such as methadone, is responsible. In such instances, frequent doses of naloxone are needed.

Unfortunately, treatment is often delayed as homemade remedies—never appropriate—are typically tried first. Coffee is urged on the person as a stimulant. The person may be slapped or doused with cold water. Fluids are forced down the throat to induce vomiting. Salt may be injected under the skin in an effort to "draw out" the heroin. Such measures serve only to seriously delay proper treatment and to worsen the situation if vomiting is induced. The acute fatal reaction need not cause death if prompt and correct measures are taken.

Other Complications

Infections

Infections are the most common complications of heroin use because contaminated material is often injected into the body under unsterile conditions. Almost every organ system can be affected.

Infection of the heart valves (endocarditis) often results in significant destruction of the valve with a progressive impairment of heart function. Surgical replacement of the damaged valve is often required.

Multiple pulmonary infections are frequent. They can range from pneumonia to lung abscesses, formed when pieces of contaminated material travel from the veins through the right side of the heart and into the lungs. Infections can also occur in the muscles, bones, and brain. All have chronic, often disastrous complications.

Localized infections at the injection site are particularly common. Abscesses beneath the skin from skin popping, track marks (veins clotted from infections), and puffiness of the arms and hands from old infections are all signs of injecting contaminated material and/or using unsterile needles. Most recently, instances of tetanus and botulism have appeared in intravenous drug users who inject subcutaneously or intramuscularly.

Liver Disease

Hepatitis B, a viral infection of the liver, has long been known to be regularly transmitted through shared needles. Laboratory evidence of liver dysfunction due to hepatitis exists in up to 75 percent of users. The illness may subside or become chronic and ultimately lead to cirrhosis. Since many heroin addicts also drink large quantities of alcohol, the role of alcohol in chronic liver disease must also be considered. More recently, hepatitis C, initially identified in 1988, also has been shown to be prominent among those who inject drugs, accounting for almost two-thirds of hepatitis C infections. It is not only more prevalent than HIV infection but is more common than hepatitis B as well. Insidious in its progression, hepatitis C infection, which can exist over fifteen to twenty-five years in up to 75 percent of people exposed to the virus, has become among the most common reasons for liver failure and transplantation. All persons with a history of intravenous drug use should be tested for antibodies to hepatitis C (Anti-HCV), and, if positive, one should measure the presence of virus in their system (HCV RNA), reviewing with a physician whether treatment is warranted.

Effects on the Immune System

Heroin use also affects the immune system; enlargement of the lymph nodes is a routine finding in users. The many immunological abnormalities also identified in heroin users are highly likely to increase susceptibility to all infections, including AIDS (Chapter 18). Transmission of HIV by shared needles is the most recent in a long line of complications associated with heroin dependency, with intravenous drug use representing up to one-third of all new cases of AIDS.

Effects on the Central Nervous System

Multiple and sometimes deadly effects of heroin use involve the central nervous system: overdose reactions with depression and coma, paralysis caused by destruction of the spinal cord lining (demyelination), local nerve impairment, and extensive muscle damage following injection of contaminated mixtures. Some of those complications can be severe enough to cause considerable disability, impairing use of the arms or legs.

Effects on the Cardiovascular System

In addition to endocarditis, abnormal cardiac rhythms and acute inflammation of the blood vessels (vasculitis) may be attributed to heroin. Even after a valve is replaced surgically, the compulsive use of heroin may destroy the prosthetic valve and create the need for yet another open-heart surgery.

Kidney Disease

Chronic heroin use affects the kidneys by persistent blood in the urine and disease of the kidney cells, causing renal shutdown. Long-term hemodialysis is a real possibility for addicts.

Endocrinological Disturbances

Disturbances in the endocrine system range from lowered blood sugar to difficulty with sexual functioning in men. Women who use heroin are especially prone to complications of childbirth and the reproductive system (Chapter 19). Menstrual irregularities include amenorrhea (failed periods) and infertility from disruption of normal ovarian function. The increased sexual activity of women heroin addicts who need money to support their habit results in frequent exposure to venereal disease. This may lead to pelvic infections that cause scarring of the fallopian tubes and subsequent infertility. Scarring of the fallopian tubes also places women at additional risk during conception and childbirth.

THE CHALLENGE OF TREATING HEROIN ADDICTION

Just as with other addictive behaviors, treating heroin addiction is filled with frustration. Understanding why someone turns to drugs in general, and to heroin in particular, is a valuable point of departure. It should be noted that not everyone who uses heroin becomes addicted to it. "Chipping," the injection of heroin on weekends or twice a week, can occur for long periods without producing physical dependency or addiction. Yet progression to continuous use is accompanied by addictive behavior and physical dependency. As described in Chapter 3, successful treatment must address both psychological and sociological issues as well as the physiological changes caused by heroin (Table 12.7).

Several treatment approaches are available for treating heroin addicts (Table 12.8). Despite considerable effort, no one has been able to define a single treatment profile that works for everyone. So no one form of therapy is clearly better than any other. Each approach can prove effective under a specific circumstance. A melding or integration of several approaches may be needed to come up with the best plan for each person.

Detoxification and Withdrawal

Abstinence can be achieved solely by discontinuing heroin use, but withdrawal symptoms will occur in varying intensity depending on the level of dependency. The symptoms, in order of increasing intensity, include anxi-

TABLE 12.7. Principles for Treating Heroin Addiction

Address reasons for starting heroin use

Address physiological changes produced by heroin dependency

Address both short- and long-term changes produced by abstinence and withdrawal

Decrease reinforcement associated with heroin use

Eliminate conditioning or environmental effects that promote use and accentuate drug craving

Change long-term behavior to maximize chance of remaining abstinent

Provide training and help develop skills needed for productive participation in society

TABLE 12.8. Approaches for Treating Heroin Addiction

Detoxification
Psychotherapy and other outpatient programs
Therapeutic communities
Maintenance therapy
Opiate antagonists
Narcotics Anonymous and other self-help groups
Acupuncture

ety, craving for the drug, restlessness, insomnia, gooseflesh, running nose, perspiration, yawning, muscle and bone pain, abdominal cramps, and fever. These symptoms are at the least uncomfortable and usually lead to drug-seeking behavior within hours of withdrawal. Withdrawal symptoms should never be allowed to develop in someone dependent on heroin or other opiates, unless this negative effect is part of a conditioned-behavior therapy (aversion therapy). Even then, permitting withdrawal to occur is controversial.

Short of just stopping drug use (cold turkey), detoxification is the simplest and quickest way to become abstinent (Chapter 6). Detoxification allows the blood level of heroin (morphine) to be gradually lowered, decreasing the tolerance threshold to slowly prevent withdrawal symptoms. It is essential to emphasize, however, that detoxification is not a treatment for heroin addiction but only the first step in the process to become and remain abstinent. Failure to realize this will result in a considerable risk of recidivism once a person has successfully detoxified. To combat the perceived heroin epidemic of the 1970s, several cities developed clinics that could provide detoxification services on relatively short notice. Referral was then made to a treatment facility. Such clinics gave immediate relief to those on long waiting lists to enter programs and to others who believed they could remain drug free if they could avoid withdrawal without entering a formal treatment program. Many successfully completed the detoxification process, but just as many returned to heroin use after several days.

A variety of techniques can be used in the detoxification process (Table 12.9). The simplest is to provide oral methadone in decreasing doses (by approximately 10 to 15 percent each day) until detoxification is complete. This process can take eight to ten days and can be accomplished without difficulty, allowing time to assess what further assistance can be provided to enhance rehabilitation. Detoxification from methadone maintenance programs requires a longer time frame and is discussed later.

Rapid Detoxification

In an attempt to shorten the detoxification process without producing symptoms, clonidine (Catapres) has been used to diminish the effects produced by hyperactivity of the noraderenegic neuronal system during withdrawal. As discussed in Chapter 3, opiates inhibit secretion of norepinephrine by depressing the activity of the locus coeruleus (LC) cells. When these cells become tolerant to chronic opiate exposure, they must work harder to produce the body's normal quota of norepinephrine. To maintain an equilibrium, the number of binding sites in the LC also increases. When heroin is suddenly discontinued, the "restraints" are removed; the cells become hyperactive and greatly increase the secretion of norepinephrine, with clinical signs of withdrawal following.

Clonidine (Catapres), used to treat high blood pressure, is quite effective in blocking norepinephrine release. By thus decreasing norepinephrine ac-

TABLE 12.9. Detoxification

Principles	Protocols	Time
Minimize or suppress withdrawal symptoms	Ultrarapid	24 hours
Is not a therapy for addiction	Rapid	3-6 days
Provides only a respite from addiction	Regular	14-180 days*
No difference in abstinence between those detoxified and those not detoxified		
Must be followed by treatment regimen		

*For persons in methadone maintenance who wish a slow detoxification.

tivity, clonidine suppresses the signs and symptoms of opiate withdrawal, allowing a relatively quick detoxification without opiates. The drug was considered to be particularly valuable with people on low-dose methadone therapy, because methadone detoxification and withdrawal can take weeks or months. By adjusting the dose of clonidine and adding a narcotic antagonist such as naltrexone or naloxone to quickly displace all of the opioids from the opioid receptors, withdrawal symptoms can be minimized and withdrawal accomplished within three days. The use of a transdermal clonidine patch has also been found quite helpful, allowing continuous delivery of clonidine at a relatively constant dose.

When clonidine was first used in detoxification, the medical community had great hopes that it might be given to anyone who didn't want further treatment or a prolonged detoxification. But side effects and complications quickly appeared. Most common was substantially lowered blood pressure. Managing that often required a medical setting. Feelings of sedation, depression, insomnia, and muscle pains were also reported. Since some of these symptoms are the same as those seen during withdrawal, the precise role played by clonidine was unclear. Other drugs with similar capabilities of suppressing norepinephrine secretion continue to be studied. They include lofexidine, guanfacine, and guanabenz (Wytensin).

Ultrarapid Opioid Detoxification (UROD)

Still not satisfied with a three-day detoxification process, several physicians developed an "ultrarapid" opioid detoxification protocol that allows a person under general anesthesia to have all of the opioid rapidly displaced from the receptors while diminishing symptoms through the use of clonidine and anesthesia. Since the person is anesthetized, there is no awareness of discomfort, and within twenty-four hours the person is awakened and allowed to leave, hopefully to begin the rehabilitative effort with naltrexone as a maintenance drug to prevent euphoria if heroin is taken. Initially started abroad, a number of clinics offering UROD have appeared in this country, charging between $3,000 to $10,000 for the twenty-four-hour detoxification process. Since UROD involves general anesthesia, not surprisingly, there has been considerable controversy about its safety as well as its long-term effects. Despite claims of proponents as to its safety and effectiveness, few, if any, well-designed studies have appeared in the literature. Deaths have been reported with this technique, and the altered tolerance resulting from naltrexone may increase the risk of a heroin overdose, if the naltrexone is discontinued. In addition, since detoxification itself is not an end to therapy, the need to detoxify a person within twenty-four hours has also been questioned. As a result of these issues, better designed studies are needed to assess safety and efficacy before UROD can be recommended as a routine detoxification procedure.

Tetrodotoxin

Tetrodotoxin (Tetrodin) is a potent toxin defensively secreted by the puffer fish indigenous to the waters surrounding Japan. Tetrodotoxin blocks the sodium currents and is believed to have potential as a potent analgesic and as an effective agent in detoxification from heroin addiction without withdrawal symptoms and without producing physical dependence. Its effectiveness is currently being evaluated through clinical trials in Canada.

Psychotherapeutic Approaches

Because intense depression and anxiety are often seen in heroin addicts, early treatment efforts focused on the reasons for starting drug use. These attempts at psychotherapy were less than successful. Freud noted that addicts were poor candidates for psychoanalysis because they lacked the necessary character and discipline. Psychiatrists and psychologists have certainly been discouraged by the antisocial personality traits of many addicts and in general have avoided treating those who are dependent on heroin. Heroin users often have difficulty forming meaningful relationships and not infrequently are aggressive and manipulative. So it's easy to understand the lack of enthusiasm when it comes to treating heroin addiction with a purely psychotherapeutic approach.

However, although many heroin addicts have antisocial characteristics, just as many are depressed and anxious. The latter inject heroin as much to relieve their pain and anxiety as to obtain a high. For that reason, they can benefit from psychotherapy, in combination with other approaches. One such use of modified psychotherapy is the counseling provided at drug-free outpatient units. These facilities sometimes use former heroin addicts as counselors or employ trained therapists. These settings have little structure, and whether meaningful, ongoing relationships can be established in such a brief time frame remains to be demonstrated.

Residential (Therapeutic) Communities

Probably the best-known treatment approaches for heroin addiction are therapeutic communities, or TCs (Chapter 6). Their great appeal lies in their effort to establish a drug-free environment while helping a person achieve abstinence. Heroin addiction is seen not as the primary problem but as a symptom. The problem is the person, not the drug. The focus is on letting the individual develop a socially productive, drug-free lifestyle.

According to TC philosophy, that kind of substantive life change can take place only in a live-in environment that provides a social, learning context through role modeling and identification with others. Those others may be staff or peers, almost all of whom have overcome a similar problem. The addict is helped to examine the reasons he or she started taking drugs and the kinds of stresses to expect on returning to the former environment. Outside influences are minimized during residency and are dealt with at a later time when the person in treatment is better prepared to cope.

The induction phase at most therapeutic communities lasts up to two months, followed by the primary treatment phase of up to twelve months and a reentry phase of up to two years. The induction phase, which orients a person to the rules and regulations of the community, is probably the most difficult to accept. It's when relationships are formed within the community and specific duties are assigned.

In the primary treatment phase, the person gets a full and varied schedule, including educational and vocational chores. Understanding the conditions surrounding heroin use is part of the educational objective. An orderly, regimented environment is provided for those whose search for drugs made chaos of their lives. Part of the treatment is the confrontation technique, a process that challenges those who are not living up to the standards of the community. It's an emotionally draining process that is difficult for many people to tolerate. Individual changes are carefully monitored, with feedback and support constantly provided.

The reentry phase prepares the person to rejoin the community at large. Appropriate educational and vocational counseling tries to pinpoint the stresses and frustrations likely to be encountered. During the early reentry phase, the individual remains mainly within the TC as discharge plans are developed. In the late reentry phase, residents are allowed to move freely in the outside community in full-time jobs or educational activities.

Approximately 14 percent of all patients in federally funded facilities for drug dependency are admitted to TCs. The success rates of TCs are comparable to those of other programs. Of those who complete the process, about 70 percent achieve favorable outcomes, with 30 percent able to remain drug free. The dropout rate, especially in the early stages of therapy, is high, however, with successful abstinence related to time spent in treatment. After treatment is completed, people are encouraged to participate in networks that strengthen the resolve to remain abstinent.

Maintenance Therapy

The concept of maintenance therapy for heroin addiction is far from new. In the late 1800s and early 1900s, physicians freely prescribed morphine and opium preparations were widely available in a variety of over-the-counter preparations. But the 1914 Harrison Act suddenly diminished the availability of opium preparations, and physicians became wary of prescribing opiates. In 1919, physicians were prevented from prescribing opiates solely to maintain a dependency. To provide relief for the unknown number of addicts, at least forty-four clinics were opened in cities across the United States to dispense heroin or provide prescriptions for heroin or morphine. The precise number of people treated at these facilities nationwide is unknown, but in New York City about 7,000 people were registered in one year. The effectiveness of legal distribution of heroin or morphine in preventing crime and allowing addicts to engage in socially productive activities was never documented. But the public considered the legal maintenance of these addicts immoral, and outrage over such activity led to the closing of all the clinics by 1924.

Maintenance therapy—demonstrated to be effective in treating heroin dependency—is no less controversial today. Supporters promote maintenance as a way to help people become functioning members of society. Critics say that, at best, it's another form of opiate dependency. Much of the controversy stems from ignorance of the rationale of maintenance therapy, its effectiveness, and its limitations.

Basis for Maintenance Therapy

The lessons learned from laboratory models (Chapter 3) and observation of heroin addicts provide the rationale behind maintenance therapy (Table 12.10). Five premises are involved.

Premise 1. Dependency produces biochemical and physiological changes that make it difficult for a formerly dependent person to remain abstinent. These changes involve the development of tolerance to opiates and are

TABLE 12.10. Rationale for Maintenance Therapy in Heroin Addiction

Heroin-produced biochemical changes in the body make abstinence difficult to achieve and maintain.

Therapy facilitates normal functioning by providing doses at tolerance threshold. Maintaining tolerance prevents discomfort of withdrawal.

Slow elevation of tolerance threshold prevents a high from injection of street heroin.

With drug-seeking behavior eliminated and comfort level maintained, rehabilitative effort can begin.

Slow detoxification from maintenance therapy, accompanied by supportive services, can result in prolonged abstinence.

responsible for the severe distress of withdrawal. In the nontolerant, non-opiate user, the opiate receptors control the body's response to stress by synthesizing and releasing endorphins and enkephalins. Used repeatedly, heroin occupies the receptor sites, decreasing synthesis of the natural opiates and affecting normal endocrine and immune functioning.

As tolerance develops, a fixed dose of heroin has less and less effect on the system. But at the same time, the cells that secrete the neurotransmitter norepinephrine become less active, requiring more cells to work at the task of maintaining constant levels of norepinephrine in the body. So long as heroin is injected, the system is regulated by the "outside" influence. But the equilibrium is disturbed when blood and brain heroin levels drop. The natural opiates that regulate secretion of norepinephrine are gone, as is the inhibiting effect of the heroin, and norepinephrine pours out of the cells. The increased levels are responsible for withdrawal symptoms, narcotic craving, and, most often, a rapid return to heroin use.

Premise 2. A conditioning effect due to the action of heroin on the brain and the environment where heroin is injected makes it difficult to remain drug free. Placing someone who has been drug free back in an environment where he or she previously used heroin can lead to craving for the drug, withdrawal symptoms, and a return to heroin use.

Premise 3. A heroin user can function normally when blood levels of morphine do not exceed the tolerance threshold (Chapter 3). Indeed, many people seemingly lead functional lives even when they are dependent. Function is impaired only when the tolerance threshold is exceeded or the blood levels of morphine drop too rapidly below this threshold, resulting in withdrawal. Thus, maintaining the individual at the tolerance threshold avoids withdrawal and decreases drug-seeking behavior due to physiological changes or the conditioning effect.

Premise 4. Slowly raising the tolerance threshold with appropriately administered opiates produces neither a high nor an overdose. A threshold can be raised enough in that way to prevent a high from injection of street heroin. Without the high, the conditioning and reinforcement of injection begin to disappear, since the individual is disinclined to spend money on something that doesn't produce the desired effects.

Premise 5. With heroin-seeking behavior eliminated and the individual maintained at a comfortable tolerance threshold, it is possible to examine the reasons for initial drug use, to isolate the steps that must be taken to prevent relapse, and to identify the kind of training required to help the person become a functioning member of society. Once the lifestyle has changed and heroin is no longer being used, the tolerance threshold can be slowly lowered through detoxification, with abstinence being maintained.

The objectives of maintenance therapy are also quite clear (Table 12.11). Unlike other forms of therapy, however, prevention of heroin use is achieved by having a person maintain a tolerance threshold sufficient to prevent the injection of even extremely pure heroin to produce a high, thereby eliminating the incentive to resort to illicit drug use.

Choice of Opiate in Maintenance Therapy

All opiates (narcotics) can be interchanged if given in equivalent doses. So theoretically, any opiate can be used in maintenance therapy. In fact when maintenance therapy was first considered, some utilized long-acting propoxyphine (Darvon) or Lomotil for maintenance, under the mistaken impression they were not true narcotics. The ideal drug, however, would have to fulfill certain criteria (Table 12.12). It would have to be (a) in a form that can be taken orally to break the behavior associated with injection; (b) relatively long-acting, so the receptor-neurotransmitter system is regulated correctly and can return to a state of equilibrium; and (c) readily absorbed to provide consistent serum levels, with a specific dose taken up by body tissues and released in the blood at a constant level to increase the time and decrease the intensity of withdrawal if it were abruptly discontinued.

TABLE 12.11. Objectives of Maintenance Therapy

Prevent opiate withdrawal
Prevent drug craving or drug hunger
Normalize physiological function
Maintain at tolerance threshold to prevent euphoria
Prevent recurrent illicit opiate use
Address psychological and sociological issues leading to drug use
Maintain abstinence when drug free

TABLE 12.12. Profile for a Potential Pharmacotherapeutic Agent for Treatment of Addiction

1. Effective after oral administration
   - Minimum systemic bioavailability after oral administration > 35 percent
   - Optimal systemic bioavailability after oral administration > 70 percent
2. Long biological half-life in humans
   - Plasma apparent terminal half-life > 20-24 hours
3. Minimal side effects during chronic administration
4. Safe—no true toxic or serious adverse effects
5. Efficacious for a substantial percentage of persons with the disorder

Heroin Maintenance

Use of heroin and/or morphine for maintenance therapy has some advocates. However, that approach is impractical. To be effective, those drugs would have to be injected several times a day. When injected frequently, they can cause wide fluctuations of mental states because of their constantly changing levels in the brain. Further, the need to prescribe syringes for injections would allow a greater risk for HIV and hepatitis virus transmission. Diversion would also be a significant problem, especially if the heroin were taken by a nontolerant person. Even as tolerance increases, the injection of greater quantities of a short-acting opiate would continue to affect functions.

In England, when government-approved maintenance programs were established in the late 1960s, heroin was the drug first prescribed. However, as expected, although chemically pure heroin was administered, users continued to supplement their habits by injecting heroin from other sources, and the incidence of needle-transmitted hepatitis was still quite high. In addition, due to overprescribing, a black market in heroin soon developed. As problems of heroin as a maintenance drug became apparent, most programs in England switched to methadone, initially by injection but later in oral form in the 1970s.

Recently, however, in Europe, several attempts at heroin maintenance have resurfaced for those who have rejected methadone maintenance, the most prominent in Switzerland, when on June 13, 1999, a majority of Swiss voters endorsed a plan to allow heroin addicts to receive heroin under medical supervision. An initial evaluation of the Swiss effort revealed that prescription of injectable heroin as maintenance therapy is feasible. Although significant reductions in consumption of other illicit drugs were reported, these were self-reports not confirmed by urinalysis. Yet, one-third of the group continued to use marijuana, 6 percent had daily illicit heroin use, 5 percent had daily cocaine use, and 9 percent had daily benzodiazepine use. These findings have encouraged other countries to study the use of heroin as a maintenance drug as well. However, it must be remembered that, since heroin is a short-acting drug, it is quite difficult to be maintained on it while leading a socially productive life. Although there would be benefits to society such as a decrease in crime, ultimately, providing a drug that must be taken frequently by injection to maintain function and that is accompanied by a high does not allow an individual to achieve his or her potential. In addition, by legalizing such efforts, heroin maintenance sends a poor message to the young, the group that ultimately will perpetuate heroin dependency.

Methadone Maintenance

When maintenance therapy was first initiated, with one exception, all medically available oral opiates had to be given every four to six hours and had a variable absorption from the gastrointestinal tract, which caused blood levels to fluctuate. The exception was oral methadone. In reviewing the requirements for a maintenance agent, Vincent Dole, Marie Nyswander and Mary Jeanne Kreek concluded in 1964 that methadone met all of these requirements.

Methadone (Chapter 11) is about equal in potency to morphine but is much longer acting. When taken by mouth, it sustains plasma levels for approximately twenty-four to thirty-six hours. It is rapidly absorbed from the gastrointestinal tract, 99 percent is bound in the tissues, and levels in the tissues and the blood are quickly equalized. As the methadone blood level falls, more is released from the tissues to sustain a steady supply in the bloodstream. The methadone keeps the opiate receptors occupied, allowing behavior to normalize and receptor-neurotransmitter functions to continue at consistent levels. That is why methadone works in maintenance therapy. However, it is quite important to realize that there is a great deal of individual variability in the metabolism of methadone, with the blood levels varying up to sevenfold on a constant oral dose of methadone in different persons. It is usually agreed that a concentration of methadone of 400 ng/ml is needed to be consistently effective. This can usually be obtained with a daily methadone dose of 80 to 120 mg per day. However, it must be emphasized that, depending on a person's metabolism of methadone, medical status, and coexisting medications, a daily dose of greater than 120 mg may be required.

The concomitant use of other drugs that enhance methadone metabolism can cause blood levels of methadone to fall, causing discomfort and, at times, a return to heroin use. These drugs include rifampicin (used to treat tuberculosis), carbamazepine, phenytoin, and phenobarbital (used to treat epilepsy), some steroids, spironolactone (a diuretic), and ritonavir and nalfinavir (used to treat AIDS). Infection with hepatitis C has also been found to often result in the need to increase the dose of methadone, with one study suggesting that the methadone requirement may be 50 percent greater.

On the other hand, some drugs inhibit the breakdown of methadone and serve to increase its concentration in the blood. These drugs include benzodiazepines such as Valium, Procardia (used to treat hypertension), and fluoxetine (an antidepressant). Grapefruit juice has also been reported to increase methadone levels in the blood, although this remains to be confirmed.

Before its use in maintenance therapy, methadone was the drug of choice for controlling such chronic painful conditions as severe deforming arthritis and cancer, and in detoxification from opiate dependency. Its effectiveness in detoxification had been demonstrated at the U.S. Public Health Service

Hospital in Lexington, Kentucky, in 1946. Ironically, for a number of years after methadone was approved for maintenance, physicians weren't permitted to use it for pain control because of public concern about its potential for inappropriate use. Reason finally prevailed, and methadone once again was prescribed for chronic pain control.

Effectiveness of Methadone Maintenance

The pilot program for methadone maintenance was initiated at Rockefeller University using volunteer "hard-core" criminals over the age of twenty-one who had been addicted for at least four years and had been unable to kick their habits. Methadone was administered in an orange-flavored commercial drink, Tang, in slowly increasing amounts up to a daily maintenance dose of 80 to 100 milligrams. The subjects consistently said they had no need to seek out heroin and felt rather normal throughout the day.

The group reported that, for the first time since becoming heroin addicts, they were able to focus on non-heroin-related activities such as seeking educational or vocational training, and establishing social relationships. Arrest rates dropped significantly, and the medical complications of heroin use were no longer seen. Essential parts of treatment were careful monitoring of urine for use of heroin and other mood-altering drugs, frequent clinic visits, medical evaluations, and counseling services.

Minimal standards for methadone programs were established by the Food and Drug Administration and the National Institute on Drug Abuse in keeping with the Narcotics Treatment Act of 1974, followed by a slow but steady increase in use of methadone for maintenance. The number of people on methadone maintenance peaked in 1977, with 80,000 persons nationwide. The number of people in treatment declined through the 1980s for a variety of reasons, including failure of funding to keep pace with increasing costs of living, availability of other treatment approaches, and a persistent public opinion that maintenance therapy is morally wrong. According to the Substance Abuse and Mental Health Services Administration, over the past decade the number of persons receiving methadone or LAAM has increased so that, as of 1997, approximately 138,000 persons were on maintenance therapy, with 98 percent receiving methadone. About 25 to 30 percent of those now in treatment for opioid dependency are receiving methadone maintenance.

Evaluation of Methadone Programs

Since its inception, methadone programs have been perhaps the most carefully monitored treatment modality in modern medicine. Evaluations have consistently demonstrated the effectiveness of this approach, with success rates being directly linked to the amount of time spent in treatment. Evaluations have consistently found improvement in social function, decreases in both use of heroin and other illicit drugs, decreases in criminal activity, and increases in employment. Medical indicators of success, such as mortality rates, decreased transmission of hepatitis and HIV, and outcome of infants born to women maintained on methadone have also been documented. The effectiveness of well-run programs has been noted by a number of scientific groups, including the Institute of Medicine, and an expert panel of the National Institute of Health on Effective Medical Treatment of Heroin Addiction. These groups have recommended that access to methadone be expanded, accompanied by appropriate funding.

Success rates are directly linked to the amount of time spent in treatment. Of all available approaches, methadone maintenance consistently retains the most people in treatment for the greatest period of time; 65 to 90 percent of those admitted stay for at least one year.

Hundreds of thousands of addicts have completed methadone maintenance programs. Some do extremely well and go on to lead drug-free, productive lives. Others can't tolerate requirements of the program or have adverse effects and drop out of treatment. Still others can't easily become detoxified and prefer long-term maintenance.

Yet, despite the scientific evidence, less than 20 percent of the estimated 600,000 heroin addicts in this country are in methadone maintenance, and methadone still receives considerable public criticism. The most recent example of this was a directive by the mayor of New York City to phase out methadone programs run by the city so that no one is treated for longer than three months. Later, the Addiction Free Treatment Act of 1999 was introduced in the U.S. Senate, which, if passed, would have limited methadone maintenance to six months, with immediate termination from treatment if a person tested positive for any illicit substance. To understand this paradox, it is necessary to look at the adverse effects of methadone as well as the reasons for the public criticism of this successful treatment modality.

Adverse Effects of Methadone

As is the case with any drug, people who take methadone regularly may experience a variety of feelings—some based on the drug's pharmacological properties, some due to an individual's sensitivity. Like other opiates, methadone frequently causes slowing of bowel activity and constipation. A proportion of methadone is excreted in sweat and sometimes causes excessive sweating on hot days. Other side effects include difficulty in sexual function in both men and women, weight gain, insomnia, and bone pain. But those symptoms are present to varying degrees in many persons before and during heroin use. Any reactions to methadone must be specifically assessed.

When combined with other mood-altering drugs in the alcohol-barbiturate-tranquilizer group, methadone can produce a depressant effect on the central nervous system—that is, sedation. Sedation may also result when methadone is taken irregularly or in doses greatly above tolerance level. Of course, a methadone maintenance dose can be fatal in a nontolerant person. This can occur if a child accidentally takes a parent's methadone or if someone takes a single large dose to get high. Fortunately, overdose of methadone by a nontolerant individual is quite infrequent.

Misconceptions About Methadone Maintenance

The continuing bad public image of methadone maintenance leads many of those on methadone to hide this fact. As a result, successes are not always visible, while failures are well publicized. Patients on maintenance loitering around clinics tend to contribute to the negative image of methadone. People don't realize that the persons engaged in such activities probably represent less than 10 percent of a clinic's total enrollment. The issue of diversion of methadone is also important and must be addressed. When patients are allowed the privilege of taking home medications, some will appear on the street. In most instances, street methadone is utilized by heroin addicts who want to prevent withdrawal reactions or to detoxify themselves from heroin in a nonsupervised setting. Nonetheless, this is a real issue. Fortunately, with the appearance of LAAM (discussed later), this problem might well be resolved as there would no longer be a need for take-home methadone.

The major reason, however, that the public acceptance of methadone maintenance is discordant with the results of such treatment is related to the feeling in our society that "narcotics are bad" and to take such drugs indicates a personal weakness. This is the reason why patients in pain are more often than not treated inadequately, resulting in needless suffering, even though we rapidly embrace other mood-altering drugs such as antidepressants and major tranquilizers, while shunning the concept of long-term treatment with opioids. This, perhaps, is the most difficult obstacle to overcome in allowing the public to adequately evaluate methadone maintenance.

Methadone maintenance has obvious limitations. Methadone allows development of tolerance to other opiates, but not to nonopiate mood-altering drugs. So people on maintenance may use and misuse substances such as alcohol, sedatives, and cocaine, just as others do.

The success of methadone maintenance is often judged on the basis of abstinence from all drugs. But persons on methadone have the same stresses and anxieties as those who are not. The only difference is that they can no longer relieve those stresses by injecting heroin. So without accompanying supportive services, people on methadone act much like those who never took heroin: they may turn to other mood-altering drugs. In fact, supportive services are essential to maximize the success of persons on methadone maintenance. Some individuals in government want to provide methadone maintenance without appropriate rehabilitative services. Their thinking is that methadone will decrease the spread of HIV and AIDS by cutting the number of heroin injections, and that cutting off the services will save money. But injecting cocaine is a preferred method of administration by heroin users and will spread AIDS as effectively as mainlining heroin.

It is often said that people on methadone maintenance continue to inject heroin. To prevent heroin highs, the daily methadone dose must be at least 60 to 80 milligrams, with a range of 80 to 120 milligrams per day most effective. But such doses are the exception rather than the rule. A study by the National Institute on Drug Abuse revealed that in 69 percent of the programs surveyed, the methadone dose was less than 30 milligrams—despite awareness that a low dose is commonly associated with poor retention rates as well as continued heroin use. At a daily dose of 34 milligrams or less, 35 percent of persons will use heroin at least once a week, whereas at a daily dose of 80 milligrams or more there is virtually no heroin use.

Why are inadequate doses prescribed? Partly because of fear that "potent doses" of methadone will be diverted to the street, but mainly due to ignorance of methadone pharmacology combined with the belief that less is better. In fact, inadequate doses of methadone may promote heroin use. Some patients clear methadone from their systems more rapidly than usual, thus exposing them to varying degrees of withdrawal during each day. The result is drug-seeking behavior and the perception that methadone is not working. The simple solution is to increase doses needed on a case-by-case basis.

Heroin users with severe psychological problems will continue to have them while on methadone. In such cases, psychotherapy and perhaps the use of other psychotropic medications may often be needed as well. But careful medical follow-up has revealed no serious consequences of long-term methadone administration. (By the same token, chronic use of opiates under sterile conditions has never been associated with significant adverse physical effects.) Although methadone maintenance may pose certain problems, a program that has worked for hundreds of thousands of people should not be condemned. Methadone maintenance is not the only realistic answer to rehabilitation, although for many it's the most practical, whether alone or in combination with other services.

Levo-Alpha Acetyl Methadol (LAAM)

LAAM, an anesthetic analgesic related to methadone but much longer acting, has been shown to be effective in opioid maintenance in a number of clinical trials. The advantage of LAAM over methadone is that it does not have to be taken any more frequently than every forty-eight hours, allowing persons to decrease their attendance at clinics, diminishing loitering and eliminating the need for take-home medication, thereby decreasing the potential for diversion as well as methadone overdose when the methadone is taken by nontolerant persons. In addition, it allows much more mobility for those on maintenance therapy. Many maintenance programs have begun to slowly switch their clients from methadone to LAAM. Recently, reports have been received of serious disturbances in cardiac rhythm in some patients taking LAAM. This disturbance, termed Torsades de Pointes (ventricular tachycardia), was seen in persons with a slight abnormality in their electrocardiograms (a prolonged QT interval) prior to starting LAAM. As a result, it is now recommended that all persons receive an electrocardiogram before initiating LAAM maintenance, with those having prolonged QT intervals ineligible for LAAM maintenance.

Buprenorphine

Buprenorphine is a synthetic opioid agonist-antagonist (Chapter 11) developed for control of pain. It is a potent analgesic with an affinity for the mu receptor. Due to its antagonist qualities, it is felt to be less likely to cause an overdose and, perhaps, less likely to cause dependency and addiction. However, initially, buprenorphine was preferred by heroin addicts over heroin, and at present it is a leading drug of abuse in Australia and New Zealand, as well as European countries.

When taken by injection, buprenorphine is 25 to 50 percent more potent than morphine in providing analgesia, although it has a relatively short half-life due to its avidity for the opioid receptors. However, is released slowly from the receptors, resulting in a rather long duration of action and a mild withdrawal syndrome. Although its bioavailability is diminished when swallowed, if taken sublingually it is absorbed rather well. A number of clinical trials have demonstrated that buprenorphine is similar to methadone as an effective maintenance agent. Combining buprenorphine and a pure antagonist to prevent its misuse also is theoretically quite attractive. Time will tell whether the acceptability of buprenorphine will allow it to be increasingly utilized in maintenance therapy. However, the two forms of buprenorphine, a sublingual tablet (Subutex) and a sublingual tablet containing buprenorphine and naltrexone (Suboxone), will soon be available. However, as the recent experience with OxyContin has demonstrated, the potential for abuse of the pure buprenorphine tablet is quite real. In fact, in areas where buprenorphine is being used for maintenance, a "street value" for the drug already exists.

Narcotic Antagonists

Naltrexone

As noted earlier, an opiate with purely antagonist properties can displace such opiates as heroin from the brain receptor sites, thus preventing a high from injected heroin. Until the early 1980s, there was no pure narcotic antagonist safe enough to make testing feasible. After considerable research, the National Institute on Drug Abuse approved naltrexone (Trexan) for treatment of opiate dependency. Before administering naltrexone, the person must be detoxified with either methadone or clonidine. Detoxifying with clonidine allows naltrexone to be taken much sooner, because several days must pass after the last dose of methadone before naltrexone can be used.

Administered orally, naltrexone has been consistently effective in preventing the high associated with heroin injection for up to seventy-two hours. But it must continue to be taken to be effective, and long-term therapy of up to a year may be required. If naltrexone is stopped and heroin is injected, a high will result. Consequently, many studies evaluating naltrexone have documented a high attrition rate—sometimes no different from that of a placebo. As many as 40 percent of those treated stop the drug after one month in order to experience the heroin high.

Widespread use of naltrexone poses some difficulties:

- Detoxification and subsequent abstinence must precede treatment, not easy tasks for someone craving heroin.
- The blocking action is easily overcome by an extremely large dose of heroin or by omitting one or more doses of naltrexone.
- Unless accompanied by intensive support, use of naltrexone fails to address the other principles involved in successful rehabilitation.
- High doses may induce liver injury.
- It may deplete naturally produced opiates, increasing heroin sensitivity if injections are resumed.

The ability of naltrexone to block effects of the body's natural opiates may prevent the neurotransmitter system from returning to normal, perpetuating persistent feelings of discomfort. Naltrexone appears to be most valuable for the limited number of people who are highly motivated to remain abstinent.

Self-Help Groups

Narcotics Anonymous (NA), like Alcoholics Anonymous and similar self-help groups, is a valuable resource. It offers group support for heroin addicts and people dependent on medically prescribed opiates. Groups are also available to help family members better understand addiction and ways of coping with those who are addicted. A fair degree of commitment is required for those who wish to remain drug-free immediately after detoxifying from opiates, so NA, when combined with other modalities, can be extremely useful in promoting abstinence.

Acupuncture   .

Acupuncture, the insertion of needles into critical parts of the body, has been a mainstay of Chinese medicine for more than 2,000 years. A variety of ailments are believed to be effectively treated when the needles are placed in specific sites. The effectiveness of many of these procedures hasn't been consistently demonstrated, however.

In the early 1970s, doctors in Hong Kong found acupuncture effective in relieving withdrawal symptoms in opium addicts undergoing surgical procedures. Subsequently, a number of physicians have been using acupuncture needles with or without electrical stimulation to detoxify individuals from heroin without medication and to keep them heroin free after detoxification. In most programs, needles are placed at specific points in the ear and stimulated with electrical pulses for approximately thirty minutes a day. The treatment period varies but usually lasts at least several weeks.

The exact mechanism that makes acupuncture effective in decreasing withdrawal symptoms is unknown. But several limited studies have shown it to be associated with an increase in the body's secretion of endorphin (met-enkephalin). That phenomenon is believed to compensate for the lack of heroin once injection has ceased, as well as for the suppressed levels of naturally occurring met-enkephalin during heroin use.

To date, probably thousands of people have been treated with acupuncture. Its supporters are convinced of its ability to diminish craving and withdrawal and to help maintain abstinence. But there have been few rigorous studies assessing the clinical effectiveness of acupuncture. Support for such studies should be provided.

Needle and Syringe Exchange Programs (SEPs)

As of 1997, approximately 113 SEPs were operating in the United States. Of the 100 SEPs that participated in a survey, 52 were operating within the laws of their states, 16 were illegal but tolerated, and 32 were illegal and operating underground. These programs exchanged a total of 17.5 million syringes. Demographic data suggest that participants in SEPs are high-risk drug users yet have a lower rate of HIV infection and, when referred to short-term treatment, better outcomes than nonparticipants. At present, the use of needle exchange programs remains quite controversial. Although perceived by its critics as promoting heroin use, its advocates view it as a valid harm reduction technique. In fact, needle exchange, similar to detoxification, may be the only way to reach some heroin addicts who do not recognize the need to stop injecting. While participating in the exchange process they can also receive information and assistance that may allow them to become more receptive to treatment. At the exchange programs, in addition to providing needles and syringes, condoms can be provided to decrease the transmission of sexually transmitted diseases and ways to decrease high-risk behaviors can be discussed. Referrals to drug treatment centers can also occur.

In 1995, the National Academy of Sciences and the Institute of Medicine evaluated ongoing needle exchange programs and found them to be effective without encouraging illegal drug use. In 1997, an independent consensus panel committee of the National Institute of Health also confirmed these findings, stating "there is no longer any doubt that these programs work." In fact, exchange programs have been found to be extremely effective in limiting the transmission of HIV infection, which has continued to rise among intravenous drug users. Nonetheless, public acceptance of needle exchange programs has not been high. In 1997, Congress banned the use of federal funds for needle exchange programs until 1998. Subsequent funding was to be provided if the Secretary of Health and Human Services determined that exchange programs were effective in preventing the spread of HIV without encouraging the use of illegal drugs. Indeed, although the Department of Health and Human Services stated that "the scientific evidence indicates that needle exchange programs did not encourage illegal drug use and can, in fact, be part of a comprehensive public health strategy to reduce drug use through effective referrals to drug treatment counseling," the administration decided that federal funding for these programs should still be withheld. This decision was made despite a Harris Poll Survey reporting that 71 percent of Americans surveyed supported needle exchange programs, in addition to professional groups, such as the American Bar Association and the United States Conference of Mayors. Hopefully, the shortsightedness of the federal government concerning these programs will have been reversed by the time of this publication and programs that are well run with appropriate safeguards will be able to receive federal support.

MEASURING TREATMENT EFFECTIVENESS

Much has been published about treatments for heroin addiction, but most evaluations have been descriptive. Still to be done are carefully designed studies that incorporate control groups and sufficient follow-up. Outcomes are often obtained by users' self-reports; and prior socioeconomic status bears on the ability to engage in productive activity. Both these facts can skew results. What's more, some programs that focus on treating heroin addiction may have many clients who use or are dependent on other mood-altering drugs.

With such cautions in mind, most large-scale evaluations of different treatment approaches yield similar results, with time spent in treatment being the most important predictor of success (Chapter 6). After appropriate time in treatment, heroin use and criminal activity decrease, and social productivity increases. By two or three years after discharge from a treatment program, heroin use may be infrequent. But other mood-altering drugs, mostly alcohol, can take its place. Excessive alcohol use remains the most common form of drug use in society today, so it's difficult to attribute to program failure the former heroin addict's turning to alcohol.

In spite of our advances in neurobiology, much more investigation is needed to explore the biology of heroin addiction and effective treatments. In that regard, basic research and clinical evaluation make good partners. As succinctly stated by Dr. Vincent P. Dole, one of the methadone maintenance pioneers at Rockefeller University, in the *Journal of the American Medical Association,* "It is not necessary to await an ultimate reduction of addictive behaviors to molecular terms before effective treatment can be provided. On the contrary, effective treatment, empirically found, can lead to a better understanding of molecular processes" (p. 3029).

Chapter 13

Amphetamines, Amphetamine-like Drugs, and Caffeine

Stimulants have been in wide use by all societies from the beginning of organized cultures, being described by the Chinese 5,100 years ago. They're taken to increase wakefulness and ability to concentrate, and to become more alert, decrease fatigue, and elevate mood. Their effects vary from a mild feeling of well-being to intense exhilaration and euphoria. The intensity depends on the specific drug, how it's taken, and the user's psychological status at time of consumption. Stimulants consistently reduce appetite and give one the perception of being able to take on herculean tasks. Continued intense use, however, results in irritability, depression, and physical and mental deterioration. Ultimately, paranoid behavior may appear.

Stimulants are among the easiest drugs to obtain. They may be legally prescribed for medical reasons, then purposely misused. They can be easily manufactured in clandestine laboratories, becoming an integral part of the street drug trade. Finally, they may be purchased over-the-counter as diet aids or as inhalers for asthma. Current inappropriate use of the illicit stimulants is not great. Stimulants used in our daily lives—coffee, tea, soft drinks, and cigarettes—are consumed far more frequently by the majority of people in the United States. Almost all stimulants, however, including those legally available, have a potential for dependency and inappropriate use. The degree to which this can happen may vary greatly (Table 13.1).

AMPHETAMINES

The first amphetamine was synthesized in 1887, but amphetamines did not become a part of physicians' practices until the late 1920s. When marketed in 1932, it was known as benzedrine and was produced as tablets, inhalers, and injectables. Since then, amphetamines and related substances have become a regular in the pharmaceutical marketplace. Initially, they were prescribed for narcolepsy, a condition that causes sleep without warning at any time. Their positive stimulant effects led to their use in treating

TABLE 13.1. Common Stimulants

Substance	Illicit Use	Rx Required	Dependency Potential	Dependency Potential Psychological	Physical*	Frequent Daily Use
Amphetamine	+	+	+	++++	+ / –	+
Methamphetamine	+	+	+	++++	+ / –	
Caffeine	–	–	–	+	–	+
Cocaine	+	–	+	++++	+	+
Nicotine	–	–	+	+++	++	+
Stimulants for weight loss	– / +	Varies with drug	+	+++	++ / –	+

– = No association
+ = Association
++ = Moderate association
+++ = Marked association
++++ = Severe dependency
* = Manifest withdrawal when use stops

depression and suppressing appetite. They're still used for narcolepsy as well as a relatively small number of other medical problems, including obesity and attention-deficit disorder, a condition of early childhood and adolescence marked by hyperactivity, impulsive behavior, and inability to focus on a subject (Table 13.2).

In the 1950s and early 1960s, amphetamines were widely used by people who needed to stay awake or to exhibit peak performance for long periods, such as long-distance truck drivers, athletes, servicemen on extended tours of duty, and students studying for examinations. In 1962 the Food and Drug Administration estimated that enough amphetamines were produced that year to supply everyone in the United States with one 250 milligram tablet. Because there were no appropriate controls, about half of that quantity was believed to be used illicitly. At that time, nineteen companies manufactured these drugs, nine of them not requiring proof of proper FDA registration of buyers. Most of the amphetamines on the street came from these legitimate manufacturers.

Others, of course, took amphetamines specifically for their mood-altering effects. Initially users swallowed the pills, but soon many people began experimenting with intravenous use. Early on, amphetamines were mixed with heroin (speedballs or splash), but young people soon began using them alone. When taking high doses of pills, or mainlining for several days at a stretch, the user would go virtually without sleep or food until becoming unable to function.

TABLE 13.2. Medical Uses of Stimulants

Severe depression unresponsive to antidepressant drugs
Pain relief, in conjunction with narcotic drugs
Hyperactivity in children
Motion sickness
Parkinsonism unresponsive to other drugs
Weight loss
Narcolepsy
Urinary incontinence

By the late 1960s, recognition of amphetamines' severe adverse effects led to them being placed in Schedule II, markedly restricting their availability. With the 1970 Controlled Substances Act, mandatory quotas on production were imposed. By 1972, most of the amphetamines in the street trade were being obtained through smuggling or by synthesis in clandestine laboratories.

Street Preparations

By 1975, only 10 percent of street samples sold as amphetamines actually contained the drug. The rest were mixtures of caffeine and amphetamine-like substances, such as ephedrine, pseudoephedrine, or phenethylamine, used for weight loss or treatment of asthma or coughs. These products were marketed under such names as black beauty, Penthouse, and Hustler, and some were advertised openly in counterculture magazines. There are also a number of amphetamine look-alike drugs on the street (Table 13.4). These are not real amphetamines but when taken in large doses can produce serious adverse reactions.

Speed's negative publicity came just when the young were becoming increasingly disillusioned with the government's inability or unwillingness to provide accurate information concerning U.S. involvement in Southeast Asia. This probably accounted for a certain amount of disbelief that amphetamines had adverse effects and an acting out through increased experimentation. Other legitimate stimulants also began finding their way to the street (Table 13.4). Use of amphetamines and amphetamine-like drugs decreased considerably through the 1980s. Nevertheless, in the 2000 Monitoring the Future Survey, 10.5 and 4 percent of high school seniors admitted using amphetamine and methamphetamine (ice) respectively, in the preceding year.

TABLE 13.3. Short-Term Effects of Amphetamines

Increased wakefulness
Decreased fatigue
Increased ability to concentrate
Decreased appetite
Sense of exhilaration, euphoria
Increased respiration
Hyperthermia

Effects on the Body

The major effects of amphetamines stem from their action on the central nervous system, heart, and blood vessels (Table 13.5). Amphetamines also stimulate the reward system of the brain (Chapter 4), which in turn intensifies the need to continue taking them. Amphetamines are readily absorbed from the intestinal tract and distributed to the tissues. Their affinity for lipid-containing tissues allows them to rapidly enter the brain as well as other organs. When amphetamines are injected directly into the bloodstream or inhaled, effects can be seen within seconds. Metabolism occurs in the liver, although much of the drug may be eliminated unchanged. As a result, the effects of the amphetamines may last from eight to twelve hours, depending on the specific drug. When amphetamines are taken frequently and intravenously, extremely high levels can accumulate.

An oral dose of 10 to 15 milligrams daily makes an individual more alert and able to perform mental or physical tasks with a greater degree of self-confidence and a higher level of activity. Whether tasks are performed more accurately remains unclear. Perfectly clear, however, is that one can work longer without fatigue or can quickly recover from fatigue. Respiration is stimulated and the appetite depressed—more from not wanting food than from an increased body metabolism. Cardiovascular consequences include a rise in blood pressure and rapid, sometimes irregular, heart rates.

Patterns of Use

Intravenous use is characterized by a quick onset of euphoria, described as an immediate "rush" or "flash" sensation. That's followed by a feeling that anything can be accomplished and a perception of physical, mental, and sexual prowess. The perception usually greatly exceeds the reality. Desire for food or sleep is absent. Mainlining the drug in runs can ultimately lead to

TABLE 13.4. Commonly Used Amphetamines and Amphetamine-like Drugs

Drug	Trade Name	Street Name
Amphetamines	Aderall, Benzedrine, Delcobese, Fetamine, Obetrol	Bennies, Blue Angels, Crank, Crisscross, Crossroads, Hearts, Lip Poppers, Peaches, Pep Pills, Pinks, Rosas, Roses, Speed, Splash, Trusters, Truck Drivers, Uppers, Ups, Wake-ups, Whites
	Desbutaal	
	Dexedrine, Ferndex Oxydess, Spancap	Caplets, Dexies, Oranges
	Biphetamine Diphetamine	Footballs
	Curban*, Dexamyl*, Eskatrol*	
	Desoxyn, Methadrene	Crystal, Mets, Water, Minibennies, Mollies, Chris/Christine
Methamphetamine crystal		Crystal, Crank, Ice, LA Ice
Methylphenidate	Ritalin	
Catha edulis Forsk (Khat)		Kitty Kat
Phenmetrazine	Preludin	Pocket Rockets, Ludies
Other commonly prescribed pills for weight loss§	Adipex, Bacarate, Cyclort, Didrex, Ionamin, Plegine, Pondimin, Pre-sate, Sandrex, Tenuate, Tepanil, Voranil	
Drugs used to prevent sleep	Ban, Drowz, Kirkaffeine, NoDoz, Stim-250, Tireno, Vivarin	
Ephedrine, phenyl-propanolamine	Variety of decongestant medications and antiasthmatic drugs	Usually sold on the street as Speed

* No longer available
§Many other weight-reduction pills are available. Although they are not structurally similar to amphetamines, they still have varying degrees of stimulant effects.

TABLE 13.5. Toxic Effects of Amphetamines

Acute

Behavioral
    Hyperactivity
    Euphoria
    Impaired judgment
    Delirium
    Acute psychotic reactions: paranoid reactions, hallucinations, suicidal or
        homicidal behavior, convulsions

Nausea or vomiting

Rise in body temperature

Marked rise in blood pressure

Irregularities in cardiac rhythm

Hemorrhages in brain or skull

Shock

Chronic

Weight loss

Chronic skin lesions

Psychotic states, especially paranoia

Heart disease

When used intravenously: hepatitis; HIV infection; infections of skin, subcuta-
    neous tissue, heart valves, and lungs; hemolytic anemia; clotting of veins
    and small arteries of brain and retina; allergic reactions; emboli in lungs;
    destruction of muscle tissue

---

extreme paranoid behavior. In that state, depending on the setting and the mainliner's personality, aggressive behavior may be directed at those perceived as threatening. Runs can continue for several days, usually ending in exhaustion. Next come prolonged periods of sleep, followed by bouts of eating and depression ("crashing"), which may last several days, accompanied by increasing craving for the drug until the cycle begins again.

Runs can also develop with oral use of amphetamines when taken in high doses (1,000 milligrams or more, every few hours). Sometimes depressants such as alcohol or sleeping pills are taken to counteract the hyperactivity generated by amphetamines.

Tolerance, Dependency, and Addiction

The effects of intravenous amphetamine and methamphetamine use by needle or smoking are similar to those of cocaine. In research settings, cocaine addicts are frequently unable to distinguish intravenous cocaine from intravenous amphetamine (Chapter 14). Not all the effects of amphetamines are subject to tolerance, but initial weight loss and mood alterations are. So an impressive increase in dosage is necessary to achieve the same effect. Psychological dependency also develops.

Withdrawal appears after a high degree of dependency. It usually consists of restlessness, anxiety, and depression accompanied by prolonged periods of sleep.

Adverse Effects

Toxic effects of amphetamines depend on patterns of use, whether taken with other mood-altering drugs, the degree of tolerance developed, the underlying medical disorders, and sometimes the conditions under which they're taken (Table 13.5).

The most severe effects occur with large intravenous doses. Symptoms of acute intoxication are restlessness, hyperactivity, delirium, acute psychotic reactions, a significant rise in temperature, and intermittent seizures and convulsions. Because amphetamines can cause rises in body temperature, a particular risk exists when the drug is taken during hot weather. Effects on the heart can result in a marked rise in blood pressure, sometimes accompanied by rupture and hemorrhage of small arteries in the brain. Irregular heartbeats may develop, sometimes causing fatal arrhythmias. People with heart disease are obviously at greater risk.

Amphetamines are often taken with depressant drugs such as alcohol, barbiturates, and benzodiazepines to modify the stimulant effect. Combinations with heroin (splash, speedball) are also common (Chapter 11).

Massive doses of amphetamines are rarely taken intentionally. But large quantities can be taken unknowingly when consuming other street drugs that contain pure amphetamines as well as other stimulants. Bleeding in the brain can result from the extreme increase in pressure in the cerebral arteries. Alternatively, the system may be so stimulated as to result in complete loss of blood pressure (shock), extreme elevation of temperature, convulsions, coma, and death. Chronic amphetamine use produces significant weight loss, skin lesions, and psychotic reactions similar to schizophrenia. Psychotic reactions with oral amphetamine use don't usually appear until the drugs have been taken for several months or as a manifestation of an intense run. Once they do, however, they reappear quickly with recurrent use.

Damage to blood vessels in the brain and heart with intravenous injection has been reported. Intravenous use of amphetamines, with its likely contaminants, adulterants, and unsterile needles, subjects the user to all the complications that accompany heroin use, including: hepatitis; skin, lung, and heart valve infections; destruction of blood vessels; and transmission of the human immunodeficiency virus (HIV) through either shared needles or unprotected sex spurred by an increased libido.

Treatment

Treatment of acute amphetamine reactions is usually directed toward preventing seizures, controlling body temperature, and quieting the person while the acute behavioral changes subside over several days. Appropriate tranquilizers are given for psychotic reactions or when behavior can't be controlled, resulting in violence. Depression and lethargy once the drug has been eliminated from the body are common and must be addressed to prevent an early return to the drug. Long-term treatment is more difficult to manage than just dealing with the acute effects of the drug, but it's of utmost importance to maintain abstinence. An uncommon sequel to amphetamine use is the appearance and subsequent persistence of a previously unrecognized psychological disorder such as manic depression. There are no effective medications to date to prevent recidivism. Cognitive and behavioral intervention have been found most effective in maintaining abstinence.

Methamphetamine

One of the more recent drugs appearing on the street is smokeable methamphetamine (ice, LA ice, crank), first appearing in Hawaii and on the West Coast. Although methamphetamine was available as a performance-enhancing drug as early as World War II, its availability on the street was mainly in oral or intravenous form and was quite prominent in the 1960s. In the late 1980s, a smokable, relatively pure form of methamphetamine became prominent in the West and Southwest. Deaths due to methamphetamine increased threefold between 1991 and 1994, with admissions to emergency rooms doubling between 1989 and 1995. The 1996 NHSDA estimated that 4.9 million people, mostly in cities in the West, Southwest, and Hawaii, had tried methamphetamine at some time during their lives.

Unlike cocaine, crystal methamphetamine is quite easy to make in home-based laboratories utilizing large quantities of ephedrine, pseudoephedrine, phenylpropanolamine, or other over-the-counter stimulants at extremely low cost with less than sophisticated equipment. The cost of producing one pound of methamphetamine sold as "rocks" or chunks, is estimated at $700. On the street it will yield $225,000, making it obvious why ice is more attractive to the drug dealer than crack. Its street price, ranging from $10 to $30 a dose, makes it more attractive to buyers than cocaine, and its effects last much longer. In response to the ease with which methamphetamine can be synthesized, in 1996 Congress passed the Comprehensive Methamphetamine Control Act to restrict the accessibility of chemicals used to make the drug.

Methamphetamine, smoked by inhaling the vapors from heated crystal through a straw, can produce a high within three to five minutes as the drug reaches the brain quite rapidly, more so than by injection, which requires fifteen to twenty minutes for an effect. The high is accompanied by a strong rush that rapidly subsides. Since methamphetamine's half-life is twelve hours and its metabolism is associated with the production of pharmacologically active metabolites, its effects last much longer than crack's, with a half life of ten to twelve hours. Acute psychotic behavior, severe paranoia, incoherent speech, hallucinations, and uncontrollable behavior lasting up to forty-eight hours are frequent side effects.

Methamphetamines exert their mood-altering effects by acting on the neurotransmitter system in the brain (Chapter 4), causing increased release of dopamine, serotonin, and norepinephrine from brain cells, blocking both their uptake and the activity of the enzyme responsible for their metabolism. It's the increased levels of those neurotransmitters that result in many of the behavioral effects peculiar to this type of drug. With time, these neurotransmitters become depleted, and toxic substances are produced by their breakdown. The toxic effects of methamphetamine are considerable, with a single dose given to a laboratory animal being shown to cause damage to dopamine-containing neurons as well as hyperthermia and convulsions. Recent brain imaging studies in humans suggest that the potential for similar changes exists.

Methcathinone

Methcathinone or Cat, as it is called on the street, is a clandestinely-produced analog of both methamphetamine and cathinone. Its effects are quite similar to methamphetamine. It can be taken either orally or dissolved in water and injected intravenously.

AMPHETAMINE-LIKE DRUGS

Methylphenidate

Methylphenidate (Ritalin, Methylin, Metadate) is a Schedule II drug that has been used for several decades to treat children and adults with hyperactivity manifested by difficulty in maintaining attention (attention deficit disorders). Its pharmacological effects are similar to those of amphetamines, although it is believed to have a greater effect on mental than on motor activity. It's generally used in conjunction with behavioral therapy and dietary regimens. In 2000, about 9 million prescriptions were written for these agents, with sales of $253.6 million.*

Methylphenidate is taken orally or dissolved in water and injected when used inappropriately. Although considered a reasonable treatment for hyperactivity, with an estimated 800,000 children taking it, its safety and efficacy over long-term use, according to some, have not been demonstrated. Moreover, complications are possible and the potential for misuse exists, just as with continued use of any stimulant. So tolerance, psychological dependence, and abnormal behavior may occur in some users. Psychotic reactions have been reported with intravenous use. In one survey of 1,183 records of adolescents seen at an outpatient substance abuse treatment center, methylphenidate misuse increased from 3 percent in 1992 to 20 percent in 1996. However, when medically supervised, its effects on hyperactivity and attention deficit disorders are quite beneficial, and it has helped many children with these conditions to function normally.

Ephedrine

Far less potent than amphetamine, ephedrine is a stimulant contained in a large variety of decongestants and antiasthmatic medications. Its easy availability has resulted in its being sold as amphetamine on the street.

Khat

Grown in the highlands of East Africa and the Middle East, khat *(Catha edulis)* is a shrub whose leaves, when chewed, produce an effect somewhat less intense than but similar to that of amphetamine. Its use dates back to the tenth century and is still well accepted as a traditional social activity in areas of Yemen, Somalia, and parts of Ethiopia. Reports of its use have appeared in England. In the United States its use is extremely limited.

The usual method of consumption is chewing the shoots or leaves of the plant within four days of harvesting. Of the plant's chemical substances, the phenylalkylamine cathinone is believed to be primarily responsible for the mood-altering effect, which is described as euphoria, anorexia, heightened libido, increased socialization, and enhancement of concentration. Khat can induce craving and a certain degree of tolerance. Although physi-

---

*The New York Times, August 19, 2001, A1, 30.

cal dependence has not been reported, it is extremely habituating with continued use. In Yemen it has been estimated that approximately 80 percent of men, 60 percent of women, and increasing numbers of children under ten years of age chew khat on a fairly regular basis. On the day following khat use, drowsiness and dysphoria can occur. The most common adverse effects are esophageal and gastric irritation accompanied by constipation. Severe and unusual reactions include malnutrition, hypothermia, and hyperventilation.

Phenylpropanolamine

Phenylpropanolamine is commonly used as a nasal decongestant and appetite suppressant in over-the-counter and some prescription medications. It first appeared on the street as an "illicit amphetamine" but is now available mainly through legal purchase. It has minimal stimulant properties in the dosages recommended for treatment of congestion, but some sensitive people do report feeling high. If used in large doses, it causes a definite amphetamine-like effect, though usually not as pronounced. Recent studies have demonstrated that the use of phenylpropylene in appetite suppressants and cough medications is an independent risk factor for hemorrhagic stroke in women.

Other Ephedra Alkaloids

In addition to phenylpropanolamine, a variety of other ephedra alkaloids are available in health food stores as dietary supplements. These alkaloids (referred to as ma huang) are widely consumed to enhance energy and lose weight. Recently, reports to the Food and Drug Administration have been made concerning adverse effects associated with these substances. These have ranged from mild cardiac rhythm abnormalities to hemorrhagic stroke, hypertensive episodes, seizures, muscle degeneration, and in pregnant women premature delivery and spontaneous abortion.

Death resulted in three of eleven cases that were definitely related or probably related, and in seven of fifteen cases that were possibly related to taking substances containing ephedra alkaloids. Although the number of adverse events compared to the number of people taking these substances is small, nonetheless, for some people, use of these drugs presents a real risk.

Appetite Suppressants

Other stimulant drugs used mostly for weight reduction have the potential for inappropriate use, but far less so than the amphetamines. Some, such as phenmetrazine (Preludin) tablets, have considerable potential for misuse and have been taken orally, or crushed, mixed with liquid, and injected. The tablet contains talc, which presents a particular problem when injected: it can block the small blood vessels in the eyes, lungs, and brain. Inappropriate use of phenmetrazine is well known; users describe the effects as similar to those of amphetamines.

Other appetite suppressants (Table 13.6), although associated with a low potential for dependency, can still be misused. In some instances, people taking appetite suppressants do become dependent because of their mood-altering effects. Their widespread availability can initiate drug use in young people. Between 1993 and 1995 in Texas, the Texas Food and Drug Administration received approximately 500 adverse event reports on persons who consumed dietary supplements containing ephedrine, pseudoephedrine, norephedrine, and methylephedrine. All these substances are stimulants and act in a manner similar to that of amphetamine. Unfortunately, since these substances are sold as natural food products, consumers are often unaware of their ingredients or assume that since the products are "natural," no untoward events can occur. Because they are considered food products, they are not under the Food and Drug Administration's aegis and, therefore, tests on their safety for consumption are not required. When taken by people with underlying heart disease they can be quite dangerous, even when not subject to abuse.

Dexfenfluramine, Fenfluramine, and Phentermine

These drugs, which are chemical congeners of amphetamine, are considered effective in promoting short-term weight loss. In 1959, the Food and Drug Administration approved phentermine (Adepix, Fastin, Lonamin) and in 1973 fenfluranime (Pondimin) as single drug therapy for short-term weight reduction. More recently, in 1996, the FDA approved the use of dexfenfluramine (Redux) for up to twelve months' treatment of obesity. Un-

TABLE 13.6. Nonprescription Weight-Reduction Pills

Acutrim
Appedrine
Control
Dexatrim
Grapefruit diet plan with Diadex
Maximum Strength Dexatrim
Maximum Strength Dex-A-Diet Capulets
Phenoxine
Phenyldrine
Spray U Thin
Unitrol

fortunately, the desire of many to lose weight as quickly as possible and to maintain this weight loss for as long as possible has resulted in use of a combination of these drugs, with phentermine and fenfluranime (phen-fen) being the most common. By 1997, the total number of prescriptions for these drugs exceeded 14 million, with the length of treatment often greater than that suggested.

Although both fenfluramine and dexfenfluramine have been shown in animals to damage serotonin-containing neurons, with damage lasting for weeks after the drug is discontinued, it was initially unclear whether such damage would occur in humans. However, the use of these drugs was accompanied by reports of a rare but often fatal condition, primary pulmonary hypertension (PPH), which culminates in severe failure of the right side of the heart and an inability to breathe. An international study published in 1996 found the use of these drugs within the previous year to be associated with a tenfold greater risk of developing PPH, with the risk increasing to twentyfold if the drug was used longer than three months.

In July 1997, heart valve damage was reported in women who had been dieting with phen-fen, with symptoms often appearing late in the course of the disease, after severe valve damage had occurred. Although a direct cause-and-effect relationship between phen-fen and valvular disease remained to be conclusively demonstrated, the Food and Drug Administration issued an advisory warning, and the pharmaceutical companies ceased their marketing. Recently, three separate studies have observed a relationship between use of these drugs and heart valve regurgitation, with one study reporting a prevalence as high as 25 percent in patients receiving the phen-fen combination as compared to a 1.3 percent prevalence among controls. However, a subsequent study reported only a small and nonsignificant difference in persons using these drugs and a control population. A separate multicenter control study found no association between use of this drug and mitral valve disorders. Aortic valve dysfunction was reported to be associated with its use only if duration of treatment exceeded six months. These findings suggest that there is a slight, significant association with long-term use; however, the valvular damage, if present, is mild and tends to improve with time. Although these drugs are often misused rather than abused, in the true sense of the word, nonetheless, the potential adverse effects with inappropriate use are of concern. These drugs should be prescribed only in refractory cases of obesity and for only a short time. It is important to emphasize that of 5 million persons using these pills between 1996 and 1998, approximately 25 percent of users were not overweight. Persons who are to begin their use should make certain they have no preexisting valvular disease that has gone undetected. Persons who have used these drugs should contact their physicians to make certain that no damage has occurred.

Nonprescription Dietary Aids

In addition to prescription medications for weight loss, a variety of non-prescription dietary aids is available on the market (Table 13.6). Although abuse and dependency are rare, misuse of these drugs in an attempt to achieve maximum weight loss is not infrequent.

Herbal Medications

A variety of herbal remedies promoted as weight-reduction agents may contain natural stimulants. Few, if any, have been adequately evaluated for either efficacy or safety. Recently, a Chinese herb *(Aristolochia fangchi)* has been associated with kidney failure and carcinoma of the urinary tract. Although these complications have been reported only in Europe, Japan, and Taiwan, this herb is available in the United States in capsule form.

CAFFEINE

Caffeine is consumed in some form by more than 90 percent of the U.S. population. Most who drink caffeine-containing beverages experience minimal deleterious effects, but those who consume unusually large quantities are prone to adverse effects and reactions similar to but of less intensity than those produced by amphetamines and cocaine.

Caffeine exists in many natural substances (Table 13.7). It's one of three drugs classified as methylated xanthines. The others are theophylline, found in smaller concentrations in tea, and theobromine, found in chocolate and cocoa. All three are stimulants, but caffeine is the most potent. Caffeine is in coffee, tea, chocolate, some soft drinks, and many over-the-counter medica-

TABLE 13.7. Natural Sources of Caffeine

Source	Location
Cocoa tree	North and South America
Coffee beans	North and South America, Ethiopia, Arabia, Turkey
Tea leaves	China, Japan, India
Kola nuts	West Africa
Ilex plant	South America
Cassina	North America

tions used for pain relief or as central nervous system stimulants. The amount of caffeine consumed in such beverages as coffee or tea varies with the strength of the brew and the amount consumed (Table 13.8).

Effects on the Body

Caffeine is easily absorbed. Peak concentrations appear in the blood within fifteen to forty-five minutes. It's quickly distributed to the central nervous system, subsequently metabolized in the liver, and excreted in the urine. Caffeine elimination is enhanced by smoking.

The popularity of caffeine results from its positive effects on the central nervous system (Table 13.9). These effects are variable, depending on a person's susceptibility and the quantity of caffeine consumed. Nevertheless, one to three cups of coffee can produce an elevation of mood, decreased fatigue, increased mental and physical work capacity, ability to think more clearly, and occasional relief of headaches and anxiety. In fact, investigators at Walter Reed Army Institute of Research found that 600 milligrams of caffeine given to volunteers after forty-eight hours of sleep deprivation improved cognitive performance and alertness similar to 20 milligrams of amphetamine without adverse effects. Caffeine gum containing 50 milligrams of caffeine per stick is also available, with 80 percent of the caffeine absorbed within five minutes.

TABLE 13.8. Caffeine Content of Common Beverages, Chocolate, and Over-the-Counter Medications

Product	Unit of Measure	Caffeine (mg/unit)
Coffee*		
Ground	cup (8 oz)	80-190
Instant	cup	30-100
Decaffeinated	cup	3-5
Tea*	cup	20-90
Cocoa	cup	6-42
Cola	12 oz	40-50
Chocolate	bar	25
Medications		
Analgesics	tablet	15-100
Stimulants	tablet	100-200

*Caffeine content depends on strength of brew.

TABLE 13.9. Positive Effects of Caffeine on the Central Nervous System

---

Elevates mood
Decreases fatigue
Increases psychological and physical work capacity
Enhances rapid, clearer thought
Relieves headache
Stimulates respiration

Caffeine, however, affects other parts of the central nervous system and other organ systems. It constricts blood vessels in the brain. It increases the heart rate, raises blood pressure slightly, dilates arteries in the lung, relaxes smooth muscles in the respiratory tract, induces acid secretion in the stomach (perhaps causing heartburn), and increases urine flow through its diuretic action.

A Habit or an Addiction?

Whether caffeine can be considered a dependency-producing drug capable of inducing withdrawal symptoms is unclear. But there's no question that caffeine is habituating. Millions of people feel they can't "get going" without their morning cup of coffee. That need is sometimes work-related, and the desire for coffee during recreational hours is not as great.

Dependency and accompanying withdrawal are quite unusual. However, in one study, chronic coffee drinkers were given beverages containing caffeine doses of 25, 50, and 100 milligrams. Those who drank the lower-dosed coffee quickly increased consumption to reach 100 milligrams.

Other studies involving coffee drinkers who consume large quantities of caffeine have shown that withdrawal reactions occur when caffeine is replaced with a placebo. The subjects experienced anxiety, headaches, increasing irritability, and decreased alertness.

Adverse Effects of Caffeine

Determining what is an excessive level of caffeine is difficult. Toxic effects may appear after consumption of 500 milligrams (approximately four cups of coffee) or after as little as 250 milligrams in susceptible persons. Symptoms of caffeinism are restlessness, flushing, gastrointestinal disturbances, increased rapidity of speech, nervousness, insomnia, confusion, and irritability.

Severe toxic effects (caffeine poisoning) are rare, but abnormalities in cardiac rhythm, extreme agitation, seizures, and death have been reported following ingestion of 5 to 10 grams of caffeine (approximately twenty-five to fifty cups of coffee). Severe effects have also been reported from as little as 1 gram. Even 500 milligrams can be toxic, especially in children who, with their low body weights, may consume excessive amounts in soft drinks or chocolate. Adverse effects appear quickly in such cases. Individual susceptibilities vary greatly, so it has not been possible to establish a precise relationship between the particular effect and the amount of caffeine consumed. Underlying medical disorders or personality traits can accentuate the appearance of such effects.

Increased irritability, difficulty sleeping, and increased gastric secretions are the most common manifestations of excessive caffeine use. But even low doses can have an impact on muscle coordination. More than five cups of coffee (or equivalent) a day can lead to difficulty in concentrating. Heartburn—the symptoms of gastric secretion—can be so severe in those who drink many cups of coffee that a heart condition may be suspected. Current popular thinking is that decaffeinated coffee prevents such symptoms. But decaffeinated coffee is only slightly less potent than regular coffee in stimulating gastric secretions. Coffee can also be particularly hazardous for those with, or prone to, peptic ulcer disease. The symptoms diminish or disappear when caffeine consumption is decreased or stopped.

Caffeine has also been suggested, but not confirmed, as a risk factor in certain cancers of the kidney, urinary tract, esophagus, and larynx. Also controversial is the relationship between caffeine and the ability of a woman to conceive easily and have an uncomplicated pregnancy and delivery (Chapter 19).

The effects of caffeine on the heart and blood vessels have been studied extensively, but with varied and contradictory findings: People who drink excessive amounts of coffee tend to be smokers, drink alcohol, and often are high-powered, hard-driving individuals, all of whom tend to have a high incidence of cardiovascular problems. At present, no reliable evidence exists that proves caffeine is a significant risk factor in coronary artery disease. Excessive caffeine may perhaps elevate cholesterol levels. However, studies have shown that moderate coffee consumption has no adverse effect on serum cholesterol. Caffeine doesn't appear to cause persistent elevation of blood pressure or increase frequency of hypertension. In reasonable amounts, it doesn't interfere with treatment of hypertension.

Even if a positive relationship between caffeine and coronary heart disease were identified, the question would remain: is caffeine an independent risk factor, or does its excessive use simply accompany high-risk behavior? A prudent recommendation for those with, or at high risk for, serious heart disease who wish to drink coffee is to consume only moderate amounts.

Chapter 14

Cocaine

I expect it [cocaine] will earn its place in therapeutics by the side of morphine and superior to it. I have other hopes and intentions about it. I take very small doses of it regularly against depression and against indigestion and with the most brilliant success.

Sigmund Freud

Cocaine is obtained from leaves of the *Erythroxylon coca* shrub. Evidence of coca leaf use dates back to 3000 B.C. in Ecuador. In the Inca Empire, dating from the thirteenth century A.D., the emperor acknowledged the right of his subjects to choose the coca leaf above silver or gold. Even though cocaine was known to be a stimulant and an anesthetic, it was considered integral to the religious rituals of the Incas. When the Spanish conquered the Incas in the sixteenth century, recognizing its capability to increase physical endurance on a short-term basis, they began to include coca leaves with the Inca workers' wages.

Cocaine was isolated in 1844 and its pharmacological effects first studied in 1880. A subsequent study provided a comprehensive review of cocaine's action in the central nervous system. Sigmund Freud was a cocaine enthusiast who promoted its use for a wide variety of disorders, including those of the digestive tract and respiratory system, as well as for sexual dysfunction, treatment of opium and alcohol addiction, and as a local anesthetic. The enthusiasm for cocaine continued into the early twentieth century, when it was widely available in over-the-counter preparations and elixirs. Cocaine was used in more than sixty cola drinks at the time. The makers of Coca-Cola removed cocaine from the drink around 1906 and replaced it with caffeine. It is alleged that today's Coca-Cola is still flavored with a "nonnarcotic" extract of the coca plant. Over the next two decades, the adverse effects of cocaine became increasingly well known, and it was one of the proscribed drugs included in the Harrison Narcotic Act of 1914.

Until the 1970s, cocaine use was generally concentrated among people in the arts and those who could afford it. Because cocaine was believed to be neither physically addictive nor capable of causing serious physical complications, aside from irritation and ulcers of the nasal passages, even medical opinion was tolerant. The combined use of cocaine and heroin was an exception, but that was also deemed insignificant when compared to heroin use alone.

The use of cocaine increased at a truly remarkable rate in the late 1970s, in part because of new restrictions on amphetamines and their decreased availability. In 1972, 14 percent of adolescents and 48 percent of young adults reported having tried marijuana. But less than 2 percent of adolescents and only 9 percent of young adults had tried cocaine. From 1976 to 1986 the National Institute on Drug Abuse reported a fifteenfold increase in emergency room visits for cocaine use, in cocaine-related deaths, and in admissions to treatment facilities. In 1986, more than 3 million people were using cocaine regularly, and 15 percent of the U.S. population had tried it. Of those, 40 percent were between the ages of twenty-five and thirty. In 1987, data from the National Institute on Drug Abuse suggested that as many as 6 million Americans were using cocaine regularly, with 1 million dependent on this drug.

Two of the more recent surveys revealed that regular use of cocaine among teenagers has stabilized. In the 2000 Monitoring the Future Survey, 5 percent of twelfth graders reported using cocaine and 2 percent used crack within the past year. The overall prevalence of cocaine use, however, varies greatly, depending on location and age group. In some cities, up to 40 percent may have experimented with cocaine use as early as junior high school. The 1999 National Household Survey on Drug Abuse estimated that there were approximately 934,000 new users of cocaine in 1998. Although data suggest that the use of crack has diminished, anecdotal evidence suggests that the use of powder cocaine, particularly among white and blue-collar workers, may be quietly increasing.*

PATTERNS OF USE

The earliest form of cocaine use was chewing coca leaves, still a common method in countries where the coca plant is grown. Cocaine shows up in the blood within five to ten minutes after chewing coca leaves and is accompanied by a considerable mood-altering effect (Table 14.1). Coca tea is consumed by many in South America. However, the interest of North Americans in coca tea is also considerable. Data from the National Enterprise Institute of Peru, which sells coca tea, estimated that in 1990, of 5.7 million bags of coca tea sold, 500,000 were purchased by American tourists. A coca

---

*The New York Times, August 21, 2000, B1, 2.

TABLE 14.1. Time Lag Between Cocaine Consumption and Onset of Effects

Method of Administration	Time (Seconds)
Chewing leaves or swallowing	300-600
Sniffing	120-180
Mainlining (intravenous)	15-30
Smoking (freebase cocaine or crack only)	6-8

tea bag is believed to contain approximately 5 mg of cocaine, with 80 percent of this remaining in the tea. Consumption of one cup of tea can result in detectable concentrations of cocaine in the urine for at least twenty-four hours. Although the consumption of a cup of coca tea is usually associated with minimal, if any, euphoric effects, detectable concentrations of cocaine will remain in the urine for at least twenty hours. The lack of a high is not surprising, as the quantity of cocaine that is absorbed into the blood stream after drinking a cup of coca tea is less than 5 nanograms per millileter. Six bags of tea per day would result in blood levels not exceeding 25 nanograms per milliliter. In contrast, a person who uses coca paste, injects cocaine, or freebases crack can achieve blood levels greater than 5,000 nanograms.

Coca Paste and Powder

An intermediate product in the making of cocaine is coca paste. The paste, though impure, can contain 40 to 85 percent cocaine, plus a number of solvents (alkaloid bases, potassium permanganate, sulfuric acid) used in the extraction process. Coca paste can produce behavioral effects identical to those seen with other forms of cocaine. Coca paste (pasta, bazooka) smokers are uncommon in the United States, but increased availability of the paste could lead to a subset of users with a tendency to progress to freebase.

Cocaine sold on the street is initially prepared from coca paste and cut with adulterants (Table 14.2). Cocaine in powder form (with purity ranging from 30 to 90 percent) can be sniffed (snorted) or dissolved in water and injected. But it can't be smoked directly because it is quickly destroyed by heat. When sniffed, about 60 percent is absorbed through the blood vessels in the nose and transmitted through the veins to the heart and lungs, and then carried by the arteries to the rest of the body. This process takes only two to three minutes to produce an effect, with peak levels occurring within thirty minutes. When cocaine is taken orally, the absorption process occurs in seven to fifteen minutes. When it is injected directly into the veins (mainlining), effects are apparent within fifteen to thirty seconds.

TABLE 14.2. Cocaine Adulterants

Ascorbic acid
Aspirin
Benzocaine
Butacaine
Caffeine
Cornstarch
Flour
Herbicides
Heroin
Lactose
Lidocaine
Manganese carbonate
Magnesium sulfate
Mannitol
Procaine
Quinine
Salicylamide
Stimulants: ephedrine, diet pills, amphetamines, phenylpropanolamine
Talc
Tetracaine

Freebasing and Crack

Waiting two or three minutes for a drug to take effect doesn't seem burdensome. Yet freebase cocaine was developed to produce a quicker, higher-intensity high. In about the time it takes to finish this page, a reader can be on a crack high (Table 14.1). Initially, freebase cocaine was processed by using ether, a highly flammable solvent, to produce a relatively heat-resistant, smokable substance. Freebase kits rapidly became available on the streets and in head shops, with total sales estimated in the tens of millions of dollars. But the ether caused a number of explosions, and it was taken out of the production process. Instead the cocaine is mixed with ammonia or baking soda and water and heated. The product is crack or rock, so called because of the cracking sound made during both processing and smoking as well as its rocklike appearance. Other names include ready rock, crystal, and when sold in three-inch sticks, french fries (Table 14.3). Crack is purer than street cocaine but still contains impurities, including varying amounts of baking soda.

Crack can be smoked in a pipe or crushed and mixed with tobacco and smoked in cigarette form or dissolved in water or alcohol, heated, and then cooled and injected. Inhaling the smoke introduces the cocaine directly into the lungs and subsequently into the left side of the heart, bypassing the

TABLE 14.3. Street Names for Cocaine

Type of Cocaine	Street Name
Cocaine hydrochloride	Blanco, Blow, C, Caine, Coca, Coke, Cola, Flake, Girl, Gold Dust, Heaven Dust, Lady Line Muser, Nose Candy, Paradise, Perico, Peruvian Flake, Polvo, Snow, Toot, White
Crack (freebase)	Bazooka, Crack, Crystal, French Fries, Fry Daddie, Ready Rock, Rock, Space Base
Crack or Cocaine and Alcohol	Liquid Lady
Crack and Heroin	Moonrock, Tar
Crack and PCP	Space Cadet, Tragic Magic

veins. An effect is produced within six to eight seconds (Table 14.1). The high is intense but lasts only minutes; by comparison, the effect of snorting peaks between fifteen and forty minutes. Crack is easy and inexpensive to manufacture. The result has been a significant drop in the street price of cocaine since the late 1980s. In 1990 the cost of 1 gram of cocaine was $40 to $100; when it was cut and sold as crack, each smoking unit cost $5 to $20, depending on location of the supplier. Because crack's extremely short-lived, intensely pleasurable high results in a constant craving, the compulsive user can easily spend $500 a day on the drug.

Stages of Cocaine Use

The Rush

A cocaine rush is followed by a stimulation phase of increased alertness, feelings of sexual prowess, and euphoria (Table 14.4). The high associated with cocaine or crack is so pleasurable and so distorts perceptions that the user quickly feels that anything can be accomplished. Social or recreational users tend to take the drug sporadically and may not escalate their use. However, the pleasurable effects of the drug may result in a progression in its use in order to cope with stress. The relief obtained in turn results in more frequent use. When the drug is taken in other than social or recreational settings, the initial effects may give way to dysphoria (unhappiness or sadness), restlessness, and irritability within thirty minutes. That state often leads to depression, which produces enough discomfort to necessitate a rapid return to the drug. Appetite suppression often accompanies cocaine use, with unexplained weight loss at times being the first objective sign of cocaine use. Correspondingly, after the drug is eliminated from the system there is often hunger and a craving for sweets.

TABLE 14.4. Stages of Cocaine Use

Intoxication
   Rush-euphoria
   Increased alertness, energy, confidence, intellectual functioning, sexual
      performance
Restlessness, anxiety
Repeat use to relieve negative feelings and regain high
Binge behavior
Crash
   Despair, anxiety, increased appetite, depression, desire but inability to
      sleep
Withdrawal
   Decreased energy, impaired intellectual functioning, muscle pains, tremors
Return to use
   At risk when in environment of prior use

The Runs

Recurrent cocaine use results in binges of constant sniffing, smoking, or injecting. Binges can last from hours to days, with cocaine being taken as frequently as every ten minutes. Similar runs are seen with amphetamines, but their effects last much longer; cocaine must be taken far more often than the amphetamines. With frequent use, tolerance to some of the effects of cocaine such as euphoria may occur, requiring an increasing dose or frequency of use to obtain the same high. Tolerance to the cardiac effects, however, does not occur, placing the chronic user at greater risk for adverse reactions.

The Crash

For a recurrent user, the inevitable crash comes at the point when judgment is virtually destroyed and the body is run down from the consistent, repetitive use of cocaine. A crash manifests itself as despair, anxiety, a tremendous desire to sleep, severe depressive symptoms, and a huge appetite. Sedatives or alcohol are sometimes taken to facilitate sleep, which is not easily achieved.

Withdrawal

Decreased energy, impaired intellectual functioning, muscle pains, and tremors appear twelve to ninety-six hours after the crash. These and other withdrawal symptoms can last several weeks (Table 14.5). Behavior becomes more normal during this time, but the craving for cocaine can resur-

TABLE 14.5. Types of Cocaine Abstinence Syndromes

Setting	Term	Duration
Immediately following a binge or run	Crash	Hours to several days
Upon becoming abstinent	Withdrawal	One week to three weeks
Within weeks of remaining abstinent	Craving	Weeks to months

face. The depression accompanying the crash quickly brings the user back to the realities of life, including all its frustrations and unfulfilled needs. Nothing seems right; everything is a burden. For some, reality becomes overwhelming. This depression often causes even those who are drug free to succumb to the lures (positive-reinforcement effects) of cocaine. Despite the will to abstain, they often quickly return to the drug if they meet former fellow users or find themselves in an environment associated with cocaine use.

Craving

As described in subsequent pages of this chapter, after weeks of abstinence from cocaine, former heavy users experience a powerful urge to resume cocaine use that is reinforced when encountering situations in which prior use occurred. This is perhaps the most difficult time to reman cocaine free and must be addressed if successful rehabilitation is to be maintained.

COCAINE METABOLISM

The bioavailability of cocaine depends on the way it is taken. When consumed orally, as it is absorbed from the gastrointestinal tract, cocaine passes through the liver with 70 to 80 percent of the dose metabolized. As a result, the level in the blood slowly increases to a peak within one hour. When snorted or sniffed, the absorption of cocaine is slightly delayed due to its ability to constrict blood vessels in the nose as well as a relatively low permeability of nasal mucosa. However, it initially does not pass through the liver for metabolism and an effect is therefore seen within three to five minutes, with peak blood levels in ten to twenty minutes, subsequently dropping rapidly within an hour. Intravenous use delivers the dose immediately into the bloodstream so that its bioavailability is 100 percent, compared to 30 percent with swallowing or snorting. The effects of intravenous use can be seen within thirty seconds, lasting for ten to twenty minutes. Smoking crack produces the quickest high, as the drug is absorbed directly in the lungs and then taken to the brain within seconds. However, smoking reduces the bioavailability to less than 30 percent.

Once in the body, cocaine is rapidly broken down, mainly by enzymes in the plasma (esterases), although metabolism in the liver may also occur. These breakdown (metabolic) products are mainly inactive and are excreted in the urine. They do, however, provide a basis for the laboratory detection of cocaine use by urine testing. An exception to the inactivity of cocaine metabolites occurs when cocaine is taken together with or after alcohol. The alcohol inhibits the normal metabolism of cocaine and as a result a substance called cocaethylene is produced. Cocaethylene is an extremely toxic compound, more so than cocaine, with a special proclivity for the heart and blood vessels.

DEPENDENCY, TOLERANCE, AND ADDICTION

Cocaine increases energy, restores confidence, makes one feel able to face any task, increases intellectual functioning, relieves boredom, and increases sexual performance.

Unfortunately, the pleasurable mood-altering effects are extremely short-lived, often leading to binge behavior or runs. Use often progresses from occasional to daily to compulsive. The risk of addiction is directly related to the time it takes cocaine to reach peak levels and the duration of the effect. Thus freebasing and IV use are associated with a much greater risk than sniffing, which in turn has a greater risk than chewing, with coca tea having the least risk of compulsive use.

Most of those who try cocaine once or twice don't become compulsive users. But the dependency potential of cocaine is great. Use can begin (as with a cocktail) simply as a means of deriving some pleasure and relaxation after a long day. Soon, however, use can become more frequent and more expensive. Rather than using cocaine just to relax after work, it may be taken to get started in the morning, and then to make the day more tolerable. Wide mood swings become noticeable. The user may be devoting all of his or her energies to getting more of the drug.

The Craving for Cocaine

Like other stimulants, cocaine inhibits the reuptake of neurotransmitters in areas of the brain believed to be responsible for behavior. These neurotransmitters include norepinephrine, serotonin, and dopamine. The release of dopamine is thought to stimulate the brain's reward mechanisms, or pleasure centers. As part of a normal cycle, the released dopamine is reabsorbed or metabolized. Cocaine not only facilitates dopamine release but also blocks its reabsorption, thus preventing a feedback mechanism from stopping dopamine production. The result is first an increase in dopamine transmission, but ultimately a depletion of its stores in the brain. The initial increase of dopamine surrounding the brain results in overstimulation, manifested as euphoria, or the cocaine high. As the dopamine supply becomes depleted, depression sets in, followed by a craving for the drug. In laboratory animals, this stimulation of the pleasure centers results in continual self-administration of the drug until death. The addictive potential of cocaine is exceptional.

On that basis, it's believed that since chronic cocaine use inhibits dopamine activity, activating dopamine can mediate the cocaine high. By depleting dopamine, serotonin, and norepinephrine, long-term cocaine use results in an increased sensitivity of the neurons to those neurotransmitters. This increased sensitivity (to the now increased levels of norepinephrine and dopamine) causes withdrawal symptoms when cocaine use suddenly stops. The subsequent craving that occurs has been localized through imaging studies and has been seen to occur in the limbic reagions of the brain, the amygdala, and anterior cingulate. Drugs able to block limbic system activity may assist in decreasing activity. Long-term use also increases sensitivity of the brain to cocaine's non-mood-altering effects. Termed reverse tolerance, this phenomenon, brought on by even small amounts of cocaine in chronic users, shows up as hyperactivity and even convulsions.

ADVERSE EFFECTS OF COCAINE

Adverse effects of cocaine may occur during acute use (Table 14.6), with cocaine withdrawal, or with chronic use. These effects are frequent and at

TABLE 14.6. Acute Toxic Effects

Behavioral effects: irritability, aggressive behavior, delirium, hallucinations, psychosis (including paranoid behavior)
Increased blood pressure and heart rate
Irregular heart rhythms, sometimes fatal
Chest pain, with increased potential for heart attacks
Increased potential for stroke
Ischemia and infarctions of the liver, kidney, spleen
Elevated body temperature (malignant hyperthermia)
Rupture of brain aneurysms
Brain hemorrhage
Seizures and convulsions
Loss of consciousness
Coma
Respiratory and circulatory collapse
Death

times may be fatal. They can develop at any time, depending on how the cocaine is taken (Table 14.7), the dose used, the presence of underlying medical disorders (Table 14.8), the environment in which cocaine is taken, and the contaminants or adulterants with which the cocaine may be mixed.

Behavioral Effects

Acute adverse effects of cocaine on behavior include increasing irritability, aggression, delirium progressing to hallucinations such as bugs under the skin (coke bugs), flashing lights (snow lights), extreme agitation or paranoia, impaired judgment, and loss of conditional reflexes (disinhibition). The user is quick to argue and quick to fight. A perceived slight can result in acting out behavior against those who are often unaware and uninvolved. Judgment can be severely impaired without the user realizing it. Inappropri-

TABLE 14.7. Adverse Effects of Cocaine, by Route

Intranasal (Snorting or Sniffing)	Intravenous (Mainlining)	Inhaling and Freebasing
Sinusitis	AIDS	Pulmonary infections
Running nose	Hepatitis	Coughing up blood
Upper respiratory infections	Infection of heart valves	Asthma
Ulceration of nasal septum	Multiple skin infections	Voice loss
	Pulmonary infections	Chest pains
	Acute allergic reactions	Burns*
		Eye irritation

*Freebasing only

TABLE 14.8. At-Risk Conditions

Medical Disorder	Risk
Abnormalities in blood vessels in brain	Brain hemorrhage, stroke
High blood pressure	Brain hemorrhage, stroke
Epilepsy or potential for seizure disorders	Convulsions
Coronary heart disease	Heart attacks (often fatal), serious disturbances in heart rhythm
Disease of heart valves, including mitral valve prolapse	Serious disturbances in heart rhythm, infection of valves (endocarditis) if cocaine injected
Psychological disorders	Psychotic reactions

ate decisions are made. The user may be impossible to relate to in any meaningful way, and at times anger may be excessive.

Such a stimulant effect is desired by those engaged in antisocial behavior. According to data from the National Institute of Justice on male and female arrests in Washington, DC, in May 1989, 65 percent of those arrested tested positive for cocaine. By comparison, in a similar survey in May 1984, the rate was 18 percent. Adverse behavioral effects of cocaine are common and can result in harm to others even in the absence of criminal intent. According to the Cocaine 800 Hotline Survey, 19 percent of the respondents had been in auto accidents while using cocaine. In New York City from 1984 through 1987, cocaine or its metabolites were detected in 18 percent of autopsies in motor vehicle fatalities. Drivers between the ages of sixteen and forty-five were thirteen times more likely to use cocaine. Statistically, this means that at least one of four drivers in this age group who were killed in such accidents in the city had used cocaine within forty-eight hours of death.

Effects on the Heart and Vascular System

Acute use of cocaine can result in severe and even fatal effects on the cardiovascular system. Cocaine has long been known to cause an increase in blood pressure and heart rate. Frequent use, or even sporadic use with high doses, can result in irregular heart rhythms, including ventricular fibrillation, which without immediate intervention is fatal. Acute increases in blood pressure may lead to dissection of the aorta. The ability of cocaine to constrict the arteries leading to the heart muscle can result in decrease of blood flow, which is associated with heart attacks, especially in those with underlying heart disease. This risk is greatly increased if alcohol is taken before cocaine use (estimated to occur in up to 9 million cocaine users) due to the production of cocaethylene. Cigarette smoking and concomitant cocaine use add an extra burden on the heart due to the constricting effect on the coronary arteries caused by tobacco. It has been estimated that over 64,000 persons are seen in emergency rooms annually with symptoms of chest pain related to cocaine use, with approximately 6 percent of those patients actually sustaining a myocardial infarction. Correspondingly, in some urban areas, emergency rooms have reported up to 25 percent of persons with chest pain having urines positive for cocaine or its metabolite with up to 6 percent having positive blood tests indicative of myocardial infarctions. One study of younger patients with cocaine-associated myocardial infarctions found one-third to have negative angiograms, with the remaining demonstrating evidence of coronary artery disease. Interestingly, the cardiac effects of cocaine may not be seen until several hours or more after cocaine use. This may be related to the effects of cocaine metabolites on the coronary arteries.

Effects on the Central Nervous System

A direct effect of cocaine on the central nervous system can be a marked increase in body temperature, producing what is termed "malignant hyperthermia." Correspondingly, consumption of cocaine in areas where the ambient temperature is high (88°F-31°C or above) has been associated with a significant increase in mortality from cocaine overdose. Increases in blood pressure, accompanied by constriction of the arteries to the brain, may also result in strokes, seizures, convulsions, and coma. Studies using imaging techniques (PET scans) have demonstrated defects in the brain, resulting from a decrease in dopamine receptors during acute cocaine use, which can persist from months to a year after abstinence has been achieved. Interactions have also been described with other neurotransmitters, including GABA, serotonin, and glutamate as well as with nitric oxide. The relationship of these changes to the craving for cocaine frequently reported by those who remain abstinent has not yet been clearly defined.

Effects on Persons with Coexisting Psychological Disorders

Since cocaine itself can often cause psychotic syndromes, not infrequently the presence of an underlying psychological disorder that precedes cocaine use can go undetected. Persons with underlying depression, anxiety disorders, and borderline states often find relief with cocaine, which in turn may worsen the underlying problem or superimpose upon it an acute paranoid state. The ability to separate primary psychological disorders from those caused by cocaine becomes quite important in the treatment of cocaine dependency, as failure to recognize these conditions will result in failure of the therapeutic efforts.

Effects on the Respiratory System

Complications in the lungs resulting from cocaine's effects on blood vessels or from an allergic reaction to contaminants in the cocaine can result in the lung tissue filling with fluid (pulmonary edema) and death by lack of oxygen (anoxia). If injected, infected material may remain in the lungs, causing pneumonia or a condition termed septic pulmonary emboli.

Effects on Reproduction and Sexual Activity

Cocaine use is accompanied by both increased libido and an impairment of judgment. As a result, the user is at risk for contracting sexually transmitted diseases and HIV. Women who conceive and use cocaine can expose their fetuses to increased risk from cocaine as well as sexually transmitted diseases and HIV (Chapters 18 and 19).

Unusual Effects of Cocaine Use

Among the more unusual effects of cocaine use are impaired blood circulation to the bowels, resulting in a severe impairment of intestinal circulation and in gangrene; sudden death during sexual activity from rapid absorption of large amounts of cocaine applied directly to the penis or the vagina; gangrene from injection directly into the urethra of the penis; and a condition called body packer syndrome seen in cocaine smugglers.

The body packer syndrome is a consequence of smugglers or "mules" swallowing large amounts of cocaine in rubber containers or condoms to escape detection on entering the country. Once the smuggler eludes customs, a mild laxative is taken and the packs are excreted. This method of transport can result in blockage of the intestines and/or acute cocaine overdose and death, if the packets leak or rupture.

Adverse Effects During Withdrawal

Adverse and even fatal reactions have been reported hours and days after using cocaine or during withdrawal. In one study of presumably healthy young men being withdrawn from cocaine, up to 38 percent showed decreased blood flow to the heart muscle. The relationship between myocardial infarctions and withdrawal from cocaine has been the subject of an increasing number of articles. In one study of men who developed chest pain between one and a half and eighteen hours following cocaine use, approximately 30 percent developed actual heart attacks. The reasons for myocardial infarctions developing in the absence of cocaine in the body need to be more clearly determined. However, it is believed that two factors may play a role in this delayed reaction. The first hypothesis involves a sudden replenishment by the body of neurotransmitters depleted by cocaine, more specifically catecholamines. This results in a marked stimulation of the heart and vascular system. The second hypothesis is that the metabolite benzoylecgonine, produced when cocaine is broken down in the body, can be detected days after cocaine has been eliminated. It may also explain the lingering effects of cocaine on the brain, such as headaches, seizure, or strokes, which also can occur hours or days later.

Even in the absence of the severe effects of withdrawal, discontinuing cocaine after dependency is frequently accompanied by dysphoria, fatigue, insomnia, increased appetite and, at times, psychomotor agitation. These symptoms can develop within several days after stopping use, may be accompanied by drug craving, and are different from the symptoms seen during the crash after cocaine runs and binges.

Effects on Users with Underlying Medical Disorders

Even relatively small amounts of cocaine can have adverse effects in persons with underlying medical disorders. People with epilepsy, coronary artery disease, liver disease, diseases of the heart valves, rhythm disturbances, or psychological disorders are most susceptible. In one study of people undergoing coronary angiograms, very low doses of cocaine decreased the diameter of the left coronary artery (which supplies blood to most of the heart) by 8 to 12 percent.

Unfortunately, not infrequently people may be unaware that they have such conditions. For example, more than 500,000 people have silent coronary artery disease, and many of them would experience a cardiac complication if they took cocaine. Mitral valve prolapse, a condition seen in up to 10 percent of the population, may also predispose someone to irregular heart rhythms when cocaine is used. The drug has also been responsible for psychotic reactions in people not known to have prior psychological disturbances. Whether such psychotic behavior results from cocaine alone or would have appeared eventually without cocaine use has not been clearly determined.

Effect of Adulterants and Substitutes

Adulterants in cocaine mixtures cause many adverse effects. Quinine, when injected, causes increased tissue destruction and abscess formation. Manganese carbonate can cause Parkinson-like symptoms, and such stimulants as antiasthmatic medications, amphetamines, and diet pills can increase toxicity to the central nervous system. An herbicide used to curtail growth of the coca leaf was found in one batch of cocaine and caused eye irritation and gastrointestinal disturbances. Other substances mixed with cocaine include all those found in heroin mixtures (Table 14.2). Allergic reactions to a number of such adulterants can occur quite easily, often with fatal results.

Sometimes a substance sold as cocaine may contain no cocaine, but instead a substitute capable of producing similar effects. The most potent are the amphetamines, particularly ice, the methamphetamine derivative (Chapter 13). Other substitutes include less potent stimulants such as ephedrine and phenylpropanolamine, and the anesthetics lidocaine, benzocaine, procaine, and tetracaine. These anesthetic drugs, especially lidocaine, may be associated with seizures when larger doses are injected.

Chronic Adverse Effects of Cocaine Use

Consistent use of cocaine may produce a variety of local complications, depending on the way the cocaine is taken. These may range in intensity from a runny nose and sinusitis resulting from snorting, to severe lung and heart valve infections, to hepatitis and the transmission of the AIDS virus from intravenous use. Use of coca paste has been associated with psychotic behavior, including hallucinations and suicidal or homicidal attempts. Complications to the heart and lungs from inhaling the solvents used to make the paste may also occur. Cocaine taken in any form has considerable effects on pregnancy and the newborn (Chapter 19). General nonspecific symptoms reported by cocaine users include chronic insomnia, fatigue, headaches, sinus infections, disrupted sexual function, nausea and vomiting, depression, anxiety and irritability, paranoia, loss of interest in all but drug-related activities, and marked difficulty in function (Table 14.9). This is believed to be due to a chronic depletion of neurotransmitters. One recent study of brain damage in chronic cocaine users found that 50 percent have a condition called cerebral atrophy, a shrinkage of brain tissue. Long-term use of cocaine has also been reported to cause cardiac enlargement with decreased function.

Effects of Cocaine in Combination with Other Drugs

Cocaine may also be used with other drugs to reduce its stimulant effect or to offset the sedative effect of another drug. Using cocaine with alcohol, especially when driving, is particularly dangerous, for the depressant effect of alcohol lasts much longer than the stimulant effect of cocaine. Since both substances can reduce awareness, judgment, and reaction time, they represent a particularly dangerous combination. As discussed earlier, use of cocaine with alcohol also produces an extremely toxic substance, cocaethylene. Cocaine use has also been shown to enhance sensitivity to the benzodiazepines, even at low doses.

TABLE 14.9. Effects of Chronic Cocaine Use

Depression	Nausea and vomiting	Panic attacks
Insomnia	Disruption in sexual function	Postcocaine dysphoria
Fatigue	Increased anxiety, irritability	Cocaine psychosis
Severe headaches	Inability to function	Malnutrition
Loss of consciousness		

Effects of Cocaine on the Nonuser

As the need for more and more cocaine escalates, so does the user's need for money. Discretionary personal funds are the first to go, followed by depletion of money necessary for family responsibilities. When pleas to family and friends eventually fail, the user often turns to illicit activities to get money. The safety of entire neighborhoods is severely compromised when the sale and use of cocaine and other drugs become prevalent. Residents are afraid of venturing out of their apartments. Complaints to the police can bring reprisals from dealers. Warfare between dealers for distribution rights can turn neighborhoods into battlegrounds. To evade the law, dealers recruit children into the distribution chain. Lured by the relatively risk-free quick money, many youngsters begin to deal crack and soon find themselves users who are dependent on and bound to their supplier.

To many readers, this may seem overly dramatic, an updated version of a Dickens novel. But it's bitter reality to the many people who have seen their children's emotional and physical lives destroyed by crack. The added misfortune is that this drama is often played out in economically depressed areas, where residents struggling simply to survive also have to face the overwhelming drug burden. Worse yet, their plight is accompanied by much outside sympathy but little actual support.

TREATMENT OF COCAINE DEPENDENCY

Treatment of Acute Toxic Reactions and Withdrawal

The treatment of acute toxic reactions to cocaine varies with the specific manifestations. In many cases, just keeping the person in a quiet environment and providing reassurance suffices. For acute psychosis and/or hallucinations, a major tranquilizer and neuroleptic agent such as haloperidol (Haldol) can be used. Seizures can be controlled with benzodiazepines. But it is important to take the person to a hospital as quickly as possible. Depending on the specific manifestation of cocaine toxicity, treatment should be directed toward the organ system involved.

Treatment of withdrawal is often supportive, with benzodiazepines being used only when needed. Since depression is the hallmark of withdrawal, assessment should be made to make certain a suicide risk is not present.

Long-Term Treatment

Treating the chronic cocaine user physiologically, psychologically, and behaviorally is highly challenging, but far from impossible. As described by

Arnold Washton, PhD, to achieve long-term abstinence usually requires passage through five distinct phases.

Phase 1 consists of withdrawal—usually lasting two to four days, but sometimes two weeks—accompanied by irritability and urgent craving for cocaine. Phase 2, lasting one to four weeks, finds the person feeling quite well and even convinced that the problem has been resolved. Only a minimal craving for cocaine is present. Phase 3 may last for two months and shows up as depression, anxiety, inability to concentrate, and a sharp escalation of craving for the drug. This is when the person is at greatest risk of returning to the drug, especially in social settings of prior use where alcohol, cocaine, and other drugs are being consumed. Phase 4 begins three to four months after abstinence starts and is marked by a return to normal functioning with only occasional cravings for cocaine, unless the person is in high-risk settings. Phase 5 sees almost complete normalization of behavior or development of another addictive behavior such as excessive drinking.

A variety of forms of treatment are available. There are therapeutic communities (Chapter 6) and programs that offer a twenty-eight-day inpatient stay followed by outpatient care. Patients may be offered a shorter inpatient time plus the outpatient care, or perhaps a program of outpatient care exclusively. Pharmacological therapies are also available but often not satisfying. Each form of treatment has advantages and risks. But the treatment most cost effective and acceptable to the greatest number of those seeking treatment is outpatient care preceded by a brief inpatient stay.

Nonpharmacological Therapies

Inpatient care

Inpatient treatment is recommended for management of cocaine addiction when: (a) the person can't stop using cocaine even for short periods; (b) dependencies on other mood-altering drugs exist, requiring detoxification; (c) a severe psychological or medical problem exists (psychotic paranoid behavior, suicidal or homicidal thoughts, or severe heart, liver, or lung disease); or (d) there are accompanying problems such as lack of a support system whereby the person can provide self-care, lack of motivation to attend any outpatient therapy, or a history of failed outpatient therapy.

Inpatient treatment specifically for cocaine use is similar to outpatient treatment, except that it also allows other problems requiring hospitalization to be treated. Preexisting psychological disturbances should be recognized and treated. Mood disorders, which increase susceptibility to inappropriate cocaine use, have been found in up to half of those who do use cocaine excessively. Most important, and often the most difficult problem to address, is the development of adequate support systems. Unless the person can be kept from returning to the environment in which he or she used cocaine, successful rehabilitation is rare. Therapeutic communities, which provide a readily available residence phase and then continuous support on an outpatient basis, can therefore be effective.

Outpatient Treatment

The three stages of outpatient treatment begin with the immediate and complete cessation of cocaine and other drug use. Gradually decreasing the quantity of cocaine doesn't work because the mood-altering effects and reinforcement continue, and use will resume at its prior level. Use of other mood-altering drugs must be stopped as well because they, too, provide a positive conditioning effect and a desire to continue using cocaine. They also lower inhibitions, thus increasing susceptibility to returning to cocaine. Frequent urine testing may be necessary for effective monitoring as well as providing incentives for abstinence. Several therapy or counseling sessions a week help provide support and encouragement, and can address the craving and reasons for having started cocaine use. To be most successful, these sessions should be part of a structured program that includes instruction in stress management and relaxation techniques. That can be provided as part of individual or group therapy run by professional therapists, or through such self-help groups as Cocaine Anonymous and Narcotics Anonymous.

The second stage focuses on prevention of relapse. It requires a change in lifestyle: learning to avoid the factors associated with cocaine use, detecting the early warning signs of craving, and handling the feelings of defeat after instances of sporadic use. Building self-esteem and coping with unavoidable situations linked to prior cocaine use are some of the other problems that are tackled.

The final stage is consolidation, usually beginning after a year of treatment. It consists largely of continuing individual, group, or self-help therapy. The length of this stage depends on a person's needs. As with other drug dependencies, relapse is almost certain if drug use was initiated because of inability to function in society. Sufficient supports, such as retraining and vocational and family counseling, must also be part of the consolidation stage.

Pharmacological Therapies

Directed primarily toward relieving acute symptoms in the early phase of withdrawal, as well as depression, pharmacological therapies were also developed to prevent the craving for cocaine.

Since many of cocaine's effects result from increased levels in the brain of the neurotransmitter dopamine, which is depleted with chronic cocaine use, selective drug therapy tries to block those effects with a "nonaddicting" drug, and then to replenish the depleted neurotransmitters. Other drugs are prescribed to prevent the depression that accompanies withdrawal. These drugs, if effective, may well decrease the reinforcing effects of cocaine and therefore lessen the craving for it.

Increasing Dopamine Effects

Both bromocriptine (Parlodel) and amantadine (Symmetrel) were initially thought effective in relieving the craving and dysphoria in the first phase of cocaine withdrawal. Bromocriptine, a dopamine agonist, significantly increases energy and relieves depression. Side effects may include headaches, dizziness, and sedation. Amantadine can cause release of dopamine and norepinephrine from neuronal pleasure centers and was thought to be effective in treating acute symptoms of withdrawal. However, large clinical trials with these drugs were quite disappointing, with the drugs no more effective than placebos.

In efforts to directly influence production of dopamine, the substance from which dopamine is made, L-tyrosine, has been administered in a preparation (Tropamine) that also contains L-tryptophan, L-glutamine, L-phenylalanine, and a variety of vitamins and minerals. One study suggested that Tropamine can reduce withdrawal symptoms and help put patients remaining in treatment at ease. Unfortunately this has not been shown to be of significant value in subsequent evaluations. In addition, L-tryptophan food supplements have been associated with eosinophilia-myalgia syndrome, a rare disorder with a variety of symptoms, including itching, fatigue, muscle pains, tenderness and cramps, joint pains, weakness, and, at times, shortness of breath. As a result, the Food and Drug Administration ordered a recall of all such products in November 1989, followed by a warning to the public in March 1990 not to use them.

Antipsychotic Drugs

Neuroleptics, a group of drugs classed as major tranquilizers, are believed to block the euphoria of cocaine and amphetamines through their dopamine-inhibiting effects and to reduce self-administration of cocaine in laboratory animals. Two such drugs are chlorpromazine (Thorazine, Promaz) and fluphenazine (Prolixin, Permitil). But their side effects make it unlikely that people will take them voluntarily for any period, and the unpleasant feeling they produce may even promote cocaine use. Under study is another drug in this group, flupenthixol, which may turn out to be more successful. At low doses it acts as an antidepressant and can be administered as a slow-release, long-acting injectable. Haloperidol (Haldol), an antipsychotic drug with fewer side effects than the other major tranquilizers, has been used with apparent success in Japan to prevent a return to cocaine use. Much more research is needed in this area.

Antidepressants

Certain tricyclic antidepressants have been used both to treat depression and to reduce the craving for cocaine. They include desipramine (Norpramin, Pertofrane) and imipramine (Tofranil, Janimine, Pramine). They've been especially effective during the second phase of withdrawal. Their use in treatment, however, requires careful monitoring because some—notably amitriptyline (Elavil)—have a well-known history of inappropriate use. The antidepressants trazodone (Desyrel, Trazon, Trialodine) and buspirone (BuSpar) may also be helpful in relieving withdrawal and promoting abstinence.

Miscellaneous Drugs

A variety of other drugs are in various stages of evaluation for treatment of cocaine dependency. They include lithium, pemoline, bupropion, pergolide, ritanserin, sertraline, and several stimulants. One of the stimulants, methylphenidate (Ritalin), has known potential for inappropriate use and so carries its own risks. As noted previously, this is an extremely effective drug for hyperactivity and, when recommended by a physician, should not be withheld for fear of dependency. It recently has been reported to diminish both cocaine craving and cocaine use.

Buprenorphine (Buprenex), an agonist-antagonist marketed to control pain (Chapter 11), has decreased cocaine self-administration in animals. In humans it has been suggested that the use of buprenorphine and Antabuse (disulfiram) might be effective in reducing cocaine use in opiate-dependent persons. Mazindol (Mazanor, Sanorex), a dopamine blocker used to treat compulsive eaters, has also been suggested for cocaine addiction. None of these drugs has been proven successful, and some may be associated with dependency risks of their own.

Carbamazepine, an anticonvulsant medication, has been suggested as an adjunct in decreasing cocaine use through decreasing craving. However, subsequent studies were unable to demonstrate that carbamazepine is any more effective than placebos.

Maintenance Therapy

Since oral consumption of coca leaves through chewing or tea drinking have not been associated with the usual signs of cocaine dependence, and studies involving physiological changes and reactions to psychological tests have fallen within normal range, it has been suggested that low-dose cocaine maintenance with coca tea or specially prepared tablets would be successful in diminishing cocaine use as well as prolonging abstinence. One study found that coca tea consumption in conjunction with counseling diminished frequency of relapse by 80 percent and extended abstinence from an average of 32 days before treatment to 217 days after treatment. Further study is necessary, however, prior to recommending this as a course of therapy.

Acupuncture

Acupuncture has been used for a number of addictions, with heroin being most prominent. A randomized controlled trial of acupuncture for cocaine use revealed that those who remained in the active protocol were significantly more likely to have negative urine for cocaine than either the "sham" acupuncture group or the group treated with relaxation techniques (53.8 percent versus 23.5 percent versus 9.1 percent, respectively). However, retention among these three groups was less in the acupuncture group than the other two (46 percent versus 63 percent versus 81 percent). These results, however, are promising, and more well-designed studies on the use of acupuncture in cocaine dependency are warranted.

Vaccine Development

Since to date no specific pharmacological agent has been proven to be exceedingly effective in preventing cocaine use, attention has recently been focused on developing a vaccine against cocaine. In a laboratory model, antibodies to cocaine can be developed that would block the effects of cocaine on the nerve terminals. This approach is theoretically doable and investigators are actively pursuing ultimate clinical trials.

Chapter 15

Nicotine

Smoking Causes Lung Cancer, Heart Disease, Emphysema, and May Complicate Pregnancy.

Quitting Smoking Now Greatly Reduces Serious Risks to Your Health.

Smoking By Pregnant Women May Result in Fetal Injury, Premature Birth, and Low Birth Weight.

Cigarette Smoke Contains Carbon Monoxide.

surgeon general's warnings on cigarette packages

Evidence of tobacco use appears in Mayan stone carvings from 2,500 years ago. Explorers to the New World found Native Americans inhaling smoke from pipes or rolls of leaves to produce mood-altering effects. After tobacco was brought to Europe and elsewhere, it was either smoked, chewed, or ground to be used as snuff. No matter how it was consumed, tobacco's positive reinforcing—and even addicting—qualities became well known.

Papal bulls prohibiting its use were issued by Popes Urban VIII and Innocent X between 1640 and 1650. Also in the 1600s, Bavaria, Saxony, Zurich, and Japan initiated measures first to restrict and then to prohibit its use. The prohibitions were unsuccessful, so severe penalties, including mutilation, were imposed. In Russia and Constantinople, the penalty was death. Ultimately, all those efforts proved futile.

Chewing tobacco and snuff were popular in the United States through the early 1900s. The social stigma of spitting and the transmission of tuberculosis through this route soon led to decline of the practice, accompanied by a significant increase in cigarette smoking. At first, people rolled their own by hand, but then went on to use an 1884 invention—the mechanical cigarette rolling machine. Cigarettes soon became widely available to both adults and children. By 1921, reaction was so strong that fourteen states had enacted legislation prohibiting cigarettes. As with Prohibition, it soon became evident that smoking habits couldn't be legislated, and all such legislation was repealed by 1927.

In 1964, the first of many reports on smoking and health was released by the surgeon general's Advisory Committee on the Health Consequences of Smoking. It can probably be credited as the first major contributor in reducing cigarette consumption. The report detailed many of the unpublicized effects of smoking and was followed by a definite but short-lived decrease in cigarette consumption. But smoking gradually increased again over the next decade.

Since the late 1960s, the surgeon general's office has been joined by all major health-related organizations in trying to limit smoking. Many government agencies have funded education and prevention programs as part of the effort. The 1985 Comprehensive Smoking Education Act unequivocally emphasized the need and obligation of tobacco manufacturers to inform the public of the hazards of smoking. That warning, plus identification of chemical substances in cigarettes, was displayed on each package. To emphasize those facts, the Department of Health and Human Services legislated a mandatory public education program monitored by the Interagency Committee on Smoking and Health. The committee included representatives from the public sector, major health organizations active in promoting a nonsmoking theme, and research agencies dealing with the adverse effects of smoking. The National Cancer Institute and the National Institute on Drug Abuse were part of this group.

A report of the surgeon general in 1989 recognized smoking as an addiction and clearly identified tobacco as another addictive drug—albeit a legal one. The recognition by the surgeon general of the addictive properties of smoking tobacco, however, seems to have lagged far behind that of the tobacco industry, as has been recently demonstrated in a multitude of "secret" documents that have been released over the last several years. These documents suggest that not only did the industry know nicotine was addictive but, in fact, in some instances considered manipulating the amount of nicotine in cigarettes to increase this dependency. Perhaps this is not surprising, considering an estimated $47 billion per year tobacco industry and a rapidly growing $50 million export market. However, such actions are indefensible and in no small part have been responsible for the industry continually being under siege by states' attorneys for the costs of tobacco-related illnesses.

As a result of these disclosures, the industry considered reimbursing the states a total of $368.5 billion for the cost of providing smoking-related health care services. Initially for a variety of reasons, not the least of which was intensive lobbying, including contributions to legislators of both parties, the settlement floundered. However, after reopening discussions the four largest tobacco makers concluded a $206 billion settlement with forty-six states in November 1998 to resolve the increasing number of suits by individual states. This agreement differed from those initially proposed as it involves considerably less money and does not provide for any penalties if underage smoking is not reduced. It also was accompanied by a significant increase in the price of a pack of cigarettes, which over twenty-five years would completely cover the cost of the settlement.

The Food and Drug Administration and Tobacco Regulations

Until 1995, the Food and Drug Administration had not attempted to establish its authority to regulate the tobacco industry. However, in 1996, following an intensive study of the industry, the FDA decided that it did have the authority to regulate tobacco products as devices that delivered drugs to consumers. To initiate its regulatory authority, the FDA published a series of rules to diminish children's access to tobacco. As might be expected, this decision was immediately challenged by the tobacco industry, with the litigation reaching the Supreme Court. On March 21, 2000, in a five-to-four decision, the Supreme Court upheld the tobacco industry's claim.

CIGARETTE SMOKERS TODAY

From 1976 to 1998, the population of adult cigarette smokers in the United States decreased from 37 to 24 percent—the lowest ever recorded. However, as of 1998, an estimated 47 to 57 million Americans—still 24 percent of the population age eighteen or older—were current smokers. This figure is quite similar to 1995 data. More important is the NHSDA finding that between 1990 and 1997 among persons ages twelve to seventeen years, the rule of initiation of first use increased from 100.9 to 159.2 per 1,000 new users. The 2000 Monitoring the Future Survey reported 15 percent of eighth graders and 31 percent of twelfth graders to be current smokers. More than 3,000 persons under eighteen years of age each day become daily smokers. The Center for Disease Control has estimated that, if current trends continue, 5 million children under eighteen years old in the year 2000, will ultimately die prematurely as adults due to their initiating smoking in adolescence.

The 1989 surgeon general's report estimated that without the educational efforts there might have been 91 million smokers in 1985 instead of 50 million. That success, however, seems related to educational background and socioeconomic status. People with a high school education account for 35 percent of smokers; those with postgraduate college education account for only 17 percent. One of our national health objectives for the year 2010 is to reduce the prevalence of current smokers to no more than 12 percent. However, it is unlikely this will be reached. A study projecting trends in cigarette smoking to the year 2000 suggested that 22 percent of the adult population, or 40 million people, would be smokers at that time. This is 7.2 million fewer smokers than is actually believed to exist.

Since 80 percent of smokers begin before age eighteen, with 53 percent rapidly becoming daily smokers, the prevalence of smoking among teenagers assumes special importance. Although smoking among adults has decreased over the past several years as noted above, there is a considerable way to go before we can feel complacent. Most important, although it was previously thought that if smoking did not begin before the age of eighteen the chances were quite good the person would never smoke, a recent survey among college students did not confirm this. This survey found that the thirty-day prevalence of smoking increased among college students from 22 percent in 1993 to 28 percent in 1997, with 28 percent starting after age nineteen and 18 percent having made more than five attempts to quit. Of equal concern is the finding that past-month smoking increased in African-American students by 80 percent and among Hispanic students by 34 percent between 1991 and 1997, reversing the consistent decline among these groups that had previously existed.

AVAILABLE NICOTINE PRODUCTS

Low-Nicotine Cigarettes

Efforts to meet public demand for a "safer cigarette" have greatly reduced the tar and nicotine content of cigarettes since the 1950s. Between 1955 and 1987, average tar yield per cigarette fell from 34 to 13 milligrams; the average nicotine yield from 2 to 0.9 milligrams. The most recent efforts have included cigarettes containing 0.1 milligrams of nicotine or less, with tar levels as low as 1 milligram.

The preliminary data suggesting that the new type of cigarettes may be less hazardous assume that smokers won't change their smoking patterns. The fact is, to get the same amount of nicotine, many who use low-yield cigarettes take more frequent puffs, inhale more deeply, and smoke a greater number of cigarettes. The use of additives to enhance flavor and the deletion of irritants may attract more smokers, especially adolescents. The inability to see sidestream smoke may give the impression that smoking is less dangerous. Such gimmicks may mislead heavy smokers into thinking that switching to the low-yield nicotine and tar cigarettes is safe. Hughes has noted that of eighty-four smokers of cigarettes containing less than 0.5 mg nicotine, only 35 percent were able to stop smoking for one week and only 8 percent for six months. However, even determining the actual tar and nicotine yields of a specific brand may not be easy. Ronald Davis, MD, and associates, in a survey of 160 cigarette brands, found tar yield listed on only 14 percent and nicotine yield on only 11 percent. As the tar yield of a brand increased, it was less likely to be shown. No cigarette yielding 11 mg or more of tar disclosed that on the package.

Nonetheless, cigarette companies continue to pursue the development of not only low-nicotine cigarettes but smokeless cigarettes as well. One such product, called Eclipse, is said to deliver nicotine primarily by heating rather than burning tobacco, creating an aerosol-containing nicotine, as well as other substances, thereby eliminating 95 percent of secondhand smoke and many, but not all, of the carcinogens produced by burning. While this may lower the risk of bronchogenic cancer, the production of carbon monoxide, which is essentially unchanged or slightly increased, along with the effects of nicotine, maintains the cardiovascular risk associated with smoking. A study by the Massachusetts Department of Public Health found that the Eclipse cigarette, while not burning tobacco, nonetheless contained 734 percent more acetaldehyde and 475 percent more acrolein, two agents known to be associated with cancers, than the company's low-tar brand.* The safety and acceptability of such products remain to be determined, as does an answer to the question of whether such a product is merely a drug delivery system and therefore under the aegis of the Food and Drug Administration.

Smokeless Tobacco

Smokeless or spit tobacco comes in two forms: chew, which is bulky tobacco sold in pouches, and snuff, which is finely ground tobacco packaged in tins. The popularity of smokeless tobacco among the young is also increasing. Even when general use of this product declined in the 1920s, athletes continued to use it over the next two decades. It was particularly popular with baseball players, who appreciated chewing tobacco's ability to produce saliva to keep their mouths moist and their gloves soft. By the 1950s, smoking had pretty much replaced chewing and was, in fact, advocated by many athletes in cigarette advertisements.

In the early 1970s, smokeless tobacco began to appear again with some frequency on the ball fields, both as a chew and as a snuff (dip). Snuff is a ground tobacco product placed between the gum and the cheek. Pluck is a chewing tobacco sold loose in a container or as a solid chunk. These products are advertised as alternative methods of nicotine use, and a number of brands have appeared on the market.

A survey of male college baseball players revealed that 40 percent used smokeless tobacco regularly, compared with 3 percent who smoked ciga-

---

Boston Globe, October 4, 2000.

rettes. In a survey of 265 players on seven major league teams, 34 percent were current users of smokeless tobacco; 17 percent past users. Of the current users, 93 percent took snuff, either alone or in combination with chewing tobacco, and 8 percent used chewing tobacco alone. Of the current users, 15 percent were also smoking approximately ten cigarettes per day. Although 28 percent of the players admitted that smokeless tobacco was very harmful, and 65 percent believed it was somewhat harmful, almost 30 percent said they couldn't stop because they were "hooked."

In the past, tobacco companies aggressively promoted smokeless tobacco, and their campaigns worked. The use of snuff increased by 55 percent between 1978 and 1985, a time when cigarette sales were decreasing. By 1985, men under age nineteen were the heaviest users of smokeless tobacco, compared with 1970, when men over age fifty-five were the greatest users. In the younger group, the proportion of men between the ages of seventeen and nineteen who used oral snuff rose from 0.3 to 2.9 percent; the proportion for chewing tobacco rose from 1.2 to 3 percent—a tenfold and threefold increase, respectively. The 2000 Monitoring the Future Survey found almost 8 percent of high school seniors to be current smokeless tobacco users. The NHSDA 1999 Survey reported 7.6 million people to be current users of smokeless tobacco.

Cigars

Cigars, often considered safer than cigarettes, still can deliver substantial amounts of nicotine and are associated with cancer of the oral cavity, esophagus, and lung. Public interest in smoking cigars has increased considerably over the past several years, with approximately 4.5 billion cigars smoked in the United States in 1996, representing an increase in consumption of 45 percent since 1993, with sales of premium cigars increasing by over 75 percent between 1993 and 1998. The 1999 NHSDA reported 12.1 million persons twelve years or older to be current cigar smokers. In addition, cigar smoking now involves women, as well as men, and has become much more popular among teenagers. In 1996, an estimated 6 million fourteen- to nineteen-year-olds reported smoking cigars in the previous year, representing 4.3 percent of males and 1.7 percent of females. Of these students, 69 percent did not smoke cigarettes. Adolescent boys now smoke cigars more frequently than chewing smokeless tobacco. This is of considerable concern, not only due to the adverse effects of such activities, but also, since the surgeon general's warning does not have to be placed on cigar products, teenagers may not be aware of the dangers in cigar smoking or the nicotine content of cigars (Table 15.1).

TABLE 15.1. Average Nicotine Content of Cigarettes

	Tar (mg)	Carbon Monoxide	Nicotine (mg)
Filter cigarette	16	14	1.1
Cigar	37	96	9.8
Filter small cigar	24	38	3.8
Premium cigar	44	97	13.3

Source: Adapted from Ingersoll, B. "U.S. Regulators to Raise a Stink About Cigars." *Wall Street Journal,* February 9, 1998, B1.

Although considered safer than cigarettes, since one may not inhale, in fact, daily cigar smokers have risks of cancer similar to those who inhale cigar smoke, having a greater risk than cigarette smokers for cancer and double the risk of chronic obstructive lung disease. The risk of coronary disease is also increased. Even among cigar smokers who do not inhale, those who smoke one or more cigars a day have an increased risk of oral cancer and of laryngeal cancer compared to nonsmokers. In addition, due to their size, burning cigars results in the delivery of many more carcinogens in the smoke than cigarettes and higher levels of carbon monoxide that may persist for hours. As a final note on the prominence of cigars, a recent article in *The New York Times* described a trend among some chefs to lace food with cigar and pipe tobacco.* One restaurant's recipe, which served twelve, called for 12 tablespoons of tobacco. This might result in as much as 60 mg of tobacco per serving (1 gram of cigar tobacco has 10-20 mg). This practice, which at best seems quite foolish, may have adverse effects on nontolerant persons with underlying medical conditions such as heart disease.

Blunts

A product being seen with increasing frequency on the street is a "blunt" cigar. Blunts are cheap cigars whose insides have been hollowed out and replaced with marijuana in order to develop a more potent high. Indeed, it has been suggested that the increase in purchases of inexpensive cigars has been fueled by their use in blunting. This was accentuated when several brands were actually labeled blunts, which led to allegations that companies were trying to compete in the illicit blunt market. Denials were accompanied by withdrawal of these brands from the marketplace.

The New York Times, January 31, 2001, F2.

Bidis

Bidis, small cigarettes wrapped in tobacco leaves, have been smoked since the beginning of the twentieth century in India, where it is estimated that eight bidis are smoked for every regular cigarette. Exported into this country in the mid-1990s, they are available in multiple flavors, costing $1.50 to $4.00 for a package of twenty. A survey in Massachusetts in the spring of 1999 found that of 642 youths surveyed, 40 percent were lifetime users of bidis, 16 percent current smokers, and 8 percent heavy smokers.

Bidis are popular as they cost less, taste better, and are easier to purchase than regular cigarettes. Unfortunately, they also produce three times the amount of carbon monoxide and nicotine and five times the amount of tar compared to regular cigarettes, making users more likely to experience all of the adverse effects associated with cigarette smoking.

Kretek

Originally indigenous to Indonesia, kreteks are cigarettes containing approximately 60 percent tobacco and 40 percent cloves. Kretek is an Indonesian term meaning crackles, sounds produced when cloves burn. Kreteks are packed more densely than regular cigarettes and therefore burn more slowly, lasting about twice as long. The risks associated with their use are the same as seen with regular tobacco-containing products. A number of brands are available wholesale on the Internet.

Both bidis and kreteks are viewed by the Centers for Disease Control and Prevention as a growing public health problem among the young. The CDC's 1999 survey of tobacco use among middle and high school students revealed that 5 percent of those surveyed had used bidis and 5.8 percent had smoked kretek, figures quite close to the 6.6 percent of youths reported to have used smokeless tobacco.

INGREDIENTS IN TOBACCO

More than 4,000 substances are generated by smoking. Approximately 500 are in tobacco, and 3,500 are released when the tobacco is burned. At least forty-three substances are believed to be able to cause cancer. Of most concern are nicotine, carbon monoxide, and "tar" (the material remaining after water and nicotine are removed).

Nicotine, the active ingredient in tobacco, was first isolated in 1828 at the University of Heidelberg in Germany. Its chemical formula was determined in the 1840s, and it was synthesized before the 1890s. By the early 1900s, nicotine was considered the reason for tobacco's popularity. The nicotine content of a cigarette can vary from 0.2 to 5 percent. When smoked, a cigarette delivers from 0.1 to 2 milligrams of nicotine. Pipe and cigar tobacco smoke contain greater amounts of nicotine, but the smoke is usually not inhaled, and absorption of nicotine occurs mainly through the mucous membrane of the mouth.

Some cigarette manufacturers identify the nicotine, tar, and carbon monoxide content, but relating these figures to individual clinical patterns of smoking is difficult, if not impossible. The amounts of tar, nicotine, and carbon monoxide inhaled depend on the number of puffs, depth of inhalation, and number of cigarettes smoked. Filters can trap a small quantity of gas and particles, but neither low tar nor low-nicotine cigarettes actively reduce the amount of carbon monoxide that is produced. Traps near the top of the cigarette are designed to reduce tar and carbon monoxide, and appear to be effective in laboratory settings. But they're far less so during actual smoking. In fact, although the average tar yield in cigarettes decreased between 1954 and 1994 from 37 mg to 12 mg, the relative risk of lung cancer increased. This paradoxical finding may be related to an increase in the number of filter cigarettes smoked, deeper inhalation of the smoke, or blocking the vents in the filter with one's fingers. It has been estimated that as many as 60 percent of smokers are unaware of the presence of vents in filter tip cigarettes or that the tar yield increases considerably when the vents are blocked.

Smoke

A cigarette emits three types of smoke: (a) mainstream, inhaled directly by the smoker; (b) sidestream, produced by the tobacco burning between puffs; and (c) environmental, the combination of sidestream and exhaled mainstream smoke. Sidestream smoke has the same constituency as mainstream smoke but has higher concentrations of carbon monoxide. Because it's produced at a lower combustion temperature, it contains more of smoke's organic constituents, including those considered carcinogenic. Environmental smoke is largely diluted by air and aged to varying degrees before it's inhaled by nonsmokers (passive smokers) and smokers. About 85 percent of environmental smoke consists of sidestream smoke.

Each puff of a cigarette contains about 0.25 milligrams of nicotine, and each cigarette lasts an average of ten to twelve puffs. How much nicotine is absorbed through the mucous membranes of the mouth and pharynx depends on the pH (alkalinity/acidity) of the material being smoked. Cigarette tobacco has a low pH (low alkalinity), so there's little absorption. But the air-cured tobaccos used in pipes, cigars, and smokeless products have a higher pH, so absorption through the membranes of the mouth, pharynx, and respiratory and gastrointestinal tracts is far greater. Regardless of pH, inhalation results in rapid absorption in the lungs; 90 percent of the nicotine is absorbed and begins to reach the brain in eight to ten seconds. The absorption rate from swallowing or chewing is 25 to 50 percent. Because blood nicotine levels accumulate—but decline slowly—chronic smokers may have nicotine in their systems twenty-four hours a day.

Smokeless Nicotine

Moist snuff contains 12 to 16 milligrams of nicotine per gram, and plug tobacco about 25 milligrams per gram. Blood nicotine levels produced with smokeless tobacco are equivalent to those from smoking, but they're reached more slowly and sustained longer. Typically, smokeless nicotine levels plateau at thirty minutes and decline over two hours. Snuff can deliver two to three times the nicotine of a cigarette; eight to ten dips of snuff (or plugs of tobacco) deliver the same amount of nicotine as thirty to forty cigarettes.

Pharmacological Effects of Smoking

Nicotine is an unusual stimulant; its mechanism of action is different from that of other drugs. It readily crosses the blood-brain barrier, acting on specific binding sites in the central nervous system, spinal cord, and autonomic nervous system.

Nicotine produces many effects on the body (Table 15.2). It decreases muscle tone and increases the concentration of several hormones, including acetylcholine, dopamine, norepinephrine, corticosteroids, and pituitary hormones. It increases blood pressure, heart rate, and serum levels of cholesterol (all considered risk factors for cardiac disease). However, the blood pressure response can vary. The carbon monoxide in cigarettes causes formation of carboxyhemoglobin, cutting the amount of oxygen delivered to the tissues. Nicotine is metabolized primarily in the liver, secondarily in the kidneys and lungs. Excretion in the urine varies depending on pH content. With regular use, nicotine levels accumulate and persist while the smoker is sleeping, though some decline occurs. Although nicotine's half-life is relatively short, being under three hours, its metabolite continine has a half-life of up to twenty hours and is often used as an index of smoking activity.

Heavy smoking also interferes with the action of many medications (Table 15.3). In some cases, nicotine's stimulant effect on enzymes in the liver causes increased metabolism of the other drugs. The stimulation may also result from the additive effect of nicotine and the other drugs.

Smoking provides many pleasures. It increases alertness, facilitates mental prowess, and is credited with maintaining a degree of calm and muscle relaxation even in stressful situations. Relief from stress is one of the most

TABLE 15.2. Effects of Smoking

Cardiovascular system*
    Increases blood pressure, heart rate; constricts blood vessels
    Palpitations, arrhythmias
Central nervous system
    Increases alertness
    Decreases skeletal muscle tone (relaxation)
    Facilitates mental processes
    Decreases appetite
    Decreases irritability
    Increases secretion of neurotransmitters, norepinephrine, dopamine
    Nausea and vomiting§
Hematologic
    Increases clotting ability of blood*
    Decreases capacity of hemoglobin to deliver oxygen to tissues*
Gastrointestinal
    Nausea, vomiting, diarrhea
Irritates linings of bronchial tissue and lungs; irritates olfactory receptor cells in
    nasal lining, with diminished sense of smell†
Metabolic
    Increases free fatty acids,* glycerol, lactate
    Increases low-density cholesterol (LDL)*
    Decreases high-density cholesterol*
    In women: earlier menopause and increased risk of osteoporosis
Neurotransmitter and hormonal function
    Increases norepinephrine, epinephrine, vasopressin, growth hormone,
        ALTH, cortisol, prolactin, endorphin, serotonin
    Decreases prostaglandin release
Peridontal disease
Neuromuscular
    Relaxes some muscle groups
Respiratory
    Cough, hoarseness, wheezing, sneezing, sinusitis

---

*Adds to risk of coronary heart disease and heart attacks
§Occurs with early exposure
†Hypothesis observed for decrease in sense of smell

common reasons given for smoking. Nicotine improves mood and even improves performance. It can also reduce the pain threshold. Weight loss is a secondary effect. The reason some women give for starting to smoke is to control their weight; in general, a smoker's weight is six to ten pounds less than that of a nonsmoker of comparable age and height.

The weight loss in smokers is believed to reflect the increased expenditure of energy resulting from the effect of nicotine on the body's metabolism. One study showed that male smokers spent less energy accomplishing

TABLE 15.3. Interactions of Nicotine with Other Drugs

Drug	Effects with Nicotine
Acetaminophen	Diminished
Aminophylline (theophylline)	Diminished
Antidepressants Imipramine (Tofranil, Janimine, SK Pramine)	Diminished
Benzodiazepines (Librium, lorazepam, Alzapam, Ativan, Valium)	Diminished
Warfarin (Coumadin)	Diminished
Estrogens	May increase viscosity of blood
Furosemide	Diminished
Insulin	Slows absorption from subcutaneous site
Glutethimide	Diminished
Narcotic agents	Diminished
Nifedipine (Procardia)	Diminished
Oral contraceptives	Increases risk of stroke and premature myocardial infarction in women
Propranolol (Inderal)	Diminished
Theophylline	Diminished

a fixed task when deprived of nicotine. So it may be that cutting off nicotine decreases the metabolic rate, which results in a weight gain. Part of the weight gain can also be attributed to increased eating, the alternative means for satisfying oral needs.

DEPENDENCY, TOLERANCE, ADDICTION, AND WITHDRAWAL

Dependency and Addiction

The dependency-producing effect of tobacco was first demonstrated in 1942, when injectable solutions of nicotine were found to suppress craving in smokers. The researcher, Dr. Lennox Johnston, concluded that "smoking tobacco is essentially a way of administering nicotine, just as smoking opium is a way of administering morphine." Tobacco dependency wasn't listed in the *Diagnostic and Statistical Manual of Mental Disorders* (DSM-III) until 1980. It was changed to "nicotine dependence" in 1987.

Nicotine meets the same criteria for dependency as narcotics (opiates), alcohol and other central nervous system depressants, and cocaine. Indeed it has been shown that nicotine affects similar neurotransmitters as other dependency-producing drugs, initially activating but then desensitizing dopamine neurons. This desensitization may be responsible for the tolerance that smokers develop associated with the need to increase the number of cigarettes smoked. Also, the first cigarette of the day is most pleasurable as the desensitization decreases with increased time between cigarettes. However, cross-dependency doesn't occur between nicotine and other mood-altering agents. Alcoholics can substitute minor tranquilizers or sedatives for alcohol, and people dependent on stimulants can substitute antidepressants. But smokers who use other drugs continue to smoke.

In some individuals, dependency develops rapidly. The body apparently adjusts to its own nicotine level, with chronic smokers consuming fewer high-nicotine cigarettes and more low-nicotine cigarettes to be comfortable. Controlled use of some mood-altering substances such as alcohol is common, but less than 10 percent of chronic smokers can manage with fewer than five or six cigarettes a day. Tobacco smokers fulfill the definition of "addict" in the true sense of the word. They defy sanctions prohibiting its use, and when necessary spend all available resources to get it—even in the presence of illnesses clearly made worse by smoking. When tobacco supplies in post-World War II Germany were rationed (two packs per day for men and one for women), heavy smokers bartered food for tobacco, searched the streets for cigarette butts, and begged passersby for a cigarette. In one study of 1,000 persons in treatment for alcohol or drug dependency, 57 percent said cigarettes would be harder to give up than their primary drug of abuse, even though they felt the pleasurable effects from that drug were greater than from smoking. Nicotine in fact does have a number of pleasurable effects when initially used, including increasing alertness, enhancing mood, and controlling weight.

Despite all that's been known for decades about tobacco, its addictive qualities are often denied. Many consider it habituating, rather than dependency-producing. As discussed earlier (Chapters 3 and 4), habituation is but one step on the road to dependency. In its dependency-producing potential, nicotine is like the more commonly feared drugs, such as alcohol, heroin, and cocaine. The 1989 report of the surgeon general's Advisory Committee on the Health Consequences of Smoking appropriately recognized that fact. The report concluded that cigarettes and other forms of tobacco, due to their nicotine content, cause an addiction manifested by pharmacological and behavioral changes similar to those of heroin and cocaine including the inability to stop smoking despite experiencing severe adverse consequences such as emphysema, cancer, or a heart attack.

The advances in neurobiology over the past several years have clearly defined the ways in which addictive behaviors develop with smoking. Nicotine activates the nicotine receptors affecting the brain's reward system, resulting in an increase in levels of dopamine similar to that seen with other stimulants, such as cocaine. Levels of an enzyme that breaks down dopamine (monoamine oxidase B) are also diminished, which further enhances dopamine levels. In addition, nicotine can enhance the release of enkephalins.

Withdrawal

Withdrawal syndromes vary greatly in intensity and are apparent in up to 80 percent of smokers who quit. They include irritability, anxiety, restlessness, sleep disturbances, headaches, cravings for cigarettes, increased appetite, weight gain, and an assortment of nonspecific gastrointestinal complaints. Symptoms can start within twenty-four hours after smoking stops, peak in forty-eight hours, and persist for weeks to months.

As with other dependency-producing drugs, the symptoms can be rapidly suppressed by the administration of nicotine. Abstinence is difficult but can be achieved. The relapse rate, however, is similar to that of such other addictive substances as alcohol and heroin.

ADVERSE EFFECTS OF SMOKING

As the chief cause of avoidable deaths in the United States, nicotine can be considered the most dangerous of all mood-altering drugs. Smoking is directly responsible for an estimated 400,000 deaths each year—more than the combined deaths from AIDS, cocaine, heroin, alcohol, fire, automobile accidents, homicides, and suicides. Exposure of nonsmokers is estimated to be responsible for 53,000 deaths annually.

Mortality is directly related to the number of cigarettes smoked over time. Overall mortality for males who smoke fewer than two packs per day is 1.7 times greater than for nonsmokers. Mortality in males who smoke two or more packs per day is two times greater. Those who inhale are at greater risk than those who don't.

The most common complaints of chronic smokers are coughing (worse in the morning), shortness of breath associated with decreased exercise tolerance, and sometimes a decrease in the sense of taste and smell. Smoking primarily affects the cardiovascular and pulmonary systems, but it harms other organ systems as well (Table 15.4).

TABLE 15.4. Health Risks Associated with Tobacco

Coronary heart disease
  Heart attacks
  Increased chest pain in persons with heart disease
  Aneurysms of aorta

Increased disturbances in cardiac rhythm

Blood vessels
  Stroke due to narrowing of cerebral vessels
  Narrowing of large arteries in legs (Buerger's disease)

Lungs
  Chronic cough
  Chronic bronchitis
  Chronic lung disease (emphysema)
  Cancer of lung

Various cancers
  Larynx, esophagus, pancreas, oral cavity, bladder

Other conditions
  Nonspecific chest pain
  Peptic ulcer
  Heartburn

Pregnancy and childbirth
  Miscarriage, premature mortality, low birth weight, sudden infant death
    syndrome

Lung Disease

Smoking markedly increases the prevalence of such acute pulmonary infections as bronchitis and chronic lung disease (emphysema). Since the late 1960s, deaths from chronic lung disease have increased two to three times in women age fifty-seven or older. Smoking also greatly increases the risk of lung cancer. Of the 126,000 deaths from lung cancer in 1986, at least 80 percent were attributed to active cigarette smoking. Among people over the age of thirty-five, the relative risk of death from lung cancer to smokers compared with those who have never smoked is twenty-two times greater for men and twelve times for women. The relative-risk comparison for former smokers is nine times for men, five times for women, respectively.

Smokers also have an add-on risk of developing lung cancer from other cancer-causing agents. The risk associated with radon exposure in smokers is six to eleven times higher than in nonsmokers. A similar increase in risk has been seen with asbestos exposure and smoking. Lung cancer appears to have reached a relative plateau in men, perhaps due to the decline in male smokers since 1970. But, as noted, the rate among women seems to be increasing. In 1986 lung cancer surpassed breast cancer as a leading cause of death in women. Epidemiological studies have suggested that the risk of developing lung cancer is decreased in those who smoke cigarettes low in tar and nicotine. Nevertheless, the risk is still much greater than for nonsmokers.

Cardiovascular Disease

Smoking's adverse effects on the heart are related to the stimulant action of nicotine; an increase in cholesterol levels, norepinephrine release, and the coagulability of the blood; and by a decrease in oxygen delivery.

Most reports linking smoking to heart disease are based on studies of heart attack victims. One study documented in dynamic fashion the effect smoking may have on blood flow to the heart. Researchers in Boston used a Holter monitor to record electrical activity of the heart in twenty-four smokers and forty-one nonsmokers with known but stable coronary artery disease. Even in the absence of symptoms, the monitor can detect signs of decreased blood flow to the heart (ischemia) during everyday activities. Smokers had signs of ischemic activity three times as often and lasting twelve times longer than in nonsmokers.

Deaths due to coronary artery disease increase two- to threefold in smokers compared with nonsmokers, with chances of dying from heart disease increasing in direct proportion to how heavily one smokes, the number of years one smokes, and the specific age range studied. Deaths due to coronary artery disease are five times greater in smokers than nonsmokers between the ages of thirty-five and forty-four; four times greater for those between forty-five and fifty-four.

Smokers with coronary artery disease experience angina more frequently. They exercise less and are at increased risk for serious heart rhythm irregularities. These risks are independent of other risk factors, but the individual has a far greater chance of a heart attack if there is a family history of coronary disease and/or if the cholesterol level is elevated. In 1985, smoking accounted for 21 percent of deaths due to coronary artery disease, 40 percent of them in men and women under the age of sixty-five.

A study of 113,404 women who were followed for six years found that those who smoked more than twenty-five cigarettes a day had 5.5 times the risk for fatal heart attack, 5.8 times the risk for nonfatal heart attack, and 2.6 times the risk for angina. Smoking even one to four cigarettes a day was associated with a twofold risk of heart attack. The figures were the same for regular and low-nicotine cigarettes.

Cessation of smoking reduces the risk of death from heart attack regardless of sex or age. One study of 1,893 men and women over the age of fifty-five with known coronary artery disease revealed that those who continued smoking had a relative risk of death 1.7 times greater than those who quit.

Other Cardiovascular Effects

Other effects of smoking include aortic aneurysms, peripheral arterial disease with leg pain when walking, shorter survival after arterial grafts are placed, and increased incidence of cerebral vascular disease, including stroke.

The risk of cerebral vascular disease is directly related to the intensity of smoking being as high as up to 5.7 times in heavy smokers. Lower but still significant risks have been reported in former smokers as well as in those who live with smokers. Smoking temporarily increases blood pressure but probably isn't responsible for sustained hypertension. In the presence of hypertension, however, smoking may interfere with the effectiveness of some antihypertensive medications. It may also be associated with an acceleration of the hypertension and with stroke.

Cancer of Other Organs

Cancers of the larynx, oral cavity, esophagus, bladder, and pancreas have all been related to potential and real carcinogens in cigarette smoke. Although the effects of chewing or smokeless tobacco are believed to be directly related to some cancers, notably of the lung, larynx, oral cavity, and esophagus, controversy exists as to whether this holds true for other cancers, such as cancer of the cervix. Smokeless tobacco is associated with oral cancer and gum disease, with oral lesions seen in up to 37 percent of regular users in the seventh to twelfth grades.

Pregnancy

Women smokers of childbearing age are at risk during pregnancy as are their fetuses. Possible complications include an increased risk of miscarriage, low birth weight babies, and sudden infant death syndrome (SIDS) in the newborn (Chapter 19).

Acute Nicotine Intoxication

Acute nicotine intoxication is a rare event, associated with nausea, vomiting, abdominal pain, diarrhea, lightheadedness, headache, confusion, weakness, and tremors. In more severe stages, the pulse may be weak and rapid, blood pressure quite low, and convulsions and respiratory failure can occur. Nicotine intoxication has been reported in tobacco harvesters who absorb excessive nicotine from the dew on tobacco leaves. Accidental poisoning by ingestion of nicotine-containing pesticides is another possibility. The condition is treated by inducing vomiting to remove gastric contents and, if needed, respiratory assistance and intravenous fluids.

Passive Smoking

Most Americans don't smoke, yet the amount of cigarette smoke in the environment is considerable due to both the burning of the cigarette and the exhaled tobacco smoke of the smoker. There are two main ways of determining the exposure of nonsmokers to environmental tobacco smoke. The first is through survey techniques; the second through actual measurements of co-nicotine in the serum or saliva. Co-nicotine is a major metabolic product of nicotine, with serum levels reflecting an exposure to nicotine over a period of one to two days. Surveys have revealed that almost two-thirds of nonsmokers report some daily exposure to cigarette smoke; 37 percent of adult non-tobacco users live in a home with at least one smoker or work in an environment where tobacco smoke exists. Of children between the ages of two months to eleven years, 43 percent were found to be living with at least one smoker. Of nontobacco users, 88 percent were found to have detectable levels of co-nicotine. These levels were associated with either the number of smokers in the household or the hours exposed at work. Most passive-smoking exposure is to sidestream smoke, which contains a greater concentration of carbon monoxide than mainstream smoke, and smaller particles that are more likely to reach the smallest and most distant portions of the lungs.

In 1986, the nineteenth surgeon general's Advisory Committee on the Health Consequences of Smoking concluded that passive smoking can cause disease in healthy nonsmokers. The most common and least severe adverse effects are unpleasant odors, headaches, eye irritations, and such respiratory effects as cough and bronchitis in people who are particularly sensitive. Whether these discomforts can result in chronic disabilities is not yet clear.

Compared with children of nonsmokers, children of parents who smoke appear to have an increased frequency of respiratory and middle ear infections. There is also an increase in hospitalizations for bronchitis and pneumonia in the first year of life. The rate of lung-function development is also slightly lower. In addition, a child whose mother smokes may run twice the risk of developing acute upper-respiratory infections.

However, more serious effects of passive smoking exist, with passive smoking estimated to increase the risk of death from heart disease by about 20 percent. An estimated 35,000 to 40,000 persons each year die of heart attacks due to environmental tobacco smoke exposure. To place this in perspective, lung cancer linked to environmental tobacco smoke is reported to cause only 3,000 to 4,000 deaths annually. Exposure to environmental tobacco smoke has also been shown to increase the risk of lipid deposition in the cerebral and carotid arteries with subsequent potential for strokes and atherosclerosis in the aorta and the peripheral circulation.

TREATMENT

Despite the overwhelming evidence of smoking's dangers, in 1986, 24 percent of smokers were not concerned about the effects of smoking, with up to 30 percent of them saying that smoking did not increase the risk of either lung or heart disease. Only 18 percent of smokers were highly concerned over the effects of smoking on their own health. Even when the hazards of smoking are recognized, however, quitting isn't easy. Remaining abstinent from cigarettes, in fact, is more difficult than quitting opioids or cocaine. Up to two-thirds of people who quit return to smoking within a few days, with less than 10 to 20 percent remaining abstinent for more than a year. Of those who do abstain for one year, one-third will relapse the following year. The easy availability of cigarettes combined with the feelings of many that smoking is essential for maintaining homeostasis mean that the majority of smokers cannot achieve abstinence without great difficulty.

The most common ways of treating tobacco dependency are simple detoxification (cutting down until the habit is eliminated), nicotine gum or nasal spray, behavioral therapy, psychological counseling, and hypnosis (Table 15.5). Formal smoking-cessation programs have also been shown to be helpful. Combining two or more of those methods has assisted many to become abstinent. However, more than 90 percent of smokers who quit do so without formal therapy. Fewer people who try to quit on their own remain abstinent on their first attempt. Under physician direction or encouragement, however, the success rate is higher. One survey reported that attempts to quit were twice as likely to occur among smokers who received encouragement from their physician to stop than among those who did not. Smokers who quit "cold turkey" were more likely to be successful than those who attempted to detoxify, as were those who quit on their own. However, since heavy smokers and smokers who had been previously unsuccessful in quitting are more likely to join cessation programs, a valid comparison is not easily made.

Nicotine Replacement

Nicotine Gum

Nicotine gum contains approximately 2 milligrams of nicotine and may be a valuable adjunct in stopping smoking. According to some profession-

TABLE 15.5. Smoking Cessation Aids

Nicotine Replacement Products		Nicotine Dose (mg)	Advantage
Nicorette gum	Nicorette	2	OTC
	Nicorette DS	4	OTC
Transdermal systems	Habitrol	17,5,35,52.5	OTC
	Nicoderm	36,78,114	OTC
	Nicotrol	8,3,16.6,24.9	OTC
	ProStep	15,30	OTC
Nicotine spray	Nicotrol NS	0.5	Rapid delivery
Nicotine inhaler	Nicotrol Inhaler		Mimics smoking
Other Agent			
Bupropion HCL	Zyban	300 mg/day*	Can be used with patch

*Slow-release procedures probably associated with less adverse effects. Immediate release may increase risk of seizures. Should start treatment one week prior to ceasing smoking.

als, nicotine gum works best when used in conjunction with a counseling program, and is taken for three to six months after smoking ceases. The gum should not be used to help decrease the number of cigarettes smoked, since a high blood level of nicotine can result. Nor should it be used until smoking has completely stopped. The nicotine is absorbed in the mouth rather than the stomach, so the gum should be chewed slowly for twenty to thirty minutes. Usually ten to fifteen pieces of the gum are chewed per day. When the gum is chewed throughout the day, average nicotine levels are approximately one- to two-thirds of those seen with smoking. Some studies have recommended 4 milligram gum, but its increased effectiveness has not been demonstrated.

There is a downside to the use of the gum. Problems include impaired absorption when taken with coffee and the possibility of long-term use being associated with dependency. It is estimated that up to one-third of those who use the gum continue for more than a year, despite advice to the contrary.

Initial success rates with the gum have not been clearly documented. In smoking-cessation programs, 27 percent of the gum users stay off cigarettes, whereas only 18 percent of those given placebos manage to do so. Among those who are treated by medical practitioners, the percentages are 9 percent and 4 percent respectively. From those numbers, it appears that the gum may be helpful in promoting abstinence when used in special centers with appropriate counseling, but not nearly so successful in general medical practice.

Adverse effects of nicotine gum include nonspecific gastrointestinal symptoms, palpitations, sore throat or mouth, and occasional hiccups. Although acute nicotine intoxication is a possibility, nicotine's slow release in the stomach and its local metabolism make that unlikely unless extremely large amounts are consumed. Nicotine gum should not be used by those with coronary heart disease, especially after a recent heart attack. Pregnant women and people with temporomandibular joint disorder also should avoid it. The gum should be used cautiously in people suffering from peptic ulcer disease and hypertension.

Transdermal Nicotine Systems

Nicotine patches that deliver doses of nicotine ranging from 7 to 22 mg per day are widely available and are effective in assisting smoking cessation efforts. However, it has been felt that the blood levels of nicotine obtained from even the 22 mg patch may be below the levels achieved by heavy smokers. Studies have recently found that patches that deliver 44 mg per day of nicotine can be more effective if a person's daily cigarette consumption is greater than forty cigarettes. In general, it is felt that those who smoke under twenty cigarettes per day can be stabilized on patches providing daily nicotine doses of 5 to 22 mg; those smoking between twenty and forty cigarettes per day on patches providing 21 to 35 mg of nicotine; and those who smoke more than forty cigarettes per day with patches providing 44 mg of nicotine.

Regardless of the patch dose that is used, however, careful physician monitoring is needed. Excessive dosage will cause nausea and vomiting. Once this occurs the patch should be discontinued and the person restarted on a lower dose to avoid acute nicotine poisoning. Local irritation at the application site can occur in one-third of patients. General systemic complaints such as headaches, insomnia, cough, or gastrointestinal disturbance can also be seen.

Nasal Spray

Nasal sprays have been found to be effective in relieving the symptoms of nicotine withdrawal. Nicotine from the spray enters the bloodstream much faster than with the patch and can provide satisfactory levels of nicotine. However, at times they can be associated with irritation of the nasal mucosa.

Nicotine Inhalers

Oral inhaling systems consist of a mouthpiece and a plastic cartridge that delivers 4 mg of nicotine from a 10 mg base. The nicotine released from the inhaler is deposited in the mouth, with approximately 2 mg of the 4 mg nicotine released being absorbed. Peak nicotine concentrations are reached within fifteen minutes. Since the absorption occurs through the mouth, levels of nicotine in the blood do not reach a peak as rapidly as from smoking a cigarette, nor are the levels as high. The number of cartridges used daily varies with the number of cigarettes smoked but in studies has ranged from a minimum of four cartridges to up to twenty cartridges per day for approximately three months. In two placebo-controlled clinical trials, the nicotine inhaler was found to be more effective than placebo at six weeks, three months, and six months, but not at twelve months.

Adverse effects of the inhaler include local irritant effects such as coughing and irritation of the mouth and throat, which may make its use hazardous in persons with asthma or chronic pulmonary disease. Occasionally, tachycardia and palpitations may occur. As a result, the product should not be used by persons who are prone to have cardiac arrhythmias. Vasospastic conditions such as Buerger's disease, angina, or Raynaud's phenomenon should also be contraindications. Other conditions that may be adversely effected by release of catecholamines, such as hyperthyroidism, pheochromo-cytoma, insulin-dependent diabetes, or active peptic ulcers are contraindications.

With the wide availability of nicotine products, such as the gum, the patch, and the inhaler as well as a variety of behavioral smoking interventions that range from brief interventions to smoking cessation programs, it often becomes difficult to decide on the most effective way to quit and remain abstinent. Indeed, it is estimated that approximately 90 percent of those who are successful in quitting do so on their own, albeit after a number of attempts. Several studies have demonstrated that, in fact, use of nicotine replacement therapy in combination with counseling may be most advantageous to those people who are unable to quit on their own.

A risk of using nicotine products is the potential to become dependent on these products rather than the cigarettes. Indeed, since the pure product is devoid of the numerous tars and carcinogens seen with smoking and are mostly available over the counter, many people have stabilized themselves on nicotine delivery systems and continue to take them far longer than recommended. It is estimated that in 1997, over-the-counter smoking cessation aids generated over $700 million. Although this pales next to the $25 billion spent on cigarettes, it is estimated that only 13 percent of all smokers use the nicotine products. Increased advertising can easily result in a marked increase in consumption, especially as the prevalence of no smoking areas in the workplace and in restaurants continues to increase.

Other Forms of Therapy

In addition to nicotine replacement, the use of antidepressants has been promoted, as smokers have a higher frequency of past or present depression that nonsmokers. Not surprisingly, smokers who are currently depressed also have greater difficulty in achieving abstinence as well as higher relapse rates once abstinence has occurred. Bupropion SR, an effective antidepressant, has been found to be helpful in achieving abstinence in clinical trials.

A study of the effectiveness of Bupropion compared to placebo revealed that 44 percent of those receiving 300 mg of Bupropion daily, as compared to 90 percent of those receiving placebo, had quit smoking by the end of the study, with abstinence rates at one year of 23 percent versus 12 percent with placebos. Nortriptyline, when used in 200 smokers, was found to double the rates of smoking cessation even if the smoker did not have a history of clinical depression. Although the mechanisms by which antidepressants may be effective have not been clearly established, it has been hypothesized that they counteract the effects of nicotine withdrawal by blocking the uptake of dopamine and serotonin.

Since the oral gratification associated with smoking has been given as a reason smokers find it difficult to quit, a vegetable-based cigarette has been distributed in Europe as an aid to abstinence. However, instances of toxicity have been reported, and it has been suggested that smoking these cigarettes exposes the smoker to the same or greater levels of carbon monoxide as tobacco cigarettes.

Finally, a nicotine vaccine that prevents nicotine from reaching the brain has recently been patented. NicVAX, found effective in animals, is undergoing preclinical trials to determine toxicity and, if proven safe, most likely will be placed in clinical trials. It is proposed that the vaccine will diminish the smoker's urged to smoke.

Effectiveness of All Forms of Treatment

The Surgeon General's 2000 Report on Reducing Tobacco Use evaluated existing, widely used froms of therapy to prevent initiation of smoking and to help smokers achieve abstinence. This report concluded:

- Educational strategies can postpone or prevent smoking onset in 20 to 40 percent of adolescents.
- Pharmacologic treatment of nicotine addiction, together with behavioral support, will enable 20 to 25 percent of smokers to remain abstinent for up to one year.
- Brief interventions by physicians, consisting of advising these patients to quit smoking, can be successful in 5 to 10 percent of cases.

- Regulation of advertising and promotion, especially directed toward the young, is very likely to reduce both prevalence and initiation of smoking.
- Restriction of minors' access to tobacco products and clean air regulations may directly influence prevalence.
- Optimally increasing levels of excise taxation of tobacco products will reduce prevalence of smoking and levels of consumption of tobacco.

Clearly, a multipronged, comprehensive approach is needed to address this issue effectively. To do so will greatly decrease the long-term, adverse effects of tobacco on both the smoker and the public.

Chapter 16

Volatile Solvents, Anesthetics, and Organic Nitrites

The use of inhalants to alter mood can be traced back to the mythology of ancient Greece. At Delphi, the pythoness—the priestess of Apollo—sat on a tripod above the cliffs, inhaling cold vapors containing carbon dioxide. This aid to meditation was soon followed by divine inspiration. Inhalation of volatile, organic solvents, however, is a relatively recent phenomenon related to our high-tech society. It wasn't noted in the medical literature and the media until 1959. The practice became widespread from then until the 1970s, when it began to decline.

Inhalants can be defined as substances whose vapors can be sniffed through the nose or "huffed" through the mouth. Excluded from this definition are substances whose vapors are produced by burning, such as nicotine or crack. Inhalants can be grouped into four general categories:

1. Volatile solvents in antifreeze, gasoline, glue, hair spray, lighter fuel, and paint thinner
2. Volatile solvents in aerosols, such as paint spray and deodorants
3. General anesthetic agents, including methylene chloride and nitrous oxide
4. Volatile nitrites such as in the amylbutyl and isobutyl groups

VOLATILE SOLVENTS

Inappropriate use of volatile solvents originated with the inhalation of gasoline fumes. Airplane glue and aerosols were used next. Indeed, many substances found in hundreds of commercial products can be misused and produce mood-altering effects (Table 16.1).

TABLE 16.1. Volatile Solvents

Solvent	Ingredients
Adhesives	n-Heptane, n-hexane, benzene, naphthalene, toluene, xylene
Aerosol sprays	Ethanol, freon, toluene, xylene
Antifreeze	Isopropanol, methanol
Degreasers	Isopropanol, methylene chloride, tetrachloroethylene, xylene, n-butyl acetate, methyl ethyl ketone, n-heptane, n-hexane, benzene, naphthalene, toluene, xylene
Gas fuels	Gasoline, methane, propane, acetylene butane, ethane, isobutane
Model cement	Ethanol, isopropanol, n-hexene, styrene, toluene, xylene, acetone
Paint thinners	Ethanol, isopropanol, methanol, n-heptane, n-hexane, methylene chloride, naphthalene, toluene, xylene, ethyl acetate, n-propylacetate acetone, methylbutyl, ketone, methyl ethyl ketone
Rubber cement	n-heptane, n-hexane, benzene, naphthalene, styrene, toluene, xylene
Spray shoe polish	Isopropanol, toluene
Typewriter correction fluid	Trichloroethylene
Window washing fluids	Methanol

Source: *The Deliberate Inhalation of Volatile Substances,* Report Series 30, No. 2. Rockville, MD: National Institute on Drug Abuse, 1978.

Patterns of Use

Inhalant users can be grouped into four major categories: (1) inhalant-dependent adults who usually use a volatile anesthetic agent, (2) organic nitrite users, (3) multiple drug users, and (4) young inhalant users.

Surveys suggest that inhalants have been used at one time by 10 to 20 percent of youngsters between the ages of twelve and seventeen, by 17 percent of people between eighteen and twenty-five, and by 4 percent of those age twenty-six or more. Those figures may vary greatly depending on the population studied, specific availabilities of inhalants, and cultural norms. Since inhalant use is a phenomenon primarily among youth, the data provided by the surveys of drug use among high school students and young adults have been most helpful.

Annual inhalant use in high school seniors rose from 3 percent in 1976 to 6 percent in 1979, then declined. It started to rise again in the early 1980s, in part due to use of amyl and butyl nitrites, and reached 7 percent in 1988, continuing to increase until 1995. At that time, an active anti-inhalant use campaign was initiated by Partnership for a Drug-Free America, and, although a direct relationship between this campaign and inhalant use cannot be confirmed, inhalant use subsequently started to decline. Nonetheless, in the 2000 Monitoring the Future Survey, 9 percent of eighth graders, 7 percent of tenth graders, and 6 percent of twelfth graders had reported inhalant use within the twelve months preceding the survey. The 1999 NHSDA reported an estimated 991,000 new inhalant users in 1998, over 2½-fold of that in 1990, with the rate of first use among ages twelve to seventeen, increasing from 11.6 to 28.1 per 1,000 potential new users during this period.

The popularity of solvent use among young people is easy to understand. Its availability, with over 1,000 potentially abusable household products, and its low cost make it readily obtainable; the small containers can be hidden easily or left in such appropriate places as a closet or garage; possession is legal; and the high is achieved within a few minutes, is more pleasant than an alcohol high, and is usually over much more quickly. In view of concerns over marijuana being a gateway drug, it is of interest that over 50 percent of the young people who use inhalants have never even tried marijuana. Use may be sporadic and ultimately come to a halt because of unexpected or unpleasant effects. Repetitive or daily use poses the greatest risk for toxicity and psychological dysfunction.

Dependency, Tolerance, and Addiction

Although tolerance does develop, physical dependency has not been clearly defined. Symptoms of irritability and anxiety, which can appear during abstinence, may be related to preexisting personality disturbances rather than to withdrawal. Habituation, however, is fairly common.

Toxic Effects

Complications, even in healthy youngsters, do occur and are sometimes fatal (Table 16.2). Minutes after inhaling, a person will become disoriented and exhilarated. When these solvents combine with body fats, they can be particularly toxic to tissues containing a high lipid concentration, such as the brain and spinal cord. The effects of many of these agents are similar to those of central nervous system depressants.

TABLE 16.2. Complications from Use of Solvents

Anemia
Aspiration
Bleeding from stomach
Cardiac arrhythmias
Chronic brain dysfunction
Coma, convulsions
Difficulty in walking
Hallucinations
Leukemia
Liver failure
Lung failure
Lung disease
Muscle damage
Nausea, vomiting
Neurological damage
Night tremors
Paralysis
Renal failure

Acute Toxic Effects

The initial high can be complicated by nausea, vomiting, sneezing, nose-bleeds, coughing, salivation, and, on occasion, loss of coordination. Depression of the central nervous system follows the high. At lower levels of intoxication, there can be a general loss of inhibitions, with subsequent impulsive behavior. Muscular coordination is diminished, and reflexes are depressed. Loss of consciousness and respiratory arrest can occur with large doses. There's also risk of brain damage. Cardiac arrest, resulting from the production of fatal heart rhythm abnormalities, is common as is death due to aspiration of vomitus. Sudden sniffing death syndrome (SSD) is also associated with aerosol inhalation. Fluorocarbons in the aerosol can sensitize the heart to epinephrine, leading to a fatal rhythm disturbance (Table 16.3). Although the precise cause of death is often difficult to determine, in one series 20 percent of deaths were felt to be due to inhalation of vomit, 15 percent to asphyxia due to use of a plastic bag, and 60 percent due to arrhythmia.

Chronic Effects

Other effects of volatile substances depend on which substance is used and how it's taken. These effects (Table 16.4) vary from an innocuous lowering of the blood count to severe depression of bone marrow, progressive neurological dysfunction and paralysis, failure of the kidneys and liver, and

TABLE 16.3. Causes of Sudden Death from Sniffing

Aspiration of vomitus
Fatal irregular cardiac rhythms
Metabolic abnormalities
Respiratory depression
Suffocation

TABLE 16.4. Toxic Effects of Solvent Use

Substance	Anemia	Leukemia	Cardiac complications	Kidney failure	Liver failure	Neurological changes	Gastro-intestinal changes
Benzene	+	+	+		+		+
Carbon tetrachloride	+					+	+
Gasoline	+					+	+
Hexane	+					+	+
Trichloro-ethylene			+	+	+	+	
Toluene	+		+	+		+	
Ketones						+	
Xylene	+						

+ = positive correlation

even leukemia. Pulmonary function is also altered, sometimes without symptoms.

Treatment

Medical complications are rare with sporadic use. Inhalants are responsible for less than 0.3 percent of emergency room visits for illicit drug use and approximately 0.4 percent of admissions for treatment of illicit drug use. So there's little experience in dealing with large numbers of those who are dependent. On the other hand, signs of chronic use include slurred speech, glazed eyes, and the smell of the inhalant, which when looked for can be easily recognized, especially by family members. Since most users are young, family support is essential; counseling and therapy are generally helpful. Unfortunately, unlike other dependencies, most inhalant users are young and come into treatment due to parental coercion and therefore are often not well motivated. Jumper Thurman and colleagues have described a comprehensive treatment plan for chronic inhalant users willing to enter treatment that includes the following:

1. A complete medical assessment with time provided for physical recovery from existing problems
2. Assessment of cognitive functioning
3. Use of a patient-peer advocate program
4. Building on existing strengths and skills
5. Developing new coping skills
6. Addressing family issues
7. Preparing for a transition back to normal functioning in the home environment

Prevention

Public policy concerning inhalant use has not been continuously promoted, probably due to the failure of the public to recognize this as a major problem compared to the use of hard core drugs such as cocaine or heroin or of drugs whose use is extremely prevalent, such as marijuana. Prevention and educational campaigns do exist, however, and warning labels appear on many products describing their abuse liability. In many instances, products have been reformulated to attempt to minimize abuse potential or have had substances added that cause irritant effects in an attempt to diminish abuse. Restricting access to these substances is extremely difficult due to their widespread use and easy availability.

Federal and state intervention to regulate the manufacture and composition of these substances has occurred, but not at a great level of intensity, as the proportion of products abused compared to those sold and not abused is exceptionally small. Harwood and colleagues, in a survey of state responses to inhalant use, found that only forty-three states had enacted legislation pertaining to inhalants, with only ten having prevention and treatment policies.

ANESTHETIC AGENTS

Ether, chloroform, and nitrous oxide were first used because they produced a high rather than for their anesthetic properties. The use of ether for recreational purposes began as early as the 1790s and was prevalent in England when the government increased the tax on alcohol. It was first taken orally; one teaspoon could produce inebriation lasting thirty minutes to an hour. Inhalation was common in a number of prestigious medical institutions in the eighteenth century. Chloroform came into use somewhat later in Europe and the United States, being first used in 1849 as an anesthetic for childbirth. Because of their toxic effects on the liver and kidneys, both ether and chloroform were gradually replaced by newer, less harmful anesthetics.

Nitrous Oxide

Nitrous oxide has been used as an anesthetic since 1845 and is now commonly used as an adjunct to local anesthesia in dental procedures. By 1976 it was again being used to get high. Within thirty seconds, nitrous oxide can produce an effect that lasts for several minutes. Because it has low potential for tolerance and doesn't produce a hangover, it was advocated as a good substitute for alcohol, especially when tolerance to alcohol existed.

When used appropriately as an analgesic, nitrous oxide offers a rapid onset of action, a rapid recovery from effects, and a minimal risk of toxicity. A 20 percent concentration of nitrous oxide can provide the same degree of analgesia as morphine. Inhalation of a 30 percent concentration, however, can sometimes cause loss of consciousness. An 80 percent concentration virtually always causes loss of consciousness, and death from coma and brain damage can result from the lack of oxygen.

Nitrous oxide is easily obtained in aerosol cans and as a propellant in small metal tubes (whippets). It's usually used by direct inhalation or from a balloon filled with the gas. Although excessive use of nitrous oxide has not been well documented, its ready availability to dentists and dental assistants has made it a particular risk among those professionals.

Nitrous oxide has relatively few physical effects on the body, although there may be an increase in blood pressure and heart rate. When taken in low doses, it has no known toxic effects on the central nervous system or other organs. Because onset of action and recovery are both fairly rapid, one can inhale nitrous oxide for short periods and function well afterward. The high is described as "floating sensations" and may be accompanied by visual hallucinations.

Tolerance has occurred with chronic use. Dependency and withdrawal similar to that of morphine can be easily measured in laboratory animals. Morphine can decrease signs of withdrawal from nitrous oxide in these animals. The relationship between nitrous oxide and the opiates is still unclear. Occasional reports in the medical literature suggest that nitrous oxide is effective in detoxification from opiates and in treating withdrawal. But whenever a mood-altering drug with known potential for inappropriate use is recommended for the treatment of another dependency, it should be viewed with caution.

Chronic use of nitrous oxide is associated with several complications (Table 16.5). Memory loss, depression, and occasional hallucinations are the most common. Those changes improve with time and subside with ab-

TABLE 16.5. Toxic Effects of Nitrous Oxide

Memory loss
Visual hallucinations
Tingling and numbness of hands and feet
Loss of finger dexterity
Weakness of muscles
Bowel and bladder symptoms
Disturbances of immune function

stinence. Such neurological changes as numbness in the hands and feet, tingling sensations, loss in finger dexterity, and other findings compatible with degeneration of nerves may also occur.

ORGANIC NITRITES

Amyl nitrite, a highly volatile substance, was used as early as 1867 to relieve pain stemming from coronary artery obstruction (angina pectoris). It served as the primary drug for angina until nitroglycerine was found to be more effective. A similar drug, butyl nitrite, has been around since the 1880s but was never used for angina. Because it was considered safe, the FDA in 1960 ruled that it was unnecessary to have a prescription in order to obtain amyl nitrite. By 1986, street use of the drug was so widespread that the decision was reversed. Butyl nitrite, often used in room deodorizers, under no such restrictions, quickly replaced amyl nitrite as a more readily available drug of use.

Amyl nitrite, isobutyl nitrite, and isopentyl nitrite (Table 16.6) are alleged to provide a general high, increase creativity and artistic ability, and enhance the male orgasmic response. Among amyl nitrite's alleged effects on sexual function are prolonged and heightened erections, relaxation of smooth muscle tone of the rectal and anal areas, and prevention of premature ejaculation.

Patterns of Use

The nitrites are generally used later in life than other mood-altering drugs, and often in combination with other agents. The average age for first use of nitrites is 25.6 years, compared with 13.9 years for alcohol, 14.6 years for glue, and 17.6 years for marijuana. But studies in 1986 revealed that about 9 percent of 3,000 high school seniors had at some time used amyl nitrite, with 1.6 percent having used it within three days of the surveys. This percentage has subsequently decreased to the extent that in 1998 only

TABLE 16.6. Nitrite Inhalants

Inhalant	Street Names*
Amyl nitrite	Poppers, Snappers
Isobutyl nitrite	Banapple Gas, Bang, Bolt, Bullet, Climax, Cryupt, Cum, Hard-on, Hardware, Highball
Isobutyl alcohol	Aroma, Joc, Kick, Liquid Increase, Locker Room
Isopentyl nitrite	Locker, Popper, Rush, Satan's Scout, Toilet Water, Vaporole

*Because commercial preparations may contain more than one nitrite, the street terminology is interchangeable.

1.4 percent of high school seniors reported using amyl or butyl nitrites within the prior year.

The incidence of nitrite use is much higher in specific high-risk groups. A study of chemically dependent adolescents revealed that 43 percent had used nitrites, and 22 percent had used them ten to ninety-nine times compared to a prevalence of 11 percent in adult polydrug users. Seventy percent of homosexual men said they used nitrites before they became concerned about the AIDS epidemic.

Adverse Effects

Smooth muscles relax after inhalation of nitrites, causing drop in blood pressure; increase in heart rate, accompanied by feelings of warmth; throbbing sensation or headache; and occasional symptoms related to heat loss. Depending on the dose, dizziness, fainting, and severe decrease in blood pressure may occur. Both the high and the headaches are probably related to widening of the blood vessels in the brain. Dilated blood vessels in the penis can cause increased engorgement and a prolonged erection.

As with any inhalant, lung irritation and acute allergic reactions are common. Contact with the skin can result in severe irritation and ulceration. When nitrites are combined with hemoglobin in the bloodstream, the oxygen-carrying capacity of the blood is impaired, and there may be a profound loss of oxygen. Increases in pressure behind the eyes, accompanied by severe eye pain, have also been reported.

The effects of nitrites on the immune system have taken on greater importance as the complications of AIDS have become more familiar (Chapter 18). No immunotoxic effects have been seen in laboratory animals after administration of amyl nitrite. But there has been a decrease in the cells believed to ward off infections (helper T cells) after twenty-one weeks of exposure. The same pattern is often seen in those at high risk for developing AIDS. When given amyl nitrite, volunteers who were negative for HIV showed no specific changes in immune function. However, acute use of amyl nitrite was associated with a decrease in blood lymphocytes and other protective elements. All returned to normal within twenty-four to ninety-six hours after discontinuing the drug. Whether this has any clinical relevance to increasing vulnerability to AIDS is uncertain. But use of nitrites by people with compromised immune systems should be avoided.

Nitrites used in combination with naturally occurring nitrogen compounds can form nitrosamines, among the most potent cancer-causing agents (carcinogens) known.

PART III:
AREAS OF SPECIAL CONCERN

Chapter 17

Multiple Drug Use

Dependency on a single drug is more the exception than the rule; multiple drug use has increased significantly since the late 1960s. Several patterns of multiple drug use can be identified (Table 17.1). Probably the most common pattern is typified by the alcohol drinker who also uses marijuana and other stimulant or depressant drugs. Another pattern results from unavailability of the primary drug, typically with regard to alcohol and other central nervous system depressants. Tranquilizers, barbiturates, or other sedatives are easily substituted for alcohol; heroin addicts who can't afford heroin may turn to such opiates as hydromorphone (Dilaudid), meperidine (Demerol), or street methadone. Multiple drugs are sometimes used to mask dependency on a person's primary drug. Alcoholics, for example, may take tranquilizers during the working day to maintain their equilibrium without smelling of alcohol. Other drugs are also used to prevent withdrawal when the primary drug is unavailable. Heroin addicts often drink excessive quantities of alcohol or take barbiturates or tranquilizers when they can't get heroin.

Certain drugs are also used to counteract particular effects of the primary drug (Table 17.2). One example is the use of central nervous system depressants by cocaine or amphetamine users to terminate runs, or to decrease the stimulant effects. It's also common to mix cocaine or amphetamines with heroin to lessen the drowsiness caused by heroin.

TABLE 17.1. Reasons for Multiple Drug Use

To maintain initial "social" drug-use behavior while progressing to illicit drugs
To substitute when primary drug isn't available
To mask signs of dependency on primary drug
To prevent withdrawal when primary drug isn't available
To diminish undesirable side effects of primary drug
To enhance effect of primary drug
To obtain a different kind of high (part of underlying psychopathology to consume whatever is available)

TABLE 17.2. Common Drug Combinations

Drug	Reason for Use	Adverse Effects
Alcohol, barbiturates, sedatives, tranquilizers	Potentiate high; prevent withdrawal; facilitate sleep following drinking binge	Depressed brain and respiratory function
Alcohol, heroin, methadone, barbiturates, sedatives, tranquilizers	Diminish narcotic withdrawal symptoms; add to narcotic high; get high when on methadone maintenance	Depressed brain and respiratory function
Alcohol, marijuana	Intensify high	Rapid heart rate; increased impaired behavior
Talwin, antihistamine	Make injection smoother; diminish irritation or veins	As with each drug
Heroin, methadone, cocaine, amphetamines	Get different type of high; decrease period of drowsiness caused by heroin	Rapid heart rate; possible heart damage
Alcohol-cocaine	Get different highs (social settings)	As with each drug
Cocaine, amphetamines, barbiturates, tranquilizers	Diminish runs; facilitate sleep	As with each drug
Hallucinogens, amphetamines	Increased intensity of trip	Marked paranoia; self-injury
Marijuana-phencyclidine	Intensify high (user may be unaware)	Marked stimulation with hallucinations

Other drugs are often taken to enhance the effects of the primary drug. Marijuana in combination with alcohol contributes to a high, as does mixing antidepressants, tranquilizers, or other central nervous system depressants.

Other combinations produce highs totally different from those of the primary drug. Heroin addicts or people on methadone maintenance frequently consume excessive quantities of alcohol or central nervous system depressants to obtain a "depressant high," or use cocaine for its stimulant effect. Those on methadone maintenance who can't get high on an opiate often turn to cocaine, alcohol, other central nervous system depressants, and even antidepressants.

In a few people, multiple drug use represents an underlying psychopathology demonstrated by a need to use any drug that produces a mood-altering effect. Such experimentation is fairly common in adolescents, but adults who adopt this behavior are usually the most difficult to treat.

Many combinations of drugs are known (Table 17.2), but some are rarely used because they produce inferior highs and severe psychological side effects. The high obtained with heroin (introversion), for example, is very different from the high from LSD (mind-blowing). The combination of cocaine or amphetamines with hallucinogens results in hallucinations and paranoia, so most multiple drug users avoid it. Other combinations, however, have equally serious—but less recognized—effects.

ALCOHOL AND OTHER DRUGS

Most future drug users try alcohol or cigarettes as their first mood-altering drugs. Marijuana and other available drugs often follow. Susceptible people may then go on to sedatives, cocaine, or opiates, with alcohol use continuing throughout this period.

The majority of people who use alcohol excessively also use at least one other drug on a regular basis. The 1999 NHSDA reported that among 12.4 million heavy drinkers, 30.5 percent were current illicit drug users. Alcohol and marijuana are the most common combination, with alcohol combined with a nonmedically prescribed psychotherapeutic drug second. Alcohol consumption in those with a history of drug dependency is also high. Surveys show that up to 60 percent of those using alcohol excessively have a co-existing drug problem. They are generally the younger members of the population.

In a survey of over 1,200 persons admitted to a level 1 trauma unit, 16 percent had a lifetime dependence on alcohol and other drugs, with 8 percent having a current dependence on multiple substances. At the time of injury, one in four persons was alcohol dependent and one in five drug dependent.

One study of United States servicemen stationed in Vietnam revealed the ease of exchanging alcohol for other drug consumption. Before enlistment, half the men were regular drinkers, another 25 percent had experienced some drinking problem, and still another 4 percent were classified as alcoholics. In Vietnam, alcohol consumption decreased significantly in 75 percent of the men. But that was accompanied by an increase in the use of opiates. Half said they had tried opiates, and 20 percent were opiate dependent. In the post-Vietnam era, opiate use decreased; alcohol use increased. Thirty-three percent of the men became problem drinkers; 8 percent were considered alcoholic.

Alcohol is the drug most often involved in multiple drug use because it can be combined with other central nervous system depressants, such as barbiturates and tranquilizers, to potentiate a high or mask an alcohol problem. The combination also prevents withdrawal symptoms and facilitates sleep following alcoholic binges. Alcohol and sleeping pills form a particularly dangerous mixture because the combined depressant effect on the brain can result in overdose. It has recently been recognized that alcohol and cocaine can be particularly dangerous. The combination of these two drugs produces a third substance called cocaethylene, which results from cocaine metabolism being inhibited. Cocaethylene is more potent than cocaine, increasing the chance of a fatal reaction up to twenty-fivefold. It also has a longer half-life and is more toxic on the heart and blood vessels. Knowledge of cocaethylene production with concomitant use of alcohol and cocaine is quite important as the use of both of these drugs is quite frequent. One study from Harvard Medical School found that 85 percent of cocaine addicts were problem drinkers. A nationwide survey of patients entering treatment programs found that 80 percent reported using cocaine in the preceding months along with alcohol. It is estimated that up to 12 million people will use both drugs in combination in a year. Simultaneous use of alcohol and cocaine is the most frequent combination seen in emergency rooms and the second most common combination in persons dying of substance abuse. Simultaneous use has been found to increase the risk of sudden death by a factor greater than twenty in persons with postmortem evidence of coronary artery disease.

The alcohol and cocaine combination affects liver function since it is well established that alcohol has a toxic effect on the liver. In addition, some cocaine-related deaths have been linked to massive liver damage. In one animal study, mice who were on a diet of alcohol were given a single dose of cocaine. Thirty percent died of severe liver damage. No serious adverse effects were seen in animals given either alcohol or cocaine alone. A direct jump from mouse to human can't be made, but it's reasonable to suspect that the same toxic reaction would occur in people. The diagnosis might be difficult because liver damage from cocaine takes considerable time to develop.

Other potential toxic effects can occur as a result of using both cocaine and alcohol. The combination of drugs may act synergistically to produce adverse effects on the brain and, if used heavily, can cause seizures.

Alcohol, of course, can't be considered a "cause" of drug use, but those who don't drink are less likely to take drugs. Drug users drink—and get drunk—more often than nondrug users. Alcohol is frequently used with other mood-altering drugs, in combinations that can potentiate the risks of alcohol alone. Such risks include accidents when driving or performing other tasks requiring muscular coordination, and antisocial behavior, including criminal acts. Pregnant women face increased risk of fetal death, complicated deliveries, and birth deformities (Chapter 19). Whereas minimal alcohol consumption may carry low risk, combining alcohol with other mood-altering drugs carries a very high-risk burden.

Narcotic (opiate) addicts often use alcohol and other central nervous system depressants to enhance a high or minimize withdrawal. One 1985 study showed that 41 percent of drug-related deaths in men were related to combinations of alcohol and other drugs. Other studies show that up to 50 percent of deaths stemming from acute fatal reactions to heroin involved alcohol.

Patients on methadone maintenance may take alcohol and tranquilizers to get high (Chapter 12). Alcohol and tranquilizers are in a different group than narcotics but are still central nervous system depressants. So the added depressant effect when they are taken together can cause coma and death. In almost all cases of overdose in patients on methadone, the responsible agent is alcohol either alone or in combination with minor tranquilizers—not the opiate.

SMOKING AND DRUG USE

Use of many mood-altering drugs is strongly associated with smoking. One of the strongest associations is smoking and drinking, with smoking rates in excessive drinkers reported as high as 90 percent and with 70 percent of alcoholics being heavy smokers. This is not surprising as either drug can enhance the mood-altering effects of the other. Illict drug use, however, is also highly associated with smoking. The 1999 NHSDA reported 41.1 percent of past-month smokers ages twelve to seventeen to have used an illicit drug as compared to 5.6 percent of adolescent nonsmokers. In the eighteen to twenty-five age-group, cigarette smokers were four times as likely to use illicit drugs as nonsmokers (31 versus 8 percent). Even adult smokers had a fourfold increase in illicit drug use as compared to nonsmokers. Cigarette use is rarely addressed in dealing with dependency on mood-altering drugs because the immediate adverse effects of the other drugs are considered far more severe and therefore deserve the full attention of patients and staff. Trying to eliminate two dependencies can dilute the effort to eliminate use of the primary drug. In addition, experiencing the intense pleasure and stress-alleviating effects of smoking while trying to abstain from alcohol, opiates, or cocaine goes a long way toward preventing a rapid return to use of the primary drug. In addition, most staff in alcohol and drug treatment facilities are unskilled in smoking-cessation techniques and often have few resources to establish such programs. Only limited evidence exists that quitting smoking helps to maintain abstinence from other drugs. However, some studies have found that those who quit smoking were more likely to maintain abstinence from alcohol than those who continued to smoke. Based on these observations many drug treatment programs have adopted a smoke-free environment policy.

The effects of smoking and alcohol consumption have been found to be synergistic with respect to increasing the risk for developing cancers of the oropharynx and upper digestive tract. This increased risk is seen with cigars as well as cigarettes. Smoking has also been found to increase the craving for illicit drugs. This association can assume importance when trying to eliminate illicit drug use by smokers.

OPIOIDS

Heroin is frequently injected along with cocaine and amphetamines to provide an initial rush and lessen the time of drowsiness. Alcohol and marijuana use are also not uncommon among heroin users.

People on methadone maintenance may use cocaine as well as alcohol, since they can't get high from heroin or other narcotics. Use of other central nervous system depressants such as diazepam (Valium) is also common. The combination of diazepam and methadone is one of the more frequent causes of overdose among those on methadone maintenance. In the laboratory, diazepam can cut in half the amount of methadone required for an animal to overdose.

Amitriptyline (Elavil) also is often used inappropriately by those dependent on opiates. That can cause a particular problem because heroin dependency is frequently accompanied by depression, which can be relieved with amitriptyline. However, inappropriate use can produce a high independent of the antidepressant effect.

COCAINE

Cocaine and central nervous system depressants are commonly used together to end runs and induce sleep in the presence of insomnia and exhaustion. Injecting cocaine while smoking marijuana has also been reported. One study found that simultaneous use of both these drugs markedly increases heart rate, a serious problem in someone with coronary heart disease. The adverse effects of cocaine and alcohol have been described earlier.

MARIJUANA

Next to alcohol and perhaps cigarettes, marijuana is the drug most often associated with multiple drug use. The overwhelming majority of marijuana smokers, however, don't use other mood-altering drugs, except for alcohol. At times, marijuana users unknowingly take PCP that has been mixed into marijuana cigarettes. The result may be a high degree of stimulation, hallucinations, and bizarre behavior not usually related to marijuana. Since the user doesn't expect such effects, they can be disturbing. Aftereffects may persist once the acute effects subside.

TREATMENT

When it comes to treatment, the multiple drug user presents many seemingly insurmountable problems. When intoxication is present, the most important first step is an accurate diagnosis of multiple drug use. Treatment of intoxication due to cocaine or heroin without recognizing alcohol dependence can lead to alcohol withdrawal later on. The presence of hallucinations or paranoia can be a sign of cocaine, amphetamine, phencyclidine, or hallucinogen toxicity. On the other hand, aberrant behavior may be due to a coexisting psychiatric state and not combined drug use. Once a patient is detoxified, most well-known treatment strategies are oriented toward a specific substance. Patients with a second dependency may meet resistance from staff members, who are unable to manage a dual dependency. Worse yet, because many staff members take a strong position on primary treatment objectives in their own areas of expertise, they may even have difficulty agreeing where to refer people with dual dependencies.

Facilities funded to treat alcoholics aren't eager to treat patients also addicted to heroin. Primary, or "pure," alcoholics are viewed as passive-aggressive, depressed people who are contrite and have strong motivation to succeed in therapy. Heroin addicts are viewed as manipulative, aggressive, and demanding—therefore capable of destroying the successful inpatient alcohol program milieu.

Facilities focused on heroin dependency (methadone maintenance) are often ill-equipped to manage the alcoholic. Abstinence programs such as Alcoholics Anonymous (AA), which have successful track records, often won't accept alcoholics who are on methadone. Residential program staff may insist that a person discontinue methadone before being treated for alcoholism. That presents an untenable problem, both for the person and, ultimately, society. Return to heroin use when methadone is prematurely terminated has run as high as 80 percent. Many AA units have now recognized this problem and are accepting persons on methadone maintenance who have drinking problems.

Cocaine use in heroin addicts, or in those on maintenance therapy, presents still different problems, particularly when antisocial personality traits exist. People in this situation need a highly structured setting during treatment, not always possible when funds are limited. Programs (mostly residential facilities) that treat multiple drug users are in short supply. The attrition rate is also fairly high because these people tend not to accept an inpatient facility for prolonged periods. Even when residential treatment is acceptable, these programs are expensive and treatment is often inadequately covered by insurance.

However, the situation isn't hopeless; much can be done to provide effective treatment for multiple users. Some steps require little additional funding but much greater flexibility. Others clearly require a funding initiative or recognition by third-party carriers that the medical and psychological problems of multiple drug use should be covered by insurance.

Chapter 18

AIDS and Drug Use

Through Deceomber 31, 2000, 774,467 cases of AIDS in the United States had been reported to the Centers for Disease Control and Prevention, with 277,400 persons alive in the United States with this diagnosis. The prevalence of AIDS had increased by 11 percent between 1995 and 1996. In 1996, the incidence and deaths due to AIDS started to decrease; however, between 1998 and 2000, these figures leveled off, and the prevalence of AIDS increased.

Of the cases of AIDS reported, injection drug use is believed to represent 25 percent, with male to male sex represented 46 percent, and heterosexual contact in 11 percent. Currently, up to one-third of AIDS infections are related to injection drug use. AIDS has now become a leading cause of death of persons between the ages of twenty-five and forty-four. In addition, it has been estimated that 800,000 to 900,000 persons may be infected with HIV with up to one-third not knowing they are infected.

HIV progressively destroys the immune system of the body, resulting in increased susceptibility to a wide variety of infections and several rare cancers, all of which can be fatal. As AIDS develops, it's also accompanied by severe mental deterioration and widespread wasting of the body. First identified in Africa as slim disease, AIDS began to be seen in the United States in 1981 and has progressed rapidly as well as globally since that time.

HIV: THE HUMAN IMMUNODEFICIENCY VIRUS

AIDS is caused by the human immunodeficiency virus (HIV), one of the lentiviruses in the retrovirus group. HIV contains RNA (ribonucleic acid), the messenger of genetic information from DNA (deoxyribonucleic acid) to the protein-forming system of the cells.

As a retrovirus, HIV has a special enzyme (reverse transcriptase) that allows it to reverse the normal flow of genetic information from DNA to RNA to protein molecules. Thus HIV's own genes are incorporated into the genetic makeup of normal cells. The viral DNA then merges with the person's gene pool and remains latent until activated to make new virus particles.

HIV comprises two types. HIV-1, responsible for AIDS, since its isolation in 1983 has been identified in the United States and throughout the world. HIV-2, first isolated in 1985, has been detected primarily in West Africa and in some AIDS patients in both Central Africa and Europe. The illness associated with Type 2 is often indistinguishable from that of Type 1. Even though HIV-2 is uncommon in the United States, those who appear ill with AIDS but test negative for the HIV Type 1 antibody should also be tested for HIV-2 infection.

HIV has been isolated from many body secretions in both men and women: blood, urine, semen, saliva, tears, breast milk, amniotic fluid, and genital secretions. HIV has been detected in those clinically ill with AIDS, as well as in those who have been exposed to the virus but show no symptoms. Although initially thought to be a slow-acting infectious agent, HIV has now been shown to be extremely active with a half life of six hours. It has the ability to replicate quite rapidly, beginning to kill CD4 T lymphocytes soon after infection. In the abscence of appropriate treatment, severe signs of AIDS will appear approximately ten years after the initial infection. However, it has been demonstrated that in some AIDS may appear quite rapidly, pursuing an aggressive, destructive course, while a small proportion of persons are infected much longer before any symptoms appear. The short half-life of HIV allows drug-resistant strains to develop quite rapidly when treatment has started in a single individual.

Infection of the immune system by HIV results in destruction of white blood cells (T lymphocytes), which usually play a major role in stimulating the immune system. T lymphocytes consist of helper cells (T4) and suppressor cells (T8). Both groups of cells actively fight infection, and each group has a role in controlling the other group's function. As HIV infections develop and clinical signs of early AIDS appear, many of the helper cells die, thus creating an inverse ratio between helper and suppressor cells. The remaining helper cells often function defectively, leaving the body susceptible to a variety of infections. Some of these infections are called opportunistic because they rarely occur in those with normal immune systems. The most common is pneumocystis carinii (PCC), a severe pneumonia, which until the late 1980s was almost uniformly fatal.

The range of severe bacterial, fungal, and viral infections affecting HIV-positive individuals as their immune systems are progressively destroyed include various pneumonias and infections of heart valves, membranes surrounding the brain and spinal cord, the skin, and the gastrointestinal tract. The most common cancer in AIDS patients is Kaposi's sarcoma, but tumors of the lymphatic system are also common. Mental deterioration (AIDS dementia), consisting of memory loss and decreased ability to concentrate, also can occur. Decreased strength in leg muscles and difficulty walking are other manifestations of the disease.

HIV Testing

HIV antibodies in the bloodstream can be readily detected. A positive result on initial screening (ELISA), confirmed by a more specific method (Western blot), provides a highly reliable indication of HIV infection. But false positives occur, especially when large numbers of people in low-risk groups are tested. The incidence of false positives in such groups may be as high as 175 per 100,000. A review of these screening tests by the Centers for Disease Control in 1989 found the accuracy rate to be 98.5 percent for ELISA and 91.6 percent for Western blot. At present, over-the-counter kits are available for home testing for HIV in the blood and urine. Most recently, an oral test has been developed that is reasonable in price and has a relatively short turnaround time. All of these tests if positive, however, must be confirmed by the Western blot technique. Quantitative tests for HIV are also available and are essential for assessing the effectiveness of therapy as well as predicting the rate of decrease in CD4 cell counts over time.

Until recently, routine testing for HIV has been quite controversial, as it was thought that there was no effective treatment, and public knowledge that an individual was HIV positive would result in severe discrimination. However, the development of combination therapy cannot only diminish the chance of developing AIDS in persons who have been exposed but, in persons with AIDS, can suppress viral replication and stabilize CD4 cell counts. Although quite expensive ($10,000 to $15,000 per year), treatment of HIV infection and high-risk exposure to HIV should be aggressive, continuous, and with multiple medications.

Unfortunately, although there are approximately 1 million persons in the United States believed to be infected with HIV, less than 50 percent have been tested, and of those known to be HIV positive, it has been estimated that only 25 percent are receiving appropriate combination therapy. It is therefore quite important for high-risk groups such as intravenous drug users (IVDUs) to undergo testing, not only for their own personal safety and treatment but also to diminish the chances of infecting others. In addition, since a considerable number of IVDUs will be HIV negative, informing them of this fact may well be an incentive for them to diminish at-risk behaviors to allow them to remain negative.

It is important to note, however, that in any high-risk group, a negative test doesn't eliminate the possibility of HIV infection. False negatives can occur if (a) HIV antibodies have not yet developed; (b) antibody formation is delayed due to failure of HIV to trigger the immune system; (c) an unusual variant (HIV-2) infection is present; or (d) quite rarely, a loss of antibodies occurs subsequent to infection while the virus remains.

Transmission of HIV and AIDS

HIV is transmitted through several routes, with a number of groups identified at high risk for HIV infection (Table 18.1). Sexual contact is a major path, with a positive relationship reported between infection and number of sexual partners. Anal-receptive intercourse appears to play a major role in transmission among both homosexuals and heterosexuals. But anal intercourse isn't essential for transmission. Sexual activity of any kind with an HIV-infected partner and without appropriate precautions can place one at risk.

The risk becomes greater as the number of sexual partners increases, mainly because the chances for contact with an HIV-positive person increase. Among other risk-increasing factors are existence of a sexually transmitted disease and failure to use condoms. Condoms are particularly important; they decrease—but don't eliminate—risk of transmitting HIV and several other sexually transmitted diseases.

The portion of non-intravenous drug users who develop AIDS each year has remained relatively stable. But the actual numbers in this category have increased considerably, by 28 percent in men and 26 percent in women between 1995 and 1996. Although the actual percentage of male heterosexual non-IVDUs with AIDS is relatively low (5 percent), with respect to women heterosexual transmission counts for over 50 percent (22,860) of AIDS cases in 1996. A large percentage of these women were known to have heterosexual contact with IVDUs.

Intravenous Drug Use and AIDS

Prevalence of HIV intravenous drug users varies greatly between different geographic areas. In New York City, up to 61 percent of samples obtained in 1986 were positive, compared with 5 percent in Colorado, 2 percent in Texas, and 10 percent in Southern California. At present, approximately one-third of intravenous drug users in New York City are felt to be HIV positive; however, this number is much higher in other countries. The Global Program on AIDS of the World Health Organization reported in 1994 that

TABLE 18.1. Groups at High Risk for HIV Infection

Gay and bisexual men
Intravenous drug users
Hemophiliacs
Heterosexual partners of HIV-infected or recognized at-risk persons
Prostitutes
Children of HIV-infected mothers
Those with genital herpes or syphilis

74 percent of drug addicts in Yangon and 84 percent in Mandalay are positive for HIV. In Southeast Asia, prevalence of HIV infection in 1996 among intravenous drug users was 45 percent and in Myanmar 70 percent. In the southwestern borders of Yunnan, China, there is an 80 percent HIV prevalence, whereas in Vietnam a 1996 survey revealed only 11 percent of intravenous drug users to be infected with HIV.

Needle sharing among IVDUs is common practice everywhere. From 70 to 90 percent of such individuals share in up to half of injection episodes, making rapid spread of HIV possible. In part this is due to the fact that distributing sterile needles to IVDUs is illegal; in part it may be due to the desire to have a shared or common experience when shooting up. Since HIV remains infectious for as long as three to five weeks in used syringes and on needles containing HIV-positive blood, and the potential for becoming infected from a single exposure to a HIV-contaminated needle or syringe is 0.67 percent, it is not surprising that sharing equipment is a major risk factor.

However, HIV infection among IVDUs is facilitated not just by needle sharing. The tendency for this group to engage in high-risk behavior, either as a means of obtaining money to purchase drugs or as a result of impaired judgment when high, also raises the risk of HIV infection.

Women and HIV Infection

Earlier studies revealed that 30 to 50 percent of female IVDUs have engaged in prostitution. So if these women are HIV carriers, they represent a large and significant pool capable of spreading the infection throughout the heterosexual community. Even women who aren't IVDUs are at particular risk for HIV infection. Indeed, the majority of women who contract HIV through heterosexual relations have an IVDU as a partner. Active protection through the use of condoms is more often male- than female-controlled. And the increasing number of women who exchange sex for crack in crack houses are at great risk.

According to the Centers for Disease Control, women with AIDS made up approximately 6.7 percent of reported cases in 1986, increasing to 18 percent in 1999. However, if one looks at the proportion of AIDS cases in women who developed AIDS from heterosexual contact with persons known to be infected with HIV or at risk of being infected, this figure increases greatly and is even higher in cities, particularly in low-income areas where HIV infection is endemic. Worse yet, the population of infected but not yet diagnosed women surely is sizable. Since not all physicians are yet attuned to early symptoms of HIV infection in women, diagnosis and early intervention may be delayed. Women of color are particularly at risk, with African-American women comprising almost 61 percent of AIDS cases reported in women in 1999, being the third leading cause of death for African-American women between the ages of twenty-five and forty-four.

Children and HIV Infection

HIV-infected women obviously play a significant role in terms of HIV-infected newborns. Except for the 20 percent who are hemophiliacs infected through blood transfusions, the overwhelming majority (virtually 80 percent) of infants with AIDS are born to mothers who have had IVDUs as sexual partners or who are themselves IVDUs.

The prevalence of HIV infection among childbearing women varies greatly, from 0.21 percent in Massachusetts to 2 percent in areas of New York City. In a study in New York State, 141,000 anonymous blood specimens were taken from men and pregnant women, and 133,781 from babies born over a six-month period. The incidence of HIV infections was startling. Depending on the geographic area, up to one in twenty-two women tested positive. Infection was twice as high in mothers in their twenties and thirties as in those in their teens and forties. In New York City, African-American mothers were many times more likely to have HIV infections than white mothers. The rates were 2.07 percent for African-American mothers, 1.66 percent for Hispanic mothers, and 0.4 percent for white mothers. When racial and geographic data were pooled, the chances of a New York City African-American mother and her baby being infected were 41 times higher than those of a white woman and her baby living outside the city.

The proportion of infants born to mothers who are HIV positive who will develop HIV infection can vary but is felt to be approximately 25 percent. However, premature rupture of the membranes is thought to approximately double the chances of HIV infection in newborns. Today, however, no correlation has been found between nursing and an increased incidence of HIV infection with mothers who are HIV positive. In a subsequent study of 276,609 newborns in New York State, 0.66 percent tested positive for HIV, with a prevalence of 1.25 percent in New York City (with rates highest in areas where intravenous drug use is also high).

The actual number of HIV-infected newborns who will develop AIDS can't be predicted with certainty. One study followed 117 infants born to HIV-positive mothers for about eighteen months after birth. By the end of this period, 27 percent of the children were seropositive for HIV or had died of AIDS. Of the thirty-two seropositives, only two remained asymptomatic. Another nine children didn't test positive for HIV but had clinical symptoms of HIV infection.

In a second study of 172 children infected with HIV perinatally, the statistics were even more ominous: half developed symptoms within the first twelve weeks; 78 percent within the first two years. Seventeen percent died in their first year; median survival time was thirty-eight months. Extrapolating these findings to the general population suggests that about one-third of the children born to HIV-positive women will develop evidence of HIV infection or AIDS by age eighteen months, with 20 percent of them having died.

Even when children born to parents who have AIDS are not infected with the virus, their parents' illness can be devastating. A national study in 1997 of 2,864 adults being treated for HIV infection found 28 percent to have children under eighteen years of age, with women much more likely than men to have children (60 percent versus 18 percent) and be living with them (76 percent versus 35 percent). Of those women younger than thirty years, 26 percent had given birth to children after the HIV infection was diagnosed. Clearly, the economic, social, and psychological costs involved with raising these children will be considerable even if they are not infected with HIV.

Adolescents and HIV Infection

The spread of HIV infection in adolescents is increasing. Whether it's related to drug use or increased sexual activity—along with or independent of drugs—is unclear. But since intravenous drug use does not appear to be the primary route of infection and 50 to 60 percent of adolescents will be sexually active by age eighteen, unprotected sex is the greatest risk factor.

The number of teenagers with AIDS is relatively small—representing less than 0.4 percent of total reported AIDS cases. But the seven-plus years of latency between infection with HIV and development of illness may increase that number. A study of 1,500 homeless and runaway teenagers in New York City revealed 7 percent to be HIV-positive, with 16 percent of those between the ages of eighteen and twenty testing positive. Between July 1989 and June 1990, the Centers for Disease Control reported an increase of 38 percent in the number of AIDS cases among teenagers. In 1995, HIV infection was reported by the CDC to be the sixth leading cause of death among persons ages fifteen to twenty-four in the United States.

Previous epidemiological surveys suggest that the education provided to adolescents about AIDS is ineffective. Although 50 to 75 percent did know that HIV could be transmitted through the blood, up to 64 percent said it could be transmitted through public toilets. Among a subset of sexually active juvenile offenders, 35 percent had never used condoms, with only 50 percent of sexually active high school students reporting that they had used condoms during their last sexual contact. The use of mood-altering drugs by teenagers also serves to impair judgment and increase at-risk behavior. Fortunately, new data provided by the 1997 Youth Risk Behavior Surveillance survey is more encouraging. This survey found that fewer high school students are engaging in behaviors placing them at risk for HIV infection. This has been accompanied by an increase in the percentage of high school students receiving HIV/AIDS education, from 83 percent in 1991 to 92 percent in 1997.

AIDS and the Elderly

Although the proportion of persons over fifty years of age with AIDS has remained stable since 1991 at approximately 11 percent of all cases reported, intravenous drug use has played an etiological role in 19 percent as compared to 26 percent of those between the ages of thirteen and forty-nine. Persons greater than fifty years of age do have an increase in AIDS-associated opportunistic infections compared to those who are younger, especially with respect to HIV encephalopathy and the AIDS wasting syndrome. A higher proportion of persons over fifty years of age with opportunistic infections will die within one month of diagnosis of AIDS, suggesting that this diagnosis may have been made later in the course of infection as compared to younger persons. These observations emphasize the need to continue surveillance for HIV infection among people at risk regardless of their age.

PREVENTING HIV TRANSMISSION

Injection of illicit drugs is a major risk factor for HIV infection, with over one-third of all new HIV cases occurring among intravenous drug users, their partners, or their children. Many attempts have been made to reduce HIV transmission through intravenous drug use. They include massive educational campaigns, harm reduction techniques such as distribution of bleach to disinfect needles, distribution of sterile needles, and expansion of available treatment programs for drug abuse. Treatment programs are obviously the preferred method for preventing the spread of HIV infection among intravenous drug users. They are usually either drug-free or methadone maintenance programs (Chapters 6, 12).

Methadone Maintenance Programs

Heroin addicts appear most likely to accept methadone maintenance, so it is essential that enough treatment slots are available. Entry into maintenance programs is usually accompanied by decreased heroin use, but many addicts still inject cocaine, continuing to put themselves at risk. Since cocaine is injected more frequently than heroin, the risk rises accordingly. In 1984, a study of patients in New York who had been on methadone maintenance continuously prior to 1978 found only 10 percent were HIV positive. The percentage rose to 47 percent for those not on continuous treatment. Even with those persons using cocaine while on methadone maintenance, high-risk needle and HIV related behaviors have been shown to decrease markedly. A subsequent study in 1993 found that over an eighteen-month period, the odds of becoming infected with HIV were 5.4 times greater in those not on methadone maintenance compared with those who were in treatment.

Continued injection of heroin by some on methadone maintenance has led critics to question the efficiency of maintenance. As noted in Chapter 12, however, failures in maintenance to prevent heroin use are primarily related to the quality of the specific program and specific methadone dose administered (Chapter 12). Good methadone maintenance programs are effective in decreasing needle use. So are therapeutic communities and ambulatory day programs. Maintenance programs, however, are more successful in attracting and keeping IVDUs for treatment. Studies have shown that residential and outpatient programs can lose 40 to 50 percent of patients in the first three months, compared with a 14 percent loss from maintenance programs. The loss rate in the latter programs can probably be lowered through appropriate staffing and closer adjustments in individual dosages. In summary, methadone maintenance has been demonstrated to be an efficient, cost-effective approach to decreasing HIV transmission. This benefit affects not only the IVDU but also the individuals who do not inject drugs.

Reduction in High-Risk Behavior

Harm reduction includes providing addicts with information about HIV transmission and how to reduce risk through changes in sexual behavior. But purely educational efforts to change behavior in IVDUs haven't been very successful. The reasons may be the heroin addict's general self-destructive nature or a feeling of helplessness stemming from the belief that infection has already taken place. Those feelings of futility and inevitability must be overcome, as less than 50 percent of IVDUs may be infected with HIV. Appropriate behavior modification may protect these people from HIV infection.

AIDS research findings have documented a deliberate reduction in high-risk behaviors once the specific risk factors are made meaningful to the drug user. Risk varies depending on total number of injections per month, percentage of injections with used needles, average number of cocaine injections per month, and frequency of sharing injection equipment with large numbers of other IVDUs. For reasons not entirely clear, cocaine injection appears to carry the greatest risk of HIV infection, with heroin next, and amphetamine injection less risky.

Directing appropriate resources to meet the needs of poor communities cannot be overemphasized. As with many communicable diseases associated with poverty, African Americans and Hispanics are at particular risk for intravenous drug use and AIDS by a factor of two to one. This is especially true for women in these groups, for whom intravenous drug use is the primary route of HIV transmission.

Needles on Demand (Syringe Exchange Programs)

Dispensing needles on request to limit HIV transmission remains controversial and politicized (Chapters 6, 12). Opponents say easy access to needles will increase intravenous drug use. Proponents say the opportunity to decrease HIV transmission is reason enough to try such an approach, and indeed studies have not documented any increased drug use associated with needle exchange. Needle exchange programs have helped diminish HIV transmission. As of 1999, there were 131 syringe exchange programs (SEP) operating in eighty-one cities, thirty-one states, Washington, DC, and Puerto Rico, with 64 percent providing on-site voluntary counseling and testing for HIV infection. One study of needle exchange in Connecticut revealed that although at the onset more than two-thirds of street syringes were positive for HIV, within three months HIV-positive syringes returned to the program decreased to less than 45 percent without any increase in the number of intravenous drug users seen. Needle exchange programs, in fact, have been evaluated by a number of independent commissions, with each evaluation demonstrating that, indeed, needle exchange is effective in decreasing HIV infection as well as hepatitis without an associated increase in the use of illicit drugs by injection. Nonetheless, as of the present writing, the federal administration has still refused to allow federal funding for development of such programs, and in many states they still remain illegal.

In addition to SEP, in 2000, several states (New Hampshire, New York, and Rhode Island) altered their laws concerning syringes, partially or completely removing penalties for syringe possession as well as the need for prescriptions to purchase syringes, thereby facilitating access to sterile "works" and further decreasing the risk of HIV transmission.

Disinfectants

An alternative to dispensing sterile syringes and needles is to disinfect them between uses. The ideal disinfectant acts quickly, is inexpensive, readily available, neutralizes viruses effectively, and is safe to the user. A solution of one part household bleach to ten parts water works best. This solution can reduce viral activity sevenfold after sixty seconds of exposure. Between June 1986 and May 1987, several thousand bottles of bleach, along with instructions for use, were dispensed in San Francisco. A follow-up survey showed that two-thirds of those who received the bleach used it for the intended purpose.

In summary, studies have shown that a variety of harm reduction techniques and increasing availability of educational programs have resulted in a continuing reduction in the behaviors of IVDUs associated with an increased risk of HIV infection. Prevention programs and harm reduction programs both deserve support in the attempt to diminish HIV infection among IVDUs.

TREATMENT OF AIDS

Initially thought to be a fatal and at times rapidly progressive disease, over the last several years AIDS and the opportunistic infections associated with it have become quite treatable. In persons potentially exposed to the virus, rapid aggressive treatment with a combination of reverse transcriptase inhibitors and HIV protease inhibitors can diminish the chances of ever becoming HIV positive. For those who are known to be HIV positive or to have AIDS, treating at the appropriate time with these agents can suppress viral replication, thereby decreasing the chances of resistant strains developing. Transmission of HIV from mother to infant can also be impressively reduced by therapy. In summary, therapy directed against HIV must be individualized, be started relatively early, be aggressive with a combination of drugs, be continuous, and be carefully monitored so that changes in therapeutic agents can be made when resistance has been shown to develop.

A variety of therapies exist for treatment of the opportunistic infection associated with AIDS which, when applied prophylactically prior to infections in high-risk individuals or quickly when infections develop, have been responsible for the decline in the annual incidence of AIDS associated with opportunistic infections.

Finally, similar to most conditions that are difficult to treat and often associated with a fatal outcome, a variety of homeopathic and nutritional therapies exist, which, although not inadequately evaluated, appear to be relatively free from harm. These include the use of macrobiotic diets, multiple vitamins, and mineral therapy as well as a variety of herbal therapies.

RELATIONSHIP BETWEEN THE USE OF NONINJECTING MOOD-ALTERING DRUGS AND HIV INFECTION

There are a number of ways that inappropriate use of mood-altering drugs may facilitate HIV infection, independent of intravenous use (Table 18.2).

TABLE 18.2. Relationship Between Heroin Use and AIDS

Facilitation of high-risk behavior, thus increasing chances for HIV infection

Transmission of HIV through needle sharing

Injection of infectious agents from contaminated drugs and through unsterile needles, worsening condition of those with AIDS

Exchange of sexual favors from HIV-infected persons for drugs

Depression of immune system, with increased susceptibility to infections in those with AIDS

Impaired Judgment

Use of mood-altering drugs, including alcohol, during sexual contact can blur judgment so that safe-sex techniques are ignored. Strong associations exist between such behavior and the types of sexual activity implicated in HIV infection. According to one study, gay men who continue high-risk behavior are twice as likely to have used alcohol and eight times as likely to have used other drugs as those who stop such behavior. Whether drug use led to high-risk sexual activity, or whether those engaged in such activity were more apt to use drugs, is unclear. But alcohol and other mood-altering drugs release inhibitions, so it's reasonable to suppose that drug consumption might contribute to failure to take appropriate precautions during sex.

Cocaine As a Specific Risk Factor

The association between intravenous use of cocaine and HIV infection is well recognized. What remains to be clearly defined, however, is whether the association is related more to frequency of cocaine injection; its use in shooting galleries, where needles are freely exchanged; the need to barter sex for cocaine; the increase in sexual activity while on cocaine; the impaired mental judgment following cocaine use that leads to other high-risk behaviors; or the effect of cocaine itself on the immune system.

Effect of Drug Use on the Immune System

Considerable laboratory and clinical evidence suggests that alcohol adversely affects immunity. Alcoholics are more susceptible to infection than nonalcoholics, and alcohol is a risk factor in development of severe pneumonia and virulent lung abscesses. When alcohol liver damage (cirrhosis) is present, susceptibility to infection increases. Tuberculosis is also more prevalent in alcoholics.

Some evidence suggests that cocaine itself may have a detrimental effect on the immune system. Markers of cell-mediated immunity in association with cocaine use have been found to be altered in other types of retroviral infections. Similar associations between cocaine use and depression of T lymphocyte helper-suppressor ratios have also been described. In experiments on the excessive use of cocaine, replication of HIV in laboratory animals was markedly increased. A link between Kaposi's sarcoma and cocaine use has also been reported, although causality hasn't been demonstrated.

Heroin has long been known to adversely affect immune function. It also significantly reduces numbers and function of T cells. In laboratory animals, marijuana can suppress certain immune functions. While this finding can't clearly extrapolate to humans, marijuana might act similarly in a person with an existing immune deficit. Whether central nervous system stimulants and barbiturates adversely affect human immune function is not known.

Volatile nitrites have been associated with changes in immune function even after relatively brief exposure. Such changes, however, haven't been consistently confirmed. Positive association between nitrite use and Kaposi's sarcoma has also been made. Combined with other chemicals, nitrites can form nitrosamines. Because nitrosamines can cause cancer, they may more easily do so in an AIDS victim with an already altered immune state. Kaposi's sarcoma has developed in habitual nitrite users, but a definite causal relationship has not been demonstrated.

SUMMARY

Continued use of mood-altering drugs might have a bearing on accelerating development of AIDS in HIV-positive individuals. One study of IVDUs in New York found that those who abstained from or markedly cut down on intravenous drug use were less likely to show progression of clinical AIDS symptoms and manifestations than those who hadn't. A large multicenter study, however, involving approximately 3,500 gay men, 38 percent of whom were HIV positive, did not find the use of any of the common mood-altering drugs to be associated with either the appearance of clinical symptoms or the speed with which AIDS developed. Compared with HIV-negative men, a significantly higher proportion of HIV-positive men had used each group of mood-altering substances more recently and more frequently during the study period. But AIDS wasn't diagnosed any earlier in the HIV-positives who also used mood-altering drugs. Alcohol consumption, seen in

90 percent of all men, was also found not to be a risk factor in the development of AIDS.

Even though use of mood-altering drugs may not increase the progression from HIV infection to AIDS, the role of mood-altering drugs in transmitting HIV, either through contaminated needles or by promoting high-risk behavior, remains a valid concern.

Studies have documented the effectiveness of treatment approaches in diminishing high-risk behavior associated with HIV transmission. Clearly, more effort is needed in providing both prevention and treatment on demand in order to diminish the transmission of this still ultimately fatal disease.

Chapter 19

Drugs, Pregnancy, and the Newborn

Behold, thou shalt conceive, and bear a son; and now drink no wine nor strong drink.

Judges 13:7

During pregnancy a woman must take responsibility for her own health as well as that of her fetus. Ideally, use of all mood-altering substances should stop at least three months before conception, with abstinence continuing throughout the pregnancy. Realistically, even when pregnancy is planned, many women who use mood-altering substances can't or don't stop.

INCIDENCE OF DRUG USE DURING PREGNANCY

Data from the National Institute on Drug Abuse suggest that many of the 56 million women of childbearing age in the United States use one or more of the following: alcohol, cocaine, marijuana, or nicotine. But defining the proportion of women at risk for drug use when pregnant isn't the same as identifying those who will continue to use drugs when pregnant. In 1992, it was estimated that 5 percent of the 4 million women who gave birth in the United States were using an illicit drug at some time during their pregnancy, with 19 percent using alcohol. At least one-third of pregnant women smoke tobacco; 60 to 90 percent use analgesics at some point during the pregnancy, and between 20 to 30 percent take sedative drugs. Data from the New York City Board of Health reveal that the risk of giving birth to an infant of low birth weight in the presence of excessive maternal drug use is 3.8 times greater than with women who do not use drugs. The risk of infant death among drug-using women is 2.6 times greater.

GENERAL EFFECTS OF DRUGS
ON PREGNANCY OUTCOME

A fair amount of knowledge has accumulated on the effects of mood-altering drugs on reproduction, pregnancy, and the newborn. Most investigators in the field agree on certain key points.

All commonly used mood-altering drugs can freely pass through the placental barrier, so any drug used by the mother is present in the fetal circulation. In general, congenital defects are usually induced during the first trimester, with the risk greatest from twenty days to two months. The risk of birth defects decreases after that time, but the fetus is still vulnerable to growth retardation and other neurological or behavioral abnormalities, which become apparent after birth.

Many mood-altering substances affect uterine contractions, causing decreased blood flow and oxygen supply to the fetus. This can result in premature labor and/or spontaneous abortion. Withdrawal from narcotics or drugs in the sedative/barbiturate category also causes uterine contractions.

Dependency-producing drugs cause the newborn to go into withdrawal, necessitating treatment of the symptoms (Table 19.1). Of course, the associ-

TABLE 19.1. Adverse Effects of Mood-Altering Drugs on Pregnancy and the Newborn

Drug	Congenital Abnormality				
	Spontaneous Abortion	Premature Delivery	Perinatal Mortality	Neonatal Withdrawal	Fetal Distress
Alcohol	+		+		++
Amphetamines		+	+		
Barbiturates, sedatives, tranquilizers				+	+
Cocaine	+	+	+		++
Heroin	+	+	+	+	++
Marijuana					+/−
Methadone				+	
Nicotine	+				+
Phencyclidine		+		+/−	+

+ = Adverse effects
+/− = Effects not consistently documented

ation of HIV and AIDS has placed infants born to intravenous drug-using women at deadly risk (Chapter 18).

A safe assumption is that any mood-altering substance used in excess during pregnancy will have a detrimental effect on the fetus. But whether minimal or even moderate use of a specific substance will cause a bad outcome is sometimes hard to determine as multiple drug use is very common. Alcohol and cigarettes are frequently used in combination with such substances as heroin, methadone, cocaine, and sedatives. Moreover, many women who use these drugs excessively are poorly nourished and don't seek adequate prenatal care and counseling.

Isolating specific drug effects in terms of future infant development has similar problems. Infants treated for withdrawal symptoms are usually given other drugs for days or weeks to alleviate symptoms. The long-term effects of these prescribed drugs aren't always measured. In addition, women with chemical dependency problems are often unable to provide adequate child care. As a result, the effect of these environmental factors on child rearing and future developmental abnormalities can't be accurately assessed.

Nevertheless, the physiological effects of specific mood-altering substances on pregnancy, fetal development, and outcome are identifiable. Before we discuss these effects for each major drug type, it should be noted that even in the "normal" course of events, without any specific identifiable risk factors, only about half of all fertilized eggs progress through a successful pregnancy and delivery. Up to half of those lost through spontaneous abortion or miscarriage are considered structurally abnormal. As many as 3 percent of newborns have one or more congenital malformations at birth; another 3 percent are diagnosed with some developmental abnormality by the end of the first year. Subtler abnormalities may not become apparent until early childhood. Because of the existence of these general patterns, we cannot simply assume that any health problems in a child born to a pregnant woman who takes drugs must be related to specific drug effects.

Alcohol

Alcohol's adverse effects on pregnancy have been observed for centuries. One of the first studies on the subject was published in the late 1800s by a doctor from Liverpool reporting the outcome of 600 children born to 100 alcoholic women.

Fetal Alcohol Syndrome

A constellation of features called the fetal alcohol syndrome (FAS) was described in 1973. FAS, found in many infants born to women who ingested substantial amounts of alcohol during their pregnancies, consists of abnormal facial characteristics, mental retardation, hyperactivity, aggressive behavior, sleep disorders, and continuing behavioral problems (Table 19.2). Associated abnormalities may include defects in the heart, genitals, kidneys, and muscles, as well as disturbances in vision. Alcohol is one of the few known mood-altering drugs definitively linked to congenital abnormalities and to pre- and postnatal growth retardation. Unfortunately, since alcohol affects these developing systems within three to six weeks after fertilization, many women who drink are unaware of their pregnancy and therefore cannot prevent these changes by abstaining. Risk of spontaneous abortion accompanying excessive alcohol consumption is also real.

As a result of these findings, the surgeon general issued an advisory warning in 1981 suggesting that alcoholic beverages be avoided by pregnant women, and that they be informed of the alcoholic content of food and medications. As a result of concern over drinking and pregnancy, the Alcoholic Beverage Labeling Act was incorporated into the Omnibus Drug Bill of 1988 requiring that warnings about the potential adverse health effects of alcohol be placed on labels for alcoholic beverages. Several states have also enacted a "point of purchase" clause, requiring information on the hazards of alcohol during pregnancy to be prominently displayed wherever alcohol is sold.

It is appropriate that physicians recommend abstinence from alcohol when a woman becomes pregnant. However, excessive alcohol consumption, which places an infant at risk, is considered more than seven drinks a week or five or more drinks in a single day. Surveys have estimated that between 10 and 15 percent of pregnant women have at least some alcohol during pregnancy, with binge drinking reported in less than 3 percent.

However, the need for complete abstinence during pregnancy has been questioned. Critics point out that many women drink varying amounts of alcohol during pregnancy, but the incidence of FAS is far lower than the number of pregnant drinkers.

TABLE 19.2. Fetal Alcohol Syndrome

Behavioral changes
    Hyperactivity, irritability

Facial changes
    Shortened opening between the eyelids
    Depressed space between nose and mouth
    Flat nose
    Small head circumference
    Thin upper lip

Growth retardation

Estimates put at approximately 36,000 the number of pregnancies adversely affected by alcohol, with 2,000 to 2,400 infants born with FAS. If we use a liberal estimate of 40,000 pregnancies adversely affected by alcohol, the risk to any given pregnant woman who drinks is 1 in 100. But the risk of having an infant with FAS approximates 1 in 1,300 with rates per 1,000 births ranging from 0.5 to 3. Both those risk ratios are lower than the risk of a congenital abnormality in the absence of any alcohol or drug use. Perhaps of greater relevance is the observation that 12 percent of all patients in long-term institutions have evidence of having had FAS at birth. Drinking during pregnancy has also been associated with other birth-related defects, including neurological and cognitive disorders.

Excessive alcohol use during pregnancy is often accompanied by use of other mood-altering drugs. The role of multiple drug use in FAS is not yet clear. One study, for example, found maternal use of marijuana to be the single best predictor of having a baby born with FAS—an even better forecaster than alcohol use.

Fear of birth defects results in some women experiencing needless concern and anxiety throughout their pregnancy if they drank alcohol before knowing they were pregnant. That can and does happen fairly often, since several weeks typically pass between conception and confirmation of pregnancy. Studies have revealed that up to 60 percent of women who drink did not know they were pregnant until after the first month of their pregnancy. By suggesting that minimal alcohol consumption always leads to impaired infants, one places drinking in the same category as those drugs that are consistently associated with risks to pregnancy, such as heavy cigarette smoking, excessive use of alcohol, and use of illicit narcotics, cocaine, and other street drugs. Minimal drinking during pregnancy should be discouraged, but it doesn't invariably increase chances of having an impaired child. Having such a misconception might even inadvertently prompt a person to use more dangerous drugs. Continued education in the hazards of drinking, however, remains important and can be quite effective. A survey of 1,000 pregnant women suggests that education on the effects of drugs during pregnancy is working. Of those women, 70 percent decreased alcohol consumption once they became pregnant. By comparison, only 14 percent stopped smoking during pregnancy.

Unfortunately, despite existing guidelines, what constitutes a safe level of alcohol consumption has not been definitely determined. Several studies have demonstrated that spontaneous abortion and low birth weight can occur even with "social" drinking. In a study of almost 500 pregnant women, researchers at the University of Washington found that moderate drinking (defined as one drink a day) was associated with a variety of symptoms in newborns, including weaknesses in heart and lung function and irritability. At age four, some of these children had attention deficiencies and slight decreases in intelligence. The same investigators documented the adverse effect of alcohol on breast-feeding infants of mothers who continued to drink. Compared with a control group, infants regularly exposed to alcohol in breast milk had slightly but significantly impaired motor control. Since it has not been possible to quantify the amount of alcohol that can be safely consumed by a woman during pregnancy, it is most reasonable for a woman to abstain from all alcohol once she learns she is pregnant.

Amphetamines

The specific effects of amphetamines are difficult to isolate because they're often used in conjunction with other mood-altering drugs. Studies have suggested that taking amphetamines, even for weight control, can be associated with low birth weight. Dependence on amphetamines has been linked to premature delivery and sometimes to prenatal mortality. In addition, emotional disturbances have been reported in children whose mothers were dependent on amphetamines during pregnancy. When the drug is injected, both woman and fetus are exposed to all the associated medical complications.

Caffeine

Both pregnant and nonpregnant women may consume large quantities of caffeine in coffee, tea, and cola beverages. The metabolism of caffeine, which freely crosses the placental barrier, is decreased during pregnancy. Since the fetus has no enzymes for its metabolism, caffeine may accumulate in the newborn for several days after birth. The effects of caffeine on pregnancy are controversial, although some investigators have reported both decreased ability to conceive, spontaneous abortion, and increased risk of low birth weight infants—other studies have not consistently confirmed these results. One of the problems in singling out the effects of caffeine is that coffee, alcohol, and cigarette smoking frequently go together—and cigarette smoking is a known independent risk factor in low birth weight infants.

A large study of 3,891 pregnant women at Yale-New Haven Hospital revealed a definite relationship between maternal coffee consumption and birth weight. Only 25 percent of the women had no caffeine intake; another 8 percent consumed the equivalent of three-plus cups of coffee per day. The latter were the only ones at significant risk for having low birth weight infants (7.3 versus 4.1 percent among non-caffeine drinkers).

Caffeine consumption correlated positively with cigarette smoking, marijuana smoking, and alcohol drinking. Yet when those variables were accounted for, the increased risk among heavy coffee drinkers remained. A more recent 2000 study found that the risk of spontaneous abortion was increased in women who consumed more than 100 mg of caffeine a day, with those consuming 500 mg or more having twice the risk as those consuming less than 100 mg. The clinical importance of these findings remains to be determined. But it is probably best for women to carefully moderate their consumption of caffeine, including coffee, teas, and cola drinks, during pregnancy or avoid all caffeine-containing beverages.

Central Nervous System Depressants

Many studies have shown that chronic maternal use of barbiturates and other central nervous system depressants can be associated with an accumulation of the drugs in fetal tissues. Infants born to mothers dependent on such drugs undergo withdrawal not unlike narcotic withdrawal. Depending on the specific drug, symptoms may not appear until several days after birth because of the prolonged half-life in the infant's blood. Acute, intermittent use during pregnancy can also be associated with adverse fetal effects. High doses prior to delivery can result in respiratory depression, failure to nurse, and lethargy at birth.

Cigarettes

The adverse effects of smoking on the reproductive system and pregnancy are well known. Less well known is whether they're related to nicotine or to the numerous constituents in cigarette smoke, including such toxins as lead, cadmium, and cyanide. Smoking has been shown to decrease fertility and to increase risk of spontaneous abortion and placental problems. These include rupture of the placenta and premature rupture of the placental membranes at birth.

Smoking can also cause growth retardation, resulting in low birth weight, and has been associated with subsequent deficits in intellectual and emotional development. Conversely, smoking has been associated with decreased incidence of maternal preeclampsia and toxemia, conditions characterized by a sudden rise in blood pressure, excessive weight gain, generalized edema, and other toxic disturbances. But when those conditions do occur in smokers, the result is increased risk of infant mortality.

The effects of passive smoking on adults are relatively well known (Chapter 15), but the effects on the fetus when a pregnant woman is exposed to cigarette smoke are not well known. For example, increased levels of thiocyanate, a by-product of tobacco smoke, have been identified in fetal tissues, but its actual effects have not been studied.

Cocaine

One nationwide survey of thirty-six hospitals found that 11 percent of women who delivered had exposed their fetuses to illegal drugs, with the most common drug being cocaine. The risks to a woman and her fetus from cocaine have been described as even greater than those from heroin (Table 19.3), with the risks increasing if the drug is used throughout the pregnancy. The risks occur whether the drug is snorted, smoked as crack, or taken intravenously—although intravenous use introduces a new set of complications. The stimulant effects and pharmacological properties are such that even a single use can result in adverse consequences.

Cocaine rapidly crosses the placental barrier. The overall effect on the placenta is to decrease blood flow to the fetus. That can result in impairment in fetal growth, an increased growth of malformations, and often excessive bleeding and fetal death. Premature labor and decreased birth weight are common. In New York City, the risk of having a low birth weight baby is four times greater in cocaine users than in women who don't take drugs. Rapid increases in maternal and fetal blood pressure may result in stroke or convulsion.

Mortality of infants born to women using cocaine in New York City has been three to six times greater than that of non-drug-using women. Cocaine is eliminated from an adult's body within forty-eight hours, but the low levels of enzymes in the fetus make metabolism there much slower. Thus co-

TABLE 19.3. Effects of Cocaine on Pregnant Women and Newborns

Women
Increased risk of:
    Spontaneous miscarriage (abortion)
    Decreased growth of fetus
    Premature birth
    Premature separation of placenta (abruptio placenta)
    Decreased uterine blood flow
Newborns
Low birth weight
Irritability
Tremors
Neurological abnormalities
Stroke
Damage to small intestines
Possible congenital heart and kidney deformities
Sudden infant death syndrome (SIDS)
More complicated and prolonged hospitalization

caine may remain in fetal tissues for several days. Norcocaine, one of cocaine's breakdown products, is equally toxic and is recirculated throughout the amniotic fluid.

At birth, newborns whose mothers have used cocaine are hypersensitive and irritable, crying at the least stimulation. Conversely, they may appear oversedated. The incidence of sudden infant death syndrome also increases. Maternal cocaine use can interfere with parent-child bonding, and neurological impairment can persist into early childhood. Subsequent psychological and social development may also be impaired. Children who have inhaled crack or cocaine smoke in their homes become drowsy, unable to stand, or even suffer seizures. Such passive exposure results in considerable blood levels of cocaine with potentially serious effects on the brain and heart. Persistent, subtle, cognitive defects have been reported in children as old as six and seven years old.

The effects of cocaine on the fetus and newborn appear to be quite damaging. Yet, these findings have recently been challenged as observations from studies that were poorly controlled, and for the most part, published in nonpeer-reviewed journals, and therefore not subject to sufficient scientific scrutiny. Regardless of the intensity of the physical effects of cocaine on the newborn, cocaine use by a woman during and after pregnancy must be addressed in a comprehensive manner, including prevention and careful assessment of the newborn with follow-up care and treatment, as appropriate.

Heroin and Methadone Maintenance

Illicit heroin use can expose the woman and her fetus to withdrawal and overdose. Both phenomena carry great risk for the fetus (Table 19.4). Consequently, heroin users who become pregnant are apt to experience an increased incidence of spontaneous abortion and stillbirth. Other complications include fetal distress during labor, narcotic withdrawal and low birth weight, and decreased growth rates when the infant is three to six months old. At one year of age, heroin-exposed babies have been found to be vola-

TABLE 19.4. Complications of Heroin Use in Pregnant Women

Abortion
Breech presentation
Infection of amniotic fluid
Intrauterine death
Placental insufficiency
Premature labor
Premature rupture of membranes
Toxemia

tile, easily frustrated and quick to temper tantrums. Sleep disturbances and impulsive behavior leading to hyperactivity were also noted.

The best solution for a pregnant woman addicted to heroin is gradual detoxification and subsequent abstinence. In practice, however, that's often unrealistic. Clinical experience has revealed that up to 70 percent of pregnant women who are detoxified from heroin resume their habits by the time they reach the third trimester. So to prevent heroin use (and clearly as a second choice), low doses of methadone have been used in maintenance therapy. Methadone prevents the "peak and valley" plasma levels of morphine in the fetus seen with heroin injection and, in addition to decreasing the risk of infections associated with heroin injection, facilitates acute prenatal care as the woman is seen in clinic or on regular visits for her methadone.

Numerous studies have tried to define the effects of methadone on the fetus, the newborn, and the developing infant. Methadone, like all narcotics, crosses the placental barrier, is found in fetal tissues, and results in newborn withdrawal 100 percent of the time. Pharmacological treatment is warranted in 60 to 80 percent of such cases. Withdrawal is sufficiently mild in the rest to allow supportive treatment only.

Mothers maintained on methadone who don't use other drugs and are appropriately followed throughout the pregnancy can deliver infants without significant problems. The babies may have slightly decreased birth weight, but their neonatal complication rate is the same as that of babies born to nondependent women. Follow-up studies indicate that children born to women on methadone may exhibit a higher incidence of minor neurological abnormalities and somewhat lower scores on developmental evaluations during their first three years. When compared with scores in a control group, however, those differences tend to regress toward normal.

No uniform long-term effects in infants whose mothers have been maintained on methadone have been consistently found. But many women on methadone also use other mood-altering drugs, including heroin and cocaine. Home environments may differ greatly, also making comparative evaluations difficult. Maintaining a woman on methadone is not preferable to abstinence, and the decision to prescribe methadone is made only after realizing how difficult—if not impossible—it is for many women to remain abstinent when pregnant. The medical use of methadone, however, is far safer than continued heroin use.

Hallucinogens, Phencyclidine, and Ecstasy

Lysergic Acid Diethylamide (LSD)

Isolated reports have linked LSD with congenital malformations, but there is no consistent evidence that it causes such abnormalities.

Phencyclidine (PCP)

Use of PCP during pregnancy has rarely been associated with malformations, but its frequent combination with other mood-altering drugs makes studying its singular effects in pregnancy difficult. Incidence of PCP use in high-risk pregnancies has been estimated at 7 to 12 percent. Premature labor, fetal distress, and low birth weight have been described in women who use PCP.

Abnormal findings in the newborn consist of increased tremors, irritability, altered nursing reflex, and poor attention span. Those symptoms are similar to the withdrawal symptoms in infants of heroin-dependent mothers. But PCP is stored in the fetal tissues, so it's possible that the irritability may be due to its release rather than representing withdrawal from the drug. Agitation and restlessness can continue for several months. Several follow-up studies observed consistent borderline abilities in fine motor development, language, and in social adjustment. However, by two years of age those differences had regressed toward normal.

Ecstasy

In the past, little data were available concerning the effects of maternal Ecstasy use on the newborn. However, a recent study in England of 176 pregnant women who took Ecstasy alone or in combination with other drugs during their pregnancy had a significantly increased risk of giving birth to infants with congenital malformations, involving mainly the cardiovascular and musculoskeletal systems.

Marijuana

Use of marijuana during pregnancy may affect the fetus through a number of mechanisms. Marijuana is highly fat soluble and is absorbed by the tissues, so a single administration may remain in the placenta and fetal tissues for up to thirty days. Physiological effects resulting in increased heart rate and blood pressure may adversely affect placental blood flow. Smoking marijuana, like smoking cigarettes, results in elevated carbon monoxide levels in the blood. These levels are higher with marijuana than those from regular cigarettes because of the practice of inhaling deeply and holding the breath. The frequent use of marijuana with other drugs can result in an additive adverse effect on the fetus.

Early studies failed to conclusively demonstrate that the incidence of congenital malformations increased in infants exposed to marijuana during gestation. Deficiencies in central nervous system functioning and congenital malformations were reported by some investigators, but not confirmed by others. In the newborn, abnormal sleep and arousal patterns were reported but tend to disappear within a month. Although there is no conclusive evidence that marijuana alone is responsible for congenital abnormalities, when combined with other drug use the risk is increased. One study found marijuana use to be the most highly predictive factor in infants born with FAS. Much higher levels of THC are being detected in marijuana; the result may be more fetal and neonatal problems.

HUMAN IMMUNODEFICIENCY VIRUS

Infection and Pregnancy

Maternal HIV infection is intimately linked with illicit drug use, be it actual intravenous injections by the woman, heterosexual contact with an HIV-infected partner, or exchange of sex for crack. HIV crosses the placental barrier, and it is believed that virtually all new HIV infections in children are due to perinatal transmission of HIV. Through 1993, an estimated 15,000 HIV-infected children were born to HIV-positive women in the United States. Globally, it is estimated that each year 2.3 million women infected with HIV give birth, with 350,000 children infected with HIV through perinatal transmission. Not all cases of perinatal HIV transmission, however, will result in AIDS. As of September 1997, there were 7,310 cases of AIDS in the United States due to perinatal transmission. This represents approximately 1 percent of the 626,334 AIDS cases reported to the Centers for Disease Control. Children with perinatally acquired AIDS are disproportionate to the ethnic composition in this country, with 61 percent non-Hispanic African Americans, 24 percent Hispanic, and 14 percent non-Hispanic white.

Fortunately, the numbers of perinatally transmitted AIDS are declining due to the increased testing of pregnant women at risk, with subsequent treatment of the women with zidovudine (ZOV) and other, newer antiretroviral agents. HIV-infected newborns are now receiving appropriate antiretroviral therapy as well. In addition, evidence has been presented that since 70 percent of cases of transmission of HIV to the fetus occur during labor and delivery, cesarean section can offer a means of diminishing the risk. Finally, the recognition that HIV-positive mothers who breast-feed can transmit the virus has resulted in an elimination of this practice in areas where appropriate nutrition to the infant can be provided. In developing countries where nutritional supplements are not available, the risk of HIV transmission in breast milk (3.2 per 100 child years of breast-feeding) must be weighed against the risk of morbidity and mortality when breast-feeding is stopped.

TREATMENT OF DRUG USE AND DEPENDENCY DURING PREGNANCY

Therapy for women who use mood-altering drugs while pregnant should be essentially the same as that for nonpregnant women on drugs. However, emphasis must be placed on the adverse effects that continued drug use will have, not only on the woman, but on the fetus, the newborn, and even on the child's subsequent development. As discussed earlier in this chapter, it is best for women to abstain from all mood-altering drugs while pregnant. For those women dependent on opiates who are unable or unwilling to remain abstinent, methadone maintenance is a viable alternative.

Treatment has been shown to be effective in decreasing the complications associated with maternal drug use. In one study, 95 percent of women in treatment for substance abuse had uncomplicated drug-free births, with 75 percent who successfully completed treatment remaining drug free. Of these women, 65 percent had their children returned from foster care and 40 percent eliminated or reduced their dependence on welfare.

Frustration over the inability to convince women who are pregnant to abstain from illicit drug use during their pregnancies has resulted in an increasing number of communities viewing the pregnant woman as a criminal rather than a victim of drug dependency. A number of states have initiated criminal proceedings against women who continue to use drugs during their pregnancy as well as charges of child neglect once the infant has been born. In 1989 Florida became the first state to convict a woman of "drug delivery" to her infant, sentencing her to fourteen years on probation. In May 1990, a New York State appeals court ruled that the presence of cocaine in an infant's system, combined with a mother's admission of drug use, was sufficient to require a hearing on child neglect.

However, these decisions pale against the actions of a South Carolina court who brought up a pregnant woman using crack on charges of murder by child abuse for killing her unborn son. The woman pleaded guilty to involuntary manslaughter for using crack and was given a three-year suspended sentence and 200 hours of community service. Other state supreme courts have ruled that a fetus is not a person under criminal law and have not sustained such criminal charges.

Advocates of pursuing criminal charges against drug-dependent pregnant women maintain that the infant's rights are as important as the mother's. Not surprisingly, opponents argue vehemently for "free choice" of the pregnant woman to use or not use drugs. When faced with the possibility that criminal charges may be leveled against them, pregnant women who are drug-dependent may steer clear of adequate prenatal care programs or deny drug use, delivering the babies without their physicians' knowledge that they are using drugs.

Treatment of the Dependent Newborn

Treatment of the newborn dependent on mood-altering substances is important and should be administered promptly. In many cases, supportive care is all that is necessary. Depending on the drug used, the level of dependency, and the effect that the drug has had on fetal development, much more may be required. Infants born dependent on opiates may require a slow detoxification to prevent the effects of withdrawal. Infants born to mothers who use cocaine have been found to suffer the most complications and require the most assistance, often including prolonged intensive care while in the hospital as well as supportive services and special education programs for learning disabilities as they get older. It is important to emphasize, however, that the appearance of illness in an infant born to a mother using mood-altering drugs may not be related to drug use but may be the result of an independent problem. Careful evaluation is therefore always mandatory.

PREVENTION OF DRUG USE DURING PREGNANCY

The economic and social costs of caring for an infant born to a woman who uses mood-altering substances have been identified. Estimates put the cost of medical care for such infants at 50 to 100 times greater than for a healthy infant. A 1990 report from the Office of the Inspector General in the Department of Health and Human Services, studying approximately 9,000 babies in eight major cities born to women who used cocaine, estimated the cost of hospitalization as well as foster care during the first five years of these children's lives at half a billion dollars. In New York City, mothers who use drugs were responsible for more than a threefold rise in cases of child abuse during the period from 1980 to 1988.

Since there may be several million women of childbearing age who use or are dependent on illicit substances and who will give birth at some future date, projections of costs to care for their infants are staggering. Hence it becomes critically important to develop outreach programs to get pregnant drug users into counseling (Table 19.5), to give these women early and proper prenatal care, to identify developmental problems in their infants as early as possible, and to establish appropriate home environments that allow for placement of these children in foster care if necessary.

TABLE 19.5. Principles to Follow in Counseling Women About Drug Use During Pregnancy

---

Be direct, straightforward and accurate

Stress the positive effects of abstinence, not just the negative effects of continued drug use

Do not predict the outcome with certainty

Tailor the message to the person

Develop individualized assessment of risk

Try to motivate an abstinence approach

Refer to treatment when maintaining abstinence not likely

Source: Modified from Cook, P.S., Peterson, R.C., and Moore, D.T. "Alcohol, Tobacco and Other Drugs May Harm the Newborn." Rockville, MD: U.S. Department of Health and Human Services DHHS (Adm) 90-1711, 1990.

Chapter 20

Drugs and Sports

Show me a good and gracious loser and I'll show you a loser.

Knute Rockne

As a group, athletes are neither more nor less prone to take mood-altering substances for recreational use than others. Drinking, smoking, chewing tobacco, and drinking caffeine-containing beverages are common behaviors in most groups, including athletes. Drugs taken by athletes for restorative effects, such as analgesics to relieve pain or steroids for specific medical conditions (diabetes or asthma), are the norm. There are also several types of drugs athletes use primarily to enhance performance: stimulants, anabolic steroids, synthetic growth hormone, and erythropoietin. In addition, the ability of a group of drugs called beta-blockers to decrease anxiety and slow heart rate has resulted in use of these agents as well by certain athletes. Although the exact prevalence of such use is difficult to determine precisely, over the past several years their use has appeared in the media involving virtually all sports and both professional and amateur athletes.

STIMULANTS

Stimulants such as amphetamines and cocaine, taken to heighten concentration, combat fatigue, and increase aggressiveness, muscular coordination, and physical prowess, are at times also taken "defensively" to compete against opponents who also use stimulants. They're detrimental both to daily functioning and ironically to performance on the field. Prolonged use results in elevated blood pressure, an increased risk of heart attack or stroke, psychotic behavior, and addiction. Bromontan, an immune stimulant produced only in Russia and initially used by Russian cosmonauts and probably the military, was detected during the 1996 Olympic Games and subsequently added to the list of proscribed drugs.

ANABOLIC STEROIDS

Steroids are naturally occurring substances found in hormones and certain vitamins. They are divided into the female sex hormones (estrogen and progesterone); cortical hormones of the adrenal gland (cortisone, deoxycorticosterone, and dehydroepiandrosterone [DHEA]); hormones from the middle of the adrenal gland (aldosterone); hormones synthesized by the liver and/or gallbladder; anabolic/androgenic steroids; and vitamin D^3 (cholecalciferol).

The anabolic/androgenic steroids are produced naturally in the body. Males produce 2 to 10 mg of testosterone a day; females much less, as these hormones are responsible for masculine characteristics. In the natural state they are responsible for the maturing of the male reproductive system, growth of body hair, deepening of voice, and sex drive. Anabolic steroids were first promoted during World War II, when the Germans supplied them to their troops to increase aggressiveness and fitness. These drugs (Tables 20.1, 20.2) are basically derivatives of testosterone, the male hormone. They were initially developed to increase body mass and muscle strength without causing the excessive masculine characteristics (androgenic effects) associated with natural testosterone. But all these drugs, to some degree, have varying androgenic effects, depending on extent and duration of use.

Anabolic steroids are approved for a variety of medical conditions. Since they are testosterone derivatives, they can stimulate sexual development in men with diminished testicular function, stimulate production of red blood cells in bone marrow in certain anemias, and diminish symptoms of hereditary angioedema, an uncommon allergic condition. They have very limited

TABLE 20.1. Oral Anabolic Steroids and Androgens

Brand Name	Generic Name
Dianabol,* Methandroid	Methandrostenolone
Mestoranum	Mesterolone
Anavar	Oxandrolone
Anadrol 50	Oxymetholone
Maxibolin, Orabolin	Ethylestrenol
Winstrol	Stanozolol
Android-F, Halotestin	Fluoxymesterone
Android, Metandren, Oreton Methyl, Vigorex, Virilon, Testred	Methyltestosterone

*Discontinued March 1982

TABLE 20.2. Injectable Anabolic Steroids and Long-Lasting Androgens

Brand Name	Generic Name
Anabolin, Androlene, Durabolin, Hybolin, Nandrobolic	Nandrolone phenylproprionate
Analone, Androlone-D, Deca-Durabolin, Hybolin Decanoate, Decolone, Neo-Durabolic, Nandrobolic L.A.	Nandrolone decanoate
Everone, Andryl, Andro LA, Delatestryl, Delatest, Everone, Durathate Testostroval, Testrin PA, Testone LA	Testosterone enanthate
Andro-Cyp, Andronaqla, Andronate, Depo-Testosterone, Duratest, depAndro Testa-C, Testadiate-Depo, Testoject LA, Testred	Testosterone cypionate
Testex	Testosterone propionate

usefulness as additional therapy in treating demineralization of bone (osteoporosis).

Anabolic steroids used as performance enhancers have been refined to accentuate the body-building properties of testosterone while diminishing its masculinization effects (Table 20.3). Their first use by athletes was reported in 1954, and despite adverse publicity use has increased over time. Frequent users are usually interested in improving muscle mass and body strength.

Prevalence of Use

Mounting evidence suggests that anabolic steroid use by athletes in the United States is equal to illicit drug use. Prevalence, however, varies by sport, and frequency varies by season. One survey of 3,400 male teenagers at Pennsylvania State University found that 7 percent had taken steroids. A National Collegiate Athletic Association (NCAA) survey found that one-third of players tested positive for steroids, with 25 percent having received the drugs through physicians' prescriptions. Only 4 percent of all athletes admit using anabolic steroids, but epidemiological surveys indicate that the actual figure may be four times higher. Approximately 1 million Americans are estimated to have taken steroids nontherapeutically, with up to 260,000 adolescents believed to have used or to be using these drugs. A report from the National Institute on Drug Abuse estimates that as many as 175,000 teenage girls have taken an anabolic steroid at least once in the past year, a 100 percent increase since 1991. The 2000 Monitoring the Future study

TABLE 20.3. Supposed Benefits of Anabolic Steroids

Enhanced physical appearance
Increased aggressiveness
Enhanced self-confidence
Increased lean-muscle mass
Decreased muscle recovery time
Decreased muscle injury healing time
Prolonged endurance

---

found 3 percent of eighth graders and 3.5 percent of twelfth graders have taken anabolic steroids at least once, with 45 percent of seniors reporting easy availability.

Of 546 football players surveyed, 3.3 percent were positive in March and April, compared with 1 percent postseason. The National Football League has estimated that 6 percent of its players have taken steroids. Nearly half of 250 surveyed weight lifters admitted taking steroids sometime during their careers. Other surveys suggest that 80 to 100 percent of international body builders experiment with these drugs at some time.

Anabolic steroid use was first detected in Russian athletes in the mid-1950s, and in Americans shortly thereafter. But it wasn't until 1976 that the magnitude of the problem was acknowledged on an international level. At that time, the International Olympic Committee initiated routine urine testing to screen for steroids.

Steroid Economics

As with the production and sale of illicit drugs, steroid use has created a considerable economic enterprise to meet the demand. The U.S. government has identified Europe, South America, and Mexico as possible points of origin, in addition to many clandestine laboratories in the United States. Considerable profit can be realized from sales of homemade steroids, whose synthesis is relatively easy. The U.S. Food and Drug Administration estimates that black market sales may be $400 million annually. Steroids may be obtained in different ways: legitimate prescriptions or veterinary products may be diverted, or steroids may be synthesized outside the United States, packaged under recognized brand names, and smuggled back into the country. Since 1990, steroids have been listed as a Schedule II drug of the Federal Controlled Substances Act. Nonmedical possession is punishable by up to one year in prison, with distribution punishable for up to five years in prison and a fine of $250,000. Nonetheless, steroids are reported to be readily available at commercial gyms or from "friends." In addition, the over-the-counter, nonprescription pharmaceutical market allows "sports supplements" containing androgenic steroids to be readily available. This was estimated to generate $800 million in sales in 1998.

Patterns of Use

There are a variety of ways that anabolic steroids may be used, giving rise to a new vocabulary associated with the drugs (Table 20.4). Anabolic steroids may be taken orally or by injection. The oral preparation methandrostenolone (Dianabol) was the most popular of these drugs at first. But in 1987, its manufacturer, Ciba-Geigy, withdrew it after its misuse as an appetite stimulant for young children in third world countries was discovered. Generic methandrostenolone, however, is still available.

Injectable steroids are now more popular because they need to be administered less frequently and have a relatively low association with liver toxicity. Prescriptions from physicians may play a role in obtaining the drugs, but most come from nonprescribed sources such as pharmaceutical houses, friends in the health professions, or associates from other countries where drug purchases are less stringently regulated than in the United States.

The body produces 4 to 10 milligrams of naturally occurring steroids per day. Anabolic steroids, however, are usually taken in increasing doses through a technique called pyramiding. When several drugs are taken, it's called stacking. The drugs are taken in a cyclic manner for four to eighteen weeks, with subsequent drug-free periods of one to twelve months. Doses may range from 10 to 2,000 milligrams daily, which is up to 200 times the usual dose prescribed for specific medical conditions.

TABLE 20.4. Use of Anabolic Steroids

Blending	Mixing different drugs
Cycling	Taking multiple doses over a specific time frame, then stopping and starting again
Doping	Use of steroids as well as other nonfood substances to improve performance
Megadosing	Taking massive amounts of anabolic steroids
Shotgunning	Taking anabolic steroids randomly in large doses
Stacking	Using a combination of anabolic steroids, often in combination with other drugs
Tapering	Decreasing the dose to avoid withdrawal effects

Androstenedione

Androstenedione, a gonadal and adrenal androgen, has been produced as a nasal spray in Europe and is now available in tablet form in the United States. It is believed to enhance athletic performance through its being a precursor of testosterone. Although studies have shown large doses can elevate testosterone levels, its effect on improving athletic performance remains to be demonstrated.

Dehydroepiandrosterone (DHEA)

Most recently, DHEA, an adrenal androgen that is a steroid precursor of androgens and estrogens, has been promoted as a miracle drug able to prevent aging, enhance libido, strengthen the immune system, retard memory loss, burn fat, and build muscle mass. It has also been promoted as an antidote to a compromised immune system, cancer, heart disease, diabetes, Alzheimer's disease, and Parkinson's disease. Allowed to be distributed by the U.S. Dietary Supplement Health and Education Act of 1994, this drug has become increasingly popular despite little evidence of its effectiveness in accomplishing any of its listed uses. In addition, evidence suggests that large doses of DHEA may be associated with masculinization in women and increased risk of ovarian cancer. In men, an association with prostate cancer has been suggested.

Supposed Benefits of Anabolic Steroids

Athletes take anabolic steroids for a variety of reasons, some of which have never been proven valid (Table 20.3). The drugs are claimed to increase muscle mass; decrease muscle recovery time; allow more frequent training sessions; decrease healing time after injury, thus allowing earlier return to practice; and increase the hemoglobin concentration in the bloodstream, thus allowing more oxygen intake to prolong the duration of exercise. The perceived psychological effects—increased aggressiveness, for one—are believed to contribute to the competitive edge.

Studies to determine what role, if any, anabolic steroids have in improving performance have produced conflicting results. One comprehensive review of twenty-five published studies noted that when increases in strength occurred, the changes were accompanied by increases in body size and weight.

In one study, biopsies of abdominal muscles were taken from normal volunteers who had been given stanozolol before undergoing elective surgery. An increase was found in the size of the muscle fibers responsible for increasing strength after long-term aerobic exercise (Type I); muscle fibers thought to be responsible for increasing strength after body building (Type II) weren't affected.

The American College of Sports Medicine, after reviewing all published evidence of anabolic steroid effects on athletic performance, and noting that the evidence was far from conclusive, found that these drugs can increase muscular strength in excess of that seen with training alone and increase lean body mass in association with diet and exercise. But they cannot increase the capacity for aerobic work. Most recently, in a randomly assigned study with placebo or testosterone it was clearly demonstrated that testosterone, especially when combined with strength training, can significantly increase fat-free mass, muscle size, and strength. In this study an increase of 22 to 38 percent in muscle strength was observed.

Adverse Effects of Steroids

Although the ability of anabolic steroids to increase muscle strength and performance in sports requires more study, the adverse effects of large doses are already well defined. Taken in excess on a chronic basis, steroids can produce a number of severe and sometimes long-lasting abnormalities (Table 20.5).

Abnormal liver function can be detected in blood tests on athletes engaged in intense training, with or without steroids. Those using steroids who exhibit increased signs of liver dysfunction appear to revert to normal when the drugs are discontinued. Oral steroid preparations are associated with a much higher incidence of liver disease. Cancer of the liver after steroid administration has also been reported.

Adverse effects on the cardiovascular system include an increase in low-density lipoprotein levels and up to a 30 percent decrease in high-density levels, increasing the statistical risk of heart attack with long-term use. Hypertension may also occur.

The adverse effects of chronic administration are difficult to assess because it's unethical to administer anabolic steroids in doses athletes ordinarily take over long periods of time. Most users, however, believe the practice is so widespread that any adverse effects would be readily seen. But such long-term effects as those associated with cardiovascular disease may not become apparent for years—particularly in people currently in excellent physical condition.

The behavioral effects of anabolic steroids are becoming better recognized, with subjective changes reported by up to 30 percent of regular users. Euphoria, increased motivation, and a sense of well-being have been described. But so have impaired judgment and increased aggressiveness. Psychiatric disturbances ranging from depression to paranoia have been reported in up to 22 percent of anabolic steroid users.

TABLE 20.5. Side Effects of Anabolic Steroids

General

Liver abnormalities,* rarely including liver cancer

Alters blood cholesterol levels predisposing to coronary artery disease
(decreases high-density lipoproteins, increases low-density lipoproteins)

Disturbs electrolyte concentration; retaining sodium, potassium chloride,
phosphate, water, may promote hypertension

Acne

Increases blood pressure

Personality changes

Increases susceptibility to infections, notably tuberculosis, hepatitis, and AIDS

Men

Prepubertal
Increases hair production
Increases skin pigmentation
Decreases height due to early closure of growth plates in bones
Increases penis size and frequency of erections

Adult
Inhibits testicular function with testicular atrophy
Enlarges breasts
Male-pattern hair loss
Enlarges prostate
Frequent erections

Women
Male-pattern hair loss
Menstrual irregularities
Deepens voice, may be permanent
Enlarges clitoris
During pregnancy, masculinizes fetus with possible birth defects

---

*Some anabolic steroids

Some reports also suggest development of an addictive state, just as is seen with the more commonly recognized dependency-producing drugs, including compulsive use, failure to stop despite awareness of adverse psychological effects, withdrawal or abstinence symptoms with craving to resume use, and once steroid-free, switching to other mood-altering substances when steroids are unavailable. Such observations indicate that—at least for some long-term, high-dose users—stopping use is far from easy, both psychologically and physiologically.

Persistent high doses taken by young people have the potential for as yet unknown long-term adverse effects. Premature closure of the growth plates in the bones of adolescents whose bone growth may not be complete is one possibility. Another is premature suppression of sperm production, now known as a temporary complication of anabolic steroid use.

Curbing Steroid Use

The Omnibus Drug Bill of 1988 prohibits distribution of anabolic steroids for any human use other than treatment of disease and requires a prescription. The penalties are up to six years in prison for distributing to those under age eighteen and up to three years for distributing to those over eighteen. Seizure and forfeiture of assets also await illegal distributors.

Many states have also introduced penalties or have classified anabolic steroids as Schedule II drugs. Penalties vary by state but may include prison sentences, and loss of license when physicians are involved. Such controls diminish diversion of these drugs by physicians, but they have little effect on illicit trade as long as people want to use them.

GROWTH HORMONE

Synthesis of human growth hormone has opened a new door to its inappropriate use in sports. Naturally secreted by the anterior pituitary gland, growth hormone has a number of physiological effects, including stimulation of protein synthesis. As such, it is essential for achieving normal growth potential. A deficit of growth hormone in childhood results in dwarfism. Fortunately, pituitary growth hormone can now be synthesized through biotechnology, all but eliminating that condition. Two synthetic growth hormone products—somatrem (Protropin) and somatropin (Humatrope)—are commercially available, albeit at exorbitant cost.

The prevalence of use of these new hormones in athletics is not yet well known. But they do increase body growth and strength, and are difficult to detect in urine tests. That makes them logical as favored substances of inappropriate use, limited only by their considerable expense. According to reports, they are already being given to many athletes. Though the drugs are newly synthesized and not easily available, one physician of the United States Sports Academy was able to obtain a supply from two drug companies he contacted.

Excessive natural production of growth hormone causes well-known complications (Table 20.6). In childhood it results in gigantism; in adults it causes acromegaly, a condition associated with elevated blood sugars, increased cholesterol concentrations, high incidence of heart disease, impo-

TABLE 20.6. Effects of Increased Secretion of Growth Hormone

In children Gigantism
In adults Elevated blood sugar Elevated cholesterol Elevated blood pressure Heart disease Impotence Increased bone growth of forehead, jaw, hands, and feet

tence, and overgrowth of the bones in the forehead, jaws, hands, and feet. Since growth hormones have never been given to people with normal supplies, their adverse effects when used by athletes is still unknown. Potential adverse effects, however, have been categorized (Table 20.7).

ERYTHROPOIETIN

The use of intravenous infusions of red blood cells to enhance athletic performance (blood doping) has long been known although infrequently used because of the inherent risks associated with intravenous infusions. Recently, the human hormone erythropoietin, which stimulates the production of red blood cells from the bone marrow, has been synthesized through recombinant DNA techniques and marketed as epoetin (Epogen). Epoetin is used for the treatment of severe anemias, most commonly those caused by chronic kidney failure. The availability of epoetin and its demonstrated ability to increase red blood cells, resulting in an increase in oxygen to the muscles and enhanced performance, has resulted in reports of its use by athletes. Unlike traditional blood doping, which requires withdrawal of an athlete's own blood to be reinfused before a meet and which must be done in the presence of those trained in blood-storage techniques, epoetin can be self-administered. Since there are a number of adverse effects due to increased red cell volume, including high blood pressure, convulsions, and increased clotting of blood in the tissues leading to pulmonary embolism, heart attacks, or strokes, the use of this drug may be quite dangerous. The American Medical Association Council on Scientific Affairs has strongly recommended against epotin use to enhance athletic performance.

TABLE 20.7. Potential Adverse Effects of Synthetic Growth Hormone

---

Development of antibodies to growth hormone
Hypothyroidism
Increased incidence of leukemia

Metabolic Effects
Impaired serum glucose levels and diabetes
Increase in serum free fatty acids
Body retention of sodium, potassium, and phosphorus

DETECTING AND PREVENTING
INAPPROPRIATE DRUG USE BY ATHLETES

Although technological advances in testing techniques might make one think that inappropriate use of drugs by athletes would be fairly easy to document, such is not the case. Certain drugs, such as stimulants and synthetic steroids, can be easily detected in urine. However, if the athlete knows the timing of the test the drug can be flushed from the system, especially when short-acting preparations are used. In an attempt to avoid detection by their appearance, men on anabolic steroids may take pituitary hormone to diminish testicular atrophy and then antiestrogens to combat the breast enlargement that might occur. Urine tests routinely detect anabolic steroids, so athletes try various ruses to avoid detection. They may consume only oral steroid preparations and quit a week or two before testing. They may use diuretics to dilute the urine. At times urines are spiked with epitestosterone so that the normal ratio of testosterone to its free analogue, epitestosterone, is not disturbed. Newer, structurally different drugs are tried in the hope that they can't be detected by current tests. Refinements in urine testing, however, have kept up. Current technology allows steroid detection at a concentration of one part per billion. Water-soluble steroids can be detected up to four days after use; fat-soluble drugs, up to two weeks. Random testing is much more valuable in detecting steroid and stimulant use but is rarely performed.

Detection of synthetic growth hormone or erythropoietin is much more difficult, as the body normally secretes these hormones. Although erythropoietin use can be presumed in the presence of an elevated red cell count or hematocrit, in fact the range of normal values for these determinations is so wide that one can increase one's hematocrit by 20 percent without exceeding the allowable limit. In addition, the endurance effect of erythropoietin is believed to last about two weeks after the last dose, which makes detection even more difficult. However, a blood test to detect EPO has been developed and was used in conjunction with urine testing by the IOC in all participants in the Sydney games. Recently, a test has been proposed as effective in detecting doping with human growth hormone; however, validation of this technique remains to be determined.

A campaign is underway to limit substance abuse in sports. As with other forms of drug use, prevention is the most effective way of diminishing use. Toward that end, educational programs in high schools have been shown to be effective, and owners of major professional teams have also expended considerable effort. In international competition, the Olympic Committee lists more than 3,000 drugs that can disqualify an athlete from competition and has initiated urine testing at all games at an annual cost of over $33 million. Moreover, the United States and the Soviet Union have signed a memorandum of agreement to test each other's Olympic athletes on a semiannual basis. Yet critics have alleged that the International Olympic Committee has not done enough and has set limits for detection high enough to allow some degree of doping without detection, yet able to boost performance levels by 5 to 10 percent, providing an essential edge.

The National Football League has recently become the first professional sports association to ban anabolic steroid use. Players whose urine tests positive for steroids are subject to further testing at any time. A second positive test results in a month's suspension; a third in dismissal from the league. The National Basketball Association, National Hockey League, and major league baseball have all to varying degrees stated their intolerance of the use of mood-altering drugs. The corresponding players' associations have voiced similar concerns, emphasizing the importance of rehabilitation as well as sanctions.

On an international level, the IOC has created the World Antidoping Agency to make recommendations concerning detecting illicit drug use and has begun testing for EPO. However, tests for other previously untested substances, such as human growth factor, remain to be instituted.

Unfortunately, inconsistencies remain among different sports as to what drugs or prescribed medications are premissible for athletes to take.

A clear-cut, consistent statement concerning the use of a performance-enhancing substance by all leagues, both amateur and professional, would go a long way in emphasizing the importance of compliance.

Appendix A

Drug Use Reporting Sources

Client Oriented Data Acquisition Process (CODAP)
  Collects demographic data on drug-free and on-maintenance persons entering treatment programs throughout the United States. Sponsored by the National Institute on Drug Abuse.

Community Epidemiology Work Group (CEWG), *Epidemiologic Trends in Drug
Abuse,* December 1988
  Combines data from a variety of sources, to develop current trends in and pat-
  terns of drug use. Sponsored by the National Institute on Drug Abuse.

Drug Abuse Warning Network (DAWN)
  Reports from selected emergency rooms and medical examiners' offices
  throughout the United States. Sponsored by the National Institute on Drug
  Abuse.

Drug Use, Drinking and Smoking: National Survey Results from High School, College, and Young Adult Populations, 1975-2000 Monitoring the Future Surveys.
  Conducted annually by Lloyd Johnston, MD, and colleagues at the University
  of Michigan. Uses representative samples of approximately 45,000 students
  in 435 schools, as well as college students and young adults up to eleven years
  after high school. Sponsored by the National Institute on Drug Abuse.

Food and Drug Administration (FDA) Annual Review of National Drug Use
  The FDA collects data on the use of prescription drugs by indication, classification of drugs, and characteristics of prescribing physician.

National Disease and Therapeutic Index (NDTI)
  Data collected quarterly from individual physicians containing drug orders
  for patients for forty-eight-hour period.

National Drug and Alcoholism Treatment Unit Survey (NDATUS)
  Census of all drug abuse and alcoholism treatment facilities in the United
  States. Sponsored by the National Institute on Drug Abuse and the National
  Institute on Alcohol Abuse and Alcoholism.

National Household Survey on Drug Abuse (NHSDA)
  Conducted every several years since 1971. It is a general population survey
  that in 1999 included a survey of more than 70,000 persons, with household
  members age twelve and above. Sponsored by the National Institute on Drug
  Abuse.

National Prescription Audit (NPA)
> Produced by the trade journal *Pharmacy Times*. Lists the top 200 drugs dispensed from retail pharmacies to patients, based on a nationwide survey of 2,000 retail pharmacies reporting on approximately 36 million prescriptions filled.

NCADI's PREVLINE Web site: <http://www.health.org>
> Provides online information concerning prevalence of substance abuse nationwide.

New York Times-CBS News Survey
> A survey based on telephone interviews with 824 adults in the continental United States. Phone numbers selected by computer. Results differ no more than plus or minus three percentage points from those obtained had all adults been surveyed.

Parents Resource Institute for Drug Education (PRIDE) Survey
> Administered annually to a large group of schools and students throughout the country.

Youth Risk Behavior Surveillance System (YRBSS)
> Includes national, state, territorial, and local school-based surveys of high school students, 1990, 1991, 1993, 1995, 1997—Centers for Disease Control and Prevention.

Appendix B

List of Common Names for Drugs*

When using this guide, it is important to remember that street names may vary from one geographic area to another. In addition, one street name can refer to two or more different drugs, and a street name may come to mean a completely different drug or combination of drugs.

Street Name—Drug Name (Drug Group**)

Abyssiniantia—Marijuana (M)
Acapulco Gold—Marijuana (M)
Acapulco Red—Marijuana (M)
Ace—Marijuana (M) cigarette, Phencyclidine (H)
Acid—LSD (H)
AD—Phencyclidine (H)
Adam—MDMA (Ecstasy) (S) (H)
African Black, Bush, or Woodbine—Marijuana (M)
Ah-pen-yen—Opium (N)
Aimies—Amphetamine (S), Amyl Nitrite (I)
AIP—Heroin from Afghanistan, Iran, Pakistan (N)
Airplane—Marijuana (M)
Alice B. Toklas—Marijuana Brownie (M)
Alpha-ET—Alpha-Ethyltyptamine (H)
Amidone—Methadone (N)
Amoeba—Phencyclidine (H)

Amp—Amphetamine (S); Marijuana (M) dipped in formaldehyde or embalming fluid, sometimes laced with Phencyclidine (H) and smoked
Amys—Amyl Nitrite (I)
Angel Dust, Hair, or Mist—Phencyclidine (H)
Angie—Cocaine (S)
Angolo—Marijuana (M)
Animal—LSD (H)
Animal Tranquilizer—Phencyclidine (H)
Antifreeze—Heroin (N)
Apache—Fentanyl (N)
Apple Jacks—Crack, Cocaine (S)
Aries—Heroin (N)
Aroma—Nitrite Inhalant (I)
Aroma of Men—Isobutyl Nitrite (I)
Astro Turf—Marijuana (M)
Atom Bomb—Marijuana (M) mixed with Heroin (N)
Atshitshi—Marijuana (M)

---

*This list contains names obtained from the author's personal experience and from a variety of sources, including street terms, drugs and the drug trade, Office of National Drug Control Policy, Drug Policy Information Clearing House, and the National Institute on Drug Abuse.

**Drug groups indicated in parentheses: (AC) = Anticholinergic, (H) = Hallucinogen, (H/S) = Hypnotic/Sedative, (I) = Inhalant, (M) = Marijuana or Marijuana Group, (MDMA) = Methylenecioxymaphetamine, (N) = Narcotic or Opioid, (S) = Stimulant.

Aunt Hazel—Heroin (N)
Aunt Mary—Marijuana (M)
Aunt Nora—Cocaine (S)
Aunti Emma—Opium (N)
Aurora Borealis—Phencyclidine (H)
B-40—Cigar with Marijuana (M) dipped in liquor
B-Bombs—Amphetamines (S), MDMA (Ecstasy) (S) (H)
B.J.'s—Crack, Cocaine (S)
Baby—Marijuana (M)
Baby T—Crack, Cocaine (S)
Back Breakers—LSD (H) and strychnine
Back Dex—Amphetamines (S)
Bad—Crack, Cocaine (S)
Badrock—Crack, Cocaine (S)
Ball—Crack, Cocaine (S) or Mexican Black Tar Heroin (N)
Bam—Amphetamine (S), Depressant (H/S)
Bamba—Marijuana (M)
Bambalacha—Marijuana (M)
Bambita—Desoxyn or Amphetamine derivative (S)
Banano—Marijuana (M) or tobacco cigarettes laced with Cocaine (S)
Banapple Gas—Nitrite Inhalant (I)
Bang—Nitrite Inhalant (I)
Barbs—Barbiturate (H/S)
Barrels—LSD (H)
Bart Simpson—LSD (H) or Heroin (N)
Bartman—LSD (H)
Base—Cocaine paste (S)
Baseball—Crack, Cocaine (S)
Basuco—Cocaine (S); coca paste residue sprinkled on regula or Marijuana (M) cigarettes
Bathtub Crank—Methamphetamine (S)
Bathtub Speed—Khat (S)
Battery Acid—LSD (H)
Bazooka—Crack, Cocaine (S)
Bazulco—Cocaine (S)
Beam Me Up Scottie—Phencyclidine (H), Crack, Cocaine (S)
Beans—Crack, Cocaine (S), Mescaline (H), Amphetamine (S), Depressants (H/S)

Beast—Heroin (N), LSD (H)
Beat—Crack, Cocaine (S)
Beautiful Boulders—Crack, Cocaine (S)
Beavis & Butthead—LSD (H)
Bebe—Crack, Cocaine (S)
Beemers—Crack, Cocaine (S)
Belushi—Cocaine (S) and Heroin (N)
Belyando Spruce—Marijuana (M)
Bennie—Amphetamine (S)
Berkely Boo—Marijuana (M)
Bernie—Cocaine (S)
Bhang—Ganga (M)
Bidis—Cigarettes (S)
Big Bag—Heroin (N)
Big C—Cocaine (S)
Big Chief—Peyote (H)
Big D—LSD (H)
Big H—Heroin (N)
Big M—Morphine (N)
Bikers Coffee—Methamphetamine and coffee (S)
Bill Blass—Cocaine (S)
Bing—Enough drug for one injection
Bings—Crack, Cocaine (S)
Birdhead—LSD (H)
Birdie Powder—Cocaine (S), Heroin (N)
Biscuits—Barbiturate (H/S)
Biscuits—MDMA (Ecstasy) (S) (H)
Biscuits and Raven—MDMA (Ecstasy) (S) (H)
Biscutt—Methadone (N)
Black Birds, Bombers, Cadillacs—Amphetamine (S)
Black Gold—Marijuana (M)
Black Gunion—Marijuana (M)
Black Hash—Opium (N), Hashish (M)
Black Mo/Black Moat—Highly potent Marijuana (M)
Black Mollies—Amphetamine (S)
Black Pearl—Heroin (N)
Black Russian—Opium (N) mixed with honey
Black Star—LSD (H)
Black Sunshine—LSD (H)
Black Tar—Heroin (N)
Blacks—Amphetamine (S)
Blanco—Heroin (N)

Blanket—Marijuana (M)
Blockbusters—Barbiturate (H/S)
Blotter—LSD (H)
Blotter Acid—LSD (H), Phencyclidine (H)
Blotter Cube—LSD (H)
Blow—Cocaine (S)
Blow—Inhalant
Blows—Heroin (N)
Blue—Crack, Cocaine (S), Depressants (H/S)
Blue Angels—Amphetamine (S) or Depressants (H/S)
Blue Birds—Barbiturate (H/S)
Blue Cap—LSD (H)
Blue Cheer—LSD (H)
Blue Clouds—Amtyl (Amobarbital Sodium) capsules (H/S) (M)
Blue de Hue—Marijuana (M) from Viet Nam
Blue Devils, Dolls, Bullets—Barbiturate (H/S)
Blue Dots—LSD (H)
Blue Heaven—LSD (H) or Barbiturate (H/S)
Blue Kisses—MDMA (Ecstasy) (S) (H)
Blue Lips—MDMA (Ecstasy) (S) (H)
Blue Madman—Phencyclidine (H)
Blue Sage—Marijuana (M)
Blue Sky Blond—High potency Marijuana (M)
Blue Velvet—Narcotic/Antihistamine
Blues—Barbiturate (H/S)
Blunt—Cigars hollowed out and filled with Marijuana (M)
Bo—Marijuana (M)
Bo-bo—Marijuana (M)
Bohd—Marijuana (M), Phencyclidine (H))
Bolasterone—Injectable steroids (S)
Bolivian Marching Powder—Cocaine (S)
Bollo—Crack, Cocaine (S)
Bolt—Amphetamine (S), Isobutyl Nitrite (I)
Bomb—Crack (S), Heroin (N), large Marijuana (M) cigarette
Bomber—Marijuana (M) cigarette

Bombitas—Heroin/Amphetamine (N)
Bone—Marijuana (M), Crack (S)
Bonecrusher—Crack (S)
Bonita—Heroin (N)
Book—100 dosage units of LSD (H)
Boom—Marijuana (M)
Boomers—Psilocybin/Psilocin (H), LSD (H)
Boppers—Amyl Nitrite (I)
Botray—Crack, Cocaine (S)
Boubou—Crack, Cocaine (S)
Boulder—Crack, Cocaine (S), $20 worth of Crack
Boulya—Crack, Cocaine (S)
Bouncing Powder—Cocaine (S)
Boy—Cocaine (S), Heroin (N)
Boy Jive—Heroin (N)
Bozo—Heroin (N)
Brain Damage—Heroin (N)
Brain Pills—Amphetamines (S)
Brick—Crack, Cocaine (S), Marijuana (M)
Brick Gum—Heroin (N)
Britton—Peyote (H)
Broccoli—Marijuana (M)
Broja—Heroin (N)
Brown—Heroin (N)
Brown Bombers—LSD (H)
Brown Crystal, Rhine, Sugar—Heroin (N)
Brownies—Amphetamine (S)
Bubble Gum—Crack, Cocaine (S)
Bud—Marijuana (M)
Buda—Marijuana (M); joint filled with Crack (S)
Buddha -Potent Marijuana (M) spiked with Opium (N)
Bullet—Nitrite Inhalant (I)
Bullets—Barbiturate (H/S)
Bullion—Crack (S)
Bullyon—Marijuana (M)
Bumblebees—Amphetamine (S)
Bump—Crack, Cocaine (S), Ketamine (H))
Bundle—Heroin (N)
Bunnies—MDMA (Ecstasy) (S) (H)
Burese—Cocaine (S)
Burnese—Cocaine (S)

Buscuso—Cocaine paste (S)
Bush—Marijuana (M), Cocaine (S), Phencyclidine (H)
Businessman's Special, DMT—Hallucinogen (H)
Busy Bee—Phencyclidine (H)
Butler—Crack, Cocaine (S)
Butt Naked—Phencyclidine (H)
Butter—Marijuana (M), Crack (S)
Butter Flower—Marijuana (M)
Buttons—Peyote (H)
Butu—Heroin (N)
Buzz Bomb—Nitrous Oxide (I)
C—Cocaine (S)
C-Dust, Game—Cocaine (S)
C & M—Cocaine (S), Heroin (N)
C.S.—Marijuana (M)
Caballo—Heroin (N)
Cabona—Inhalant
Caca—Heroin (N)
Cactus—Peyote (H)
Cadillac—Cocaine (S), Phencyclidine (H)
Cadillac Express—Khat (S)
Caine—Cocaine (S)
Cakes—Round Discs of Crack (S)
California Sunshine—LSD (H)
Cambodian Red—Marijuana (M)
Came—Cocaine (S)
Camel—LSD (H)
Can—Marijuana (M)
Canade—Heroin (N)/Marijuana (M) combination
Canadian Black—Marijuana (M)
Canamo—Marijuana (M)
Canappa—Marijuana (M)
Cancelled Stick—Marijuana (M)
Candles—LSD (H)
Candy—Crack, Cocaine (S), Amphetamine (S), Depressants (H/S)
Candy Blunt—Blunts dipped in cough syrup (N)
Cannabinol—Phencyclidine (H), Marijuana (M)
Caplets—Amphetamine (S)
Caps—Heroin (N), Psilocybin/Psilocin (H), Crack (S)
Carga—Heroin (N)

Carmabis—Marijuana (M)
Carne—Heroin (N) or Cocaine (S)
Carnie—Cocaine (S)
Carrie—Cocaine (S)
Cartucho—Marijuana (M) cigarettes
Casper—Crack (S)
Cat—Methcathinone (S)
Cat Valium—Ketamine (H)
Catha—Cathinone (S)
Catnip—Marijuana (M) cigarette
Cavite All Star—Marijuana (M)
Cecil—Cocaine (S)
Cest—Marijuana (M)
Chalk—Methamphetamine (S)
Champagne—Combination of Cocaine (S) and Marijuana (M)
Chandoo/Chandu—Opium (N)
Charas—Ganga (M)
Charley—Heroin (N)
Charlie—Cocaine (S)
Chat—Cathinone (S)
Cheeba—Marijuana (M)
Cheeo—Marijuana (M)
Cheery Top—LSD (H)
Chemical—Crack, Cocaine (S)
Cherry Meth—Gamma Hydroxybutyrate
Chewies—Crack, Cocaine (S)
Chicago Black, Green—Marijuana (M)
Chicken Powder—Amphetamine (S)
Chief—LSD (H), Mescaline (H)
Chieva—Heroin (N)
China Cat—High potency Heroin (N)
China Girl, Town—Fentanyl (N)
China White—Heroin (N), Fentanyl (N), synthetic Heroin
Chinese Molasses—Opium (N)
Chinese Red—Heroin (N)
Chip—Heroin (N)
Chippy—Cocaine (S)
Chips—Tobacco or Marijuana (M) cigarettes laced with Phencyclidine H)
Chira—Marijuana (M)
Chiva/Chieva—Heroin (N)
Chocolate—Marijuana (M), Opium (N), Amphetamine (S)
Chocolate Chips—LSD (H)

Chocolate Ecstasy—Crack (S) made brown by adding chocolate milk during production

Chocolate Rock—Crack (S) smoked together with Heroin (N)

Chocolate Tide—Marijuana (M)

Choe—Cocaine (S)

Cholly—Cocaine (S)

Chris/Christina—Amphetamine (S)

Christmas Rolls—Depressants (H/S)

Christmas Tree—Marijuana (M), Amphetamine (S), Depressant (H/S)

Chronic—Marijuana (M), Marijuana mixed with Crack (S)

Chunky—Marijuana (M)

Churus—Marijuana (M)

Cid—LSD (H)

Cigarette Paper—Packet of Heroin (N)

Cigarrode Cristal—Phencyclidine (H)

Circles—Rohypnol (H/S)

CJ—Phencyclidine (H)

Clarity—MDMA (Ecstasy) (S) (H)

Clicker—Crack (S) and Phencyclidine (H); Marijuana (M) dipped in formaldehyde and smoked

Clickums—Marijuana (M) cigarette laced with Phencyclidine (H)

Cliffhanger—Phencyclidine (H)

Climax—Amyl or Butyl Nitrite (I)

Climb—Marijuana (M) cigarette

Cloud 9—Ephedra (S) or Crack (S)

Co-pilot—Amphetamine (S)

Coca—Cocaine (S)

Coco Rocks—Crack (S) mixed with chocolate pudding

Cody—Cocaine (S)

Coffee—LSD (H)

Cola—Cocaine (S)

Colombian—Marijuana (M)

Colorado Cocktail—Marijuana (M)

Columbo—Phencyclidine (H)

Columbus Black—Marijuana (M)

Combol—Cocaine (S)

Conductor—LSD (H)

Contact Lens—LSD (H)

Cookies—Crack (S)

Coolie—Cigarette laced with Cocaine (S)

Cotton Brothers—Cocaine (S), Heroin (N) and Morphine (N)

Courage Pills—Heroin (N), Depressants (H/S)

Crack—Crack, Cocaine (S)

Crackers—LSD (H); Talwin (N) and Ritalin (S) combination injected

Crank—Crack, Cocaine (S), Heroin (N), Amphetamine (S), Methamphetamine (S), Methcathinone (S)

Crap—Heroin (N)

Crazy Coke, Eddie—Phencyclidine (H)

Crazy Weed—Marijuana (M)

Crib—Crack, Cocaine (S)

Crimmie—Cigarette laced with Crack (S)

Crink—Methamphetamine (S)

Cripple—Marijuana (M) cigarette

Cris—Methamphetamine (S)

Crisscross—Amphetamine (S)

Croak—Crack (S) and Methamphetamine (S)

Crop—Low quality Heroin (N)

Cross Tops—Amphetamine (S)

Crosses—Amphetamine (S)

Crossroads—Amphetamine (S)

Crown Crap—Heroin (N)

Crumbs—Tiny pieces of Crack (S)

Crunch & Munch—Crack, Cocaine (S)

Crying Weed—Marijuana (M)

Cryppie—Marijuana (M)

Crypt—Amyl or Butyl Nitrite (I)

Crypto—Methamphetamine (S)

Crystal—Crack, Cocaine (S), Amphetamine (S), Methamphetamine (S), Phencyclidine (H)

Cube—Narcotic (N)

Cube-D—LSD (H)

Culican—Marijuana (M)

Cum—Nitrite Inhalant (I)

Cupcakes—LSD (H)

Cyclone—Phencyclidine (H)

Dagga—Marijuana (M)

Dance Fever—Fentanyl (N)

Dank—Marijuana (M)

Date Rape—Gamma Hydroxybutyrate

Dead on Arrival—Heroin (N)

Death Wish—Heroin (N)

Debs—Amphetamine (S), MDMA (Ecstasy) (S) (H)
Deca-Duabolin—Injectable steroids
Decadence—MDMA (Ecstasy) (S) (H)
Deeda—LSD (H)
Delatestryl—Injectable steroids
Demolish—Crack (S)
DET—Dimethyltryptamine (H)
Detroit Pink—Phencyclidine (H)
Devil's Dandruff—Crack (S)
Devil's Dust—Phencyclidine (H)
Dexies—Amphetamine (S)
Diamonds—Amphetamines (S), MDMA (Ecstasy) (S) (H)
Dice—Crack, Cocaine (S)
Diesel—Heroin (N)
Ding—Marijuana (M)
Dinkie Dow—Marijuana (M)
Dino—MDMA (Ecstasy) (S) (H)
Dip—Crack, Cocaine (S)
Dirt—Heroin (N)
Disco Biscuit—Depressants (H/S), MDMA (Ecstasy) (S) (H)
Disks—Methadone (N)
Ditch—Marijuana (M)
DMA—MDMA (Ecstasy) (S) (H)
DMT—Dimethyltryptamine (S) (H), Phencyclidine (H)
DOA—Crack (S), Heroin (N), Phencyclidine (H)
Doctor—MDMA (Ecstasy) (S) (H)
Dog Food—Heroin (N)
Dollies—Methadone (N)
Dolls—Amphetamines (S), Depressants (H/S) MDMA (Ecstasy) (S) (H)
DOM—MDMA (Ecstasy) (S) (H)
Domes—LSD (H)
Domex—Phencyclidine (H), MDMA (Ecstasy) (S) (H)
Dominoes—Amphetamine (S)
Don Juan—Marijuana (M)
Doo Doo—Heroin (N)
Doob—Marijuana (M)
Dooley—Heroin (N)
Dope—Heroin (N) or Marijuana (M)
Dors and 4's—Combination of Doriden (H/S) and Tylenol 4
Doses—LSD (H)

Dots—LSD (H)
Double Bubble—Cocaine (S)
Double Cross—Amphetamine (S)
Double Dome—LSD (H)
Double Yoke—Crack, Cocaine ((S)
Dover's Deck—Opium (N)
Doves—MDMA (Ecstasy) (S) (H)
Downers—Barbiturate (H/S)
Downs—Barbiturate (H/S)
Dr. Feelgood—Heroin (N)
Drag Weed—Marijuana (M)
Dragon—LSD (H)
Dream Gum, Stick—Opium (N)
Dreamer—Morphine (N)
Dreck—Heroin (N)
Drink—Phencyclidine (H)
Drivers—Amphetamine (S), MDMA (Ecstasy) (S) (H)
Drops—Hypnotic/Sedative
Duby—Marijuana (M)
Dugga—Ganga (M)
Duke—Heroin (N)
Dummy Dust—Phencyclidine (H)
Dust—Heroin (N) or Cocaine (S) or Phencyclidine (H)
Dust of Angels—Phencyclidine (H)
Dusted Parsley—Phencyclidine (H)
Dusting—Phencyclidine (H) or Heroin (N) added to Marijuana (M) and Cocaine (S)
Dx M—Dextromethorphan (N)
Dynamite—Heroin (N)
Dyno—Heroin (N)
E—MDMA (Ecstasy) (S) (H)
Earth—Marijuana (M)
Eastside Player—Crack (S)
Easy Lay—Gamma Hydroxybutyrate
Ecstasy—MDMA (S) (H)
Egg—Crack, Cocaine (S)
Electric Kool Aid—LSD (H)
Elephant—Marijuana (M) or Phencyclidine (H)
Elvis—LSD (H)
Embalming Fluid—Phencyclidine (H)
Emsel—Morphine (N)
Erth—Phencyclidine (H)
Essence—MDMA (Ecstasy) (S) (H)
Estuffa—Heroin (N)

Eve—Hallucinogen (H)
Evening's Delight—Heroin (N)
Everclear—Cocaine (S), Gamma Hydroxybutyrate
Ex—MDMA (Ecstasy) (S) (H)
Eye Opener—Crack (S) or Amphetamine (S)
Famous Dimes—Crack, Cocaine (S)
Fantasia—Dimethyltryptamine (H)
Fastin—Amphetamine (S)
Fat Bags—Crack, Cocaine (S)
Fatty—Marijuana (M) cigarette
Felix the Cat—LSD (H)
Ferry Dust—Heroin (N)
Fields—LSD (H)
Fire—Crack (S) and Methamphetamine (S)
First Line—Morphine (N)
Fizzies—Methadone (N)
Flake—Cocaine (S)
Flamethrowers—Cigarette with Cocaine (S) and Heroin (N)
Flat Blues—LSD (H)
Flea Powder—Heroin (N)
Flex—Fake Crake (Rock Cocaine)
Flower—Marijuana (M)
Foo Foo—Cocaine (S)
Fool Pills—Barbiturate (H/S)
Foolish Pleasure—Heroin (N)
Footballs—Amphetamine (S)
Forget All—Rohypnol (H/S)
Forget Me Pill—Rohypnol (H/S)
Forwards—Amphetamine (S)
Fours—Narcotic (N)
French Blues—Amphetamine and Cocaine (S)
French Fries—Crack, Cocaine (S)
Fresh—Phencyclidine (H)
Friend—Fentanyl (N)
Frios—Marijuana (M) with Phencyclidine (H)
Frisco Special—Cocaine (S), Heroin (N), LSD (H)
Frisco Speedball—Cocaine (S), Heroin (N), LSD (H)
Friskie Powder—Cocaine (S)
Fry Daddy—Crack, Cocaine (S), Marijuana (M)

Fu—Marijuana (M)
Fuel—Marijuana (M) mixed with insecticides
Funk—Heroin (N)
Furra—Heroin (N)
G—Gamma Hydroxybutyrate
Gaggler—Amphetamine (S), MDMA (Ecstasy) (S) (H)
Gallup—Heroin (N)
Gangster Pills—Depressants (H/S)
Gank—Fake Crack
Gash—Marijuana (M)
Gato—Heroin (N)
Geek-Joints—Cigarettes or cigars filled with tobacco and Crack (S); Marijuana (M) cigarette with Crack (S) or powdered Cocaine (S)
Geep—Methamphetamine (S)
Gelatin Chips—LSD (H)
Georgia Home Boy—Gamma Hydroxybutyrate
Ghanja—Marijuana (M)
GHB—Gamma Hydroxybutyrate
Ghost—LSD (H)
Gib—Gamma Hydroxybutyrate
Gift-of-the-Sun—Cocaine (S)
Giggle Weed—Marijuana (M)
Girl—Cocaine (S)
Glacines—Heroin (N)
Glad Stuff—Cocaine (S)
Glass—Methamphetamine (S)
Glo—Crack (S)
Glory—Hallucinogen (H)
Go—Amphetamine (S)
God's Drug—Morphine (N)
God's Flesh—Psilocybin (H)
Gold Dust—Cocaine (S)
Golden Dragon—LSD (H)
Golden Eagle—4-Methylthioamphetamine (S) (H)
Golden Girl—Heroin (N)
Golden Leaf—Very high quality Marijuana (M)
Golf Ball—Crack (S)
Golpe—Heroin (N)
Goma—Narcotic (N)
Goma de Mota—Ganga (M)
Gondola—Opium (N)

Good—Phencyclidine (H), Heroin (N)
Good and Plenty—Heroin (N)
Goodfellas—Fentanyl (N) or Amphetamine (S)
Goof Ball—Cocaine (S), Heroin (N)
Goof Balls—Barbiturate (H/S)
Goofy's—LSD (H)
Goon—Phencyclidine (H)
Gorilla Biscuits—Phencyclidine (H)
Gram—Hashish (M)
Granulated Orange—Methamphetamine (S)
Grape Parfait—LSD (H)
Grass—Marijuana (M)
Gravel—Crack (S)
Great Bear—Fentanyl (N)
Great Tobacco—Opium (N)
Green—Inferior quality Marijuana (M), Ketamine (H), Phencyclidine H)
Green Balls—Marijuana (M)
Green Double Domes—LSD (H)
Green Dragons—Barbiturate (H/S)
Green Frogs—Hypnotic/Sedative
Green Leaves—Phencyclidine (H)
Green Tea—Phencyclidine (H)
Green Wedge—LSD (H)
Greenies—Amphetamines (S), MDMA (Ecstasy) (S) (H)
Gremmies—Combination of Cocaine (S) and Marijuana (M)
Grey Shields—LSD (H)
Griefo—Marijuana (M)
Griefs—Marijuana (M)
Grievous Bodily Harm—Gamma Hydroxybutyrate
Griff—Marijuana (M)
G-riffic—Gamma Hydroxybutyrate
Grit—Crack (S)
Groceries—Crack, Cocaine (S)
Guma—Opium (N)
Gungeon—Marijuana (M)
H—Heroin (N)
H & C—Heroin (N) and Cocaine (S)
H-Bomb—MDMA (Ecstasy) (S) (H) mixed with Heroin (N)
H Caps—Heroin (N)
Hail—Crack (S)
Haircut—Marijuana (M)

Half Moon—Peyote (H)
Hamburger Helper—Crack (S)
Happy Dust, Powder—Cocaine (S)
Happy Sticks—Phencyclidine (H)
Happy Trails—Cocaine (S)
Hard Ball—Crack, Cocaine (S)
Hard Candy—Heroin (N)
Hard Line—Crack, Cocaine (S)
Hard-on—Nitrite Inhalant (I)
Hard Stuff—Heroin (N), Opium (N)
Hardware—Nitrite Inhalant (I)
Harry—Heroin (N)
Harsh—Marijuana (M)
Hash—Hashish (M)
Hash Oil—Marijuana (M)
Hats—LSD (H)
Haven Dust—Cocaine (S)
Hawaiian—Marijuana (M)
Hawaiian Sunshine—LSD (H)
Hawk—LSD (H)
Hay—Marijuana (M)
Haze—LSD (H)
Hazel—Heroin (N)
He-man—Fentanyl (N)
Head Drugs—Amphetamines (S)
Headlights—LSD (H)
Heart On—Butyl Nitrate
Hearts—Amphetamine (S)
Heaven and Hell—Phencyclidine (H)
Heaven Dust—Cocaine (S)
Heavenly Blue—LSD (H)
Helen—Heroin (N)
Hell—Crack (S)
Hemp—Marijuana (M)
Henry—Heroin (N)
Her—Cocaine (S)
Hera—Heroin (N)
Herb—Marijuana (M)
Herb and Al—Marijuana and alcohol
Herbal Ecstacy—Ephedra (S)
Herone—Heroin (N)
Hessle—Heroin (N)
Highball—Nitrite Inhalant (I)
Hikori—Peyote (H)
Hinkley—Phencyclidine (H)
Hironpon, Hiropon—Smokable Methamphetamine (S)
Hits—Hypnotic/Sedative

Hoa—Phencyclidine (H)
Hocus—Marijuana (M), Opium (N)
Hog—Phencyclidine (H)
Hombre—Heroin (N)
Homegrown—Marijuana (M)
Homicide—Heroin (N) Cut with Sco-
polamine (AC) or strychnine
Honey Blunts—Marijuana cigars
with honey
Hooch—Marijuana (M)
Hooter—Cocaine (S), Marijuana (M)
Hop/Hops—Opium (N)
Horse—Heroin (N)
Horse Heads—Amphetamine (S)
Horse Tranquilizer—Phencyclidine (H)
Horsebite—Heroin (N)
Hospital Heroin—Dilaudid (N)
Hot Cakes—Crack (S)
Hot Dope—Heroin (N)
Hot Ice—Methamphetamine (S)
Hows—Morphine (N)
Hubbas—Crack (S)
Huff—Inhalants
Hug Drug—MDMA (Ecstasy) (S) (H)
Hunter—Cocaine (S)
Hydro—Amphetamine (S), Marijuana
(M), MDMA (Ecstasy) (S) (H)
Iboga—Amphetamine (S)
Ice—Amphetamine (S)
Ice Cube—Crack, Cocaine (S)
Icing—Cocaine (S)
Ill—Phencyclidine (H)
Indian Boy—Marijuana (M)
Indian Hay—Marijuana (M)
Indians—Mescaline (H)
Indigo—Marijuana (M)
Iranian Heroin—Heroin (N)
Isda—Heroin (N)
Issues—Crack, Cocaine (S)
Itog—Phencyclidine (H)
J—Marijuana (M)
Jacblaster—Butyl Nitrite (I)
Jackpot—Fentanyl (N)
Jam—Amphetamine (S) or Cocaine (S)
Jamaican—Marijuana (M)
Jamaican Gold—Marijuana (M)
Jane—Marijuana (M)
Jay Smoke—Marijuana (M)

Jee Gee—Heroin (N)
Jeff—Khat (S)
Jelly Bean—Amphetamine (S)
Jet—Ketamine (H)
Jet Fuel—Phencyclidine (H)
Jib—Gamma Hydroxybutyrate
Jim Jones—Marijuana (M)
with Cocaine (S) and Phencycli-
dine (H)
Jive—Marijuana (M)
Jive—Heroin (N)
Joc—Nitrite Inhalant (I)
Johnson—Crack, Cocaine (S)
Joint—Marijuana (M)
Jolly Bean—Amphetamine (S)
Jolly Green—Marijuana (M)
Jones—Heroin (N)
Joy—Heroin (N)
Joy Flakes—Heroin (N)
Joy Juice—Depressants (H/S)
Joy Powder—Cocaine (S), Heroin (N)
Joy Smoke—Marijuana (M)
Jugs—Amphetamine (S)
Juice—Phencyclidine (H), steroids
Juice Joint—Marijuana (M) cigarette
sprinkled with Crack (S)
Juja—Marijuana (M)
Ju-Ju—Marijuana (M) cigarette
Junk—Cocaine (S), Heroin (N)
K—Phencyclidine (H)
K-Blast—Phencyclidine (H)
Kali—Marijuana (M)
Kangaroo—Crack (S)
Kaps—Phencyclidine (H)
Karachi—Heroin (N), Phenobarbital
(H/S), and Methaqualone (H/S)
Karo—Codeine (N) cough syrup
Kat—Khat (S)
Kate Bush—Marijuana (M)
Kaya—Marijuana (M)
Kee—Marijuana (M)
Kentucky Blue—Marijuana (M)
Ket—Ketamine (H)
Key—Marijuana (M)
KGB (Killer Green Bud)—Marijuana
(M)
Khat—Methcathinone (S), MDMA
(Ecstasy) (S) (H)

Kibbles & Bits—Small crumbs of Crack (S)
Kick—Nitrite Inhalant (I)
Kiddie Dope—Prescription drugs
Kif—Ganga (M)
Killer—Marijuana (M), Phencyclidine (H)
Killer Joints—Phencyclidine (H)
Killer Weed—Phencyclidine (H)
Kilter—Marijuana (M)
Kind—Marijuana (M)
King—Cocaine (S)
King Bud—Marijuana (M)
King Ivory—Fentanyl (N)
King Kong Pills—Depressants (H/S)
King Tut—LSD (H)
King's Habit—Cocaine (s)
Kiss of Death—Heroin (N)
Kitty Kat—Amphetamine-like (S)
Kleenex—MDMA (Ecstasy) (S) (H)
Knockout Drugs—Chloral Hydrate in alcohol (H/S)
Kools—Phencyclidine (H)
Kryptonite—Crack (S)
Krystal—Phencyclidine (H)
KS—Marijuana (M) and Phencyclidine (H)
Kumba—Marijuana (M)
La Bamba—Heroin (N)
La Glass—Methamphetamine (S)
LA Ice—Amphetamine (S)
La Rocha—Rohypnol (H/S)
Lace—Cocaine (S) and Marijuana (M)
Lactone—GBL
Lady—Cocaine (S)
Lady Line Muser—Cocaine (S)
Late Night—Cocaine (S)
Laughing Gas—Nitrous Oxide (I)
Lay Back—Depressants (H/S)
LBJ—Heroin (N), LSD (H), Phencyclidine (H)
Leak—Marijuana (M)/Phencyclidine (H) combination
Leaky Bolla—Phencyclidine (H)
Lean—Codeine (N) cough syrup
Leapers—Amphetamine (S)
Lemon 714—Phencyclidine (H)
Lemon Drop—Methamphetamine (S)

Lemon Drop—Methamphetamine (S) with a dull yellow tint
Lemons—Methaqualone (H/S)
Lenos—Phencyclidine (H)
Lens—LSD (H)
Lethal Weapon—Phencyclidine (H)
Liberty Caps—Psilocybin (H)
Lid—Marijuana (M)
Lip Poppers—Amphetamine (S)
Liquid E—Gamma Hydroxybutyrate
Liquid Ecstasy—Gamma Hydroxybutyrate
Liquid Increase—Nitrite Inhalant (I)
Liquid X—Gamma Hydroxybutyrate
Loads (Setups)—Heroin (N)
Loaf—Marijuana (M)
Locker—Nitrite Inhalant (I)
Locker Room—Nitrite Inhalant (I)
Locoweed—Marijuana (M)
Looderstar— Khat (S)
Love Boat—Phencyclidine (H)
Love Drug—MDMA (Ecstasy) (S) (H)
Love Leaf—Marijuana (M)/Phencyclidine (H) combination
Love Pearls—Alpha-ethyltryptamine (H)
Love Pills—Alpha-ethyltryptamine (H)
Love Trip—Mescaline (H) and MDMA (Ecstasy) (S) (H)
Lovelies—Marijuana (M) with Phencyclidine (H)
Lovely—Phencyclidine (H)
Lovers' Speed—MDMA (Ecstasy) (S) (H)
Lubage—Marijuana (M)
Lucy in the Sky with Diamonds—LSD (H)
Ludes—Hypnotic/Sedative
Ludies—Amphetamine-like (S)
M & M—Depressants (H/S)
M.J.—Marijuana (M)
Machohina—Ganga (M)
Mad Dog—Phencyclidine (H)
Madman—Phencyclidine (H)
Magic—Heroin (N)
Magic Dust—Phencyclidine (H)
Magic Mushroom—Psilocybin (H)
Magic Smoke—Marijuana (M)

Magnums—Amphetamine (S)
Mama Coca—Cocaine (S)
MAMs—MDMA (Ecstasy) (S) (H)
Man—LSD (H)
Manhattan Silver—Marijuana (M)
MAO—Amphetamine (S), MDMA
　(Ecstasy) (S) (H)
Marathons—Amphetamine (S)
Marching Powder—Cocaine (S)
Mari—Marijuana (M) cigarette
Marshmallow Reds—Depressants
　(H/S)
Mary Jane—Marijuana (M)
Maui Wauie—Marijuana (M)
Maui-Wowie—Marijuana (M), Meth-
　amphetamine (S)
Max—Gamma Hydroxybutyrate
　dissolved in water and mixed
　with Amphetamines (S)
Maxibolin—Oral steroids
Mayo—Cocaine (S), Heroin (N)
MDEA—Hallucinogen (H)
MDM—Hallucinogen (H)
MDMA—Methylenedioxyamphet-
　amine (S) (H)
Mean Greens—Hypnotic/Sedative
　or Phencyclidine (H)
Meg—Marijuana (M)
Mellow Yellow—LSD (H)
Merck—Cocaine (S)
Mesc—Peyote (H)
Mescal—Peyote (H)
Meth—Methamphetamine (S)
Meth Cathinone—Khat (S)
Methatriol—Injectable steroids
Methlies Quik—Methamphetamine (S)
Methyltestosterone—Oral steroids
Mets—Amphetamine (S)
Mexican Brown—Heroin (N)
Mexican Crack—Methamphetamine
　(S)
Mexican Green—Marijuana (M)
Mexican Mud—Heroin (N)
Mexican Reds—Barbiturate (H/S)
Mexican Speedballs—Crack (S) and
　Methamphetamine (S)
Mexican Valium—Rohypnol (H/S)
Mexicana—Hallucinogen (H)

Mickey—MDMA (Ecstasy) (S) (H)
Mickey Doctor—MDMA (Ecstasy) (S)
　(H)
Mickey Finn—Alcohol and Chloral
　Hydrate (H/S)
Micro Dots—Narcotic (N)
Microdot—LSD (H)
Midnight Oil—Opium (N)
Mighty Joe Young—Depressants (H/S)
Mighty Mezz—Marijuana (M) cigarette
Mighty Quinn—LSD (H)
Mind Detergent—LSD (H)
Minibeenies—Amphetamine (S)
Mint—Phencyclidine (H)
Miss Emma—Morphine (N)
Missile Basing—Crack liquid and
　Phencyclidine (H)
Mister Blue—Morphine (N)
MJ—Marijuana (M)
Mo—Marijuana (M)
Mojo—Cocaine (S), Heroin (N)
Mollies—Amphetamine (S)
Monkey Dust—Phencyclidine (H)
Monkey Juice—Methadone (N)
Monster—Cocaine (S)
Moon—Mescaline (H)
Moon Gas—Inhalants
Moonrock—Crack, Cocaine (S), Her-
　oin (N)
Mooters—Marijuana (M) cigarette
Mootie—Marijuana (M)
More—Phencyclidine (H)
Morf—Morphine (N)
Morning Shot—Amphetamine (S),
　MDMA (Ecstasy) (S) (H)
Morotgara—Heroin (N)
Morph—Morphine (N)
Mortal Combat—Heroin (N)
Mosquitos—Cocaine (S)
Mota—Marijuana (M)
Mother—Marijuana (M)
Mother's Little Helper—Depressants
　(H/S)
MPPP—Fentanyl (N)
MPTP—Narcotic (N)
Mr. Blue—Morphine (N)
Mr. Natural—LSD (H)
Mud—Heroin (N), Opium (N)

Muggles—Marijuana (M)
Mulke—Khat (S)
Murder 8—Fentanyl (N)
Murder One—Heroin (N) and Cocaine (S)
Mushroom—Psilocybin (H)
Mutha—Marijuana (M)
Muzzle—Heroin (N)
Nail—Marijuana (M) cigarette
Nanoo—Heroin (N)
Natural Sleep 500—Gamma Hydroxybutyrate
Nature Formula 1—Ephedrine (S)
Nebbies—Depressants (H/S)
New Acid—Phencyclidine (H)
New Addition—Crack, Cocaine (S)
New Jack City—Fentanyl (N)
Nice and Easy—Heroin (N)
Nick—$5 bag of Marijuana (M)
Nigh—Nitrous Oxide (I)
Nigra—Marijuana (M)
Nimbies—Depressants (H/S)
Nineteen—Amphetamine (S), MDMA (Ecstasy) (S) (H)
Nods—Codeine (N) cough syrup
Noise—Heroin (N)
Nose Candy, Powder, Stuff—Cocaine (S)
Nose Drops—Liquified Heroin (N)
Nubs—Peyote (H)
Nugget—Amphetamine (S)
Nuggets—Crack, Cocaine (S)
Number—Marijuana (M) cigarette
Number 1—Heroin (N)
Number 2—Heroin (N)
Number 3—Heroin (N)
Number 4—Heroin (N)
O.D.—Marijuana (M)
O.J.—Marijuana (M)
O.P.P.—Phencyclidine (H)
Ogoy—Heroin (N)
Oil—Heroin (N), Phencyclidine (H)
Old Steve—Heroin (N)
One and Ones—Talwin (N) and Ritalin (S) combination injected
One Way—LSD (H)
One-Fifty-One—Crack (S); Crack sprinkled on tobacco

Oolies—Marijuana (M) cigarette with Crack (S)
Optical Illusions—LSD (H)
Orange Barrels, Cubes, Haze, Micro, Wedges—LSD (H)
Orange Sunshine—LSD (H)
Oranges—Amphetamine (S)
Organic Quaalude— Gamma Hydroxybutyrate
Original Herbal X—Ephedrine (S)
Outerlimits—Crack (S) and LSD (H)
Owsley—LSD (H)
OxiContin—a semi-synthetic opiate (N)
Oxy—OxyContin (N)
Oxy 80s—OxyContin (N)
Oxycet—OxyContin (N)
Oxycotton—OxyContin (N)
Oyster Stew—Cocaine (S)
Ozone—Marijuana (M); Phencyclidine (H) and Crack (S) cigarette; Marijuana cigarette; Phencyclidine (H)
P—Peyote (H) or Phencyclidine (H)
P-Dope—Heroin (N)
P-Funk—Crack (S) mixed with Phencyclidine (H); Heroin (N)
Pack—Marijuana (M), Heroin (N)
Pajao—Barbiturate (H/S)
Pakistani Black—Marijuana (M)
Panama Cut, Gold Red—Marijuana (M)
Panama Red—Marijuana (M)
Panatella—Large Marijuana (M) cigarette
Pancakes and Syrup—Combination of Glutethimide and Codeine (N) cough syrup (H/S)
Pane—LSD (H)
Pangonadalot—Heroin (N)
Paper Acid—LSD (H)
Paper Blotter—LSD (H)
Parabolin—Oral steroids, veterinary steroid
Parachute—Crack (S) and Phencyclidine (H) smoked; Heroin (N); smokable Crack and Heroin mixture

Paradise, White—Cocaine (S)
Pasta—Cocaine paste (S)
Pat—Marijuana (M)
PCP—Phencyclidine (H)
Peace—Phencyclidine (H), LSD (H)
Peace Pill—Phencyclidine (H)
Peaches—Amphetamine (S)
Peanut—Depressants (H/S)
Peanut Butter—Methamphetamine (S);
  Phencyclidine (H) mixed with
  peanut butter
Pearl—Cocaine (S)
Pearls—Amyl Nitrite (I)
Pearly Gates—LSD (H)
Pebbles—Crack, Cocaine (S)
Peep—Phencyclidine (H)
Peg—Heroin (N)
Pellets—LSD (N)
Pen Yan—Opium (N)
Pep Pills—Amphetamine (S)
Percio—Cocaine (S)
Percolators—Narcotics (N)
Perfect High—Heroin (N)
Peruvian Flake, Lady—Cocaine (S)
Peter—Depressants (H/S)
Peter Pan—Phencyclidine (H)
Peth—Depressant (H/S)
Phennies—Depressants (H/S)
Phenos—Depressants (H/S)
Piece—Cocaine (S)
Pig Killer—Phencyclidine (H)
Piles—Crack, Cocaine (S)
Pimp—Cocaine (S)
Pin—Marijuana (M)
Pink Blotters—LSD (H)
Pink Hearts—Amphetamine (S)
Pink Ladies—Barbiturate (H/S)
Pink Panther, Robots, Wedges,
  Witches—LSD (H)
Pinks—Amphetamine (S)
Pinks and Grays—Darvon (N)
Pit—Phencyclidine (H)
Pitillo—Cocaine paste (S)
Pitzu—Impure Morphine Base (N)
Pixies—Amphetamine (S)
Plastivil—Hypnotic/Sedative
PMA—Hallucinogen (H)
Pocket Rockets—Amphetamine-like (S)

Pod—Marijuana (M)
Point on Point—Heroin (N)/Scopol-
  amine (AC)
Poison—Heroin (N), Fentanyl (N)
Pollutants—Amphetamines (S),
  MDMA (Ecstasy) (S) (H)
Polo—Mixture of Heroin (N)
  and motion sickness drug
Polvo—Cocaine (S)
Pony—Crack, Cocaine (S)
Poor Man's Heroin—Talwin (N)
  and Ritalin (S) combination injected
Poor Man's Pot—Inhalants
Pop—Amyl or Butyl Nitrite (I)
Popper—Nitrite Inhalant (I)
Pot—Marijuana (M)
Potato—LSD (N)
Potato Chips—Crack (S) cut with
  benzocaine
Potlikker—Marijuana (M)
Powder Diamonds—Cocaine (S)
Pox—Opium (N)
Predator—Heroin (N)
Press—Cocaine (S)
Pretendo—Marijuana (M)
Primbolin—Injectable and oral steroids
Prime Time—Crack, Cocaine (S)
Primo—Crack (S); Marijuana (M)
  mixed with Crack; Crack and Heroin
  N); Heroin, Cocaine (S) and tobacco
Primo Square—Marijuana (M) joint
  laced with Crack (S)
Primos—Cigarette laced with Heroin
  (N) and Cocaine (S)
Product—Crack, Cocaine (S)
Proviron—Oral steroids
Puffy—Phencyclidine (H)
Pulborn—Heroin (N)
Pure Love—LSD (H)
Purple Haze—LSD (H)
Purple Hearts—Barbiturates (H/S)
Purple Rain—Phencyclidine (H)
Pussy Juice—Alcohol and Metronidazole
Qat—Khat (S)
Quack—Hypnotic/Sedative
Quads—Hypnotic/Sedative
Quartz—Smokable Methamphetamine
  (S)

Quas—Depressants (H/S)
Quat—Cathinone (S)
Queen Ann's Lace—Marijuana (M)
Quicksilver—Isobutyl Nitrite (I)
Quill—Cocaine (S), Heroin (N), Meth-
amphetamine (S)
Rainbow—LSD (N)
Rainbows—Depressants (H/S)
Rainy Day Woman—Marijuana (M)
Rambo—Heroin (N)
Rane—Cocaine (S), Heroin (N)
Raven—MDMA (Ecstasy) (S) (H)
Ready Rock—Crack, Cocaine (S)
Red Birds—Barbiturate (H/S)
Red Chicken—Heroin (N)
Red Cross—Marijuana (M)
Red Devils—Barbiturate (H/S)
Red Dirt—Marijuana (M)
Red Eagle—Heroin (N)
Red Lips—LSD (H)
Red Phosphorus—Amphetamine (S)
Red Rock—Heroin (N)
Red Rock Opium—Heroin (N), Barbi-
tal (H/S), strychnine, and caffeine S)
Red Rum—Heroin (N), Barbital (H/S),
strychnine, and caffeine (S)
Red Stuff—Heroin (N), Barbital (H/S),
strychnine, and caffeine (S)
Redneck Cocaine—Methamphetamine
(S)
Reds—Amphetamine (S)
Reds—Barbiturate (H/S)
Reefer—Marijuana (M)
Regular "P"—Crack, Cocaine (S)
Rest in Peace—Crack, Cocaine (S)
Reynolds—Rohypnol (H/S)
Rhapsody—MDMA (Ecstasy) (S) (H)
Rhine—Heroin (N)
Rhythm—Amphetamine (S)
Rib—Rohypnol (H/S)
Righteous Bush—Marijuana (M)
Roach—Marijuana (M)
Roach 2—Rohypnol (H/S)
Roaches—Rohypnol (H/S)
Road Dope—Amphetamine (S)
Roapies—Rohypnol (H/S)
Robutal—Rohypnol (H/S)
Roca—Crack (S)

Roche—Rohypnol (H/S)
Rock—Crack, Cocaine (S)
Rocket Fuel—Phencyclidine (H)
Rockets—Marijuana (M) cigarette
Rocks of Hell—Crack, Cocaine (S)
Rojo—Barbiturate (H/S)
Rompums—Marijuana (M) with horse
tranquilizers (H/S)
Roofies—Rohypnol (H/S)
Rope—Rohypnol (H/S) or Marijuana
(M)
Rophies—Rohypnol (Flunitrazepam)
(H/S)
Rosa—Amphetamine (S)
Ruffies—Rohypnol (H/S)
Running—MDMA (Ecstasy) (S) (H)
Rush—Cocaine (S); Isobutyl Nitrite (I);
Inhalants
Rush Snappers—Isobutyl Nitrite (I)
Russian Sickles—LSD (H)
Rz's—Rohypnol (H/S)
Sacrament—LSD (H)
Salt—Heroin (N)
Salt and Pepper—Marijuana (M)
Salty Water—Gamma Hydroxybutyrate
Sandoz—LSD (H)
Sandwich Bag—$40 bag of Marijuana
(M)
Satan's Scout—Nitrite Inhalant (I)
Satan's Secret—Inhalants
Sativa—Marijuana (M)
Scaffle—Phencyclidine (H)
Scat—Heroin (N)
Schmeck—Cocaine (S)
Schmiz—Methamphetamine (S)
Schoolboy—Cocaine (S), Codeine (N)
Scissors—Marijuana (M)
Scooby Snacks—MDMA (Ecstasy) (S)
(H)
Scoop—Gamma Hydroxybutyrate
Scootie—Methamphetamine (S)
Scorpion—Cocaine (S)
Scott—Heroin (N)
Scotty—Cocaine/Crack (S)
Scrabble—Crack, Cocaine (S)
Scruples—Crack, Cocaine (S)
Scuffle—Phencyclidine (H)
Seccies—Barbiturate (H/S)

Seccy—Depressants (H/S)
Second to None—Heroin (N)
Seeds—Marijuana (M)
Seggy—Depressants (H/S)
Sen—Marijuana (M)
Seni—Peyote (H)
Seren Fourteens—Methaqualone (H/S)
Serenity—Hallucinogen (H)
Sernyl—Phencyclidine (H)
Serpico 21—Cocaine (S)
Sess—Marijuana (M)
Seven-Up—Crack, Cocaine (S)
Shabu—Ice, Crack, Cocaine (S), Meth-
amphetamine (S), MDMA Ecstasy)
S) (H)
Shake—Marijuana (M)
She—Cocaine (S)
Sheet Rocking—Crack (S) and LSD
(H)
Sheets—Phencyclidine (H)
Sherman Sticks/Tanks—Phencyclidine
(H)
Sherms—Crack, Cocaine (S),
Phencyclidine (H), cigars dipped in
or laced ith Phencyclidine (H)
Shit—Heroin (N)
Shmeck/Schmeek—Heroin (N)
Shoot—Heroin (N)
Shrooms—Psilocybin (H)
Sightball—Crack, Cocaine (S)
Silly Putty—Psilocybin (H)
Simple Simon—Psilocybin/Psilocin (H)
Sinsemilla—Marijuana (M)
Skag—Heroin (N)
Sketch—Methamphetamine (S)
Skid—Heroin (N)
Skuffle—Phencyclidine (H)
Skunk—Marijuana (M)
Sleeper—Heroin (N), Depressants
(H/S)
Sleeping Pills—Barbiturate (H/S)
Sleet—Crack, Cocaine (S)
Sleigh Ride—Cocaine (S)
Slime—Heroin (N)
Smack—Heroin (N)
Smears—LSD (H)
Smoke—Marijuana (M); Crack, Co-
caine (S); Heroin (N) and Crack

Smoking Gun—Heroin (N) and Co-
caine (S)
Smurf—Cigar dipped in embalming fluid
Snap—Amphetamine (S)
Snappers—Nitrite Inhalant (I)
Sniff—Amyl or Butyl Nitrite (I)
Snop—Marijuana (M)
Snorts—Phencyclidine (H)
Snow—Cocaine (S) or Amphetamine
(S)
Snow Pallets—Amphetamine (S)
Snow Seals—Cocaine (S) and Amphet-
amine (S)
Snowball—Cocaine (S) and Heroin (N)
Snowcones—Cocaine (S)
Snowmen—LSD (H)
Snuff—Tobacco (S)
Soap—Gamma Hydroxybutyrate
Soapers—Hypnotic/Sedative
Soda—Cocaine (S)
Soles—Hashish (M)
Soma—Phencyclidine (H)
Somali Tea—Methcathinone (S)
Somatomax—Gamma Hydroxybutyrate
Space Ball—Phencyclidine (H) and
Crack (S)
Space Base—Crack (S) dipped in
Phencyclidine (H); hallowed out ci-
gar refilled with Phencyclidine (H)
and Crack (S)
Space Cadet—Crack, Cocaine (S),
Phencyclidine (H)
Sparklers—Amphetamine (S)
Special K—Ketamine (H)
Special la Coke—Ketamine (H)
Speed—Amphetamine (S)
Speedball—Cocaine (S) mixed with
Heroin (N); Crack (S) and Heroin
smoked together; Methylphenidate
(Ritalin) (S) mixed with Heroin;
Amphetamine (S)
Speedboat—Marijuana (M),
Phencyclidine (H), and Crack (S)
combined and smoked
Spider Blue—Heroin (N)
Splash—Amphetamine (S)
Spivias—Amphetamine (S), MDMA
(Ecstasy) (S) (H)

Spliff—Large Marijuana (M) cigarette
Splivins—Amphetamine (S)
Spores—Phencyclidine (H)
Sporos—Methaqualone (H/S)
Spray—Inhalants
Square Time Bob—Crack, Cocaine (S)
Squirrel—Combination of
    Phencyclidine (H) and Marijuana
    (M) prinkled ith Cocaine (S) and
    smoked; Marijuana, Phencyclidine,
    and Crack (S) ombined and smoked;
    LSD (H)
Stack—Marijuana (M)
Star—Cocaine (S), Amphetamine (S),
    Methcathinone (S)
Stardust—Cocaine (S) or Phencyclidine
    (H)
Stat—Khat (S)
Stick—Marijuana (M)
Sting—Heroin (N)/Scopolamine (AC)
STP—Hallucinogen (H)
Stones—Crack (S)
Stoppers—Depressants (H/S)
Stove Top—Crystal Methamphetamine
    (S), Methamphetamine (S)
Straw—Marijuana (M) cigarette
Strawberries—Depressants (H/S)
Strawberry Fields—LSD (H)
Strawberry Shortcake—Amphetamine
    (S), MDMA (Ecstasy) (S) (H)
Studio Fuel—Cocaine (S)
Stumblers—Barbiturate (H/S)
Sugar—Crack, Cocaine (S), Heroin
    (N), LSD (H)
Sugar Block—Crack, Cocaine (S)
Sugar Cubes—LSD (H)
Sugar Weed—Marijuana (M)
Suicide—Heroin (N)
Sunshine—LSD (H)
Super—Phencyclidine (H)
Super Acid—Ketamine (H)
Super Buick—Dextromethorphan (N),
    Scopolamine (AC)
Super C—Ketamine (H)
Super Cools—Phencyclidine (H)
Super Grass—Phencyclidine (H); Mari-
    juana (M) with Phencyclidine;
    arijuana

Super Ice—Methamphetamine (S)
Super Joint—Phencyclidine (H)
Super Kools—Phencyclidine (H)
Super Pot—Phencyclidine (H)
Superman—LSD (H)
Surfer—Phencyclidine (H)
Sustanon 250—Injectable steroids
Sweet Dreams—Heroin (N)
Sweet Jesus—Heroin (N)
Sweet Lucy—Hashish (M)
Sweeties—Amphetamine (S)
Swishers—Cigars in which tobacco is
    replaced with Marijuana (M)
Synthetic Cocaine—Phencyclidine (H)
Synthetic THT—Phencyclidine (H)
T—Cocaine (S), Marijuana (M)
T-Birds—Hypnotic/Sedative
T-Buzz—Phencyclidine (H)
T.N.T.—Heroin (N); Fentanyl (N)
T's and B's—Talwin (N) and Amphet-
    amine (S)
T's and Blues—Talwin (N) and Anti-
    histamine (S)
Tabs—LSD (H)
TAC—Phencyclidine (H)
Tail Lights—LSD (H)
Taking a Cruise—Phencyclidine (H)
Talco—Cocaine (S)
Tango and Cash—Fentanyl (N)
Tar—Crack, Cocaine (S), Heroin (N)
Tardust—Cocaine (S)
Tea—Marijuana (M), Phencyclidine (H)
Teenager—Cocaine (S)
Teeth—Cocaine (S)
Tens—Amphetamine (S), MDMA (Ec-
    stasy) (S) (H)
Tension—Crack, Cocaine (S)
Tex Mex—Marijuana (M)
Texas Tea—Marijuana (M)
THC—Tetrahydrocannabinol (M)
The Beast—Heroin (N)
The C—Amphetamine (S),
    Methcathinone (S)
Thing—Main drug interest at the mo-
    ment
Thirteen—Marijuana (M)
Thirty-Eight—Crack (S) sprinkled on
    Marijuana (M)

Thrusters—Amphetamine (S)
Thumb—Marijuana (M)
Thunder—Heroin (N)
Tic—Phencyclidine (H) in powder form
Tic Tac—Phencyclidine (H)
Tick Tick—Methamphetamine (S)
Ticket—LSD (H)
Tish—Phencyclidine (H)
Tissue—Crack, Cocaine (S)
Titch—Phencyclidine (H)
Tits—Black Tar Heroin (N)
TMA—MDMA (Ecstasy) (S) (H)
T.N.T.—Heroin (N) or Fentanyl (N)
Tocas Tea—Marijuana (M)
Tongs—Heroin (N)
Tooies—Barbiturate (H/S)
Toolies—Barbiturate (H/S)
Toot—Cocaine (S)
Tootsie Roll—Heroin (N)
Top Gun—Crack, Cocaine (S)
Top Shelf—Heroin (N)
Topi—Mescaline (H)
Tops—Peyote (H)
Torch—Marijuana (M)
Tornado—Crack, Cocaine (S)
Torpedo—Marijuana (M) and Crack (S)
Toxy—Opium (N)
Toys—Opium (N)
TR-6s—Amphetamine (S)
Tragic Magic—Crack, Cocaine (S),
  Phencyclidine (H)
Tran Q—Phencyclidine (H)
Tranquility—Hallucinogen (H)
Tray—$3 bag of Marijuana (M)
Trees—Barbiturate (H/S)
Troop—Crack (S)
Trophobolene—Injectable steroid
Tropicana—Marijuana (M)
Truck Drivers—Amphetamine (S)
Tuiys—Barbiturate (H/S)
Turbo—Marijuana (M) and Crack (S)
Turkey—Cocaine (S), Amphetamine
  (S)
Turned On—Introduced to drugs; under
  the influence
Tweak—Cocaine (S) or Methamphet-
  amine (S)
Tweeker—Methcathinone (S)

Twenty-Five—LSD (H)
Twenty-Twenty—Amphetamine (S)
Twist—Marijuana (M) cigarette
Twisters—Small plastic bags of Heroin
  (N) secured with a twist tie
Twistum—Marijuana (M) cigarette
U.S.P.—Amphetamine (S), MDMA
  (Ecstasy) (S) (H)
Ultimate—Crack, Cocaine (S)
Ultimate Xphoria—Ephedra (S)
Uncle Milty—Depressants (H/S)
Unkie—Morphine (N)
Unotque—Marijuana (M)
Uppers—Amphetamine (S)
Ups—Amphetamine (S)
Utopiates—Hallucinogens (H)
V—Valium (H/S)
Vaporole—Nitrite Inhalant (I)
Vega—Cigar wrapping refilled with
  Marijuana (M)
Viper's Weed—Marijuana (M)
Vita-G—Gamma Hydroxybutyrate
Vitamin K—Ketamine (H)
Vodka Acid—LSD (H)
Wac—Phencyclidine (H) on Marijuana
  (M)
Wack—Phencyclidine (H)
Wacky Weed—Marijuana (M)
Wafers—Methadone (N)
Wake and Bake—Marijuana (M)
Wake-ups—Amphetamine (S)
Water—Amphetamine (S)
Wave—Crack (S)
Wedge—LSD (H)
Weed—Marijuana (M)
Weed—Phencyclidine (H)
West Coast—Methylphenidate (Ritalin)
  (S)
West Coast Turnarounds—Amphet-
  amine (S), MDMA (Ecstasy) (S) (H)
Wet—Blunts mixed with Marijuana
  (M) and Phencyclidine (H);
  ethamphetamine (S)
Whack—Crack, Cocaine (S); Heroin
  (N) and Phencyclidine (H);
  rack/Phencyclidine mixture or Mari-
  juana (M) laced with insecticides
Wheels—MDMA (Ecstasy) (S) (H)

Whiffledust—Amphetamine (S), MDMA (Ecstasy) (S) (H)
Whippets—Nitrous Oxide (I)
White—Cocaine (S)
White Crosses—Amphetamine (S)
White Ghost, Girl, Horse, Lady, Mosquito, Sugar, Tornado—Cocaine (S)
White Junk, Nurse, Stuff—Heroin (N)
White Lemons—Methaqualone (H/S)
White Lightning—LSD (H)
White Mole—Amphetamine (S)
Whites—Amphetamine (S)
Whiteout—Isobutyl Nitrite (I)
Whiz Bang—Cocaine (S) and Heroin (N)
Wicked—Heroin (N)
Wicky Stick—Phencyclidine (H), Marijuana (M) and Crack (S)
Wigits—MDMA (Ecstasy) (S) (H)
Wild Cat—Methcathinone (S) mixed with Cocaine (S)
Window Panes—LSD (H)
Wings—Cocaine (S), Heroin (N)
Winstrol—Oral steroids
Winstrol V—Veterinary steroids
Witch—Heroin (N)
Wobble Weed—Phencyclidine (H)
Wolf—Phencyclidine (H)
Wolfies—Rohypnol (H/S)
Wollie—Rocks of Crack (S) rolled into a Marijuana (M) cigarette or in a cigar
Wonder Star—Methcathinone (S)
Woolah—Cigar filled with Marijuana (M) and Crack (S)
Woolies—Marijuana (M) and Crack (S) or Phencyclidine (H)

Working Man's Cocaine—Methamphetamine (S)
Worm—Phencyclidine (H)
Wrecking Crew—Crack, Cocaine (S)
X—MDMA (Ecstasy) (S) (H)
XTC—MDMA (Ecstasy) (S) (H)
Yale—Crack, Cocaine (S)
Yayoo—Crack, Cocaine (S)
Yellow Barn—Methamphetamine (S)
Yellow Bullets—Depressants (H/S)
Yellow Dimples—LSD (H)
Yellow Fever—Phencyclidine (H)
Yellow Jackets—Barbiturates (H/S)
Yellow Roach—Benzodiazepines (H/S)
Yellow Submarine—Marijuana (M)
Yellow Sunshine—LSD (H)
Yen Pop—Marijuana (M)
Yerba—Marijuana (M)
Yesco—Marijuana (M)
Yimyom—Crack, Cocaine (S)
Ying Yang—LSD (H)
Zacatecas Purple—Marijuana from Mexico (M)
Zambi—Marijuana (M)
Zay—A mixture of Marijuana (M) and other substances within a cigar; blunts
Ze—Opium (N)
Zen—LSD (H)
Zero—Opium (N)
Zigzag—LSD (H)
Zip—Methamphetamine (S) or Cocaine (S)
Zombie—Phencyclidine (H)
Zombie Weed—Phencyclidine (H)
Zonkers—Barbiturates (H/S)

Selected Bibliography

Preface

Blendon, R. J. and Young, J. T. "The Public and the War on Illicit Drugs." *Journal of the American Medical Association* 279(1988): 827-832.

Brecher, E. M. *Licit and Illicit Drugs: The Consumers Union Report on Narcotics, Stimulants, Depressants, Inhalants, Hallucinogens, and Marijuana—Including Caffeine, Nicotine, and Alcohol.* Boston: Little, Brown, 1972.

Butterfield, F. "Drug Treatment in Prisons Dips as Use Rises, Study Finds." *New York Times,* January 6, 1999, A14.

"Drugs of Abuse: Cannabis." *Drug Enforcement* 6(1979): 34-37.

"Drugs of Abuse: Depressants." *Drug Enforcement* 6(1979): 18-19.

"Drugs of Abuse: Hallucinogens." *Drug Enforcement* 6(1979): 28-31.

"Drugs of Abuse: Narcotics." *Drug Enforcement* 6(1979): 10-17.

"Drugs of Abuse: Stimulants." *Drug Enforcement* 6(1979): 24-27.

Goodman Gilman, A., Goodman, L. S., Rall, T. W., et al., eds. *Goodman and Gilman's The Pharmacological Basis of Therapeutics,* Eighth Edition. New York: Pergamon, 1990.

Morin, R. and Brassaro, M. A. "Communication Breakdown on Drugs: Poll Finds a Generation Gap on Extent of Problems, Parental Role." Washington Post–ABC News Poll, *The Washington Post,* March 4, 1997, p. A01.

National Institute on Drug Abuse. *Drug Abuse and Drug Abuse Research II: The Triennial Report to Congress from the Secretary's Department of Health and Human Services.* Rockville, MD: National Institute on Drug Abuse, 1984. DHHS Publication No. (ADM) 85-1372.

National Institute on Drug Abuse and National Institute on Alcohol Abuse and Alcoholism. *Economic Costs of Alcohol and Drug Abuse.* Rockville, MD: National Institutes of Health, 1988.

Schuckit, M. A. *Drug and Alcohol Abuse: A Clinical Guide to Diagnosis and Treatment.* New York: Plenum Medical Book Co., 1979.

Secretary of Health and Human Services. *Ninth Special Report to the US Congress on Alcohol and Health.* Washington, DC: Government Printing Office, 1997. NIH Publication no. 97-4017.

Wessel, D. and Cummings, J. "Treasury Pegs Smoking's Economic Cost." *Wall Street Journal,* March 26, 1998, A3.

Wilford, B. B. *Drug Abuse: A Guide for the Primary Care Physician.* Chicago: American Medical Association, 1981.

Chapter 1

Alcohol and Health: Seventh Special Report to the United States Congress from the Secretary of Health and Human Services. Rockville, MD: U.S. Department of Health and Human Services, 1990.

Avom, J., Dreyer, P., Connelly, K., et al. "Use of Psychoactive Medication and the Quality of Care in Rest Homes." *New England Journal of Medicine* 320(1989): 227-232.

Barnes, D. M. "Drugs: Running the Numbers." *Science* 240(1988): 1729-1731.

Bell, C. S. and Battjes, R. *Prevention Research: Deterring Drug Abuse Among Children and Adolescents.* NIDA Research Monograph 63, Rockville, MD: U.S. Dept. of Health and Human Services, Public Health Service, Alcohol, Drug Abuse, and Mental Health Administration, 1985.

Berke, R. L. "Poll Finds Many in U.S. Back Bush Strategy on Drugs." *The New York Times,* September 12, 1989, A14.

Blum, R. H. and Associates. *Utopiates: The Use and Users of LSD 25.* Stanford University. Institute for the Study of Human Problems. New York: Atherton Press, 1970.

Bradley, A. M. "Capsule Review of the State of the Art: The Sixth Special Report to the U.S. Congress on Alcohol and Health." *Alcohol World: Health and Research* 11(1987): 4-9.

Brook, J. S., Lettieri, D. J., and Brook, D. W. "Alcohol and Substance Abuse in Adolescence." Special issue of *Advances in Alcohol and Substance Abuse* 4(3/4) (1985): 1-204.

"CEOs See Drug Abuse as a Growing Problem." *American Medical News,* September 1, 1989, 20.

Community Epidemiology Work Group. *Epidemiologic Trends in Drug Abuse Proceedings.* Rockville, MD: National Institute on Drug Abuse, 1989.

Cook, R. F. "Drug Use Among Working Adults: Prevalence Rates and Estimation Methods." In *Drugs in the Workplace.* NIDA Research Monograph 91. Rockville, MD: U.S. Dept. of Health and Human Services, 1989.

Greene, J. M., Ennett, S. T., and Ringwalt, C. L. "Substance Use Among Runaway and Homeless Youth in Three National Samples." *American Journal of Public Health* 87(2) (1997): 229-235.

Greene, J. M. and Ringwalt, C. L. "Youth and Familial Substance Use's Association with Suicide Attempts Among Runaway and Homeless Youth." *Substance Use and Misuse* 31(1997): 1041-1058.

Gunby, P. "Nation's Expenditures for Alcohol, Other Drugs, in Terms of Therapy, Prevention, Now Exceed $1.6 Billion." *Journal of the American Medical Association* 258(1987): 2023.

Hoffman, J. P., Brittingham, A., Larison, C. *Drug Use Among U.S. Workers: Prevalence and Trends by Occupation and Industry Categories.* Rockville, MD: Substance Abuse and Mental Health Services Administration. Office of Applied Studies, DHHS Pub No (SMA)96-3089, 1996.

Horgan, C., Carley, S. K., Wara, K., and Strickler, G. *Substance Abuse: The Nation's Number One Health Problem.* Princeton, NJ: Schneider Institute for Health Policy. Robert Wood Johnson Foundation, 2001.

Johnston, L. D., O'Malley, P. M., and Bachman, J. G. *Drug Use, Drinking and Smoking: National Survey Results from High School, College and Young Adult Population, 1975-1988.* Rockville, MD: National Institute on Drug Abuse. Alcohol, Drug Abuse, and Mental Health Administration, 1989.

Johnston, L. D., O'Malley, P. M., and Bachman, J. G. *Monitoring the Future. National Results on Adolescent Drug Use. Overview of Key Findings 1999.* Bethesda, MD: U. S. Department of Health and Human Services, National Institutes of Health, National Institute on Drug Abuse. NIH Publication No. 00-4690, 2000.

Johnston, L. D., O'Malley, P. M., and Bachman, J. G. *Monitoring the Future. National Results on Adolescent Drug Use. Overview of Key Findings 2000.* Bethesda, MD: National Institute on Drug Abuse. NIH Publication No. 01-4923, 2001.

Johnston, L. D., O'Malley, P. M., and Bachman, J. G. (Eds.). *The Monitoring the Future Study, 1975-1995.* National Institute on Drug Abuse, Rockville, MD, NIH Pub: No 98-4140, 1997.

Jones, C. L. and Battjes, R. J. *Etiology of Drug Abuse: Implications for Prevention.* National Institute on Drug Abuse Research Monograph 56. Rockville, MD: U.S. Dept. of Health and Human Services, Public Health Service, Alcohol, Drug Abuse and Mental Health Administration, 1986.

Kaestner, E., Frank, B., Marel, R., and Schmeidler, J. "Substance Use Among Females in New York State: Catching Up with the Males." *Advances in Alcohol and Substance Abuse* 5(3) (1986): 29-49.

Kipke, M. D., Montgomery, S. B., Simon, R. R., and Iverson, E. F. "Substance Abuse Disorders Among Runaway and Homeless Youth." *Substance Use and Misuse,* 32 (1997): 965-982.

Kozel, N. J. and Adams, E. H. "Epidemiology of Drug Abuse: An Overview." *Science* 234(1986): 970-974.

Lewin, L. *Phantastica: Narcotic and Stimulating Drugs: Their Use and Abuse.* Translated by P. A. Wirth. London: Kegan Paul, Trench, Trubner, 1931. Republished London: Routledge and Kegan, 1964.

Lund, A. K., Preusser, D. F., Blomberg, R. D., et al. "Drug Use by Tractor-Trailer Drivers." *Journal of Forensic Sciences* 33 (1988): 648-661.

National Institute on Alcohol Abuse and Alcoholism. *Alcohol and Aging.* Rockville, MD: U.S. Dept. of Health and Human Services, Public Health Service, Alcohol, Drug Abuse, and Mental Health Administration, 1988.

National Institute on Drug Abuse. *Overview of the 1988 National Household Survey on Drug Abuse.* NIDA Capsules. Rockville, MD: National Institute on Drug Abuse, 1989.

Newcomb, M. D. and Bentler, P. M. *Consequences of Adolescent Drug Use.* Newbury Park, CA: Sage Publications, 1988.

Research Report to Physician Leadership on National Drug Policy (PLNDP). Brown University Center for Alcohol and Addiction Studies, Providence, RI, March 17, 1998.

Ruben, D. H. "The Elderly Alcoholic: Some Current Dimensions." *Advances in Alcohol and Substance Abuse* 5(4) (1986): 59-70.

Simonsen, L. L. "Top 200 Drugs of 1987: New Prescription Volume Increases 4.2 Percent Moving Total Rxs Up 1.4 Percent." *Pharmacy Times* 54(1988): 38-46.

Stanford Research Institute, National Institute on Drug Abuse, Services Research Branch. *The Aging Process and Psychoactive Drug Use.* DHEW Publication No. (ADM) 79-813. Washington, DC: U.S. Government Printing Office, 1979.

Substance Abuse and the American Adolescent. New York: Center on Addiction and Substance Abuse, 1997.

Substance Abuse Among Older Adults. Rockville, MD: Center for Substance Abuse Treatment, Treatment Improvement Protocol, 1997.

Summary of Findings from the 1999 National Household Survey on Drug Abuse. National Household Survey on Drug Abuse Series H-12. Rockville, MD: Department of Health and Human Services Substance Abuse and Mental Health Services Administration, 2000.

Trimble, J., Padilla, A., and Bell, C. *Drug Abuse Among Ethnic Minorities.* DHHS Publishing No. 87-1474. Rockville, MD: National Institute on Drug Abuse, 1987.

United States General Accounting Office. *Comprehensive Approach Needed to Help Control Prescription Drug Abuse Summary: Report to the Congress of the United States by the Comptroller General.* Washington, DC: U.S. General Accounting Office, 1982.

Washton, A. M. and Gold, M. S., "Recent Trends in Cocaine Abuse: A View from the National Hotline, '800-COCAINE'." *Advances in Alcohol and Substance Abuse* 6(2) (1986): 31-47.

Wechsler, H., Davenport, A., Dowdall, G., Moeykens, B., and Castillo, S. "Health and Behavioral Consequences of Binge Drinking in College. A National Survey of Students at 140 Campuses." *Journal of the American Medical Association* 272(1994): 1672-1677.

Winslow, R. "Productivity Data Indict Casual Drinking." *Wall Street Journal,* December 22, 1998, B1.

Chapter 2

Barnett, G. and Rapalla, R. S. "Designer Drugs: An Overview." In *Cocaine, Marijuana, Designer Drugs: Chemistry, Pharmacology, and Behavior,* edited by K. K. Redda, C. A. Walker, and G. Barnett. Boca Raton, FL: CRC Press, 1989.

Culhane, C. "Court Says No to Peyote." *The U.S. Journal,* September 1990, 10.

Kumar, S. "Big Health Threat from Drug Abuse in South Asia." *Lancet* 353(1999): 651.

Nahas, G. G. "A Pharmacological Classification of Drugs of Abuse." *Bulletin on Narcotics* 33(1981): 1-19.

Nichols, D. E. "Discovery of Novel Psychoactive Drugs: Has It Ended?" *Journal of Psychoactive Drugs* 19(1987): 33-37.

Chapter 3

Barnes, D. M. "The Biological Tangle of Drug Addiction." *Science* 241(1988): 415-417.

Goldstein, A. "The Pharmacologic Basis of Methadone Therapy." *Proceedings of the Fourth National Conference on Methadone Treatment.* New York: National Association on Prevention of Addiction to Narcotics, 1972.

Goodwin, F. K. "Cannabinoid Receptor Gene Cloned." *Journal of the American Medical Association* 264(1990): 1389.

Leshner, A. I. "Drug Abuse and Addiction Are Biomedical Problems." *Hospital Practice,* April 1997, 2-4.

Mathias, R. "Study Shows How Genes Can Help Protect from Addiction." *NIDA Notes* 13(6)(1999): 5, 9.

National Survey Results on Drug Use from *The Monitoring the Future Study, 1975-1995.* Edited by L.D. Johnston, P.M. O'Malley, J.G. Bachman. National Institute on Drug Abuse, Rockville, MD, NIH Pub: No 98-4140, 1997.

NIH Consensus Statement. *Effective Medical Treatment of Opiate Addiction.* 15(6) (1997): 1-38. Bethesda, MD: National Institutes of Health.

Rinaldi, R. C., Steindler, E. M., Wilford, B. B., et al. "Clarification and Standardization of Substance Abuse Terminology." *Journal of the American Medical Association* 259(1988): 555-557.

Self, D. W. "Neurobiological Adaptations to Drug Use." *Hospital Practice,* April 1997, 5-9.

Snyder, S. *Drugs and the Brain.* New York: Scientific American Books, 1986.

Stimmel B. ed. *Opiate Receptors, Neurotransmitters and Drug Dependence: Basic Science—Clinical Correlates.* New York: Haworth Press, 1981.

Stimmel, B. *Pain, Analgesia and Addiction: The Pharmacologic Treatment of Pain.* New York: Raven Press, 1983.

Stimmel, B. and Glick, S. D. "Animal-Human Correlates of Narcotic Dependence: A Brief Review." *American Journal of Psychiatry* 135(1978): 821-825.

Stimmel, B. and Kreek, M.J. "Neurobiology of Addictive Behaviors and Its Relationship to Methadone Maintenance." *Mount Sinai Journal of Medicine,* 67(5-6)(2000): 375-380.

Wickelgren, I. "Teaching the Brain to Take Drugs." *Science* 280(1998): 2045-2047.

Chapter 4

Bell, C. S. and Battjes, R. *Prevention Research: Deterring Drug Abuse Among Children and Adolescents.* NIDA Research Monograph 63. Rockville, MD: U.S. Dept. of Health and Human Services, Public Health Service, Alcohol, Drug Abuse, and Mental Health Administration, 1985.

Brook, J. S., Lettieri, D. J., and Brook, D. W. "Alcohol and Substance Abuse in Adolescence." Special issue, *Advances in Alcohol and Substance Abuse* 4(3/4) (1985): 1-204.

Calipano, J. A. "The Hunt for a Drug Free American: Look Under Every Rock and in the Mirror." Address to the National Newspaper Association, Washington DC, March 21, 1997.

Charness, M. E., Simon, R. P., and Greenberg, D. A. "Ethanol and the Nervous System." *New England Journal of Medicine* 321 (1989): 442-454.

Clarke, P. B. S. "Tobacco Smoking, Genes, and Dopamine." *Lancet* 352(1998): 84-85.

Goleman, D. "Scientists Pinpoint Brain Irregularities in Drug Addicts." *The New York Times,* June 26, 1990, C1.

Jones, C. L. and Battjes, R. J. *Etiology of Drug Abuse: Implications for Prevention.* NIDA Research Monograph 56. Rockville, MD: U.S. Dept. of Health and Human Services, Public Health Service, Alcohol, Drug Abuse, and Mental Health Administration, 1986.

Kauffman, J. F., Shaffer, H., and Burglass, M. E. "A Strategy for the Biological Assessment of Addiction." *Advances in Alcohol and Substance Abuse* 3(1-2) (1983/1984): 7-18.

"Keeping Youth Drug Free. A Guide for Parents, Grand Parents, Elders, Mentors and Other Care Givers." Rockville, MD: U.S. Department of Health and Human Services, Substance Abuse and Mental Health Services Administration Center for Substance Abuse Prevention, 1996.

Koob, G. F. and Le Moal, M. "Drug Abuse: Hedonic Homeostatic Dysregulation." *Science* 278(1997): 52-58.

Leshner, A. I. "Drug Abuse and Addiction Are Biomedical Problems." *Hospital Practice,* April 1997, 2-4.

Louis Harris and Associates, Inc., Poll. New York, September, 1997.

Marx, J. "Marijuana Receptor Gene Cloned." *Science* 249 (1990): 624-626.

Mathias, R. "Study Shows How Genes Can Help Protect from Addiction." *NIDA Notes* 13(6)(1999): 5, 9.

Morin, R. and Brossard, M. A. "Communication Breakdown on Drugs: Poll Finds Generation Gap on Extent of Problems, Parental Role." Washington Post – ABC News Poll, *The Washington Post,* March 4, 1997, A01.

National Consensus Development Panel on Effective Medical Treatment of Opiate Addiction. "Effective Medical Treatment of Opiate Addiction." *Journal of the American Medical Association* 280(1998): 1936-1942.

Newcomb, M. D. and Bentler, P. M. *Consequences of Adolescent Drug Use.* Newbury Park, CA: Sage Publications, 1988.

NIH Consensus Statement. *Effective Medical Treatment of Opiate Addiction.* 15(6) (1997): 1-38. Bethesda, MD: National Institutes of Health.

Pianezza, M. L., Sellers, E. M., and Tyndale, R. F. "Nicotine Metabolism Defect Reduces Smoking." *Nature* 393(1998): 750.

Pirisi, A. "New Insights Gained into Genetics of Alcoholism." *Lancet,* 351(1998): 1636.

Self, D. W. "Neurobiological Adaptations to Drug Use." *Hospital Practice,* April 1997, 5-9.

Senior, K. "The Need for a Cigarette: Does It Reside in the Genome." *Lancet* 353(1999): 384.

Stimmel, B. and Kreek, M.J. "Neurobiology of Addictive Behaviors and Its Relationship to Methadone Maintenance." *Mount Sinai Journal of Medicine,* 67(5-6)(2000): 375-380.

Wickelgren, I. "Teaching the Brain to Take Drugs." *Science* 280(1998): 2045-2047.

Chapter 5

Anglin, M. D. "The Efficacy of Civil Commitment in Treating Narcotic Addiction." In *Compulsory Treatment of Drug Abuse: Research and Clinical Practice,* edited by C. G. Leukefeld and F. M. Tims. NIDA Research Monograph Series 86. Rockville, MD: U.S. Dept. of Health and Human Services, ADAMHA-NIDA, 1986.

Ashery, R. S., ed. *Progress in the Development of Cost-Effective Treatment for Drug Abusers.* NIDA Research Monograph Series 58, DHHS-PUB-ADM-85-1401. Rockville, MD: National Institute on Drug Abuse, 1985.

Bullock, M. L., Culliton, P. D., and Olander, R. T. "Controlled Trial of Acupuncture for Severe Recidivist Alcoholism." *Lancet* 1 (1989): 1435-1439.

Cherpitel, C. J. "Screening for Alcohol Problems in the Emergency Room. A Rapid Alcohol Problems Screen." *Drug and Alcohol Dependence* 40(1995): 133-137.

"Court Rejects Some Drug Testing of U.S. Workers." *The New York Times,* November 18, 1990, A31.

Curran, W. J. "Compulsory Drug Testing: The Legal Barriers." *New England Journal of Medicine* 316(1987): 318-321.

De Leon, G. *The Therapeutic Community: Study of Effectiveness: Social and Psychological Adjustment of 400 Dropouts and 100 Graduates from the Phoenix House Therapeutic Community.* DHHS Publication No. (ADM) 84-1286. Treatment Research Monograph Series. Rockville, MD: U.S. Dept. of Health and Human Services, Public Health Service, Alcohol, Drug Abuse, and Mental Health Administration, National Institute on Drug Abuse, 1984.

"Drug Treatment and the Criminal Justice System." Washington DC: Office of National Drug Control Policy, September 17, 1998.

"Eosinophilia-Myalgia Syndrome—Canada." *Morbidity and Mortality Weekly Report* 39(1990): 89-91.

"Eosinophilia-Myalgia Syndrome—New Mexico." *Morbidity and Mortality Weekly Report* 38(1989): 765-767.

Ewing, J. S. "Detective Alcoholism: The CAGE Questionnaire." *Journal of the American Medical Association* 252(1984):1905-1907.

Gerstein, D. R. and Lewin, L. S. "Treating Drug Problems." *New England Journal of Medicine* 323(1990): 844-846.

Hansen, H. J., Caudill, S. P., and Boone, D. J. "Crisis in Drug Testing: Results of CDC Blind Study." *Journal of the American Medical Association* 253(1985): 2382-2387.

Hawks, R. L. and Chiang, C. N., eds. *Urine Testing for Drugs of Abuse.* NIDA Research Service Monograph 73. USPHS ADAMHA. Rockville, MD: National Institute on Drug Abuse, 1986.

Hubbard, R. L., Marsden, M. E., and Rachas, J. et al. *Drug Abuse Treatment: A National Study of Effectiveness.* Chapel Hill: University of North Carolina Press, 1989.

Hunt, G. H. and Odoroff, M. E. "Follow-up Study of Narcotic Drug Addicts After Hospitalization." *Public Heath Reports* 77(1962): 41-54.

Larson, D. B., Swyers, J. P., and McCullough, M. E. *Scientific Research on Spirituality and Health: A Consensus Report.* Bethesda, MD: National Institute of Health Care Research, 1998, pp. 68-82, John Templeton Foundation.

Marshall, E. " Testing Urine for Drugs." *Science* 241(1988): 150-152.

McLellan, A. T., Luborsky, L., and O'Brien, C. P. et al. "Alcohol and Drug Abuse Treatment in Three Different Populations: Is There Improvement and Is It Predictable?" *American Journal of Drug and Alcohol Abuse* 12(1986): 101-120.

McLellan, A. T., Woody, G. E., Luborsky, L. et al. "Increased Effectiveness of Substance Abuse Treatment. A Prospective Study of Patient-Treatment 'Matching.'" *Journal of Nervous and Mental Disease* 171(1983): 597-605.

Morris, K. "Antiepileptic Drug Blocks Rats' Taste for Nicotine." *Lancet,* 352(1998): 1835.

Musto, D. F. *The American Disease: Origins of Narcotic Control.* New Haven, CT: Yale University Press, 1973.

Nadelmann, E. A. "Common Sense Drug Policy." *Foreign Affairs* 77(1998): 111-126.

National Drug and Alcoholism Treatment Unit Survey (NDATUS) 1987: Final Report. Rockville, MD: U.S. Dept. of Health and Human Services, U.S. Public Health Service, ADAMHA National Institute on Drug Abuse and National Institute on Alcohol Abuse and Alcoholism, 1988.

NIH Consensus Development Panel. "Acupuncture." *Journal of the American Medical Association* 280(1998): 1518-1524.

O'Keefe, A. M. "The Case Against Drug Testing." *Psychology Today* 21(1987): 34-38.

Sacks, H. "Theoretical Limits of the Evaluation of Drug Concentrations in Hair Due to Irregular Hair Growth." *Forensic Salut* 70(1995): 53-61.

Schmeck, H. M. Jr. "Drug-Testing Technology Speeds Up." *The New York Times,* November 20, 1988, E7.

Simpson, D. D., Joe, G. W., Lehman, W. E. et al. "Addiction Careers: Etiology, Treatment, and 12-Year Follow-Up Outcomes." *Journal of Drug Issues* 16(1986): 107-122.

Smith, M. O. and Kahn, I. "An Acupuncture Programme for the Treatment of Drug-Addicted Persons." *Bulletin on Narcotics* 40(1988): 35-41.

Sullivan, E. and Fleming, M. "A Guide to Substance Abuse Services for Primary Care Physicians." Treatment Improvement Protocol (TIP) Series 24. Rockville, MD: U.S. Department of Health and Human Services, Public Health Service, Substance Abuse and Mental Health Services Administration, Center for Substance Abuse Treatment, 1997.

Tagliaro, F., De Battisti, Z., Smith, F. P., and Marigo, M. "Death from Heroin Overdose: Findings from Hair Analysis." *Lancet,* 351(1998): 1923-1925.

Tennant, F. "Clinical Diagnosis and Treatment of the Post Drug Impairment Syndrome." *Psychiatry Letter* 6(1982): 47-51.

Westermeyer, J. "Nontreatment Factors Affecting Treatment Outcome for Substance Abuse." *American Journal of Drug and Alcohol Abuse* 15(1989): 13-29.

Winick, C. "Some Policy Implications of the New York State Civil Commitment Program." *Journal of Drug Issues* 18(1988): 561-574.

Wolf, C. "Judge Rejects Broad Testing for Drug Use." *The New York Times,* June 7, 1990, Bl.

Chapter 6

"19 Meds for Substance Use Disorders Are in Development." *New Medicines in Development for Mental Illnesses 1998.* Pharmaceutical Research and Manufacturers of America (PhRMA).

"21 Percent of U.S. Inmates Are Called Nonviolent." *The New York Times,* February 5, 1994, Section 1, 9.

Caulkins, J. P. *Mandatory Minimum Drug Sentences: Throwing Away the Key or the Taxpayers' Money?* Santa Monica, CA: Rand, 1997.

Confronting the Drug Problem, Debate Persists on Enforcement and Alternative Approaches: A Report to the Chairman, Committee on Government Operations, House of Representatives. Washington, DC: U.S. General Accounting Office, 1993.

Donovan, D. M. "Efficacy and Effectiveness: Complementary Findings from Two Multisite Trials Evaluating Outcomes of Alcohol Treatments Differing in Theoretical Orientations." *Alcohol Clinical and Experimental Research* 23(1999): 564-572.

Egan, T. "Hard Time. Less Crime, More Criminals." *The New York Times,* March 7, 1999, Section 4, 1.

Fagan, R. "The Use of Required Treatment for Substance Abusers." *Substance Abuse* 20(1999): 249-261.

Grinspoon, L. and Bakalar, J. B. "The War on Drugs—A Peace Proposal." *New England Journal of Medicine* 330(1994): 357-360.

McLellan, A. T., Grissom, G. R., Zanis, D., Randall, M., Brill, P., and O'Brien, C. P. "Problem Service 'Matching' in Addiction Treatment: A Prospective Study in 4 Programs." *Archives of General Psychiatry* 54(1997): 730-735.

Nadelmann, E. A. "Common Sense Drug Policy." *Foreign Affairs* 77(1998): 111.

Principles of Drug Addiction Treatment. A Research-Based Guide. Bethesda, MD: National Institute on Drug Abuse, NIH Publication No. 99-4180, October 1999.

Rydell, C. P. and Everingham, S. S. *Controlling Cocaine: Supply vs. Demand Programs.* Santa Monica, CA: Rand Corporation, 1994.

Second Policy Report of the Physician Consortium on Substance Abuse Education. *Substance Abuse and Addiction: The Interface of the Health and Criminal Justice Systems.* Rockville, MD: U.S. Department of Health and Human Services, Health Resources and Services Administration, 1998.

"Substance Abuse and Welfare Reform." *Prevention Pipeline,* 11(5) September/October (1998): 9.

Swan, N. "Matching Drug Abuse Treatment Services to Patient Needs Boosts Outcome Effectiveness." *NIDA Notes* 13(5)(1999): 5, 8.

"U.N. Agency Is Wary of Prescriptions for Heroin." *The New York Times International,* April 17, 1999, A7.

Weisner, C., McCarty, D., and Schmidt, L. "New Directions in Alcohol and Drug Treatment Under Managed Care." *The American Journal of Managed Care* 5 (1999): SP57-69.

Wren, C. "Arizona Finds Cost Savings in Treating Drug Offenders." *The New York Times,* April 21, 1999, A14.

Zickler, P. "Blood-Borne Medications Could Intercept Drugs Before They Reach the Brain." *NIDA Notes* 14(2)(1999): 8-10.

Chapter 7

Addolorato, G., Balducci, G., Capristo, E., Attilia, M. L., Taggi, F., Gasbarrini, G., and Ceccanti, M. "Gamma-Hydroxybutyric Acid (GHB) in the Treatment of Alcohol Withdrawal Syndrome: A Randomized Comparative Study versus Benzodiazepine." *Alcohol Clinical and Experimental Research* 23(1999): 1596-1604.

Addolorato, G., Cibin, M., Caprista, E., et al. "Maintaining Abstinence from Alcohol with Gamma Hydroxybutyric Acid." *Lancet* 351(1998): 58.

"Alcohol and Aging." *Alcohol Alert,* 40(April 1998): 1-3. National Institute on Alcohol Abuse and Alcoholism.

Alcohol and the Impaired Driver: A Manual on the Medicolegal Aspects of Chemical Tests for Intoxication. Chicago: American Medical Association, Committee on Medicolegal Problems, 1968.

"Alcohol-Related Traffic Fatalities During Holidays—United States, 1988." *Morbidity and Mortality Weekly Report* 38(1989): 861-863.

"Alcohol-Related Traffic Fatalities Involving Children—United States, 1985-1996." *Morbidity and Mortality Weekly Report* 46/48(1997): 1130-1133.

"Alcohol and Sleep." *Alcohol Alert* 41(July 1998): 1-3. National Institute on Alcohol Abuse and Alcoholism.

"Alcohol Use in the United States." *Statistical Bulletin/Metropolitan Insurance Companies* 68(1987): 20-25.

American College of Physicians. "Disulfiram Treatment of Alcoholism." *Annals of Internal Medicine* 111(1989): 943-945.

American Psychiatric Association. *Diagnostic and Statistical Manual of Mental Disorders* (DSM-IV). Washington, DC: Author, 1994.

Anda, R. F., Williamson, D. F., and Remington, P. L. "Alcohol and Fatal Injuries Among U.S. Adults." *Journal of the American Medical Association* 260(1988): 2529-2532.

Annis, H. M. "Is Inpatient Rehabilitation of the Alcoholic Cost Effective? Con Position." *Advances in Alcohol and Substance Abuse* 5(1-2) (1985/1986): 175-190.

Banys, P. "The Clinical Use of Disulfiram (Antabuse): A Review." *Journal of Psychoactive Drugs* 20(1988): 243-260.

Blum, H. T., Nobel, E. P., Sheridan, P. J. et al. "Allelic Association of Human Dopamine D2 Receptor Gene in Alcoholism." *Journal of the American Medical Association* 263(1990): 2055-2060.

Bowen, O. R. and Sammons, J. H. "The Alcohol-Abusing Patient: A Challenge to the Profession." *Journal of the American Medical Association* 260(1988): 2267-2270.

Bradley, K. A., Badrinath, S., Bush, K., Boyd-Wickizer, J., and Anawalt, B. "Medical Risks for Women Who Drink Alcohol." *Journal of General Internal Medicine* 13(1998): 627-639.

Charness, M. E., Simon, R. P., and Greenberg, D. A. "Ethanol and the Nervous System." *New England Journal of Medicine* 321(1989): 442-454.

Cherpitel, C. J. "Brief Screening Tests for Alcoholism." *Alcohol World: Health and Research* 21(4)(1997): 348-352.

Cloninger, C. R. "Neurogenetic Adaptive Mechanisms in Alcoholism." *Science* 236(1987): 410-416.

Davidson, D., Palfai, T., Bird, C., and Swift, R. "Effects of Naltrexone on Alcohol Self-Administration in Heavy Drinkers." *Alcohol Clinical and Experimental Research* 23(1999): 195-203.

"Driving under the Influence." *Lancet* 352(1998): 1871.

"DWI Deaths Reach Historic Low." *The Nation's Health,* October (1998): 4.

Edenberg, H. J., Foroud, T., Koller, D. L., et al. "A Family-Based Analysis of the Association of the Dopamine D2 Receptor (DRD2) with Alcoholism." *Alcoholism Clinical and Experimental Research* 22(1998): 505-512.

Emrick, C. D. "Alcoholics Anonymous: Affiliation Processes and Effectiveness as Treatment." *Alcoholism (N.Y.)* 11(1987): 416-423. [Published erratum appears in *Alcoholism (N.Y.)* 12(1988): 29.]

Feinman, L. and Lieber, C. S. "Toxicity of Ethanol and Other Components of Alcoholic Beverages." *Alcoholism (N.Y.)* 12(1988): 2-6.

Fell, J. C. and Nash, C. E. "The Nature of the Alcohol Problem in U.S. Fatal Crashes." *Health Education Quarterly* 16 (1989): 335-343.

Franck, D. H. "'If You Drink, Don't Drive' Motto Now Applies to Hangovers As Well." *Journal of the American Medical Association* 250(1983): 1657-1658.

Frezza, M., di Padova, C., Pozzato, G. et al. "High Blood Alcohol Levels in Women. The Role of Decreased Gastric Alcohol Dehydrogenase Activity and First-Pass Metabolism." *New England Journal of Medicine* 322(1990): 95-99. [Published erratum appears in *New England Journal of Medicine* 322(1990): 1540.]

Gallant, D. M. "The Type 2 Primary Alcoholic." *Alcoholism: Clinical and Experimental Research* 14(1990): 631.

Garbutt, J. C., West, S. L., Carey, T. S., Lohr, K. N., and Crews, F. T. "Pharmacological Treatment of Alcohol Dependence. A Review of the Evidence." *Journal of the American Medical Association* 281(1999): 1318-1325.

Goodwin, D. W. *Alcoholism: The Facts.* New York: Oxford University Press, 1981.

Hall, W. and Zador, D. "The Alcohol Withdrawal Syndrome." *Lancet* 349(1997): 1897-1900.

Handa, K., Sasaki, J., Saku, K., et al. "Alcohol Consumption, Serum Lipids and Severity of Angiographically Determined Coronary Artery Disease." *American Journal of Cardiology* 65(1990): 287-289.

Harburg, E., Davis, D., Cummings, K. M., and Gunn, R. "Negative Affect, Alcohol Consumption and Hangover Symptoms Among Normal Drinkers in a Small Community." *Journal Studies of Alcohol* 42(1981): 998-1012.

Harwood, H., Fountain, D., and Livermore, G. *The Economic Costs of Alcohol and Drug Abuse in the United States, 1992.* Rockville, MD: U.S. Department of Health and Human Services National Institutes of Health, National Institute of Drug Abuse; Office of Science Policy and Communications; National Institute on Alcohol Abuse and Alcoholism, 1998.

Heath, A. C., Jardine, R. and Martin, N. G. "Interactive Effects of Genotype and Social Environment on Alcohol Consumption in Female Twins." *Journal of Studies on Alcohol* 50(1989): 38-48.

Heath, A. C. and Martin, N. G. "Teenage Alcohol Use in the Australian Twin Register: Genetic and Social Determinants of Starting to Drink." *Alcoholism (N.Y.)* 12(1988): 735-741.

Honan, W. H. "Campus Alcohol and Drug Arrests Rose in '96, Survey Says." *The New York Times,* May 3, 1998, A26.

Humphreys, K. and Moos, R. H. "Reduced Substance Abuse Related Healthy Costs Among Voluntary Participants in Alcoholics Anonymous." *Psychiatry Service* 47(1996): 709-713.

Kaprio, J., Koskenvuo, M., Langinvainio, H. et al. "Genetic Influences on Use and Abuse of Alcohol: A Study of 5638 Adult Finnish Twin Brothers." *Alcoholism (N.Y.)* 11(1987): 349-356.

Klatsky, A. L., Armstrong, M. A., and Friedman, G. D. "Red Wine, White Wine, Liquor, Beer, and Risk for Coronary Artery Disease Hospitalization." *American Journal of Cardiology* 80(1997): 416-420.

Kranzler, H. R. "Medications for Alcohol Dependence—New Vistas." *Journal of the American Medical Association* 284(2000): 1016-1017.

Larkin, M. "Festive Drinking's Slippery Slope Beckons." *Lancet* 352(1998): 1994.

Mäki, T., Toivonen, L., Koskinen, P., Näveri, H., Härkönen, M., and Leinonen, H. "Effect of Ethanol Drinking, Hangover and Exercise on Adrenergic Activity and Heart Rate Variability in Patients with a History of Alcohol-Induced Atrial Fibrillation." *American Journal of Cardiology* 82(1998): 317-322.

Marlatt, G. A. "Alcohol, Expectancy, and Emotional States: How Drinking Patterns May Be Affected by Beliefs About Alcohol's Effects." *Alcohol Health and Research World* 11(1987): 10-13, 80-81.

Mayo-Smith, M. F. for the American Society of Addiction Medicine Working Group on Pharmacological Management of Alcohol Withdrawal. "Pharmacological Management of Alcohol Withdrawal. A Meta-analysis and Evidence-Based Practice Guideline." *Journal of the American Medical Association* 278(1997): 144-151.

Milgram, G. G. and Consumer Reports Books. *The Facts About Drinking: Coping with Alcohol Use, Abuse and Alcoholism.* Mount Vernon, NY: Consumers Union, 1990.

Miller, W. R. and Hester, R. K. "The Effectiveness of Alcoholism Treatment: What Research Reveals." In *Treating Addictive Behaviors: Processes of Change,* edited by W. R. Miller and N. Heather. New York: Plenum Press, 1986.

Muntwyler, J., Hennekens, C. H., Buring, J. E., and Gaziano, J. M. "Mortality and Light to Moderate Alcohol Consumption After Myocardial Infarction." *Lancet* 352(1998): 1882-1885.

New Advances in Alcohol Treatment, Alcohol Alert. No. 49. Rockville, MD: National Institute on Alcohol Abuse and Alcoholism, U.S. Department of Health and Human Services, October 2000.

O'Connor, P. G., Farren, C. K., Rounsaville, B. J., and O'Malley, S. S. "A Preliminary Investigation of the Management of Alcohol Dependence with Naltrexone by Primary Care Providers." *American Journal of Medicine* 103(1997): 477-482.

O'Connor, P. G. and Schottenferd, R. S. "Patients with Alcohol Problems." *New England Journal of Medicine* 338(1998): 592-602.

Orford, J. and Keddie, A. "Abstinence or Controlled Drinking in Clinical Practice: Indications at Initial Assessment." *Addictive Behaviors* 11(1986): 71-86.

Peele, S. "Can Alcoholism and Other Drug Addiction Problems Be Treated Away or Is the Current Treatment Binge Doing More Harm Than Good?" *Journal of Psychoactive Drugs* 20(1988): 375-383.

Rivara, F. P., Mueller, B. A., Somes, G., Mendoza, C. T., Rushforth, N. B., and Kellermann, A. L. "Alcohol and Illicit Drug Abuse and the Risk of Violent Death in the Home." *Journal of the American Medical Association* 278(1997): 569-575.

Roizen, R. "The Great Controlled-Drinking Controversy." *Recent Developments in Alcoholism* 5(1987): 245-279.

Sacco, R. L., Elkind, M., Boden-Albala, B., Lin, I. F., Kargman, D. E., Hauser, W. A., Shea, S., and Paik, M. C. "The Protective Effect of Moderate Alcohol Consumption on Ischemic Stroke." *Journal of the American Medical Association* 281(1999): 53-60.

Schuckit, M. A., Irwin, M., and Mahler, H. I. M. "Tridimensional Personality Questionnaire Scores of Sons of Alcoholic and Nonalcoholic Fathers." *American Journal of Psychiatry* 147(1990): 481-487.

Secretary of Health and Human Services. *Alcohol and Health: Seventh Special Report to the United States Congress.* PHS, ADAMHA, NIAAA. Rockville, MD: U.S. Dept. of Health and Human Services, January 1990.

Secretary of Health and Human Services. *Special Report to the U.S. Congress on Alcohol and Health from the Secretary of Health and Human Services (6th).* PC A08/MF A01. Rockville, MD: Alcohol, Drug Abuse, and Mental Health Administration, 1987.

Smith-Warner, S. A., Spiegelman, D., Yaun, S. S., et al. "Alcohol and Breast Cancer in Women. A Pooled Analysis of Cohort Studies." *Journal of the American Medical Association* 279(1998): 535-540.

Stout, D. "President Promises New Fight on Drunken Driving." *The New York Times,* December 27, 1998, A26.

Surgeon General's Workshop on Drunk Driving: Proceedings. December 14-16, 1988, Washington, D.C. Rockville, MD: U.S. Dept. of Health and Human Services.

Wallack, L., Breed, W., and Cruz, J. "Alcohol on Prime Time Television." *Journal of Studies on Alcohol* 48(1987): 33-38.

Wiesbeck, G. A., Weijers, H. G., Chick, J., Naranjo, C. A., and Boening, J. on behalf of the Ritanserin in Alcoholism Work Group. "Ritanserin in Relapse Prevention in Abstinent Alcoholics: Results from a Placebo-Controlled Double-Blind International Multicenter Trial." *Alcohol Clinical and Experimental Research* 23(1999): 230-235.

Wiese, J. G., Shlipak, M. G., and Browner, W. S. "The Alcohol Hangover." *Annals of Internal Medicine* 132(2000): 897-902.

Yesavage, J. A. and Leirer, V. O. "Hangover Effects on Aircraft Pilots 14 Hours After Alcohol Ingestion: A Preliminary Report." *American Journal of Psychiatry* 143(1986): 1546-1550.

Chapter 8

"Adverse Events Associated with Ingestion of Gamma-Butyrolactone—Minnesota, New Mexico, and Texas, 1998-1999." *Morbidity and Mortality Weekly Report* 48(1999): 137-140.

"Alcohol and Sleep." *Alcohol Alert,* 41(July 1998): 1-3.

Bangsberg, D., Tulsky, J. P., Hecht, F. M., Moss, A. R. "Safety and Mobility of the Older Driver." *Journal of the American Medical Association* 278(1997): 66-67.

"Benzodiazepines: Prescribing Declines Under Triplicate Program." *Epidemiology Notes,* New York State Department of Health 4(12)(1989).

"Carisoprodol Addiction Studies Requested." *ASAM News* July/August/September, 1997, 12.

"Drug Linked to Assault Is Reformulated." *The New York Times,* October 19, 1997, A20.

"DWI Deaths Reach Historic Low." *The National Health,* October 1998, 4.

"Gamma Hydroxy Butyrate Use—New York and Texas 1995-1996." *Journal of the American Medical Association* 277(1997): 1511-1515.

Gonzalez, E. R. "Methaqualone Abuse Implicated in Injuries, Deaths Nationwide." *Journal of the American Medical Association* 246 (1981): 813-815.

Greenblatt, D. J., Shader, R. I., and Abernethy, D. R. "Drug Therapy: Current Status of Benzodiazepines." *New England Journal of Medicine* 309(1983): 410-416.

Hemmelgarn, B., Suissa, S., Huang, A., Boivin, J.-F., and Pinard, G. "Benzodiazepine Use and the Risk of Motor Vehicle Crash in the Elderly." *Journal of the American Medical Association* 278(1997): 27-31.

Marwick, C. "Coma-Inducing Drug GHB May Be Reclassified." *Journal of the American Medical Association* 277(1997): 1505-1506.

Mayo-Smith, M. F. "Pharmacological Management of Alcohol Withdrawal." *Journal of the American Medical Association* 278(1997): 144-518.

Murphy, S. M., Owen, R. T., and Tyrer, P. J. "Withdrawal Symptoms After Six Weeks' Treatment with Diazepam." Letter. *Lancet* 2 (1984): 1389.

"Prescribing of Minor Tranquilizers." *Food and Drug Administration Drug Bulletin* 10(1980): 2-3.

Rickels, K., Case, W. G., and Schweizer, E. E. et al. "Low-Dose Dependence in Chronic Benzodiazepine Users: A Preliminary Report on 119 Patients." *Psychopharmacological Bulletin* 22(1986): 407-415.

"Rohypnol (Flunitrazepam)—'Rophies.'" *NIDA Fact Sheet.* Rockville, MD: National Institute on Drug Abuse, 1997.

Roy Byrne, P. P. and Hommer, D. "Benzodiazepine Withdrawal: Overview and Implications for the Treatment of Anxiety." Review. *American Journal of Medicine* 84(1988): 1041-1052.

Shader, R. I., Anglin, C. L., et al. *Emergency Room Study of Sedative Hypnotic Overdosage: A Study of the Issues.* Treatment Research Monograph Series. DHHS Publication No. (ADM) 82-1118. Rockville, MD: U.S. Dept. of Health and Human Services, Public Health Service, Alcohol, Drug Abuse, and Mental Health Administration, National Institute on Drug Abuse, (1982).

Whitten, L. *Conference Highlights Increasing GHB Abuse.* NIDA Notes 16(2) 10, 11. Rockville, MD: National Institute of Drug Abuse, 2000.

Zvosee, D. L., Smith, S. W., McCutcheon, J. R., Spillane, J., Hall, B. J., and Peacock, E. D. "Adverse Events, Including Death, Associated with the Use of 1,4 Butanediol." *New England Journal of Medicine,* 344(2001): 87-93.

Chapter 9

Baggott, M. and Sferios, E. "Chemical Analysis of Ecstasy Pills." *Journal of the American Medical Association* 284(2000): 2190.

Bergman, R. L. "Navajo Peyote Use: Its Apparent Safety." *American Journal of Psychiatry* 128(1971): 695-699.

Boot, B. P., McGregor, I. S., and Hall, W. "MDMA (Ecstasy) Neurotoxicity: Assessing and Communicating the Risks." *Lancet* 355(2000): 1818-1821.

Burros, M. and Jay, S. "Concern Grows Over Herb That Promises a Legal High." *The New York Times,* April 10, 1996, C1, 6.

Butterfield, F. "Violence Rises as Club Drug Spreads Out Into the Streets." *The New York Times,* June 24, 2001, A1, 14.

Clouet, D. H., ed. *Phencyclidine: An Update.* NIDA Research Monograph Series 64. DHHS Publication No. (ADM) 86-1443. Rockville, MD: Dept. of Health and Human Services, Public Health Service, Alcohol, Drug Abuse, and Mental Health Administration, National Institute on Drug Abuse, 1986.

"Club Drugs." *Community Drug Alert Bulletin.* Bethesda, MD: U.S. Department of Health and Human Services, National Institutes of Health, National Institute on Drug Abuse, NIH Publication No. 00-4723, December 1999.

Cohen, R. S. *The Love Drug: Marching to the Beat of Ecstasy.* Binghamton, NY: The Haworth Medical Press, 1998.

Fields, G. "An Explosion of Chemical 'Ecstasy'." *USA Today,* October 23, 1999, 3A.

"FTC Charges False Claims in Sales of Herbal Ecstasy." *Substance Abuse Letter,* August 18, 1997.

Grinspoon, L. and Bakalar, J. B. *Psychedelic Drugs Reconsidered.* New York: Basic Books, 1979.

Henry, J. A., Fallon, J. K., Kicman, A. T., Hutt, A. J., Cowan, D. A., and Forsling, M. "Low Dose MDMA ('Ecstasy') Induces Vasopressin Secretion." *Lancet* 351(1998): 1784.

Johnston, L. D., O'Malley, P. M., and Bachman, J. G. *Monitoring the Future. National Results on Adolescent Drug Use. Overview of Key Findings 2000.* Bethesda, MD: National Institute on Drug Abuse. NIH Publicaiton, No. 101-4923, 2001.

Martin, W. R. and Sloan, J. W. "Pharmacology and Classification of LSD Hallucinogens." In *Drug Addictions II: Amphetamine, Psychotogen, and Marijuana Dependence,* edited by W. R. Martin. Berlin: Springer-Verlag, 1977, pp. 305-308.

McElhatton, P. R., Bateman, D. N., Evans, C., Pughe, K. R., and Thomas, S. H. L. "Congenital Anomalies After Prenatal Ecstasy Exposure." *Lancet* 354(1999): 1441-1442.

MDMA (Ecstasy). *NIDA Capsules,* Rockville, MD: National Institute on Drug Abuse, 1994.

Petersen, R. C. and Stillman, R. C., eds. *Phencyclidine (PCP) Abuse: An Appraisal.* Based upon papers presented at a conference held Feb. 2-28, 1978, Pacific Grove, California. National Institute on Drug Abuse Research Monograph Series 21. DHEW Publication No. (ADM) 78-728. Rockville, MD: Dept. of Health, Education, and Welfare, Public Health Service, Alcohol, Drug Abuse, and Mental Health Administration, National Institute on Drug Abuse, Division of Research, 1978.

Redda, K. K., Walker, C. A., and Barnett, G. *Cocaine, Marijuana, Designer Drugs: Chemistry, Pharmacology and Behavior.* Boca Raton, FL: CRC Press, 1989.

Riba, J. and Barbanoj, M. J. "A Pharmacological Study of Ayahuasca in Healthy Volunteers." *MAPS,* 8(1998): 12-15.

Seymour, R., Smith, D., Inaba, D., et al. *The New Drugs: Look Alikes: Drugs of Deception and Designer Drugs.* Center City, MN: Hazelden Press, 1989.

Siegel, R. K. "Herbal Intoxication: Psychoactive Effects from Herbal Cigarettes, Tea, and Capsules." *Journal of the American Medical Association* 236(1976): 473-476.

Wren, C. S. "Seizure of Ecstasy at Airport Shows Club Drug's Increase." *The New York Times,* October 29, 1999, B6.

Chapter 10

Astin, A. W., Green, K. C., and Kern, W. S. *The American Freshman: Twenty-Year Trends, 1966-1985.* Los Angeles: Cooperative Institutional Research Program. University of California, Higher Education Research Institute, Graduate School of Education, 1987.

Bachman, J. G., Johnston, L. D., and O'Malley, P. M. "Explaining Recent Increases in Students' Marijuana Use: Impacts of Perceived Risks and Disapproval, 1976 through 1996." *American Journal of Public Health* 88(1998): 887-892.

Barinaga, M. "How Cannabinoids Work in the Brain." *Science* 291(2001): 2530-2531.

Brooke, J. "5 States Vote Medical Use of Marijuana." *The New York Times,* November 5, 1998, B10.

Cohen, S. "Marijuana. Does It Have a Possible Therapeutic Use?" *Journal of the American Medical Association* 240(1978): 1761-1763.

"Dangerous Habits." *Lancet* 352(1998): 1565.

"Drugs of Abuse: Cannabis." *Drug Enforcement* 6(1979): 34-37.

Dupont, R. L., Goldstein, A. and O'Donnell, J., eds. *Handbook on Drug Abuse.* Rockville, MD: U.S. Dept. of Health, Education, and Welfare, Public Health Service, Alcohol, Drug Abuse, and Mental Health Administration, National Institute on Drug Abuse, 1979.

Fishman, R. H. B. "Israeli Government to Give Marijuana Guidelines." *Lancet* 353(1999): 388.

Flynn, K. "Arrests Soar in Crackdown on Marijuana." *The New York Times,* November 17, 1998, A1.

Gieringer, D. H. "Marijuana, Driving, and Accident Safety." *Journal of Psychoactive Drugs* 20(1988): 93-101.

Hollister, L. E. "Marijuana (Cannabis) as Medicine." *Journal of Cannabis Therapeutics* 1(2001): 5-27.

Itall, W. and Solowij, N. "Adverse Effects of Cannabis." *Lancet,* 352(1998): 1611-1616.

Kane, B. "Medical Marijuana. The Continuing Story." *Annals of Internal Medicine* 134(2001): 1159-1162.

McConnell, H. "Marijuana Anonymous." *The Journal* July/August 1989. Toronto: Addiction Research Foundation.

Mikuriya, T. H. and Aldrich, M. R. "Cannabis 1988: Old Drug, New Dangers. The Potency Question." Review. *Journal of Psychoactive Drugs* 20(1988): 47-55.

Nahas, G. "Symposium on Marijuana: Rheims, France, 22-23 July 1978." *Bulletin on Narcotics* 30(1978): 23-32.

Noble, H. B. "Report Links Heart Attacks to Marijuana." *The New York Times,* March 3, 2000, A13.

Plisko, V. W. and Stem, J. D., eds. *The Condition of Education: A Statistical Report.* Washington, DC: U.S. Government Printing Office, 1985.

Schwartz, R. H. "Marijuana: An Overview." Review. *Pediatric Clinics of North America* 34(1987): 305-317.

"Short-Term Memory Impairment in Chronic Cannabis Abusers." *Lancet* 2(1989): 1254-1255.

Stolberg, S. G. "Government Study of Marijuana Sees Medical Benefits." *The New York Times,* March 18, 1999, A19.

Stolberg, S. G. "Restrictions East for Studies on Marijuana as Medicine." *The New York Times,* May 22, 1999, A11.

Watson, S. J., Benson, J. A. Jr., and Joy, J. E. "Marijuana and Medicine: Assessing the Science Base." A summary of the 1999 Institute of Medicine Report. *Archives of General Psychiatry* 57(2000): 547-552.

Yesavage, J. A., Leirer, V. O., Denari, M., et al. "Carry-Over Effects of Marijuana Intoxication on Aircraft Pilot Performance: A Preliminary Report." *American Journal of Psychiatry* 142(1985): 1325-1329.

Zimmer, L. and Morgan, J. P. *Marijuana Myths—Marijuana Facts—A Review of the Scientific Evidence.* New York: The Lindesmith Center, 1977.

Chapter 11

Cicero, T. J., Adams, E. H., Geller, A., Inciardi, J. A., Munõz, A., Schnoll, S. H., Senay, E. C., and Woody, G. E. "A Postmarking Surveillance Program to Monitor Ultram® (Tramadol Hydrochloride) Abuse in the United States." *Drug Alcohol Dependence* 57(1999): 7-22.

Clines, F. X. and Meier, B. "Cancer Painkillers Pose New Abuse Threat." *The New York Times,* February 9, 2001, A11.

Cushman, P. "Propoxyphene Revisited." *American Journal of Drug and Alcohol Abuse* 6(1979): 245-49.

Goodman Gilman, A., Goodman, L. S., Rall, T. W., et al. eds. *Goodman and Gilman's The Pharmacological Basis of Therapeutics,* Seventh Edition. New York: Macmillan, 1985.

Lange, W. R. and Jasinski, D. R. "The Clinical Pharmacology of Pentazocine and Tripelennamine (T's and Blues)." *Advances in Alcohol and Substance Abuse* 5(4) (1986): 71-83.

McNeer, M. D. "The OxyContin Dilemma." *ASAM News,* March/April(2001): 17.

"New Warning on Propoxyphene." *Food and Drug Administration Drug Bulletin* 9(1979): 22-23.

Pasternak, G. W. "Multiple Morphine and Enkephalin Receptors and the Relief of Pain." Review. *Journal of the American Medical Association* 259(1988): 1362-1367.

Peachey, J. E. "Clinical Observations of Agonist-Antagonist Analgesic Dependence." Review. *Drug and Alcohol Dependence* 20 (1987): 347-365.

Showalter, C. V. "T's and Blues: Abuse of Pentazocine and Tripelennamine." *Journal of the American Medical Association* 244 (1980): 1224-1225.

Smith, R. J. "Federal Government Faces Painful Decision on Darvon." *Science* 203(1979): 857-858.

Stimmel, B. "Pain, Analgesia, and Addiction: An Approach to the Pharmacologic Management of Pain." *Clinical Journal of Pain* 1(1985): 14-22.

Stocker, S. "NIDA Researchers Developing Problem-Free Pain Relievers." *NIDA Notes,* November/December 1997, 7-9.

"Treatment of Dextropropoxyphene Poisoning." Editorial. *Lancet* 2 (1977): 542.

Chapter 12

Allison, M., Hubbard, R. L., and Rachal, J. V. *Treatment Process in Methadone, Residential, and Outpatient Drug Free Programs.* Treatment Research Monograph Series. DHHS Publication No. (ADM) 85-1388. Rockville, MD: U.S. Dept. of Health and Human Services, Public Health Service, Alcohol, Drug

Abuse, and Mental Health Administration, National Institute on Drug Abuse, Division of Clinical Research, 1985.

Bammer, G. "Should the Controlled Provision of Heroin Be a Treatment Option." *Addiction* 88(1993): 467-475.

Bammer, G., Dobler-Mikola, A., Fleming, P. M., and Strang, J. "The Heroin Prescribing Debate: Integrating Science and Politics." *Science* 284(1999): 1277-1278.

Barnes, D. M. "Breaking the Cycle of Addiction." *Science* 241(1988): 1029-1030.

Bartter, T. and Gooberman, L. L. "Rapid Opiate Detoxification." *American Journal of Drug and Alcohol Abuse* 148(1996): 933-935.

Brewer, E. "Ultra Rapid Antagonist-Precipitated Opiate Detoxification Under General Anesthesia or Sedation." *Addiction Biology* (1997): 291-302.

Chronic Hepatitis C: Current Disease Management. Bethesda, MD: National Institutes of Health Publication No. 99-4230, June 1999.

Comte, M. "Puffer Fish Offers Drug Possibilities for Addicts." *Business in Vancouver,* March 13-19, (2001): 10, 11.

Cooper, J. B. "Methadone Treatment in the United States." In *Methadone in the Management of Opioid Dependence: Programs and Policies Around the World,* edited by A. Arif and J. Westermeyer. Minneapolis: University of Minnesota Press, 1988.

De Leon, G. "The Therapeutic Community and Behavioral Science." In: *Learning Factors in Substance Abuse,* edited by B. A. Ray. NIDA Research Monograph 84. Rockville, MD: U.S. Dept. of Health and Human Services.

Des Jarlais, D. C., Joseph, H., Dole, V. P., and Schmeidler, J. "Predicting Post-Treatment Narcotic Use Among Patients Terminating from Methadone Maintenance." *Advances in Alcohol and Substance Abuse* 2(1) (1982): 57-68.

Des Jarlais, D. C., Marmor, M., Paone, D., et al. "HIV Incidence Among Injecting Drug Users in New York City Syringe-Exchange Programs." *Lancet* 348 (1996): 387-391.

Dole, V. P. "Implications of Methadone Maintenance for Theories of Narcotic Addiction." *Journal of the American Medical Association* 260(1988): 3025-3029.

Drug Addiction Treatment Act of 2000. Washington, DC: HR 2634-5324.

Epstein, J. F. and Gfroerer, J. C. "Heroin Abuse in the United States." ODAS Working Paper. Rockville, MD: Substance Abuse and Mental Health Services Administration, NCADI, Pub No. RP0919, August 1997.

Ginzburg, H. M. *Naltrexone: Its Clinical Utility.* National Institute on Drug Abuse Treatment Research Report. USPHS ADAMHA. Rockville, MD: U.S. Dept. of Health and Human Services, 1988.

Gold, M. S., and Dackis, C. A. "New Insights and Treatments: Opiate Withdrawal and Cocaine Addiction." *Clinical Therapeutics* 7(1984): 6-21.

Goldstein, M. S., Surber, M., and Wilner, D. M. "Outcome Evaluations in Substance Abuse: A Comparison of Alcoholism, Drug Abuse, and Other Mental

Health Interventions." *International Journal of the Addictions* 19(1984): 479-502.

Gray, J. "Puffer Fish or Cold Turkey." *Canadian Business,* April 16(2001): 17.

"Guideline for the Role and Responsibilities of Physicians in Narcotic Treatment Programs." San Francisco, CA: California Society of Addiction Medicine (1998).

Hagan, H., Des Jarlais, D. C., Friedman, S. R., Purchase, D., and Actor, M. J. "Reduced Risk of Hepatitis B and Hepatitis C Among Injecting Drug Users in the Tacoma Syringe Exchange Program." *American Journal of Public Health* 85(1995): 1531-1537.

Himmelsbach, C. "Clinical Studies of Morphine Addiction: Nathan B. Eddy Memorial Award Lecture." *National Institute on Drug Abuse Research Monograph Series* 81(1988): 8-18.

"HOV Paradoxically Increases Methadone Dose Requirement." *Addiction Treatment Forum,* IX, Fall(2000): 1, 6.

Hurley, S. F., Jolley, D. J., and Kaldor, J. M. "Effectiveness of Needle-Exchange Programs for Prevention of HIV Infection." *Lancet* 349(1977): 1797-1800.

Karel, R. "New Swiss Program Will Distribute Hard Drugs to Addicts." *Drug Policy Letter* 21: 10-11.

Mathias, R. "NIH Panel Calls for Expanded Methadone Treatment for Heroin Addiction." *NIDA Notes,* November/December 12(6)(1997): 2.

Mattick, R. P., Oliphant D., Ward, J., and Hall, W. *The Effectiveness of Other Opioid Replacement Therapies: LAAM, Heroin, Buprenorphine, Naltrexone and Injectable Maintenance in Methadone Maintenance Treatment and Other Opioid Replacement Therapies.* Amsterdam, Netherlands: Howard Academic Publishers, 1998.

Narayanaswami, K. "Parameters for Determining the Origin of Illicit Heroin Samples." *Bulletin on Narcotics* 37(1985): 49-62.

National Consensus Development Panel on Effective Medical Treatment of Opiate Addiction. "Effective Medical Treatment of Opiate Addiction." *Journal of the American Medical Association* 280(1998): 1935-1943.

Newman, R. G. "Methadone Treatment: Defining and Evaluating Success." *New England Journal of Medicine* 317(1987): 447-450.

Newmeyer, J. A., Johnson, G., and Klot, S. "Acupuncture as a Detoxification Modality." *Journal of Psychoactive Drugs* 16(1984): 241-261.

NIH Consensus Statement. *Effective Medical Treatment of Opiate Addiction.* 15(6)(1997): 1-38. Bethesda, MD: National Institutes of Health.

O'Connor, P. G. and Kosten, T. R. "Rapid and Ultrarapid Opioid Detoxification Techniques." *Journal of the American Medical Association* 279(1998) : 229-234.

Office of National Drug Control Policy (ONDCP). *Policy Paper: Opioid Agonist Treatment.* Washington, DC: Author, 1999.

Okpaku, S. O. "Psychoanalytically Oriented Psychotherapy of Substance Abuse (With Observations on the Penn-VA Study)." *Advances in Alcohol and Substance Abuse* 6(1) (1986): 17-33.

Passaro, D. J., Werner, S. B., McGee, J., Mac Kenzie, W. R., and Vugia, D. J. "Wound Botulism Associated with Black Tar Heroin Among Injecting Drug Users." *Journal of the American Medical Association* 279(1998): 859-863.

Rawson, R. A., Washton, A. M., Resnick, R. B., and Tennant, F. S. Jr. "Clonidine Hydrochloride Detoxification from Methadone Treatment—The Value of Naltrexone Aftercare." *Advances in Alcohol and Substance Abuse* 3(3) (1984): 41-49.

Report of the External Panel on the Evaluation of the Swiss Scientific Studies of Medically Prescribed Narcotics to Drug Addicts. Geneva, Switzerland: World Health Organization, April 1999.

Roehrich, H. and Gold, M. S. "Clonidine." *Advances in Alcohol and Substance Abuse* 7(1) (1987): 1-16.

Shakur, M., and Smith, M. "The Use of Acupuncture to Treat Drug Addiction and the Development of an Acupuncture Training Program." Presented at the 1977 National Drug Abuse Conference, San Francisco, California.

Simpson, D. D. and Sells, S. B. "Effectiveness of Treatment for Drug Abuse: An Overview of the DARP Research Program." *Advances in Alcohol and Substance Abuse* 2(1) (1982): 7-29.

Sorensen, J. L., Deitch, D. A., and Acampora, A. "Treatment Collaboration of Methadone Maintenance Programs and Therapeutic Communities." Review. *American Journal of Drug and Alcohol Abuse* 10(1984): 347-359.

Spanagel, R. "Is There a Pharmacological Basis for Therapy with Rapid Opioid Detoxification?" *Lancet* 354(1999): 2017-2018.

Sporer, K. A. "Acute Heroin Overdose." *Annals of Internal Medicine* 130(1999): 584-590.

Stimmel, B. *Heroin Dependency: Medical, Economic and Social Aspects.* New York: Stratton Intercontinental Medical Book Corp., 1975.

Stimmel, B. and Kreek, M.J. "Neurobiology of Addictive Behaviors and Its Relationship to Methadone Maintenance." *Mount Sinai Journal of Medicine,* 67(5-6)(2000): 375-380.

Stocker, S. "NIDA Researchers Developing Problem Free Pain Relievers." *NIDA Notes,* 12(6)(1997): 6-8.

Strain, E. C., Bigelow, G. E., Liebson, I. A., and Stitzer, M. L. "Moderate- vs High-Dose Methadone in the Treatment of Opioid Dependence. A Randomized Trial." *The Journal of the American Medical Association* 281(1999): 1000-1005.

Swarns, R. L. "Mayor Wants to Abolish Use of Methadone Programs." *The New York Times,* July 21, 1998, B1.

"Tetanus Among Injecting Drug Users—California, 1997." *Morbidity and Mortality Weekly Report* 47(8)(1998):149-151.

"Trexan: A Pharmacologic Adjunct for the Detoxified Opioid Addict." Dupont Pharmaceuticals, 1984.

"U.N. Agency Is Wary of Prescriptions for Heroin." *The New York Times,* April 17, 1999, A7.

"Update: Syringe Exchange Programs—United States, 1997." *Morbidity and Mortality Weekly Report,* Centers for Disease Control and Prevention, 47(1998): 652-655. *Journal of the American Medical Association* 280(1998): 1217-1218.

U.S. General Accounting Office. *Needle Exchange Programs: Referral Suggests Promise As an AIDS Prevention Strategy.* Washington DC: U.S. General Accounting Office, 1993.

"USA Continues Federal Ban on Needle-Exchange Funding." *Lancet* 351(1998): 1333.

Ward, J., Hall, W., and Mattick, R. P. "Role of Maintenance Treatment in Opioid Dependence." *Lancet* 353(1999): 221-226.

Wen, H. L. and Cheung, S. Y. C. "Treatment of Drug Addiction by Acupuncture and Electrostimulation." *Asian Journal of Medicine* 9(1973): 138-141.

Whitehead, P. C. "Acupuncture in the Treatment of Addiction: A Review and Analysis." *International Journal of the Addictions* 13 (1978): 1-16.

Woody, G. E., McLellan, A. T., Luhorsky, L., et al. "Sociopathy and Psychotherapy Outcome." *Archives of General Psychiatry* 42 (1985): 1081-1086.

Wren, C. S. "White House Drug and AIDS Advisors Differ on Needle Exchange." *The New York Times,* March 23, 1998, A10.

Zielbauer, P. "Doctor Defends Heroin Detoxification Procedure and Vows to Resume it." *The New York Times,* October 15, 1999, B5.

Zielbauer, P. "State Knew of Risky Heroin Treatment Before Patient Deaths." *The New York Times,* October 31, 1999, A1, 49.

Chapter 13

Abenhaim, L., Moride, Y., Bernot, F. et al for the International Primary Pulmonary Hypertension Study Group. "Appetite Suppressant Drugs and the Risk of Primary Pulmonary Hypertension." *New England Journal of Medicine* 335(1996): 609-610.

"Adverse Events Associated with Ephedrine-Containing Products: Texas, December 1993-1995." *Morbidity and Mortality Weekly Report* 45(1996): 689-693.

American Medical Association Committee on Alcoholism, Addiction and Mental Health. "Dependence on Amphetamine and Other Stimulant Drugs." *Journal of the American Medical Association* 197(1966): 1023-1027.

Berglund, B. and Hemmingsson, P. "Effects of Caffeine Ingestion on Exercise Performance at Low and High Altitudes in Cross-Country Skiers." *International Journal of Sports Medicine* 3(1982): 234-236.

Bishop, K. "Fear Grows Over Effects of a New Smokable Drug." *The New York Times,* September 16, 1989, 1.

"Cardiac Valvulopathy Associated with Exposure to Fenfluramine or Dexfenfluramine." U.S. Department of Health and Human Services. Interim Public Health Recommendations, November, 1997, *Morbidity and Mortality Weekly Report,* 46(1997): 1061-1066.

Cho, A. K. "Ice: A New Dosage Form of an Old Drug." *Science* 249(1990): 631-634.

Cowart, V. S. "The Ritalin Controversy: What's Made This Drug's Opponents Hyperactive?" *Journal of the American Medical Association* 259(1988): 2521-2523.

Devereux, R. B. "Appetite Suppressants and Valvular Heart Disease." *New England Journal of Medicine,* 339(1998): 765-767.

Fleming, A. "The FDA, Regulation and the Risk of Stroke." *New England Journal of Medicine* 343(2000): 1886-1887.

Gilbert, R. "Caffeine: Cardiovascular Effects." *The Journal—Addiction Research Foundation,* 17(5)May 1(1988): 12.

Gilliland, K. and Bullock, W. "Caffeine: A Potential Drug of Abuse." *Advances in Alcohol and Substance Abuse* 3(1-2) (1983/1984): 53-73.

Greenblatt, J. C. and Gfroerer, J. C. "Methamphetamine Abuse in the United States." Rockville, MD: Substance Abuse and Mental Health Services Administration, Center for Substance Abuse Prevention, RP0906, 1996.

Grinspoon, L. and Hedblom, P. *The Speed Culture: Amphetamine Use and Abuse in America.* Cambridge, MA: Harvard University Press, 1975.

Haller, C. A. and Benowitz, N. L. "Adverse Cardiovascular and Central Nervous System Events Associated with Dietary Supplements Containing Ephedra Alkaloids." *New England Journal of Medicine* 343(2000): 1833-1838.

Herbel, E. S. and Scala, J. "Coffee, Tea, and Coronary Heart Disease." *Lancet* 2(1973): 152-153.

Jick, H., Vasilakis, C., Weinrauch, L. A., et al. "A Population-Based Study of Appetite Suppressant Drugs and the Risk of Cardiac Valve Regurgitation." *New England Journal of Medicine* 339(1998): 719-724.

Kandela, P. "Women's Rights, a Tourist Boom, and the Power of Khat in Yemen." *Lancet* 355(2000): 1437.

Kessler, D. A. "Cancer and Herbs." Editorial. *The New England Journal of Medicine* 342(2000): 1742-1743.

Khan, M. A., Herzog, C. A., St. Peter, J. V., et al. The Prevalence of Cardiac Valvular Insufficiency Assessed by Transthoracic Echocardiography in Obese Patients Treated with Alcohol Suppressant Drugs." *New England Journal of Medicine* 339(1998): 713-718.

Lamberg, L. "Brew It or Chew It? Military Seeks Ways to Caffeinate." *Journal of the American Medical Association* 281(1999): 885-886.

Lanareth, R. "Critics Claim Diet Clinics Misuse Obesity Drugs." *Wall Street Journal,* March 31, 1997, B8.

Mark, E. J., Patalas, E. D., Chang, H. T., Evans, R. J., and Kessler, S. C. "Fatal Pulmonary Hypertension Associated with Short Term Use of Fenfluramine and Phentermine." *New England Journal of Medicine* 337(1997): 602-605.

Marsh, L. D., Key, J. D., and Payne, T. P. "Methylphenidate Misuse in Substance Abusing Adolescents." *Substance Abuse* 19(1998): 143.

McCann U. D., Seiden, L. S., Rubin, L. J., and Ricaurte, G. A. "Brain Serotonin Toxicity and Primary Pulmonary Hypertension from Fenfluramine and Dexfenfluramine. A Systematic Review of the Evidence." *Journal of the American Medical Association* 278(1997): 666-672.

"Methamphetamine: Abuse and Addiction." Rockville, MD: NIDA Research Report Series, U.S. Department of Health and Human Services, National Institutes of Health, 1998.

Morgan, J. P. "Over the Counter Medication: Availability and Issues." In *Phenylpropanolamine: Risks, Benefits and Controversies*, edited by J. P. Morgan, D. U. Kagan, and J. S. Brody. Clinical Pharmacology and Therapeutics Series, Vol. 5. New York: Praeger, 1985.

Morgan, J. P., Wesson, D. R., Puder, K. S., et al. "Duplicitous Drugs: The History and Recent Status of Look-Alike Drugs." *Journal of Psychoactive Drugs* 19(1987): 21-31.

Nencini, P. and Ahmed, A. M. "Khat Consumption: A Pharmacological Review." *Drug and Alcohol Dependence* 23 (1989): 19-29.

Nortier, J. L., Muniz Martinez, M. C., Schmeiser, H. H., Arlt, V. M., Bieler, C. A., et al. "Urothelial Carcinoma Associated with the Use of a Chinese Herb (Aristolochia Fangchi)." *New England Journal of Medicine* 342(2000): 1686-1692.

Petitti, D. B., Sidney, S., and Quesenberry, C. "Stroke and Cocaine or Amphetamine Use." *Epidemiology* 9(6)(1998): 596-600.

Rosmarin, P. C., Applegate, W. B., and Somes, G. W. "Coffee Consumption and Serum Lipids: A Randomized, Crossover Clinical Trial." *American Journal of Medicine* 88(1990): 349-356.

St. John Sutton, M. "Silver Lining to the Cloud Over Anoroxygen Related Cardiac Valvulopathy?" *Annals of Internal Medicine.* 134(2001): 335-336.

Swan, N. "Response to Escalating Methamphetamine Abuse Builds on NIDA-Funded Research." *NIDA Notes,* 11(5)(1996): 1, 5-6, 18. NIDA Pub No. 97-3478.

Walsh, J. "Psychotoxic Drugs: Dodd Bill Passes Senate, Comes to Rest in the House; Critics Are Sharpening Their Knives." *Science* 145(1964): 1418-1420.

Wehrwein, P. "More Evidence That Tea Is Good for the Heart." *Lancet* 353(1999): 384.

Weissman, N. J., Tighe Jr, J. F., Gottdiener, J. S., and Gwynne, J. T. "An Assessment of Heart Valve Abnormalities in Obese Persons Taking Dexfenfluramine, Sustained Release Dexfenfluramine or Placebo." *New England Journal of Medicine* 339(1998): 725-732.

Chapter 14

Belongia, E. A., Hedberg, C. W., Gleich, G. J. et al. "An Investigation of the Cause of the Eosinophilia-Myalgia Syndrome Associated with Tryptophan Use." *New England Journal of Medicine* 323(1990): 357-365.

Byck, R., ed. *The Cocaine Papers by Sigmund Freud.* New York: Stonehill Press, 1974.

Cave, L. J. *Cocaine/Crack: The Big Lie.* DHHS Publication No. (ADM) 87-1427. Rockville, MD: U.S. Dept. of Health and Human Services, Public Health Service, Alcohol, Drug Abuse, and Mental Health Administration, 1987.

"Controlled Substances: Uses and Effects." *Drug Enforcement* 6(1979): 20-21.

"Crack." Editorial. *Lancet* 2(1987): 1061-1062.

Culhane, C. "Dealer Stockpiling Drives Cocaine Prices Up." *The U.S. Journal,* September 1990, 10.

Egan, T. "War on Crack Retreats, Still Taking Prisoners." *The New York Times,* February 28, 1999, A1, 22, 23.

Estroff, T. W. and Gold, M. S. "Medical and Psychiatric Complications of Cocaine Abuse with Possible Points of Pharmacological Treatment." *Advances in Alcohol and Substance Abuse* 5(1/2)(1985/1986): 61-76.

Galanter, M. "Social Network Therapy for Cocaine Dependence." *Advances in Alcohol and Substance Abuse* 6(2) (1986): 159-175.

Gawin, F. H. and Ellinwood, E. H. Jr. "Cocaine and Other Stimulants: Actions, Abuse, and Treatment." *New England Journal of Medicine* 318 (1988): 1173-1182.

Gold, M. S., Dackis, C. A., Pottash, A. L. C., Extein, I., and Washton, A. "Cocaine Update: From Bench to Bedside." *Advances in Alcohol and Substance Abuse* 5(1/2) (1985/1986): 35-60.

Gold, M. S., Miller, N. S., and Jonas, J. M. "Cocaine (and Crack): Neurobiology." In J. H. Lowinson, P. Ruiz, and R. B. Millman, *Substance Abuse: A Comprehensive Textbook,* Second Edition. Baltimore, MD: William & Wilkins, 1992.

Herridge, P. and Gold, M. S. "Pharmacological Adjuncts in the Treatment of Opioid and Cocaine Addicts." *Journal of Psychoactive Drugs* 20(1988): 233-242.

Hollander, J. E. "The Management of Cocaine Associated Myocardial Ischemia." *New England Journal of Medicine* 333(1995): 1267-1272.

Hollander, J. E., Shih, R. D., Hoffman, R. S., Harchelroad, F. P., Phillips, S., Brunt, J., Kulig, K., Thode, H. C., and the Cocaine Associated Myocardial Infarction Group. "Predictors of Coronary Artery Disease in Patients with Cocaine Associated Myocardial Infarction." *American Journal of Medicine* 102(1)(1997): 158-163.

Hollander, J. E., Todd, K. H., Green, G., et al. "Chest Pain Associated with Cocaine. An Assessment of Prevalence in Suburban and Urban Emergency Departments." *Annals of Emergency Medicine* 26(1995): 1267-1272.

Isner, J. M. and Chokshi, S. K. "Cocaine and Vasospasm." *New England Journal of Medicine* 321(1989): 1604-1606.

Jenkins, A. J., Llosa, T., Montoya, I., and Cone, E. J. "Identification and Quantification of Alkaloids in Coca Tea." *Forensic Science International* 77(1996): 179-189.

Korsten, R. "The Pharmacotherapy of Relapse Prevention Using Anticonvulsants." *American Journal of Addictions* 7(1998): 205-209.

Korsten, R. "Role of Anticonvulsants to Treat Cocaine Dependence Is Unsupported." *Brown University Digest of Addiction Theory and Application,* March 1999, 6.

Lange, R. A. and Hillis, L. D. "Cardiovascular Complications of Cocaine Use." *New England Journal of Medicine* 345(2001): 351-358.

LeDuff. "Cocaine Quietly Reclaims Its Hold As Good Times Return." *The New York Times,* August 21, 2000, B112.

Levin, F. R., Evans, S. M., McDowell, D. M., and Kleber, H. D. "Methylphenidate Treatment for Cocaine Abusers with Adult Attention-Deficit/Hyperactivity Disorder: A Pilot Study." *Journal of Clinical Psychiatry* 59(1998): 300-305.

Levine, S. R., Brust, J. C. M., Futrell, N., et al. "Cerebrovascular Complications of the Use of the 'Crack' Form of Alkaloidal Cocaine." *New England Journal of Medicine* 323(1990): 699-704.

Llosa, T. "Comparison of Physiological, Psychological and Toxicological Effects Among Users of Cocaine Alkaloid by Oral Route (Coca Chewers, Coca Tablet Eaters, Coca Tea Drinkers), Cocaine Hydrochloride Users (Sniffers), Coca Paste Users (Smokers), and No Coca Nor Cocaine Users Using DSM III-R Criteria." Lima: International Institute of Information on Coca and Its Derivatives, COCAD, 1995.

Llosa, T. "The Standard Low Dose of Oral Cocaine Used for Treatment of Cocaine Dependence." *Substance Abuse* 15(1994): 215-219.

Lowenstein, D. H. and Massa, S. M. "Acute Neurologic and Psychiatric Complications Associated with Cocaine Abuse." *American Journal of Medicine* 83 (1987): 841-846.

Marzuk, P. M., Tardiff, K., Leon, A. C., et al. "Prevalence of Recent Cocaine Use Among Motor Vehicle Fatalities in New York City." *Journal of the American Medical Association* 263(1990): 250-256.

Marzuk, P. M., Tardiff, K., Leon, A. C., Hirsch, C. S., Portera, L., Iqbal, I., Kock, M. K., and Hartwell, N. "Ambient Temperature and Mortality from Unintentional Cocaine Overdose." *Journal of the American Medical Association* 279(1998): 1795-1800.

May, C. D. "Coca-Cola Discloses an Old Secret." *The New York Times,* July 1, 1988, 25.

Morris, K. "Needling Cocaine Addicts Helps Abstinence." *Lancet* 356(2000): 658.

Musto, D. F. *The American Disease: Origins of Narcotic Control.* Expanded Edition. New York: Oxford University Press, 1987.

Panikkar, G. P. "Cocaine Addiction: Neurobiology and Related Current Research in Pharmacotherapy." *Substance Abuse* 20(1999): 149-166.

Sgan, S. L. "Therapeutic Uses for Cocaine. A Historical Review." *The Pharos,* Winter 1998, 23-28.

Shenon, P. "U.S. Says Hospital Statistics Show Use of Cocaine May Have Peaked." *The New York Times,* September 1, 1990, 9.

Siegel, R. K. "Cocaine: Recreational Use and Intoxication." In *Cocaine: 1977,* edited by R. C. Petersen and R. C. Stillman. National Institute on Drug Abuse Research Monograph 33. DHEW Publication No. (ADM) 77-741. Washington, DC: Supt. of Docs. U.S. Government Printing Office, 1977, 119-136.

Trachtenberg, M. C. and Blum, K. "Improvement of Cocaine-Induced Neuromodulator Deficits by the Neuronutrient Tropamine." *Journal of Psychoactive Drugs* 20(1988): 315-331.

Virmani, R., Robinowitz, M., Smialek, J. E., et al. "Cardiovascular Effects of Cocaine: An Autopsy Study of 40 Patients." *American Heart Journal* 115(1988): 1068-1076.

Volkow, N. D. "Imaging Pharmacological Actions of Psychostimulants During Drug Addiction." Institute of Medicine Symposium on Neuroscience Research, Washington, DC, July 29, 1996.

Volkow, N. D., Wang, G. S., Fowler, J. S., Hitzemann, R., Gatley, S. J., Dewey, S. S., and Pappas, N. "Enhanced Sensitivity to Benzodiazepines in Active Cocaine Abusing Subjects. A PET Study." *American Journal of Medicine* 155(1998): 200-206.

Washton, A. M. "Structured Outpatient Treatment of Cocaine Abuse." *Advances in Alcohol and Substance Abuse* 6(2) (1986): 143-157.

Washton, A. M. and Gold, M. S. *Cocaine: A Clinician's Handbook.* New York: The Guilford Press, 1987.

Washton, A. M. and Gold, M. S. "Recent Trends in Cocaine Abuse: A View from the National Hotline, '800-COCAINE'." *Advances in Alcohol and Substance Abuse* 6(2) (1986): 31-47.

Weiss, R. D., Mirin, S. M., and Michael, J. L. "Psychopathology in Chronic Cocaine Abusers." *American Journal of Drug and Alcohol Abuse* 12(1986): 17-29.

Zickler, P. "Cues for Cocaine and Normal Pleasures Activate Common Brain Sites." NIDA Notes 16(2). Rockville, MD: Mational Institute of Drug Abuse, 2000.

Chapter 15

Abramson, J. "Tobacco Industry Steps Up Flow of Campaign Money." *The New York Times,* March 8, 1998, 1, 28.

Barry, J., Mead, K., Nabel, E. G., et al. "Effect of Smoking on the Activity of Ischemic Heart Disease." *Journal of the American Medical Association* 261 (1989): 398-402.

Benowitz, N. L. "Drug Therapy. Pharmacologic Aspects of Cigarette Smoking and Nicotine Addiction." *New England Journal of Medicine* 319(1988): 1318-1330.

Benowitz, N. L. "Health and Public Policy Implications of the 'Low Yield' Cigarette." *New England Journal of Medicine* 320(1989): 1619-1621.

Benowitz, N. L. "Treating Tobacco Addiction—Nicotine or No Nicotine?" *New England Journal of Medicine* 337(1997): 1230-1231.

"Bidi Use Among Urban Youth—Massachusetts, March-April 1999." *Morbidity and Mortality Weekly Report,* 48(1999): 796-799. *Journal of the American Medical Association* 282(1999): 1416-1417.

Brooks, J. E. *The Mighty Leaf: Tobacco Through the Centuries.* London: Alvin Redman Ltd., 1953.

Bruerd, B. "Smokeless Tobacco Use Among Native American School Children." *Public Health Reports* 105(1990): 196-201.

Burros, M. "Cigars Cuisine Puzzles Health Experts." *The New York Times,* January 31, 2001, F2.

Byrd, J. C., Shapiro, R. S., and Schiedermayer, D. L. "Passive Smoking: A Review of Medical and Legal Issues." *American Journal of Public Health* 79(1989): 209-215.

Chartbend, S. A. "Company Promotes a Nicotine Vaccine It Says Can Prevent Addiction to Smoking." *The New York Times,* May 28, 2001, C8.

Chelala, C. "Tobacco Corporations Step Up Invasion of Developing Countries." *Lancet* 351(1998): 889.

"Cigar Smoking Among Teenagers—United States, Massachusetts, and New York, 1996." *Morbidity and Mortality Weekly Report* 46(20)(1997): 433-440.

"Cigarette Advertising—United States, 1988." *Morbidity and Mortality Weekly Report* 39(1990): 261-265.

"Cigarette Smoking Among Adults—United States, 1995." *Morbidity and Mortality Weekly Report* 46(51) (1997): 1217-1220.

"Cigarette Smoking Among Adults—United States, 1997." *Morbidity and Mortality Weekly Report* 48(1999): 993-996.

"Cigarette Smoking Among Adults—United States, 1998." *Morbidity and Mortality Weekly Report* 49(2000): 881-884.

"Cigars: Health Effects and Trends." NIH Publication No. 98-4302. Bethesda, MD: U.S. Department of Health and Human Services, National Institute of Health, National Cancer Institute, New York, 1998.

Cohen, R. Y., Sattler, J., Felix, M. R., et al. "Experimentation with Smokeless Tobacco and Cigarettes by Children and Adolescents: Relationship to Beliefs, Peer Use, and Parental Use." *American Journal of Public Health* 77(1987): 1454-1456.

Cone, E. J.,and Henningfield, J. E. "Premier 'Smokeless Cigarettes' Can Be Used to Deliver Crack." Letter. *Journal of the American Medical Association* 261(1989): 41.

Dale, L. C., Hurt, R. D., Offord, K. P., et al. "High-Dose Nicotine Patch Therapy. Percentage of Replacement and Smoking Cessation." *Journal of the American Medical Association* 274(1995): 1353-1358.

Davis, R. M., Healy, P., and Hawk, S. A. "Information on Tar and Nicotine Yields on Cigarette Packages." *American Journal of Public Health* 80(1990): 551-553.

Donnan, G. A., McNeil, J. J., Adena, M. A., et al. "Smoking as a Risk Factor for Cerebral Ischaemia." *Lancet* 2(1989): 643-647.

Dwyer, J. H. "Exposure to Environmental Tobacco Smoke and Coronary Risk." *Circulation* 96(1997): 1367-1369.

Easton, A. and Wallerstein, C. "Philippines Fear They Will Be Targeted by US Tobacco Industry." *Lancet* 350(1997): 126.

Faison, S. "China Next in the War to Depose Cigarettes." *The New York Times,* August 27, 1997, A7.

Fielding, J. E. and Phenow, K. J. "Health Effects of Involuntary Smoking." *New England Journal of Medicine* 319(1988): 1452-1460.

"Filter Ventilation Levels in Selected US Cigarettes, 1997." *Morbidity and Mortality Weekly Report,* 46(1997): 1043-1050.

Fiore, M. C., Novotny, T. E., Pierce, J. P., et al. "Methods Used to Quit Smoking in the United States: Do Cessation Programs Help?" *Journal of the American Medical Association* 263(1990): 2760-2765.

Fiscella, K. and Franks, P. "Cost-Effectiveness of the Transdermal Nicotine Patch As an Adjunct to Physicians' Smoking Cessation Counseling." *Journal of the American Medical Association* 275(1996): 1247-1251.

Freedman, A. M. and Hwang, S. L. "Cigar Maker Exposes Dirty Secret of 'Bunting.'" *Wall Street Journal,* April 8, 1996, B1, 5.

Frye, R. E., Schwartz, B. S., and Doty, R. L. "Dose-Related Effects of Cigarette Smoking on Olfactory Function." *Journal of the American Medical Association* 263(1990): 1233-1236.

George, H. *Teenage Attitudes and Behavior Concerning Tobacco: Report of Findings.* Princeton, NJ: Gallop International Institute, 1992.

Glantz, L. H. and Annas, G. J. "Tobacco, the Food and Drug Administration, and Congress." *New England Journal of Medicine* 343(2000): 1802-1806.

Glantz, S. A. and Parmley, W. W. "Passive and Active Smoking. A Problem for Adults." *Circulation* 94(1996): 596-598.

Glassman, A. H., Stetner, F., Walsh, B. T., et al. "Heavy Smokers, Smoking Cessation, and Clonidine. Results of a Double-Blind, Randomized Trial." *Journal of the American Medical Association* 259(1988): 2863-2866.

Gold, M. S. and Herkov, M. J. "Tobacco Smoking and Nicotine Dependence: Biological Basis for Pharmacotherapy from Nicotine to Treatments that Prevent Relapse." *Journal of Addictive Diseases* 17(1)(1998): 7-21.

Goldsmith, M. F. "Increasing Use of Smokeless Tobacco Leads to Fears of Young Lives Being Snuffed Out." *Journal of the American Medical Association* 260 (1988): 1511-1512.

Groman, E. Bernhard, G., Blauensteiner, D., and Kunze, U. "A Harmful Aid to Stopping Smoking." *Lancet* 353(1999): 466-467.

Hall, R. L. and Dexter, D. "Smokeless Tobacco Use and Attitudes Toward Smokeless Tobacco Among Native Americans and Other Adolescents in the Northwest." *American Journal of Public Health* 78(1988): 1586-1588.

"The Health Consequences of Involuntary Smoking: A Report of the Surgeon General." DHHS (CDC) 87-8398. Rockville, MD: U.S. Dept. of Health and Human Services, Public Health Service, Centers for Disease Control, Center for Health Promotion and Education, Office on Smoking and Health, 1986.

"The Health Consequences of Smoking: Nicotine Addiction: A Report of the Surgeon General, 1988." DHHS Publication No. (CDC) 88-8406. Rockville, MD: U.S. Dept. of Health and Human Services, Public Health Service, Centers for Disease Control, Center for Health Promotion and Education, Office on Smoking and Health, 1988.

Hermanson, B., Omenn, G. S., Kronmal, R. A., et al. "Beneficial Six-Year Outcome of Smoking Cessation in Older Men and Women with Coronary Artery Disease. Results from the CASS Registry." *New England Journal of Medicine* 319 (1988): 1365-1369.

Hughes, J. R., Goldstein, M. G., Hurt, R. D., and Shiffman, S. "Recent Advances in the Pharmacotherapy of Smoking." *Journal of the American Medical Association* 281(1999): 72-76.

Hughes, J. R., Gulliver, S. B., Fenwick, J. W., et al. "Smoking Cessation Among Self Quitters." *Health Psychology* 11(1992): 331-334.

Hurt, R. D. and Robertson, C. R. "Prying Open the Door to the Tobacco Industry's Secrets About Nicotine: The Minnesota Tobacco Trial." *Journal of the American Medical Association* 280(1980): 1173-1181.

Hwang, S. L. "Drug Makers See a Risky New Role for Nicotine." *Wall Street Journal,* February 27, 1998, 2.

Hwang, S. L. and Noah, T. "RJR Is Planning Final Market Test for New Cigarette." *Wall Street Journal,* April 18, 1996, B5.

"Incidence of Initiation of Cigarette Smoking—United States, 1965-1996." *Morbidity and Mortality Weekly Report,* 47(1998): 837-840.

Ingersoll, B. "U.S. Regulators to Raise a Stink About Cigars." *Wall Street Journal,* February 9, 1998, B1.

Iribarren, C., Tekawa, I. S., Sidney, S., and Friedman, G. D. "Effects of Cigar Smoking on the Risk of Cardiovascular Disease, Chronic Obstructive Pulmonary Disease, and Cancer in Men." *New England Journal of Medicine* 340 (1999): 1773-1780.

Johnston, L. M. and Glasg, M. B. "Tobacco Smoking and Nicotine." *Lancet* 3(1942): 742.

Jordan, M. "Behind a Hot Smoke, Hard Labor." *Wall Street Journal,* August 17, 1999, A1.

Jorenby, D. E., Leischow, S. J., Nides, M. A., Rennard, S. I., Johnston, J. A., et al. "A Controlled Trial of Sustained-Release Bupropion, a Nicotine Patch, or Both for Smoking Cessation." *New England Journal of Medicine* 340(1999): 685-691.

Kessler, D. A. "The Tobacco Settlement." *New England Journal of Medicine* 337(1997): 1082-1083.

Kigotho, A. W. "Cigarette Companies Shift Their Sights to Africa." *Lancet* 350(1997): 792.

Koop, C. E., Kessler, D. C., and Lundberg, G. D. "Reinventing American Tobacco Policy. Sounding the Medical Community's Voice." *Journal of the American Medical Association* 279(1998): 550-552.

Kozlowski, L. T., Goldberg, M. E., Yost, B. A., Ahern, F. M., Aronsen, K. R., and Sweeny, C. T. "Smokers Are Unaware of the Filter Vents Now in Most Cigarettes: Results of a National Survey." *Tobacco Control* 5(1996): 265-270.

Kozlowski, L. T., Wilkinson, D. A., Skinner, W., et al. "Comparing Tobacco Cigarette Dependence with Other Drug Dependencies." *Journal of the American Medical Association* 261(1989): 898-901.

Layde, P. M. "Smoking and Cervical Cancer: Cause or Coincidence?" *Journal of the American Medical Association* 261(1989): 1631-1632.

Macay, J. "The Global Tobacco Epidemic: The Next 25 Years." *Public Health Reports* 113(1998):16-21.

Macay, J. "Predicting the Global Tobacco Epidemic." *The Brown University Digest of Addiction Theory and Application,* March 1999, 7-8.

Mackay J. "International Aspects of U.S. Government Tobacco Bills." *Journal of the American Medical Association* 281(9)(1999): 1849-1850.

Mattson, M. E., Boyd, G., Byar, D. et al. "Passive Smoking on Commercial Airline Flights." *Journal of the American Medical Association* 261(1989): 867-872.

McGinn, P. R. "Cigarette's 'Denicotined' Advertising Hit." *American Medical News,* September 8, 1989, 3.

Meier, B. "Among Cigarette Makers, Old Habits Die Hard." *The New York Times,* September 7, 1997, E3.

Meier, B. "Cigarette Makers and States Draft a $206 Billion Deal." *The New York Times,* November 14, 1998, A1.

Meier, B. "Cigarette Makers Ordered to Relinquish Documents." *The New York Times,* March 8, 1998, 1, 28.

Meier, B. "House Committee Releases 39,000 Tobacco Documents." *The New York Times,* April 23, 1998, 18.

O'Connolly, G. N., Orleans, C. T., and Kogan, M. "Use of Smokeless Tobacco in Major-League Baseball." *New England Journal of Medicine* 318(1988): 1281-1285.

Palmer, J. R., Rosenberg, L., and Shapiro, S. "'Low-Yield' Cigarettes and the Risk of Nonfatal Myocardial Infarction in Women." *New England Journal of Medicine* 320(1989): 1569-1573.

Peto, R., Chen, Z., and Boreham, J. "Tobacco—The Growing Epidemic in China." *Journal of the American Medical Association* 275(1996): 1683-1684.

Pierce, J. P., Fiore, M. C., Novotny, T. E., et al. "Trends in Cigarette Smoking in the United States. Projections to the Year 2000." *Journal of the American Medical Association* 261(1989): 61-65.

Pirkle, J. L., Flegal, K. M., Bernert, J. T., et al. "Exposure of the US Population to Environmental Tobacco Smoke. The Third National Health and Nutrition Examination Survey, 1988 to 1991." *Journal of the American Medical Association* 275(1996): 1233-1240.

"Prevalence of Oral Lesions and Smokeless Tobacco Use in Northern Plains Indians." *Morbidity and Mortality Weekly Report* 37(1988): 608-611.

"Reducing Tobacco Use. A Report of the Surgeon General. Executive Summary." *Morbidity and Mortality Weekly Report* 49(Supplement)(2000): 2.

"Resisting Smoke and Spin." Editorial. *Lancet* 355(2000): 1197.

"Reynolds to Expand Test of Low-Smoke Cigarette." (AP) *The New York Times,* May 28, 1996, D11.

Sellers, E. M. "Pharmacogenetics and Ethnoracial Differences in Smoking." *Journal of the American Medical Association* 280(1998): 179-180.

Shine, B. "Nicotine Vaccine Moves Toward Clinical Trials." NIDA Notes 15(5). Rockville, MD: National Institute on Drug Abuse, 2000.

Smothers, R. "After Years of Despair Tobacco Farmers Enjoy Prosperity of Better Times." *The New York Times,* December 15, 1994, A18.

"State-Specific Estimates of Smoking-Attributable Mortality and Years of Potential Life Lost—United States, 1985." *Morbidity and Mortality Weekly Report* 37(1988): 689-693.

Stephenson, J. A. "A 'Safer' Cigarette? Prove It Say Critics." *Journal of the American Medical Association* 283(2000): 2507-2508.

"The Surgeon General's 1989 Report on Reducing the Health Consequences of Smoking: 25 Years of Progress." *Morbidity and Mortality Weekly Report* 38(1989): 1-32.

Tanaka, T., Oka, Y., Tawara, I., Sada, T., and Kira, Y. "Acute Effects of Nicotine Content in Cigarettes on Coronary Flow Velocity and Coronary Flow Reserve in Men." *The American Journal of Cardiology* 82(1998): 1275-1278.

"Tobacco Lessons: Crossing Substance Abuse Boundaries, Part 1." *The Journal— Addiction Research Foundation* 17(7), July 1, (1988): 7.

"Tobacco Lessons: Crossing Substance Abuse Boundaries, Part 2." *The Journal— Addiction Research Foundation* 17(8), August 1, (1988): 7.

"Tobacco Use by Adults—United States, 1987." *Morbidity and Mortality Weekly Report* 38(1989): 685-687.

"Tobacco Use Among High School Students—United States, 1997." *Morbidity and Mortality Weekly Report* 47(12)(1998): 229-233.

"Tobacco Use Among Middle and High School Students—United States, 1999. *Morbidity and Mortality Weekly Report* 49(3) (2000): 49-53.

"Tobacco Use Among U.S. Racial/Ethnic Minority Groups, African Americans, American Indians and Alaska Natives, Asian Americans and Pacific Islanders, Hispanics." A Report of the Surgeon General, Executive Summary, *Morbidity and Mortality Weekly Report* 47(1998): RR18.

"Tobacco Use—United States, 1900-1999." *Morbidity and Mortality Weekly Report* 48(1999): 986-993. *Journal of the American Medical Association* 282 (1999): 2202-2204.

U.S. Department of Health and Human Services. "Preventing Tobacco Use Among Young People: A Report of the Surgeon General." Atlanta: U.S. Department of Health and Human Services, Public Health Service, CDC, National Center for Chronic Disease Prevention and Health Promotion, Office on Smoking and Health, 1994.

Warner, K. E. "Health and Economic Implications of a Tobacco-Free Society." *Journal of the American Medical Association* 258(1987): 2080-2086.

Wechsler, H., Rigotti, N. A., Gledhill-Hoyt, J., and Lee, H. "Increased Levels of Cigarette Use Among College Students—A Cause for National Concern." *Journal of the American Medical Association* 280(1998): 1673-1678.

Wickelgren, I. "Drug May Suppress the Craving for Nicotine." *Science* 282(1998): 1797-1799.

Willett, W. C., Green, A., Stampfer, M. J., et al. "Relative and Absolute Excess Risks of Coronary Heart Disease Among Women Who Smoke Cigarettes." *New England Journal of Medicine* 317(1987): 1303-1309.

Wolf, P. A., D'Agostino, R. B., Kannel, W. B., et al. "Cigarette Smoking as a Risk Factor for Stroke: The Framingham Study." *Journal of the American Medical Association* 259(1988): 1025-1029.

"Youth Tobacco Surveillance United States 1998-1999." *Morbidity and Mortality Weekly Report* 49(Supplement)(2000): 94.

Chapter 16

"Adverse Events Associated with Ingestion of Gamma-Butyrolactone—Minnesota, New Mexico, and Texas, 1998-1999." *Morbidity and Mortality Weekly Report* 48(1999): 137-140.

Beschner, G. M. and Friedman, A. S. *Teen Drug Use.* Lexington, MA: Lexington Books, 1986.

Cohen, S. "Inhalant Abuse: An Overview of the Problem." In *Review of Inhalants: Euphoria to Dysfunction,* edited by C. W. Sharp and M. L. Brehm. NIDA Research Monograph Series 15. DHEW Publications No. (ADM) 77-553. Rockville, MD: Department of Health, Education and Welfare; Public Health Service; Alcohol, Drug Abuse and Mental Health Administration, 1977.

Cohen, S. "Inhalants and Solvents." In *Youth Drug Abuse: Problems, Issues, and Treatments,* edited by G. M. Beschner and A. S. Friedman. Lexington, MA: Lexington Books, 1979.

Crider, R. A. and Rouse, B. A. "Epidemiology of Inhalant Abuse: An Update." NIDA Research Monograph Series 85. DHHS Publication No. (ADM) 88-1577. Rockville, MD: U.S. Department of Health and Human Services; Public Health

Service; Alcohol,.Drug Abuse and Mental Health Administration; National Institute on Drug Abuse, 1988.

Edwards, R. W. and Oetting, E. R. "Inhalant Use in the United States." In *Epidemiology of Inhalant Abuse: An International Perspective,* edited by N. Kozel, Z. Sloboda, and M. de La Rosa. NIDA Research Monograph 148, NIH Publication No. 95-3831. Rockville, MD: U.S. Department of Health and Human Services; Public Health Service; Alcohol, Drug Abuse and Mental Health Administration; National Institute on Drug Abuse, 1995.

Harwood, H. J., Thomson, M., Nesmith, T., Cianci, J., and Bailey, S. "Inhalants: A Policy Analysis of the Problem in the United States." In *Epidemiology of Inhalant Abuse: An International Perspective,* edited by N. Kozel, Z. Sloboda, and M. de La Rosa. NIDA Research Monograph 148, NIH Publication No. 95-3831. Rockville, MD: U.S. Department of Health and Human Services; Public Health Service; Alcohol, Drug Abuse and Mental Health Administration; National Institute on Drug Abuse, 1995.

Haverkos, H. W. and Dougherty, J. A. *Health Hazards of Nitrite Inhalants.* DHHS Publication No. (ADM) 88-1573. Research Monograph Series 83. Veteran's Administration Medical Center, Lexington, KY. Rockville, MD: National Institute on Drug Abuse, 1988.

Jumper Thurman, P., Plested, B., and Beauvais, F. Treatment Strategies for Volatile Solvent Abusers in the United States. In *Epidemiology of Inhalant Abuse: An International Perspective,* edited by N. Kozel, Z. Sloboda, and M. de La Rosa. NIDA Research Monograph 148, NIH Publication No. 95-3831. Rockville, MD: U.S. Department of Health and Human Services; Public Health Service; Alcohol, Drug Abuse and Mental Health Administration; National Institute on Drug Abuse, 1995.

Lange, W. R., Haertzen, C. A., Hickey, J. E., et al. "Nitrite Inhalants: Patterns of Abuse in Baltimore and Washington, D.C." *American Journal of Drug and Alcohol Abuse* 14(1988): 29-39.

McHugh, M. J. "The Abuse of Volatile Substances." Review. *Pediatric Clinics of North America* 34(1987): 333-340.

Ramsey, J., Taylor, J., Ross-Anderson, H. R., and Flanagan, R. J. "Volatile Substance Abuse in the United Kingdom." In *Epidemiology of Inhalant Abuse: An International Perspective,* edited by N. Kozel, Z. Sloboda, and M. de La Rosa. NIDA Research Monograph 148, Rockville, MD: National Institute on Drug Abuse. 1995, pp. 205-249.

Sharp, C. W. and Brehm, M. L., eds. *Review of Inhalants: Euphoria to Dysfunction.* DHEW Publication No. (ADM) 77-553. Research Monograph Series 15. Rockville, MD: National Institute on Drug Abuse, 1977.

Chapter 17

Andrews, P. "Cocaethylene Toxicity." *Journal of Addictive Diseases* 16(3)(1997): 75-84.

Bobo, J. K. "Nicotine Dependence and Alcoholism Epidemiology and Treatment." *Journal of Psychoactive Drugs* 21(1989): 323-329.

De Leon, G. "Alcohol Use Among Drug Abusers. Treatment Outcomes in a Therapeutic Community." *Alcoholism: Clinical and Experimental Research* 11(1987): 430-436.

Grant, B. F. and Harford, T. C. "Concurrent and Simultaneous Use of Alcohol with Cocaine: Results of National Survey." *Drug and Alcohol Dependence* 25(1990): 97-104.

Hasin, D. S., Grant, B. F., Endicott, J. et al. "Cocaine and Heroin Dependence Compared in Poly-Drug Abusers." *American Journal of Public Health* 78(1988): 567-569.

Henningfield, J. E., Clayton, R., and Pollin, W. "Involvement of Tobacco in Alcoholism and Illicit Drug Use." *British Journal of Addiction* 85(1990): 279-291.

Hoyumpa Jr., A. M. "Alcohol Interactions with Benzodiazepines and Cocaine." *Advances in Alcohol and Substance Abuse* 3(4) (1984): 21-34.

Iribarren, C., Tekawa, I. S., Sidney, S., and Friedman, G. D. "Effects of Cigar Smoking on the Risk of Cardiovascular Disease, Chronic Obstructive Pulmonary Disease, and Cancer in Men." *New England Journal of Medicine* 340 (1999): 1773-1780.

Kaufman, E. "The Relationship of Alcoholism and Alcohol Abuse to the Abuse of Other Drugs." *American Journal of Drug and Alcohol Abuse* 9(1982): 1-17.

Komblith, A. B. "Multiple Drug Abuse Involving Nonopiate, Nonalcoholic Substances. II. Physical Damage, Long-Term Psychological Effects and Treatment Approaches and Success." *International Journal of the Addictions* 16(1981): 527-540.

Kosten, T. R., Gawin, F. H., Rounsaville, B. J., et al. "Cocaine Abuse Among Opioid Addicts: Demographic and Diagnostic Factors in Treatment." *American Journal of Drug and Alcohol Abuse* 12(1986): 1-16.

McLellan, A. T., Luborsky, L., O'Brien, C. P., et al. "Alcohol and Drug Abuse Treatment in Three Different Populations: Is There Improvement and Is It Predictable?" *American Journal of Drug and Alcohol Abuse* 12(1986): 101-120.

Norton, R. and Noble, J. "Combined Alcohol and Other Drug Use and Abuse." *Alcohol Health and Research World* 11(1987): 78-80.

Randall, T. "Cocaine, Alcohol Mix in a Body to Form Even Longer Lasting More Lethal Drug." *Journal of the American Medical Association* 267(1992): 1043-1044.

Satcher, D. "Cigars and Public Health." *New England Journal of Medicine* 340 (1999): 1829-1831.

Soderstrom, C. A., Smith, G. S., Dischinger, P. C., McDuff, D. R., et al. "Psychoactive Substance Use Disorders Among Seriously Injured Trauma Center Patients." *Journal of the American Medical Association* 277(1997): 1769-1774.

Substance Abuse and Mental Health Services Administration Drug Abuse Warning Network Annual Medical Examiner Data. Washington, DC: Government Printing Office, 2000.

Yamaguchi, K. and Handel, D. B. "Patterns of Drug Use from Adolescence to Young Adulthood: II. Sequences of Progression." *American Journal of Public Health* 74 (1984): 668-672.

Zickler, P. "Nicotine Craving and Heavy Smoking May Contribute to Increased Use of Cocaine and Heroin." NIDA Notes 15(5). Rockville, MD: National Institute on Drug Abuse, 2000.

Chapter 18

AIDS 89 SUMMARY. A Practical Synopsis of the Vth International Conference, June 4-9, 1989. Philadelphia: Philadelphia Sciences Group, 1990.

"AIDS Among Persons Aged ≥ 50 Years—United States, 1991-1996." *Morbidity and Mortality Weekly Report,* 47(2)(1998): 21-27.

"AIDS and Human Immunodeficiency Virus Infection in the United States: 1988 Update." *Morbidity and Mortality Weekly Report* 38 Suppl 4(1989): 1-38.

"AIDS Trends to 1990." *City Health Information* (CHI) 9(3) New York City Department of Health, May 1990.

Balter, M. "On World AIDS Day, a Shadow Looms Over Southern Africa." *Science* 282(1998): 1790-1791.

Blanche, S., Rouzioux, C., Moscato, M. L., et al. "A Prospective Study of Infants Born to Women Seropositive for Human Immunodeficiency Virus Type 1." *New England Journal of Medicine* 320(1989): 1643-1648.

Brickner, P. W., Torres, R. A., Barnes, M., et al. "Recommendations for Control and Prevention of Human Immunodeficiency Virus (HIV) Infection in Intravenous Drug Users." *Annals of Internal Medicine* 110(1989): 833-837.

Carpentor, C. C., Fischl, M. A., Hammer, S. M., et al. "Antiviral Therapy for HIV Infection in 1997: Updated Recommendations of the International AIDS Society—USA Panel." *Journal of the American Medical Association* 277(1997): 1962-1969.

Chaisson, R. E., Bacchetti, P., Osmond, D., et al. "Cocaine Use and HIV Infection in Intravenous Drug Users in San Francisco." *Journal of the American Medical Association* 261(1989): 561-565.

Community Epidemiology Work Group. *Epidemiologic Trends in Substance Abuse.* Proceedings. Rockville, MD: National Institute on Drug Abuse, June 1989.

Cooper, J. R. "Methadone Treatment and Acquired Immunodeficiency Syndrome." *Journal of the American Medical Association* 262(1989): 1664-1668.

Curran, J. W., Jaffe, H. W., Haroy, A. M., et al. "Epidemiology of HIV Infection and AIDS in the United States." *Science* 239(1988): 610-616.

D'Aunno, T. and Vaughn, T. E. "Variations in Methadone Treatment Procedures." *Journal of the American Medical Association* 267(1992): 253-258.

Des Jarlais, D. C., Friedman, J. R., Sotheran, J. L, et al. "Continuity and Change within an HIV Epidemic Injecting Drug Users in New York City 1984-1992." *Journal of the American Medical Association* 271(1994): 121-127.

Des Jarlais, D. C. and Friedman, S. R. "AIDS and IV Drug Use." *Science* 245 (1989): 578.

Des Jarlais, D. C., Perlis, T., Friedman, S. R., Chapman, T., Kwok, J., Rockwell, R., Paone, D., Milliken, J., and Monterroso, E. "Behavioral Risk Reduction in a Declining HIV Epidemic: Injection Drug Users in New York City, 1990-1997." *American Journal of Public Health* 90(2000): 1112-1116.

Dole, V. P. "Methadone Treatment and the Acquired Immunodeficiency Epidemic." *Journal of the American Medical Association* 262(1989): 1681-1682.

Fauci, A. S. "The AIDS Epidemic." *New England Journal of Medicine* 341(1999): 1046-1050.

"Forum on AIDS Addiction, Update 1997." Chevy Chase, MD: American Society of Addiction Medicine, 1997.

Gayle, J. A., Selik, R. M., and Chu, S. Y. "Surveillance for AIDS and HIV Infection Among Black and Hispanic Children and Women of Childbearing Age, 1981-1989." *Morbidity and Mortality Weekly Report* 39 Suppl 3(1990): 23-30.

Gostin, L. O., Ward, J. W., and Baker, A. C. "National HIV Case Reporting for the United States. A Defining Moment in the History of the Epidemic." *New England Journal of Medicine* 337(1997): 1162-1167.

Gottheil, E., Lundy, A., Weinstein, S. P., and Sterling, R. C. "Does Intensive Outpatient Cocaine Treatment Reduce AIDS Risky Behaviors?" *Journal of Addictive Diseases* 17(4)(1998): 61-69.

"Guidelines for HIV Infection and AIDS in Addiction Treatment." Chevy Chase, MD: American Society of Addiction Medicine, 1998.

Hader, S. L., Smith, D. K., Moore, J. S., and Holmberg, S. D. "HIV Infection in Women in the United States. Status at the Millennium." *Journal of the American Medical Association* 285(2001): 1186-1192.

Heyward, W. L. and Curran, J. W. "The Epidemiology of AIDS in the U.S." *Scientific American* 259(1988): 72-81.

Joseph, S. C. "Current and Future Trends in AIDS in New York City." *Advances in Alcohol and Substance Abuse* 7(2) (1987): 159-174.

Kane, B. "Controlling Disease Transmission in Injection Drug Users." *Annals of Internal Medicine* 130(1999): 541-544.

Kaplan, E. H. and Heimer, R. "A Circulation Clinic of Needle-Exchange." *AIDS* 8(1994): 567-574.

Kaslow, R. A., Blackwelder, W. C., and Ostrow, D. G., et al. "No Evidence for a Role of Alcohol or Other Psychoactive Drugs in Accelerating Immunodeficiency in HIV-I Positive Individuals. A Report from the Multicenter AIDS Cohort Study." *Journal of the American Medical Association* 261(1989): 3424-3429.

Lambert, B. "New AIDS Data Show the Course of Infection." *The New York Times,* July 15, 1988, B1.

"Licensure of Screening Tests for Antibody to Human T-Lymphotropic Virus Type I." *Morbidity and Mortality Weekly Report* 37(1988): 736-740,745-747.

MacGregor, R. R. "Alcohol and Drugs as Co-Factors for AIDS." *Advances in Alcohol and Substance Abuse* 7(2) (1987): 47-71.

Magura, S., Rosenblum, A., and Rodriguez, E. M. "Changes in HIV Risk Behaviors Among Cocaine-Using Methadone Patients." *Journal of Addictive Diseases,* 17(4)(1998): 71-90.

Novick, L. F., Berns, D., Stricof, R., et al. "HIV Seroprevalence in Newborns in New York State." *Journal of the American Medical Association* 261(1989): 1745-1750.

Peterson, P., Gekker, G., Chao, C., Schut, R., et al. "Cocaine Potentiates HIV Replication in Human Peripheral Blood Mononuclear Cell Cultures." *Journal of Immunology* 146(1991): 81-84.

Pohl, M. I. and Siegal, L. "Forum on AIDS and Addictions: Update 1997." Retrieved August 31, 2001, from American Society of Addiction Medicine Web site: <http://www.asam.org/conf/aidsform.html>.

Popescu, C. B. *Answers About AIDS: A Report by the American Council on Science and Health.* New York: The Council, 1988.

Schoenbaum, E. E., Hartel, D., Selwyn, P. A., et al. "Risk Factors for Human Immunodeficiency Virus Infection in Intravenous Drug Users." *New England Journal of Medicine* 321(1989): 874-879.

Schuster, M. A., Kanouse, D. E., Morton, S. C., Bozzette, S. A., Miu, A., Scott, G. B., and Shapiro, M. F. "HIV-Infected Parents and Their Children in the United States." *American Journal of Public Health* 90(2000): 1074-1081.

Scott, G. B., Hutto, C., Makuch, R. W., et al. "Survival in Children with Perinatally Acquired Human Immunodeficiency Virus Type 1 Infection." *New England Journal of Medicine* 321(1989): 1791-1706.

Shoptaw, S., Reback, C. J., Frosch, D. L., and Rawson, R. A. "Stimulant Abuse Treatment as HIV Prevention." *Journal of Addictive Diseases* 17(4)(1998): 19-32.

Siegel, L. and Korcok, M. *AIDS: The Drug and Alcohol Connection: What Health Care Professionals Need to Know.* Center City, MN: Hazelden Press, 1989.

Stall, R. "The Prevention of HIV Infection Associated with Drug and Alcohol Use During Sexual Activity." *Advances in Alcohol and Substance Abuse* 7(2) (1987): 73-88.

Steinbrook, R. "Providing Antiviral therapy for HIV Infection." *New England Journal of Medicine* 344(2001): 844-845.

"Update: HIV and AIDS—United States, 1981-2000." *Morbidity and Mortality Weekly Report* 50(2001): 430-454.

"Update: Reducing HIV Transmission in Intravenous Drug Users Not in Drug Treatment—United States." *Morbidity and Mortality Weekly Report* 39(1990): 529, 535-538.

"Update: Syringe Exchange Programs—United States, 1998." *Morbidity and Mortality Weekly Report* 50(2001): 384-388.

Weiss, S. H. "Links Between Cocaine and Retroviral Infection." *Journal of the American Medical Association* 261(1989): 607-609.

Zaric, G. S., Barnett, P. G., and Brandeau, M. L. "HIV Transmission and the Cost-Effectiveness of Methadone Maintenance." *American Journal of Public Health* 90(2000): 1100-1110.

Zylke, J. W. "Interest Heightens in Defining, Preventing AIDS in High Risk Adolescent Population." *Journal of the American Medical Association* 262(1989): 2197.

Chapter 19

Abel, E. L. "Smoking and Pregnancy." *Journal of Psychoactive Drugs* 16(1984): 327-338.

Baquet, D. "New York City Neglect Hearings Upheld in Newborn Cocaine Cases." *The New York Times,* May 30, 1990, B3.

Bearer, C. F., Lee, S., Salvator, A. E., Minnes, S., Swick, A., Yamashita, T., and Singer, L. T. "Ethyl Linoleate in Meconium: A Biomarker for Prenatal Ethanol Exposure." *Alcohol Clinical and Experimental Research* 23(1999): 487-493.

Brody, J. E. "Cocaine: Litany of Fetal Risks Grows." *The New York Times,* September 6, 1988, 19.

Center for Substance Abuse Treatment. *Quarterly Report Data from Sampling of Grant Programs.* Bethesda, MD: Women and Children's Branch, 1995.

Chasnoff, I. J., Griffith, D. R., MacGregor, S., et al. "Temporal Patterns of Cocaine Use in Pregnancy. Perinatal Outcome." *Journal of the American Medical Association* 261(1989): 1740-1744.

Chasnoff, I. J., Landress, H. J., and Barrett, M. E. " The Prevalence of Illicit-Drug or Alcohol Use During Pregnancy and Discrepancies in Mandatory Reporting in Pinellas County, Florida." *New England Journal of Medicine* 322(1990): 1202-1206.

Chattinglus, J. "Caffeine Intake and the Risk of First Trimester Spontaneous Abortion." *New England Journal of Medicine* 343(2000): 1839-1845.

Chiang, C. N. and Lee, C. C., eds. *Prenatal Drug Exposure: Kinetics and Dynamics.* NIDA Research Monograph Series 60. DHHS Publication No. (ADM) 85-1413. Rockville, MD: U.S. Dept. of Health and Human Services, Public Health Service, Alcohol, Drug Abuse, and Mental Health Administration, National Institute on Drug Abuse, 1985.

Clouet, D. H., ed. *Phencyclidine: An Update.* NIDA Research Monograph Series 64. DHHS Publication No. (ADM) 86-1443. Rockville, MD: U.S. Dept. of Health and Human Services, Public Health Service, Alcohol, Drug Abuse, and Mental Health Administration, National Institute on Drug Abuse, 1986.

"Crack-Using Woman Admits Guilt in the Death of Her Fetus." (Associated Press) *The New York Times,* December 3, 1997, A23.

Eskenazi, B. "Caffeine—Filtering the Facts." Editorial. *New England Journal of Medicine* 341(1999): 1688-1689.

Fielding, J. E. "Smoking and Women: Tragedy of the Majority." Editorial. *New England Journal of Medicine* 317(1987): 1343-1345.

Fingerhut, L. A., Kleinman, J. C., and Kendrick, J. S. "Smoking Before, During, and After Pregnancy." *American Journal of Public Health* 80(1990): 541-544.

Frank, D. A., Augustyn, M. A., Knight, W. G., Pell, T., and Zuckerman, B. "Growth, Development and Behavior in Early Childhood Following Prenatal Cocaine Exposure. A Systematic Review." *Journal of the American Medical Association* 285(2001): 1613-1625.

"Government Policies on Alcohol and Pregnancy." Washington, DC: International Center for Alcohol Policies, Reports 6, January 1999.

Hankin, J., McCaul, M. E., and Huessner, J. "Pregnant, Alchohol Abusing Women." *Alcoholism: Clinical and Experimental Research* 24(2000): 1276-1286.

Hinds, M. deCourcy. "Drug-Laced Air Called Risk to Babies." *The New York Times,* January 31, 1990, A18.

Hingson, R., Alpert, J. J., Day, N., et al. "Effects of Maternal Drinking and Marijuana Use on Fetal Growth and Development." *Pediatrics* 70(1982): 539-546.

Hoffman, J. "Pregnant, Addicted and Guilty?" *The New York Times Magazine,* August 19, 1990, 32.

Joesoef, M. R., Beral, V., Rolfs, R. T., et al. "Are Caffeinated Beverages Risk Factors for Delayed Conception?" *Lancet* 335(1990): 136-137.

Klebanoff, M. A., Levine, R. J., DerSimonian, R., Clemens, J. D., and Wilkins, D. G. "Maternal Serum Paraxanthine, a Caffeine Metabolite, and the Risk of Spontaneous Abortion." *New England Journal of Medicine* 341(1999): 1639-1644.

Leroy, V., Newell, M.-L., Dabis, F., et al. "International Multicentre Pooled Analysis of Late Postnatal Mother-to-Child Transmission of HIV-1 Infection." *Lancet* 352(1998): 597-600.

Little, R. E., Anderson, K. W., Ervin, C. H., et al. "Maternal Alcohol Use During Breast-Feeding and Infant Mental and Motor Development at One Year." *New England Journal of Medicine* 321(1989): 425-430.

Martin, T. R. and Bracken, M. B. "The Association Between Low Birth Weight and Caffeine Consumption During Pregnancy." *American Journal of Epidemiology* 126(1987): 813-821.

"Maternal Drug Abuse—New York City." *City Health Information* 8(8), September 1, 1989, New York City Department of Health, 1-4.

McCann, J. "Heart Defects Now Seen in Cocaine Babies." *The Journal,* March 1, 1990, 5.

McElhatton, P. R., Bateman, D. N., Evans, C., Pughe, K. R., and Thomas, S. H. L. "Congenital Anomalies After Prenatal Ecstasy Exposure." *Lancet* 354(1999): 1441-1442.

"The Multiple Deficits of Prenatal Drug Abuse." *Science Focus* (New York Academy of Sciences) 3 (1988): 1, 10-11.

National Institute on Drug Abuse, Services Research Branch. "Drug Dependence in Pregnancy: Clinical Management of Mother and Child." Rockville, MD: U.S. Department of Health, Education and Welfare, Public Health Service, Alcohol, Drug Abuse, and Mental Health Administration, National Institute on Drug Abuse, Division of Resource Development, Services Research Branch, 1979.

National Pregnancy and Health Survey, Rockville, MD: National Institute on Drug Abuse, 1994.

Neerhof, M. G., MacGregor, S. N., Retzky, S. S., et al. "Cocaine Abuse During Pregnancy: Peripartum Prevalence and Perinatal Outcome." *American Journal of Obstetrics and Gynecology* 161(1989): 633-638.

Niebyl, J. R. *Drug Use in Pregnancy.* Second Edition. Philadelphia: Lea and Febiger, 1988.

"Perinatal Toxicity of Cocaine." *Medical Letter on Drugs and Therapeutics* 30(1988): 59-60.

Pinkert, T. M. *Current Research on the Consequences of Maternal Drug Abuse.* Research Monograph Series 59. DHHS Publication No. (ADM) 85-1400. Rockville, MD: National Institute on Drug Abuse, 1985.

Pinkney, D. S. "Costs Increase with Numbers of 'Crack Babies.'" *American Association World News,* April 6, 1990, 15.

Pinkney, D. S. "Drug-Addicted Newborns Increasing: MDs, Hospitals Face Care Dilemma." *American Medical News,* February 3, 1989, 2.

Plant, M. *Women, Drinking, and Pregnancy.* London: Tavistock Publications, 1985.

Richardson, G. A. "Prenatal Cocaine Exposure: A Longitudinal Study of Development." *Annals of the New York Academy of Sciences* 846(1998): 144-152.

Riley, L. E., and Greene, M. F. "Elective Cesarean Delivery to Reduce the Transmission of HIV." *New England Journal of Medicine* 340(1999): 1032-1033.

Roll, D. B., Smith, T., and Whelan, E. M. "Alcohol Use During Pregnancy: What Advice Should Be Given to the Pregnant Woman?" In *Current Controversies in Alcoholism,* edited by B. Stimmel. New York: Haworth Press, 1983.

Silverman, S. "Scope, Specifics of Maternal Drug Use, Effects on Fetus Are Beginning to Emerge from Studies." *Journal of the American Medical Association* 261(1989): 1688-1689.

Smith, S. K. "Alcohol Induced Cell Death in the Embryo." *Alcohol World: Health and Research* 21(1997): 287-295.

"Smoking and Health, a National Status Report: A Report to Congress." DHHS Publication No. (CDC) 87-8396, Rockville, MD: U.S. Dept. of Health and Human Services, Public Health Service, Centers for Disease Control, Center for Health Promotion and Education, Office on Smoking and Health, 1986.

Stratton, K., Howe, C., and Battaglia, F., eds. *Fetal Alcohol Syndrome: Diagnosis, Epidemiology, Prevention and Treatment.* Washington, DC: National Academy Press, 1996.

Streissguth, A. P., Barr, H. M., Sampson, P. D., et al. "IQ at Age 4 in Relation to Maternal Alcohol Use and Smoking During Pregnancy." *Developmental Psychology* 25(1989): 3-11.

"Update: Perinatally Acquired HIV/AIDS—United States, 1997." *Morbidity and Mortality Weekly Report,* 46(1997): 1086-1092.

Wachsman, L., Schuetz, S., Chan, L. S., et al. "What Happens to Babies Exposed to Phencyclidine (PCP) in Utero?" *American Journal of Drug and Alcohol Abuse* 15(1989): 31-39.

Zuckerman, B., Frank, D. A., Hingson, R., et al. "Effects of Maternal Marijuana and Cocaine Use on Fetal Growth." *New England Journal of Medicine* 320(1989): 762-768.

Chapter 20

Alfano, P. and Janofsky, M. "Drugs That May Build Bulk Pull Weight on Black Market." *The New York Times,* November 18, 1988, A1.

Alfano, P. and Janofsky, M. "A 'Guru' Who Spreads the Gospel of Steroids." *The New York Times,* November 18, 1988, 1.

Altman, L. K. "New Olympic Drug Test Foiled Sprinter (Ben Johnson)." *The New York Times,* October 4, 1988, 1.

Atkin, C., Hocking, J., and Block, M. "Teenage Drinking: Does Advertising Make a Difference?" *Journal of Communication* 34 (1984): 157-167.

Begley, S., Brant, M., Dickey, C., Helmstaedt, K., Nordland, R., and Hayden, T. "The Real Scandal." *Newsweek,* February 15, 1999, 48-54.

Bhasin, S., Storer, T. W., Berman, N., Callegari, C., Clevenger, B., et al. "The Effects of Supraphysiologic Doses of Testosterone on Muscle Size and Strength in Normal Men." *New England Journal of Medicine* 335(1996): 1-7.

Birchard, K. "Past, Present and Future of Drug Abuse at the Olympics." *Lancet* 356(2000): 1008.

Birchard, K. "Why Doctors Should Worry About Doping in Sport." *Lancet,* 352 (1998): 42.

Bracciale, D. and Remmers, E. G. "Athletes and Steroids: A Losing Proposition." *ACSH News and Views* 8(1987): 5, 11.

Buckley, W. E., Yesalis III, C. E., Friedl, K. E., et al. "Estimated Prevalence of Anabolic Steroid Use Among Male High School Seniors." *Journal of the American Medical Association* 260(1988): 3441-3445.

Burnat, P., Payen, A., Le Brumant-Payen, C., Hugon, M., and Ceppa, F. "Bromontan, A New Doping Agent." *Lancet* 350(1989): 963-964.

Cowart, V. S. "Blunting 'Steroid Epidemic' Requires Alternatives, Innovative Education." *Journal of the American Medical Association* 264(1990): 1641.

Cowart, V. S. "Erythropoietin: A Dangerous New Form of Blood Doping." *The Physician and Sports Medicine* 17(1989): 115-118.

Cowart, V. S. "Issues of Drugs and Sports Gain Attention as Olympic Games Open in South Korea." *Journal of the American Medical Association* 260 (1988): 1517-1518.

Cowart, V. S. "National Institute on Drug Abuse May Join in Anabolic Steroid Research." *Journal of the American Medical Association* 261(1989): 1855-1856.

"Creatine and Androstenedione: Two Dietary Supplements." *The Medical Letter on Drugs and Therapeutics* 40(1998): 105-106.

"Dehydroepiandrosterone (DHEA)." *The Medical Letter on Drugs and Therapeutics* 38(1996): 91-92.

Duda, M. "NCAA Documents Off-Season Steroid Use." *The Physician and Sports Medicine* 16(11)(1988): 40.

Goldberg, L., Elliot, D., Clarke, G. N., MacKinnon, D. P., Moe, E. et al. "Effects of a Multidimensional Anabolic Steroid Prevention Intervention." *Journal of the American Medical Association* 276(1996): 1555-1562.

Hallagan, J. B., Hallagan, L. F., and Snyder, M. B. "Anabolic-Androgenic Steroid Use by Athletes." *New England Journal of Medicine* 321(1989): 1042-1045.

Haupt, H. A. and Rovere, G. D. "Anabolic Steroids: A Review of the Literature." *American Journal of Sports Medicine* 12(1984): 469-484.

Janofsky, M. "U.S., Soviets Agree on Drug-Test Plan for Their Athletes." *The New York Times,* November 22, 1988, Al.

Johnson, W. O. "Sports and Suds: The Beer Business and the Sports World Have Brewed Up a Potent Partnership." *Sports Illustrated* 69(1988): 68-82.

Kashkin, K. B. and Kleber, H. D. "Hooked on Hormones? An Anabolic Steroid Addiction Hypothesis." *Journal of the American Medical Association* 262(1989): 3166-3170.

King, D. S., Sharp, R. L., Vukovich, M. D., Brown, G. A., Reifenrath, T. A., Uhl, N. L., and Parsons, K. A. "Effect of Oral Androstenedione on Serum Testosterone and Adaptations to Resistance Training in Young Men." *Journal of the American Medical Association* 281 (1999): 2020-2028.

Lamb, D. R. "Anabolic Steroids in Athletics: How Well Do They Work and How Dangerous Are They?" *American Journal of Sports Medicine* 12(1984): 31-38.

Ledwith, F. "Does Tobacco Sports Sponsorship on Television Act as Advertising to Children?" *Health Education Journal* 43(1984): 85-88.

Longman, J. "U.S. Report will Criticize I.O.C. on Drugs." *The New York Times,* September 8, 2000.

Longman, J. "Widening Drug Use Compromises Faith in Sports." *The New York Times,* December 26, 1998, A1, D2.

Marshall, E. "The Drug of Champions." *Science* 242(1988): 183-184.

Noble, H. B. "Steroid Use by Teen-Age Girls Is Rising." *The New York Times,* June 1, 1999, F8.

Penn, S. "Muscling In: As Ever More People Try Anabolic Steroids, Traffickers Take Over; Dope Dealers Smuggle Drugs from Mexico for Athletes and for the

Merely Vain; Sideline Business at the Gym." *The Wall Street Journal,* October 4, 1988, Al.

Scott, W. C. "The Abuse of Erythropoietin to Enhance Athletic Performance." *Journal of the American Medical Association* 264(1990): 1660.

Skolnick, A. A. "Scientific Verdict Still Out on DHEA." *Journal of the American Medical Association* 276(1996): 1365-1367.

Somerville, J. "Sports, Medical Groups Crack Down on Steroids." *American Medical News,* November 4, 1988, 4-5.

Taylor, W. N. "Growth Hormone: Preventing Its Abuse in Sports." *Technological Review,* October 1985, 14.

Whitten, P. "Strong-Arm Tactic." *The New Republic,* November 17, 1997, 10, 12.

Wu, Z., Bidlingmaier, M., Dall, R., and Strasburger, C. J. "Detection of Doping with Human Growth Hormone." *Lancet* 353(1999): 895-896.

Index

Page numbers followed by the letter "f" indicate figures; those followed by the letter "t" indicate tables.